the
scandinavian
kitchen

the scandinavian kitchen

Camilla Plum

photography by Anne-Li Engström

Kyle Books

Published in 2011 by Kyle Books,
an imprint of Kyle Cathie Ltd.
www.kylebooks.com

Distributed by National Book Network
4501 Forbes Blvd., Suite 200
Lanham, MD 20706
Phone: (800) 462-6420
Fax: (301) 429-5746
custserv@nbnbooks.com

First published in Great Britain in 2010
by Kyle Cathie Limited
www.kylecathie.com

ISBN: 978-1-906868-47-5

10 9 8 7 6 5 4 3 2 1

Text copyright © 2010 Camilla Plum
Photographs copyright © 2010
    Anne-Li Engström
Design copyright © 2010 Kyle Cathie Ltd

Design: Ketchup
Photography: Anne-Li Engström*
Food and propping: Camilla Plum
Production: Gemma John

Color reproduction by Scanhouse
Printed and bound in China

* except for pages 38: Magr
Hans/Stockfood UK; 46 bottom right:
photolibrary.com; 72: Niall
Benvie/Corbis; 73: Barry Lewis/In
Pictures/Corbis

Important notes:

Unless otherwise stated: all cream used is
heavy cream, all crème fraîche is 38% fat, all
sugar is granulated sugar, all butter is salted,
and all eggs should be organic and free-range
where possible. Salt should be sea salt and
pepper freshly ground.

Raw eggs: With eggs and all other raw foods
from animals, there is a small possibility of
Salmonella food poisoning. The risk is greater
for those who are pregnant, elderly or very
young and those with medical problems which
have impaired their immune systems. These
individuals should avoid raw and undercooked
animal foods.

Healthy people need to remember that there is
a very small risk and treat eggs and other raw
animal foods accordingly. Use only properly
refrigerated, clean, sound-shelled, fresh, grade
AA or A eggs. Avoid mixing yolks and whites
with the shell. Refrigerate broken-out eggs,
prepared egg dishes and other foods if you
won't be consuming them within an hour.

All yeast should be fresh yeast, bought from
your local bakery or supermarket.

contents

Introduction 6

Eggs & dairy 8
Eggs; Cheese, Sour milk products, Cream

Fresh fish & shellfish 24
Freshwater fish (Salmon, Eel, Pike), Saltwater fish (Norway Haddock, Cod, Herring, Mackerel, Garfish, Monkfish, Gray Mullet,), Flatfish: Fish Roe; Shellfish & Mollusks (Black Lobster; Norway Lobster; Crayfish, Shrimp, Common Crab, Oyster, Mussel)

Preserved fish 70
Dried fish, Salted fish, Smoked fish, Cured fish, Northern Anchovy

Poultry, meat, game, & offal 88
Chicken, Goose & Duck; Pork, Ham, Sausages, Lamb & mutton, Beef & veal; Game (Deer, Elk, Wild boar, Wildfowl); Offal

Vegetables 130
Cabbage & kale, Asparagus, Peas, Cucumber, Beets, Potatoes, Rutabaga, Salsify & scorzonera, Celeriac

Mushrooms 160

Herbs 168
Dill, Parsley, Tarragon, Chervil, Lovage, Horseradish, Ramsons, Nettles, Elderflower

Fruit 188
Apple, Crab apple, Pear, Cherry, Rhubarb, Plum, Sloe

Berries 210
Strawberry, Raspberry, Blueberry, Gooseberry, Cloudberry, Lingonberry, Black currant, Elderberry, Rowanberry, Blackberry, Rosehip, Sea buckthorn

Breads & grains 236
Wheat, Rye, Oats, Barley

Festive food 254

Index 268

Introduction

When researching and writing for this book I realized just how special, exotic, particular, ethnic, and diverse the ingredients and traditions of Scandinavian cooking really are.

I guess that when you grow up with certain tastes, seasonal specialties, and very fresh ingredients, it's in your bones, and feels almost universal, but Scandinavian cooking and Scandinavian ingredients are truly unique. This has become internationally recognized in the past few years. The particularity of both the cooking and ingredients of the north is now receiving global acclaim, at the same level as the other great regional cuisines of the world.

Growing conditions are the roots of any kitchen; the flavors of our food here in the north stem from cool summers and icy winters, plenty of rain, cold waters, and long summer days with endless light evenings.

These conditions produce extremely sweet berries, thin-skinned apples, firm, sweet-fleshed fish and shellfish, and slow-growing flavorful vegetables. The northern climates are perfect for mushrooms and all manner of foraging, and the huge forests, the mountains, and tundra are very much alive with game.

The flavors are fresh and intense, but not overwhelming, and this has taught us to prepare food simply, but effectively, to allow every ingredient to shine.

Scandinavian cooking achieves a delicate balance between extravagance and the humble, producing a wealth of fine tastes, seasonal daily food, and more luxurious festive food.

We are proud of our traditions, and they are mostly very much alive, some of them very local or regional. Scandinavians are eager foragers, home picklers, and home bakers, and traditions are here to stay, but also happily coexist with new ways. Young chefs and young families embrace traditions, in order to evolve them, creating fresher, lighter, even more seasonal, and local food. Environmental awareness is big, and growing and eating organic food, and eating locally and seasonally are growing fast. Small dairies and farms, smokehouses, market gardens, butchers, breweries, farmers' markets, and bakeries are increasing in numbers at a fast pace. And this means a re-creation of local specialties, keeping and evolving traditions almost lost to large-scale farming and factory food. It is taking place before our eyes, and it is very, very welcome.

This book is a reflection of the traditional, recipes worth preserving, and new techniques, dishes, and ingredients, all necessary to keep the particularity of Scandinavian cooking alive and well.

This is not a complete or even comprehensive cookbook, neither in terms of ingredients nor ways to prepare them. The subject is far too vast to cover in one book, but I do hope that the necessary choices and omissions still allow you to get a sense of the cooking of the north, and that the book will be a help in creating and recreating the special Scandinavian tastes in your own kitchen.

Camilla Plum
Denmark, May 2010

Eggs are beautifully packaged, nutritious food and have been a source of fascination to man since the earliest times. In the north Atlantic islands, where sea birds lay their eggs on narrow shelves on incredibly high and inaccessible cliffs, egg-collecting has long been the ultimate test of male cunning and bravery. While the conscientious egg-collecting habits of the indigenous people never posed a threat to the bird populations, most of the egg gathering is now prohibited. Twenty years ago seagulls' eggs were available in the spring. These beautiful, spotted eggs are a quite different and exciting experience when boiled—the yolk a deep sunset color, the white eerily opaque—and the taste is more intense and creamy than that of a hen's egg, but eating gulls' eggs is an experience lost to political correctness, I'm afraid. These days the gulls' numbers are restricted by making holes in their eggs rather than eating them. In some places, wild birds' eggs are still collected in a sustainable way; the eggs of the common guillemot and the fat chicks of the northern fulmar are eaten by people in the north as a delicacy in spring—the habit of a people used to searching for nutritious food for their families at the scarcest time of year, when winter stocks have mostly been eaten and new crops are only on their way.

Scandinavian food is unthinkable without lots of dairy products: butter for crisping fish and meat, and for sauces in which to bathe mushrooms and vegetables; cream for potatoes and herby sauces; cream and sugar for the sweet berries; and whipped cream for every dessert and cake. Cheese is eaten around the clock, and is a vital component of lots of lovely dishes. Even if, nowadays, we are more reluctant to eat massive amounts of animal fat every day, we will not demolish our traditional dishes and culinary heritage that demand the rich cream and butter. We choose to eat a little less of it and enjoy the richness of beautiful dairy products when it's necessary.

eggs & dairy

EGGS

Hen-keeping is very popular in Scandinavia and helps to keep the love of fresh eggs alive. Northern egg-eating traditions survive, but they are undoubtedly diminishing in the face of health scares and the avalanche of poor-quality conventional eggs available in the stores. It is as if we have forgotten that eggs are a delicacy, and that they make lovely dishes in their own right.

Eggs are eaten in many guises at Easter, even if the celebration of the egg as the ultimate symbol of spring and rejuvenation is out of step with modern reality. In the past, and in the case of farms like ours, you do not have eggs in winter as hens are kept in sheds without artificial light, and daylight is too low in winter to trigger egg-laying—except on sunny days with snow, when you can see exalted hens cackling with joy, scattering eggs all over the place.

Appearance and taste The taste and color of eggs are determined partially by their freshness, but most of all by the way in which the hens are kept and fed. Conventionally produced eggs or battery eggs are massively inferior to free-range organic eggs in terms of taste. Since hens are kept in a better environment on organic farms, the birds are rarely sick and this makes for a better taste in the eggs, as well as fewer harmful bacteria. Organic eggs have superior technical qualities too—to make a soufflé or cake rise well or to bind together other ingredients. The lame and insipid taste of a poor-quality egg is not what you're after if you love eggs.

A fresh egg keeps together when cracked and the yolk is bright yellow; if the hens were fed on grass the yolk will be almost orange, and the white like a thick jelly, clinging to the yolk. The taste should be fresh and not sulfuric. These eggs will fluff up an omelette in no time.

Buying and storing Officially, eggs keep for several weeks, but the fresher they are, the better they taste—and the safer they are, too. Many of the eggs on offer in the stores are mostly too old, or just not very tasty. Do not necessarily keep eggs in the refrigerator; a cool place is fine. Freshness is essential if you are using the eggs raw: you should eat them within two days of laying, which in real life means that you have to keep your own hens.

A newly laid egg is sterile inside, but there may be harmful bacteria on the outside of even very fresh eggs, which can penetrate the shell and the protective membrane inside over time. The way around this is to scald the newly laid eggs by simply putting them in a colander and pouring boiling water over them. This may seem too much trouble, but it is the only safe way to keep making ice cream, mayonnaise, and the other lovely things that we do not want to be without. If kept for more than a few days, eggs should be turned over every other day, so the yolk will stay in the middle of the egg.

Sterilized eggs, bought separated in little boxes, are not the same; they lack taste and the quality that has kept delicious dishes with raw eggs so popular since time immemorial.

Culinary uses Scandinavian kitchens have a wealth of traditional egg recipes, which provide plenty of evidence that eggs were once a treat rather than an everyday staple: these range from easy dishes mildly flavored with spring herbs to sharply flavored dishes in which mustard, vinegar, and raw onion are a welcome contrast to the fattiness of the eggs. A fresh egg served with homemade mayonnaise on rye bread with chives and chervil must be one of the prettiest sights on any lunch plate. We also have a tradition of eating raw egg yolks on blue cheese, beef tartare, pickled herrings, and smoked herrings—and lovely it tastes too.

A truly northern soup, eaten cold and a highlight of summer, is made with buttermilk, fresh eggs, vanilla, and lemon and served with crispy cookies crumbled on top—it's far better than it sounds (page 20). We also love creamy poached eggs in our chervil or nettle soup.

Sun eggs

Solæg, or sun eggs, are a much-loved Easter dish with variations all over Scandinavia, and a very pretty way to present eggs. You can eat them like all other hard-boiled eggs, but this Easter specialty is served with little bowls of chopped onion, washed salted capers, olive oil, sharp Dijon mustard, cider vinegar, and chives. It's a very social dish, taking time to eat: everyone cuts open an egg, removes the yolk, puts a little of the accompaniments in the cavity, and balances the yolk on top—to be eaten in one mouthful with rye bread, beer, and schnapps.

First, fill a saucepan with water and add plenty of the tattered dry skin of onions. The idea is that this will color the eggs as they boil: white onions produce a rich brown tan, red onions a beautiful mahogany color. Let the water and onion skin simmer for 30 minutes to extract the color. Then add the eggs (pricked at one end with a needle—so they won't crack) and boil for 8 minutes.

Remove the eggs and cool them in cold water if you wish. You can return them to the cooled onion bath for a deeper color. Rub the eggs with a little olive oil and they will appear as burnished wooden eggs. Or crack them gently on your counter and then return them to the onion bath, where they will become marbled in a few hours. Peel them and be amazed.

Thick omelette with tomatoes, chives, and bacon

Eat in spring when the eggs are perfect and the chives abundant. Serve with toasted rye bread, which is a completely different thing untoasted. The toasting brings out the caramel flavor. Leftovers are eaten the day after as a topping for open-face sandwiches.

12 bacon slices
½ stick butter
12 eggs
3–4 tomatoes, sliced

Maybe a few sliced boiled
   new potatoes
Large bunch of chives,
   finely cut

SERVES 4

In a thick cast iron skillet, fry the bacon in the butter until crisp. Remove the bacon and keep warm.

Beat the eggs and then add them to the skillet and fry in the bacon fat and butter. As soon as the eggs start to get stiff, lift the edges of the omelette and tilt the skillet so more runny egg goes underneath.

Arrange the tomato and potato slices on the omelette. Fry until the egg is still gooey and then let the heat from the skillet do the rest of the cooking.

Scatter with chives and serve immediately with the bacon.

Dirty eggs with seven greens

The name may sound strange—the "dirty" refers to the mustard-speckled sauce—but this dish is traditional and absolutely worth preserving. It dates from a time when both eggs and herbs were scarce in the winter; when spring arrived, people would be desperate for any micronutrients they could find, especially in the far north, and they would crave the bitter taste of the year's newest greens and weeds. If you know what you're looking for, you can make delicious salads or spinach-like dishes from a huge variety of greens.

The traditional seven greens might include some of the following: tiny dandelion greens (collected while they still have strange violet-purple and red colors and resemble tiny octopus), nettles, chives, sorrel, wood sorrel, scorzonera or salsify leaves, mache, parsley, ground elder, samphire, wild arugula, chervil, the last of the kale, overwintered spinach, or fava bean greens.

The eggs must be absolutely fresh as they are the *raison d'être* of the whole dish.

4 cups mixed greens

4 eggs

for the vinaigrette

¼ cup extra-virgin olive oil

2 tablespoons cider vinegar

I teaspoon honey

Salt and pepper

for the sauce

¼ stick butter

2 tablespoons
   all-purpose flour

1¾ cups whole milk

4 tablespoons coarse-grain
   Dijon mustard

2 tablespoons smooth
   Dijon mustard

Salt and pepper

SERVES 4

First of all, prepare the greens by washing them very carefully, leaving any mache and dandelion greens as whole plants, but cleaning away all roots. Let dry on a clean dish towel. Nettles must be blanched before using.

Make a vinaigrette out of the oil, vinegar, honey, salt, and pepper. Mix with the greens just before eating.

Put the eggs on to boil while you make the sauce, but since the eggs should be *almost* rather than totally hard-boiled you must keep a close eye on the time.

To make the sauce, first melt the butter in a saucepan, without letting it color. Mix in the flour and let it bubble for a minute. Add the milk a little at a time, taking care to stir it into the roux thoroughly before adding any more. Let the sauce simmer while stirring for about 10 minutes. You can add more milk if the sauce is very thick—it must be pourable.

Remove the pan from the heat and add the mustards, salt, and pepper. The sauce must not boil again after the mustards are added, or the taste will disappear.

Peel the eggs, cut them in half, and arrange cut-side up on a dish. Pour over the sauce and serve with the greens and rye bread.

TIPS

- You could use the cream dressing on page 22 instead of the vinaigrette.
- In the north, we also eat young greens with eggs and a cream sauce, but the greens go just as beautifully in an omelette or in a sandwich with eggs and mayonnaise.

Easter lamb cake

The mold is the thing in this recipe—in this case a French lamb cake pan, available in kitchenware stores—though you can use any brioche mold or even a muffin tray. The dough can be anything from ordinary loaf dough to this luscious brioche-type batter. It's as rich and eggy as dough gets, and is very liquid from all the delicious salted butter. Making brioches is not generally a job for beginners: it takes cake training to estimate the rising time, and to get them into shape without deflating them. As in all baking, you have to trust the recipe, and the method, even if it seems strange. I prefer to use an electric mixer to make brioche, but of course it can be done without it. Now, you can just go ahead!

½oz fresh yeast
4 cups flour with a high gluten content (e.g. Italian 00 flour)
1 teaspoon sea salt
2 tablespoons sugar

2 tablespoons whole milk
6 eggs
2 cups soft butter, plus extra for greasing
1 beaten egg, for glazing

Dissolve the yeast in 1 tablespoon tepid water. Put all the other ingredients except the butter and beaten egg in the mixer, or in a bowl if you are using a hand-held mixer. Work the batter at a medium speed until it is shiny and flexible. Mix in a quarter of the butter at a time, making sure that each lump is absorbed before you add the next.

When the butter is amalgamated, put the dough into an oiled bowl and cover with oiled plastic wrap. Let rise in a warm place until it has doubled in size. Punch down the dough and put it in a very cool place (the refrigerator is fine) for a minimum of 8 hours, to rise again.

Turn the dough out on to a floured counter, without deflating it. Butter the mold or molds generously with melted butter, then fill to half with the dough, still taking care not to punch or squeeze it unnecessarily. A traditional brioche is made from a ball of dough, with a smaller ball on top. This smaller ball is actually shaped like a champagne cork, stuck into an incision made in the big ball, with only the top sticking out. But you can, of course, shape your brioche as you wish, the number depending on which molds you use. Glaze the brioches with the beaten egg, then let rise in a warm place until doubled in size again.

Bake at 450°F. Small, muffin-sized brioches will need to cook for just 12 minutes, while the lamb mold will need about 25 minutes. If you are using a mold that's somewhere in between, you will need to tip the brioche out and tap the bottom with your knuckles; if it gives a hollow sound, it is ready. In fact, you should do this whichever mold you are using.

TIP

- A rich bread like this is best on the day it is baked, but it makes delicious toast for several days.

DAIRY

Dairy products are the backbone of rural self-sufficiency and farming traditions in southern Scandinavia. The cooperative movement itself is an extremely important part of Scandinavian democracy and self-understanding. It was originally invented to professionalize and upgrade the milk and milk products in Denmark and southern Sweden. In fact, it was a very early form of self-organized fair trade. The cooperative movement later became a grand affair, concerning and affecting the way all foodstuffs are traded and handled, but at the beginning it was all about milk. The movement founded 2,000 local dairies in Denmark alone, the idea rapidly spreading to all of Scandinavia.

These dairies developed an enormous variety of cheeses, in a friendly, ongoing competition, often influenced by foreign cheeses, but also building on

traditional local farm cheeses, and almost every dairy had its own methods, and its own special cheeses. Twenty to thirty years ago, most small dairies were bought by the big ones, and most were immediately closed down. The big dairies aimed for uniformity, mass production, and equality and this is what we got, instead of local, interesting cheeses. Then again, this left room in the market for many new, small, very often organic dairies producing beautiful, local, handmade cheeses with much more spirit than the factory-made, humdrum versions. Nowadays, it is very difficult to buy the real old matured cheeses, and you must work at tracking them down.

The excess of milk in southern Scandinavia has led to a varied use of milk in cooking: there is almost no dish without milk, butter, and lavish amounts of cream. A hundred years ago, and it's still so in rural areas, the main meal was served at noon, always starting with a "milk dish." There was an endless repertoire of these, often sweet dishes, soups, hot oatmeal, and rice puddings, intended to fill up hungry stomachs before the expensive meat was served. Today, a sour milk product is eaten in the morning and as snacks during the day, and almost all children, and far too many adults, drink enormous amounts of fresh milk.

Cheese

The Scandinavian tradition is for salty, full-fat, firm, or hard cheeses, often matured, some as long as two years. The last few decades have seen the production of a vast number of new soft cheeses, inspired by southern Europe, but even these are eaten in the traditional way—namely thinly sliced on bread.

Most cheeses are made from cow's milk as milking sheep and goats is rare in southern Scandinavia. In Norway, goats and cows used to be kept inside in the long snowy winters and driven to the high mountains in summer. The milk was treated and made into cheese on the spot, and brought back to the valleys in the fall. Cow's milk was skimmed and made into *Gammalost* ("old cheese"), a grainy, slightly crumbling, matured cheese, with a strong blue-cheese flavor. This is still a favorite cheese in Norway but virtually unobtainable outside the country. It is not necessarily very old, but it has extremely good keeping qualities without refrigeration.

The whey from the summer milk was sweetened with cream and boiled in cauldrons for hours to evaporate. The resulting cheese is known as Myseost or Mesost after *myse*, meaning whey in Norwegian; even today, it makes up to 30 percent of the cheese eaten in Norway. It is a true Nordic specialty, a brown, velvety, sweet cheese with a nutty, almost chocolate flavor as the milk sugars caramelize during cooking. It is somehow like peanut butter and tastes very good with jam. It's eaten thinly sliced on crispbread, and used in cooking to add sweetness and body to sauces for game and venison. You can have a dark brown Myseost made solely from goat's milk, and a lighter version made with both cow's and goat's milk. The pure goat's milk version is much better, and much more expensive.

Norwegian Jarlsberg is a fine, full-fat, creamy type of Emmenthal, and rightly famous. Sweden has a vast number of beautiful hard cheeses. The most spectacular is the Västerbottenost, the Nordic equivalent of Parmesan cheese, but quite Sweden's own. Denmark has a great variety of both firm and blue cheeses, all worth a try, as well as a specialty unique to Denmark, a smoked fresh cheese called Rygeost, made from drained junket.

Kaffeost ("coffee cheese"), or Leipäjuusto, is a round, flat, mild cow's milk cheese and a specialty of Norrland in northern Sweden and Finland. The unusual name has resulted from the cheese being added in cubes to sweetened, hot coffee, and eaten after the coffee is drunk.

Buying and storing With all these beautiful cheeses, you must choose a specialty cheese store to buy from, and a small producer rather than the huge dairy chains.

Culinary uses Scandinavians' love for extremely old, matured cheeses is mostly incomprehensible to foreigners. Old cheese is eaten in very thin slices, on bread, often with meat jelly, sliced onion, and a dripping of brown rum.

Another sensational way with cheese is an open-face sandwich consisting of blue cheese topped with a raw egg yolk and thinly sliced onion. We love open-face cheese sandwiches, which are eaten around the clock: on rye bread, which is best for matured cheeses; on white bread, preferred with yellow cheeses; or on crispbread, which is good for Myseost and hard cheeses. And we absolutely love to eat these sandwiches topped with jam—one with some nerve, i.e. black currant, blackberry, rosehip, cloudberry, or raspberry, or orange marmalade. A Northern specialty is a sandwich made with Swedish Västerbottenost melted between slices of toast with cloudberry jam. It is absolutely delicious.

Potkäse ("pot cheese") is an extremely old-fashioned but quite delicious way to use up odds and ends of cheese. The cheese is grated or cubed, then added to a clay pot with a dash of rum or schnapps. This is blended into the potkäse. If it is too dry, you can add cream, and season with salt and even sugar. It's long-lasting, pungent, but quite mellow if it's made right. Eat it as a spread on rye bread, with beer and schnapps.

Smoked fresh cheese

Known as Rygeost, this is one of very few, purely Danish specialties. It is delicious on its own on rye bread, with chives, or turned into the lovely cheese salad below. It is fairly easy to make yourself, from a store-bought or homemade junket.

If making the junket at home, follow the recipe on page 21 and leave it to set in one big bowl rather than individual ones. Once it's set, turn it into a colander lined with a clean, scalded dish towel. Leave the junket to drip for 4–6 hours until firm. The smoking is done exactly as you would for smoking fish (page 83). Turn the cheese, rounded-side up, onto a sheet of parchment paper and scatter caraway seeds across the top. Smoke for only 3 minutes, then cool.

You can also use a very fine, fresh ricotta instead of the drained junket.

Summer smoked cheese salad

This is a very summery topping for open-face sandwiches. It would be delicious if made with a beautiful sheep's or goat's milk ricotta instead, but it would not have the smoky flavor, unless you smoked it before using. Eat with toasted rye bread.

for the cream
1 cup smoked fresh cheese
½ cup crème fraîche or
   mayonnaise
Salt and pepper
A dash of cider vinegar
A pinch of sugar

for the salad
5 ripe tomatoes
1 cucumber
20 radishes
9oz boiled new potatoes
A large bunch of chives,
   finely chopped
SERVES 4

Mix the cream and season to taste; the sugar is not meant to make it sweet, but to break the acidity, the vinegar to add a little interest. Arrange the vegetables, nicely cut up, on four plates and spoon the cream on top. Scatter huge amounts of chives all over and serve. Alternatively, pile everything onto slices of rye bread.

Fresh goat cheese with berries and apple syrup

Fresh silky goat cheese is a specialty of Norway, and it's very good used in cooking. It also works well as a dessert, as the texture and slightly goaty creaminess suits the Nordic berries so well. Either serve it on a plate, with fresh cream, a lot of fresh berries, and a river of apple syrup (page 192), or mix the cream with the cheese, spoon into glasses, and top with the berries and syrup.

Sour milk products

Scandinavia is home to a number of exquisite and unique milk products, aside from all the ones available in the rest of the world.

Sour milk, like yogurt, was originally produced to make fresh milk keep, but also for its health-giving and culinary properties. The fermenting process makes milk much easier to digest. Most Scandinavians are able to digest large quantities of milk, as opposed to other races who, apart from nomads, often get sick from eating large amounts of milk products.

The ability to digest milk is taken too far in the Nordic countries, where almost every adult drinks lots of milk every day. It stems from a popular misconception that milk is the only source of calcium and that it is just basically good for you. The truth however is more complex, and milk drinking is certainly a way to get fat; obesity is now a huge problem in Scandinavia.

Långfil

A type of fermented cow's milk, *långfil* is available only in Sweden and Finland. It ferments at low temperatures over a long period, and was traditionally a way of making milk keep (and still is), to have while you are out in the wilderness tending your herd, logging or hiking, or just to take along. Lactic bacteria turns the milk sugars into long strands of polysaccharides when lightly beaten. It is an acquired taste, but quite fun, and is eaten like all the other sour milk products, with berries, rolled oats, or grated rye bread and brown sugar.

Skyr

Originally from Norway, *skyr* was taken by the Vikings to Iceland, where it is tremendously popular as an everyday health food. *Skyr* is a dense, drained milk product, essentially a fresh, unfermented cheese, much like fresh ricotta. It is often made with both rennet and lactic bacteria. It is eaten as it is, used as a topping for bread, in smoothies, and, like the Turkish Ayran, diluted with water for a refreshing drink. To enjoy as a dessert, you dilute it with milk or cream to your desired consistency... and eat it with cream, sugar, and berries. It will keep without refrigeration, and is good for taking on hikes. *Skyr* bought outside Iceland is often diluted; real *skyr* is like extremely firm, drained yogurt.

Buttermilk

The story of butter and the resulting buttermilk is closely entwined with the Scandinavian pig export business, a story told on page 100. Genuine buttermilk is the whey that's left after you have churned the butter, and the real stuff is delicious. Butter was traditionally made with sour cream, and the rich, slightly sour and thick buttermilk was drunk the minute it cooled. Modern buttermilk is usually sour skim milk and much thinner, and not at all the same. However, small independent dairies are beginning to make the real thing. Buttermilk is the basis of *kærnemælkskoldskål*, (page 20) as well as some other delicious desserts such as buttermilk jelly.

Buttermilk and sweetgrass cream with rhubarb jelly

2 sweetgrass leaves or 4 rose geranium leaves	**for the jelly**
	5 sheets of gelatin
1 cup water	2 cups rhubarb cordial (page 205) or leftover syrup from rhubarb compote or soup
for the cream	
½ cup sugar	
1¼ cups full-fat cream	
Generous ¾ cup buttermilk	A handful of edible flowers
4 sheets of gelatin	SERVES 6

Boil the sweetgrass in the water for 10 minutes, then let cool. Discard the grass.

Bring the sugar and cream to a boil, then take off the heat. Stir in the grass water and buttermilk.

Soften the four sheets of gelatin in a little cold water for a few minutes until it reaches a jelly-like consistency. Squeeze off any excess water and place in a small saucepan along with a little of the cream. Place over the lowest heat until the gelatin is completely melted, then stir in some more of the cream, making sure there are no lumps, and finally the rest of the cream.

Divide between six tall glasses or bowls, allowing room for the gelatin on top. Leave in a cool place to set.

Meanwhile, soften the gelatin for the rhubarb jelly as before, and then dissolve in the rhubarb cordial. When the buttermilk cream has set, pour or spoon over the rhubarb gelatin and let set completely. Do not put it in the refrigerator, as this will spoil the taste. Decorate with edible flowers.

Serve with the berries and cookies to crumble on top. If the berries are not quite ripe, help them along by marinating in sugar for an hour or two.

Kalvdans

A truly rural and Nordic specialty, this is a giant pancake, or rather oven cake, made with the first lactation after the cow has calved. The very first lactation is solely for the calf, but most cows give far more of this precious milk than the calf can drink, and you can celebrate the birth with a *kalvdans*, meaning "calf's dance." It's as thick as pancake batter, yellow, and very different from ordinary milk in both texture and taste.

The protein and fat content of this essential milk is so high that you don't need to add either fat or eggs; it will make a fluffy pancake on its own. Sweetening is not necessary either as the milk is very sweet, and the cake will eventually be eaten with lingonberry or cloudberry jam. You can make the cake from this milk alone, but the protein and fat content lowers dramatically over the first few days after lactation has started. Try to fry a little of the milk as you would a small pancake, and if it bakes up it's fine. If it becomes almost rubbery, add some fresh, ordinary milk.

Mix 4 cups of fresh milk from a newly lactating cow with a little salt, and pour into a buttered ovenproof dish. Bake at 400°F until set and fluffy. Eat warm with jam and maybe ice cream. This quantity feeds 4–5 people.

Buttermilk dessert

This delicious summer soup, a sweet, lemony, and much-loved concoction made from raw egg yolks, buttermilk, lemon, sugar, and vanilla is unlike anything you've ever had. The only remotely similar thing is a well-sweetened Indian lassi, and *kærnemælkskoldskål* is often drunk the same way. As a dessert, it's eaten in bowls with a special cookie that's crumbled over the top, but graham crackers or another not-too-sweet cookie will do.

Real buttermilk is thick enough to give the right consistency. If you don't have this, you can compensate by using 4 cups of buttermilk and 4 cups of a thicker sour milk product such as full-fat yogurt.

6 egg yolks	8 cups buttermilk
I cup sugar	**to serve**
I lemon	18oz strawberries,
I vanilla bean	raspberries, or blueberries
Generous ¾ cup	Cookies, for crumbling
heavy cream	SERVES 6–8

Whisk the egg yolks with the sugar until the sugar is dissolved. Slice the lemon thinly and remove any seeds. Split the vanilla bean and scrape out the seeds. Whip the cream.

Mix everything together with the buttermilk and let rest in a cool place for a couple of hours. Adjust the sugar—it may very well need more.

Swedish cheesecake

This is far from any cheesecake you know. It is a no-crust, baked, fresh cheese curd cake that you make yourself from fresh milk and rennet. It can, however, be made with ricotta or cottage cheese and be quite good, but different. It must be eaten while still tepid, with whipped cream and cloudberry, blackberry, or lingonberry jam or any type of sweet berry or fruit. The consistency is grainy and overwhelmingly flavored with almonds.

creamy layer on top, delicious with the jelly-like junket. It is eaten with grated, and sometimes toasted, rye bread and plenty of brown sugar. Traditional junket bowls are made of glass, with a blue rim (and are becoming expensive antiques), but of course any portion-size bowl will do.

It is very easy to make your own junket. The buttermilk must be very fresh to ensure that the active bacteria are still alive and well. It cannot be made if the weather is unstable, with thunder in the air.

8 cups whole milk	Generous ¾ cup heavy
1¾ cups very fresh	cream
buttermilk	MAKES 5 BOWLS

Mix the ingredients together and divide between six pretty bowls. Put a saucer on each bowl and let set, undisturbed, at room temperature. Chill when set. Save one bowl for starting the next batch; the culture will improve with age.

¼ cup all-purpose flour	Finely grated zest of 1 lemon
10 cups whole milk	2½ cups almonds, finely
1½ tablespoons	chopped
liquid rennet	3 Spanish almonds, finely
3 eggs	grated
½ cup sugar	SERVES 6–8
Generous ¾ cup heavy cream	

Mix the flour with some of the milk until smooth. Heat the rest of the milk to 99°F. Whisk in the flour/milk mixture and also the rennet. Let the mixture rest for 30 minutes to set. When it is set, whisk with a balloon whisk to break up the curds into fine grains. Pour into a colander lined with a clean cotton or linen dish towel and let it drip into a bowl until dry. Whisk the sugar and eggs until fluffy and pale, and then add to the curds, along with the rest of the ingredients. Pour into a buttered, ovenproof dish, in a 1¼–1½in layer, and bake at 350°F for about an hour.

Junket

Junket is simply milk set to a gelatin with bacteria from buttermilk, rather like a mild yogurt but with a completely different taste. It is a summer specialty in Scandinavia. The bowls are left to set, at room temperature, and in old farmhouses there are special junket shelves, under the ceiling. The junket sets quickly in the humid summer air, and is then cooled. After cooling there will be a solid,

Cream

Cream is, of course, a favorite ingredient in Scandinavia, used in cream sauces, creamed vegetables, and gratins, or simply as whipped or pouring cream to be eaten with berries, fruit, cakes, fools, and all manner of desserts. Scandinavian cream is 38% fat, which is the kind used in cooking, but you can also buy a thinner cream for coffee. There is a number of sour cream products, such as *rømme*, *gräddfil*, and *smetana*, which are variations on crème fraîche, and they can all be used in an undiscriminating way. Sour cream is a favorite accompaniment for cured herrings and new potatoes, and the very rich Norwegian dish called *rømmegrød* consists almost entirely of sour cream.

Rømmegrød

This is a madly filling dish, a velvety hot oatmeal eaten like rice pudding. The calorie density is unthinkable, but it's good after a long day's skiing in the mountains. It's traditionally served with an assortment of dried and smoked meats, cheese, and flatbread, as a whole meal, but can also be eaten more simply as a dessert, sprinkled with sugar and cinnamon.

2½ cups *rømme* or crème fraîche	Salt, to taste
¾ cup all-purpose flour	Sugar and ground cinnamon, to serve
2 cups whole milk	SERVES 8

Heat the *rømme* in a thick-bottomed saucepan and simmer for 2 minutes. Add half of the flour and whisk vigorously. Some of the cream will separate; remove with a spoon and save as this is butter! Whisk in the rest of the flour and gradually add the milk. Simmer slowly until silky smooth. Season with salt.

Serve with the reserved butter and a thick sprinkling of sugar and cinnamon.

Green salad with cream or buttermilk dressing

Before French cuisine invaded Scandinavia, this was the only way to eat lettuce. And it is still absolutely lovely, if you use big fat butterhead lettuces, preferably those with a waxy surface and pale yellow-green leaves. There is no room for other salad greens in this, except maybe a cucumber, finely sliced. It is eaten with almost any summer dish, chicken, fish, veal, and meatballs. Cream is best, and buttermilk is for the prim and virtuous. But

Generous ¾ cup heavy cream or buttermilk	3 teaspoons sugar
	Maybe a little grated lemon zest
Juice of ½ lemon	1 large or two smaller soft lettuces, to serve
½ teaspoon salt	
Ground black pepper	SERVES 4

a mixture of mostly cream and a little buttermilk is fine. Mix the dressing ingredients and let the dressing sit for a while on the counter to allow it to thicken.

When the salt and sugar have dissolved, adjust the seasoning—it must not be too sweet or lack salt.

Toss the lettuce in the dressing just before serving.

Lemon cream

A legendary Nordic dessert and everybody's favorite, when asked. It's rarely served any more, maybe because it seems that people are more scared of raw eggs than the A-bomb. But if you have access to fresh eggs, you simply must make this, a perfect ending to a spring meal. Don't even consider making it with pasteurized eggs. The charm of this simple dessert is its being made only from fresh perfect eggs, fresh perfect cream, and lemons.

3 eggs, separated	Generous ¾ cup
½ cup sugar	heavy cream
3 lemons	3 sheets of gelatin
	SERVES 4

Whisk the egg yolks and sugar until the sugar is dissolved. Grate the zest from the lemons and squeeze the juice. Whisk the egg whites until stiff, and whip the cream.

Soak the gelatin in cold water for 5 minutes. Squeeze, then melt the gelatin in a small saucepan with the water that clings to it; this will take only a few seconds. Stir in the lemon juice, making sure that it's well mixed. Add the gelatin and zest to the egg yolks while stirring, making sure it's completely amalgamated. Fold in the whipped cream, followed by the egg whites.

Divide between four glasses, and leave in a cool place to set. Eat the day it is made.

Cardamom ice cream

This is a mixture between a parfait and an ice cream, and is extremely velvety and delicious. The taste is very Nordic and it goes beautifully with apples, berries, pancakes, and cakes in general.

7 green cardamom pods	5 egg yolks
I vanilla bean	3 cups heavy cream
¾ cup sugar	SERVES 6

Bash the cardamom pods in a mortar and remove the green casings. Grind the seeds finely. Split the vanilla bean, scrape out the seeds and mix with the sugar and cardamom. Boil the emptied vanilla bean in a little water for 10 minutes, then cool.

Whisk the egg yolks and sugar until pale and frothy. Whip the cream, then combine with the egg and sugar mixture and add the vanilla liquid. Freeze in an ice cream maker, if you have one. Otherwise, pour into a big container and freeze; break the ice cream up every 30 minutes until absolutely smooth, with a balloon whisk at first, then a wooden spoon.

Scoop the ice cream out and serve it as soon as it's set. If you're not eating it straight away, wrap it well in plastic wrap and return to the freezer. Remove the ice cream from the freezer 20 minutes before you want to eat it. If—against all odds—the ice cream is crystalline, run it in a food processor to a beautiful soft ice and eat immediately.

Northern waters are still teeming with fish, even if it's not as it used to be. Overfishing of certain species is a threat to the sustainability of marine life, with the cold waters being more fragile than warm seas, and restrictions are being made on the most popular fish such as cod, herring, and salmon. This brings in new species to try, and for the adventurous it's a thrill to eat strange-looking creatures from the deep with eyes like huge silver coins, dressed in spikes and thorns.

These days, Scandinavian fish lovers are beginning to eat more humble fish, as the most popular types become more expensive. Chefs are doing their best to introduce new fish, showing us how to cook them, because even if people in the north eat lots of fish, most of us stubbornly cling to the well-known ones, despite other fish being just as delicious. Garfish, shark, Norway haddock, English whiting, ling, fork-beard, smelt, witch, dab, and pollock are slowly becoming household names. Even die-hard traditions are challenged—new fatty fish are being cured, smoked, and pickled, which is a solace to people in other parts of the world who want to try Nordic ways of preparing fish, using their local varieties. As long as you replace them with a similar species: fatty or lean meat, dense flesh or flaky, the result will be successful. And it's also a necessary challenge to find new ways with fish. Even if there are fine traditions of cooking fish in the north, we need to reinvent: crisper skin, less overcooking, more spice.

fresh fish & shellfish

The abundance and sheer quality of the fresh fish and shellfish are cornerstones in Scandinavian cooking. Cold waters provide the juiciest and tastiest fish, simply because there is plenty of food for all kinds of sea creatures, but the cold makes them grow at a slow pace, packing in nutrients and thereby taste into the flesh. Scandinavians love fish and cook them simply, to show off their exquisite flavor and firm juiciness. Buying newly caught fish straight from the fishing boats in the numerous fishing harbors is popular, and the whole environment is a mouth-watering experience, especially in summer, when families get up early in order to meet the boats as they return from sea in the morning.

Fish is regarded as a festive treat, and is served at both Christmas and New Year. It is always served in some form or other as an appetizer for grand occasions, and very few families eat fish for supper less than a couple of times a week. Shellfish is more of a treat, with expensive oysters and lobsters being served for very special occasions, while the more accessible small shrimp, crabs, and mussels are eaten outdoors in summer, when the time is right—both season-wise and because we like to eat complicated, time-consuming, beautiful food when the summer nights are long and light.

How to prepare fresh fish

The following instructions and recipes are useful for almost every fish you can lay your hands on, wherever you are in the world. Fish from warm waters are generally drier, and you will need to take extra care not to overcook it. There is no need to distinguish between freshwater fish and saltwater fish when choosing your recipe, it will work for both. But of course you will have to establish a few characteristics—is it lean or fat, flat or round, firm or loose-fleshed?—when choosing how to prepare the fish of your choice, and prepare it in a way and with accompaniments that will make the best of it.

Descaling

Any fish with scales will need to be scaled before it is cooked, unless you are baking it whole, in which case the entire skin is removed before you eat it—so the scales can be left on. Pan-frying, on the other hand, is best when the fish has its skin on, in which case the scales must be removed.

The scaling needs to be done before the fish is cut up, or it will be impossible to do. You can either ask the fishmonger to do it, or do it yourself. You'll have to do it anyway if your fish is home-caught. But do the scaling outdoors, or your kitchen will be decorated with glittery fish scales forever. It's not difficult to scale a fish, but it's messy.

Grab the fish by the tail with a wet dish towel and scrape all the scales off with a small knife or a special scaling device (which is expensive and no more effective than a knife). Hold the fish so you do not cut the skin. Scrape from tail to head contrary to the angle of the scales, which will jump and scatter in all possible directions— it's quite fun—until you are sure that every scale has gone. Feel with your fingers, stroking in the same direction, to check none are left: fish scales are not compatible with pleasurable fish eating. You can then go ahead and wash the fish, gut it, and do whatever you want with it.

Gutting

There are two ways to gut round fish. Most round fish can be gutted through the hole that opens up when you cut the throat. Don't cut off the head entirely, as the cooked fish looks much better if prepared with its head on. Stick your finger into the cavity and pull out the gut, which usually comes out in one piece. Wash the fish carefully. This method leaves a nice place to put herbs, butter, and lemon to flavor the fish.

Alternatively, you can cut open the stomach using a very sharp, pointed knife. Using the tip of the knife only, so as not to damage the gut, insert the blade into the anus of the fish and slit the belly open in a straight line all the way to the gills. Take out the gut, carefully washing away all the blood and dirt, then puncture the leathery floating sac to penetrate the vein running along the spine, to remove the blood. After a thorough rinse, dry the fish inside and out. It can all be done very quickly, once you get the knack, and then the fish is ready to cook.

If you want a whole boneless fish, as for plank fish, or for whole fried herrings, this is easily done. Once the fish is gutted and opened, remove the head. Grab the head end of the spine between your fingertips, and gently pull it backward, toward the tail. It's very easy when you see it done, and hard to describe. But it really is a simple operation that takes only a matter of seconds. Cut the spine off just above the tail, and the fish is ready to cook on the plank, or fry as it is.

Flatfish are gutted through the hole where the throat is slit. You can keep the head and dark skin on, if the fish is supposed to be baked, as you will remove these anyway before eating. If it's going to be fried, it will need to have the upper dark skin removed as this is rubbery and not good when fried. The white skin on the underside will be nice when fried. The skinning is done with a pair of pliers; first cut off the head, tail, and wavy edges with all the small bones on both sides, then grab the dark skin at the tail with the pliers, and pull straight backward. It takes some practice, but you can do it.

Filleting

You will need a long, thin, and very sharp knife. The knife must act as a prolonged finger, feeling its way through the flesh. You must work with the whole blade, not just the tip, with long, slow cuts. If you have not done this before, there is only one thing to remember—take your time. Filleting is an art, and if you hurry it will be a mess.

Flatfish are easy to fillet, as there is only a central spine with a layer of bone protruding to either side.

Remove the head, tail, and fins first. Then cut along one side of the spine, sliding the knife all the way along, under the flesh, until you have cut off the whole fillet. Repeat with the remaining fillet.

Round fish have soft bones around the cavity, which you cut along, and sometimes an extra row of bones in the fillet, which you will have to cut through. Remove the head, fins, and tail. Put the fish on its side, and cut along the spine. Slide the knife, working slowly, under the fillet, which is easy at first, but when you get to the cavity it will need care. Keep on slowly cutting the fillet from the bones until the whole fillet comes off. Turn the fish over and remove the other fillet.

Save the bones and heads for fish soup or stock.

Pre-salting

Salt extracts moisture from fish, and this generally makes it tastier, firmer, and easier to cook. Pre-salting simply involves scattering a little more salt than you normally would allow for the fish a couple of hours before cooking. Dry off any excess salt and moisture with paper towels and proceed with the recipe, without adding more salt.

Oven-baked whole fish

This way of preparing fish is useful for all whole fish on the bone. But naturally the baking time will vary enormously; you will have to test regularly for doneness during baking by sticking a pointed knife into the thickest part of the fish, right to the bone. Always cook it at 400°F. If the fish still has its head on, you must pull out the gills and wash all the blood out, as fish blood is very bitter. A whole fish does not necessarily have to be scaled, as you rarely eat the skin. You can prepare any fish this way, and it's so much easier to handle than boiled fish.

Put the whole fish, gutted and cleaned, on top of a lattice of fennel stalks, chopped shallots, and tarragon or dill fronds in an ovenproof dish. If there is room, leave the head and tail: they add to the experience. Cover the bottom of the dish with ½in of fish stock, beer, white wine, or plain water. Salt the fish inside (unless it has been pre-salted) and dot all over with butter.

Baked fish on a plate

The easiest and best way to prepare fresh fish fillets is to cook them simply in the oven. This will give an extremely clean taste that will show off the distinctiveness of any fish. If you like, you can pre-salt the fish for a couple of hours first.

If you have thin fillets of fish, you can bake them just as they are. Larger pieces, such as cod, monkfish, or salmon, are best cut into ½in slices. You can even try putting an assortment of fish on the same plate—the differences in taste and texture will stand out, and it will look good too.

The idea of this recipe is to bake each portion of fish on an individual plate for each person. If you are cooking for a large number, however, you'll probably want to cook the fish in one larger dish.

Brush an ovenproof plate with melted butter, or olive oil. Place 7oz fish on the plate in one layer and brush with more butter or olive oil. Sprinkle with salt if the fish has not been pre-salted. Make a plate for each person and bake in the oven at 400°F for about 8 minutes. The fish should be just done. If it's a little opaque in the middle, it's perfect.

The accompaniments can be a simple tomato sauce, chervil cream, caper sauce, or just melted butter, lemon, and potatoes.

Bake for 10 minutes, and then cover with parchment paper or aluminum foil for the rest of the baking time. In the oven the heat will be all around the fish, so do not try to turn it over. Bake only until the fish feels like a foam mattress, and no longer. Take it out of the oven, and insert a pointed knife at the thickest end, next to the bone. The meat should be white, pink, or gray depending on the fish, and the bone still faintly rosy, not red. At this point the fish is just done, still juicy, and will be a treat. If the flesh is still translucent, put it back into the oven again. A 2¼lb fish will take 25 minutes. If you are preparing a piece of a larger fish it will be thicker round the waist, and may take longer to cook.

Serve by peeling off the skin and removing each side as a long, firm fillet; any nasty bones should adhere to the central bone.

A very nice sauce, and also the easiest, is simply to whisk a generous piece of butter into the pan juices, flavored with lemon juice. Another simple sauce consists of melted butter, grated horseradish, and lemon. The classic mustard sauce for fish also goes well with oven-baked freshwater fish, as does caper sauce.

Perfect crisp fried fish

This method works with any kind of fish fillets with their skin still on; scaly fish must be scaled first. If the fillets have been skinned, follow the recipe above.

Dry the fish on the skin side, and make two or three slashes with a sharp knife in the skin. Heat a thick-bottomed skillet to very hot and add a layer of olive oil. Place the fillets of fish skin-side down in the pan, making sure that they do not touch each other. Flatten them with a round-bladed knife at first to stop them curling.

Here's the important part: let the fish fry only on the skin side. DO NOT prod, or move the fish! It will not stick to the pan or burn, but will be perfect. The fillets will retain a good heat all the way through. Just wait and watch for the moment when the flesh is opaque all the way through.

Serve immediately, skin-side up, sprinkled with salt at the last minute.

Plank fish

This recipe, like the following one, is for outdoor use, when you are fishing, camping, or just picnicking. Neither is a relic of the past, but used whenever northerners are out enjoying the countryside, and there is no doubt that it will produce a memorable meal, even if you are surrounded by hordes of mosquitoes, as always in the Scandinavian summer.

Plankefisk is so ethnic it's almost unbelievable, and is easy to arrange anywhere you have been lucky enough to land a fish. More importantly, it works. The fish will be delicious, lightly charred, and smoke-kissed from the fire. Traditionally birch planks are used, maybe because birch grows everywhere, but any deciduous wood will do. All freshwater fish are suitable to be cooked this way. The only other things you need are a fire, a plank of wood, a few nails, and some salt.

First scale your fish, then remove the spine. Pre-salt the fish for a couple of hours; you need it to be firm in order to stay attached to the plank. When you are ready, nail the fish to the plank with conventional nails or with the "Great Outdoors" version, tiny wooden wedges.

Place the plank very near to the fire, at a slant, and let the smoke and heat from the fire do their job. Adding heather or herb twigs to the fire will give a nice flavor to the fish, as well as perfumed smoke for you to enjoy while watching your fish cook.

If you aren't lucky enough to have a river to hand, you can try this method of cooking in an open fireplace, indoors or out, with your bought fish.

Newspaper fish

You can try this recipe with a whole herring, mackerel, or a good-sized perch, trout, or white fish, as long as it is very fresh. There is no need to scale the fish for this recipe, as you will not be eating the skin anyway.

Fill the cavity of the fish with herbs and a piece of butter, then close the cavity with a twig. Salt the fish rather heavily on the outside, add a few pats of butter, and wrap it in several pages and layers of wet newspaper. Close the package with twine. Put the package directly on glowing embers, and let it burn until there is only a single layer of newspaper left, by which time the fish will be done and delicious. Unwrap and eat, preferably with your fingers.

Fish cakes

Fish cakes are a well-loved everyday dish all over Scandinavia, with small variations from region to region. Use preferably coley or whiting, though any member of the cod family will do.

The best and most beautiful fish cakes are made with coarsely ground fish and some sort of salted, dried, or smoked pork—usually smoked bacon or fat. The meat's saltiness and fat tastes heavenly with the lean fish, adding both interest and juiciness. Smoked salmon is sometimes added for the same effect.

2¼lb white fish, coarsely ground
2 onions, coarsely grated
2 eggs
1 tablespoon coarse sea salt
1 teaspoon coarsely ground black pepper
1 bunch of parsley, chopped
1 bunch of dill, chopped

1 cup smoked bacon or pork fat, finely chopped
1 teaspoon chopped thyme
3 slices white bread, crusts removed, soaked in milk
Butter, for frying
Serves 5–6 as a main course

Simply mix all the ingredients (except the butter) in a food mixer or a large bowl until the consistency becomes gummy. Let rest for an hour.

Divide the fish mixture into cakes roughly 2oz in weight. Heat a generous lump of butter in a skillet until golden brown, and fry the fish cakes over a low heat, turning them once, so they become cooked through, before going too dark.

Eat with a tomato sauce and potatoes, or with remoulade (page 32), cucumber salad, lemon, potatoes, and melted butter. Leftovers taste good, simply on rye bread with a little lemon and remoulade.

Fish stock

To make a flavorful fish stock, you can use the bones, skin, and heads from flatfish, cod, and many other species, but beware of using very oily fish. It is alright to include a salmon head, but never use mackerel or herrings. You can make fish stock from freshwater fish, but this will need extra vegetables and maybe tomatoes or it will be bland.

Otherwise, you can use odds and ends of fish you prepare, or buy them directly from the fish market. The bones and heads from flatfish are best. Heads from round fish must have had their gills removed; either ask the fishmonger to do this, or simply cut the little piece

of skin that attaches the gills just below the chin and pull them out; you may want to use a dish towel as they sometimes have sharp edges. Flatfish have extremely bitter blood, so wash them before using, to make sure that the blood from inside has gone.

Pack the bones, skin, and heads tightly in a large pot. Fill it up with fennel, celery, parsnips, carrots, leeks, and onions. Don't worry too much about your vegetables—odds and ends will do. Make a bouquet garni from parsley stems, thyme, chervil, fennel fronds, and a bay leaf. Add some orange zest. Over low heat, let it sweat with a good lump of butter until the fish becomes white, and add wine or hard cider if you like, then cover the contents of the pan with water. Add a little salt and some whole peppercorns and bring to a boil.

Turn off the heat and let the stock sit for half an hour. Then repeat the process of boiling and resting twice more. This may seem tedious, but the effect will be that you extract all the flavor from the fish and vegetables, and none of the glue from the bones. This would seep out during a continued boiling, and would make the stock gummy and awful.

After the last rest, you whisk the contents with a balloon whisk to a papier-mâché-like oatmeal and strain through a fine sieve. The result is a delicate, scented, light stock that can be used straight away for soup, or reduced to about a third for sauces.

Mustard sauce for fish

The traditional mustard sauce for boiled or baked fish is a white sauce specked with coarse mustard. There must be plenty of it, and it must be hot. The creaminess and spiciness is a lovely, velvety foil for all the accompaniments served with traditional boiled cod or stockfish, but it's fine with a plain baked fish as well.

Melt 1 tablespoon of butter in a small saucepan, then add 2 tablespoons of all-purpose flour and stir well. Pour in 1¼ cups milk a little at a time, while whisking vigorously with a balloon whisk. You're after a thin to creamy consistency, so add some of the cooking liquid from the fish, or more milk, if necessary; let it bubble away for about 5 minutes, until the floury taste has gone.

Remove the pan from the heat and stir in 2 tablespoons each of Dijon mustard and fish mustard or coarse-grain Dijon mustard. Correct the seasoning with a pinch each of sugar, salt, and black pepper. The sauce must not boil again or the mustard will lose its taste. (Quantities serve four people.)

Simple mustard sauce

This extremely simple mustard sauce is just as good as the one above. It's richer, and perfect for lean fish and all freshwater fish.

Melt a generous lump of butter for each portion and when it is just melted take it off the heat and stir in 1 tablespoon of Dijon mustard; the sauce will thicken and then it's done. If you let it come to a boil, the spiciness diminishes—it's your own choice. It's astonishingly good.

Hollandaise sauce

Hollandaise has a natural affinity with any boiled, baked, or steamed fish.

Generous ¾ cup white wine
Generous ¾ cup white wine
  vinegar
3 shallots, finely chopped

1 teaspoon black
  peppercorns

Remoulade

This is an ever-popular cold sauce for fish and fish patties, roast beef sandwiches, fries, and cod's roe. You can buy it everywhere, but it will inevitably be too sweet and too smooth; this is a flavorful, chunky version.

Generous ⅓ cup
  mayonnaise (page 56)
Generous ⅓ cup crème
  fraîche
2 large gherkins, chopped
1 tablespoon chopped capers

2 teaspoons curry powder
1 tablespoon Dijon mustard
Cider vinegar, to taste
1 tablespoon chopped fresh
  tarragon
A little sugar (optional)

Mix all the ingredients together and adjust the seasoning. If the gherkins have no sugar, you might want to add some. The remoulade must be kept in the refrigerator and eaten within two days.

1¾ cups butter, melted
8 egg yolks

Finely grated zest and juice
    of 1 lemon
1 teaspoon sea salt

Put the wine, vinegar, shallots, and peppercorns in a small, non-reactive saucepan and boil down to a few spoonfuls. Cool.

Strain the cooled essence into a heatproof bowl placed over a small saucepan. Pour warm water into the saucepan. Place the whole arrangement on the stove, over a medium heat. The water in the pan should never boil, just tremble, or the sauce will curdle. As a precaution you can fill a heatproof bowl of a slightly bigger size with ice cubes and cold water, to put the sauce bowl into if the sauce threatens to curdle.

Melt the butter in a separate saucepan. I use salted butter, which leaves a residue of salt and buttermilk at the bottom of the pan—I always incorporate this into the sauce too, as it seems to prevent it from curdling.

While the essence is still cold, mix in the egg yolks. From now on you must focus: no telephone calls, no TV, just keep stirring with a balloon whisk, while you add the butter a very little at a time, as if for a mayonnaise. The sauce will thicken gradually, and if you wish you can reduce the hair-raising thrill of concocting your first hollandaise by moving the pan away from the heat, to recover. If it does curdle a little, add a spoonful of cold water and go on whisking. At the end, your sauce will leave tracks from the whisk, and be perfect. Add the sea salt and lemon zest and juice to taste, and leave the sauce to sit in the pan while you get ready to serve.

If all this makes you tremble, try the egg sauce, and relax.

Caper sauce

This sauce goes well with Norway haddock, ray, mullet, zander, and cod.

2 cups white wine, hard
    cider or ale
1 onion, chopped
1 fresh bay leaf
1 teaspoon fresh thyme
1 teaspoon black
    peppercorns

½ cup butter
Bunch of parsley, finely
    chopped
1 tablespoon salted capers,
    washed and chopped

Put the wine, onion, bay leaf, thyme and pepper into a saucepan and reduce to a hefty spoonful of syrup at the bottom of the pan, taking care not to burn it. When the fish is baked, pour the cooking juices into the syrup, and reduce. Whisk in the butter off the heat. Stir in the parsley and capers, and the sauce is ready.

Egg sauce with chervil and chives

This is a very easy and lovely sauce for all kinds of green spring vegetables, such as asparagus and pointed head cabbage, as well as for all smoked, fried, or baked fish— and it's a good choice if the idea of making hollandaise or mousseline sauce makes you nervous. Its zingy richness is the perfect foil for mild and delicate foods.

3 hard-boiled eggs, peeled
2 egg yolks
⅔ cup butter, melted
1 teaspoon lemon juice
1 teaspoon cider vinegar

½ teaspoon coarsely
    ground black pepper
1 bunch of chervil, chopped
1 bunch of chives, cut into
    very fine rings
SERVES 4–6

While they are still warm, put the hard-boiled eggs into a bowl and chop them up with a balloon whisk. Whip in the egg yolks followed by the melted butter. Add the lemon juice, vinegar, black pepper, and herbs and stir well. It should amalgamate into a thick, creamy, and slightly chunky sauce—if it doesn't, you can heat the sauce gently in a thick-bottomed casserole dish that is suitable for use on the stovetop, whisking non-stop until it thickens.

The sauce can now be eaten straight away. If you want to keep it warm in a bain-marie (water bath), that's fine, but the sauce cannot be reheated.

FRESHWATER FISH

Nordic rivers and lakes, and a large part of the brackish Baltic, are home to a wide variety of freshwater fish. Freshwater fishing is a very popular pastime, highly competitive, and nowadays even big business, as anglers come from all over the world to fish for giant pikes, zanders, trout, salmon, and Arctic char in the rivers and lakes throughout Scandinavia. But for many Scandinavians, fishing remains a relaxed means to provide food for your family, in a non-competitive, everyday way.

The ice season in northern Scandinavia hosts traditions of fishing together on the ice. Families meet for fish ice-skating, to have picnics, build bonfires, and prepare their catch on the spot—as *plankefisk* or simply baked in wet newspaper in the embers. All you need to bring is salt and lemon; the cold air provides the appetite and the sweet-fleshed fish all the flavor you need.

There are many local species, but pike-perch, or zander, and Arctic char (which is a huge trout) are the most hardy of freshwater fish, being able to live in Arctic fresh waters. Pike and powan are found in most of Scandinavia, while carp is rarely eaten, though it is considered a delicacy by some. Perch is abundant, as are many other local species, but they are not items of commerce even though they are eaten in quantities locally. Salmon is only a part-timer in fresh water, as it lives its adult life in the ocean, and returns to the river or lake it was hatched in only to spawn and die. Eels used to be numerous, and even fairly cheap, but they are now endangered and it is not currently advisable to eat

them from the wild. They lead the weirdest life of all fish, spending only their adult life in fresh water, returning to the sea to spawn and die.

Buying and storing The only problem when buying freshwater fish is that you have to know where they have lived. They do not all taste equally good. Fish from lakes with still water are muddy; from flowing waters they are delicious. The taste can be detected in their smell: a sweet, fresh smell indicates a good taste, while muddiness (which can also be smelled) does not. But do not misinterpret the typical odor of freshwater fish, which is very different from the sea-breezy smell of saltwater fish. The size has no influence on the taste, so a giant pike is as good as a small one.

Freshwater fish do not keep very well, and they should be cleaned and preferably eaten the same day they are bought. If this is not possible, either keep them whole (gutted and cleaned), or cut them into fillets, and green salt (page 75) or pre-salt them for the next day (page 27).

Culinary uses Freshwater fish have really nasty forked bones, seemingly spread at random through the flesh. These types of fish are generally ground to make fish cakes and quenelles—there are fine traditions in these all over the north, made from both fresh- and saltwater fish. They are mildly seasoned with thyme, pepper, and onion, and often with some kind of smoked pork, which adds a wonderful flavor, saltiness, and fat to the dish. But for good-quality freshwater fish, baking it whole with few trimmings is all that's needed to show off its wonderful characteristics. The most spectacular way to prepare fish is simply nailed to a plank of wood and cooked by the fire (*plankefisk*, page 29) in the wilderness, or indeed at home just because you want the resinous flavor from the birch plank perfuming your fish on a special occasion.

Salmon, trout, powan, and Arctic char are perfect for gravad fish (page 78). Other species are not very good to cure, and are best eaten fried, baked, or boiled. There is no real tradition of preserving freshwater fish as most are accessible all year round. Fish soup from freshwater fish can be made but it is never as good as soup made with saltwater fish.

Salmon *Salmo salar*

When I was a child in Denmark, salmon was a luxury. Now it's become cheap and tasteless, with a fatty acid content similar to that of conventionally farmed pigs. Not the healthy meat you hope for. We pay for the low price in other and less transparent ways. If you want the real thing, which means not farmed, polluted, medicated, or heavily colored, you must wait for the season, and pay what it costs to buy a line-caught, beautiful, silver creature. The reward is one of the most delicate, versatile, and delicious fish you can possibly eat. The flesh is melting and sweet, and the color of pale apricot, the qualities that made it popular in the first place.

Wild salmon used to be so numerous in northern Scandinavia that it was written in Norwegian farm boys' contracts, before the Second World War, that they should not be served wild salmon more than twice a week.

Habitat The coast of Norway is specked with marine fish farms raising thousands of tons of salmon. It's a serious source of pollution, ruining the seabed, and the raised fish are generally of low quality: with a bland taste, dyed meat, higher-than-usual fat content, and full of medicine residues. Even though it has made salmon everyday fare, there is a rising awareness that this mass production is not sustainable, and there are new ways of raising salmon, even organically, which is higher priced and of wonderful quality.

Appearance and taste Salmon are silver and black, and soft-fleshed when raw. Wild salmon have pretty, pale apricot-colored flesh, not the bright orange flesh of farmed fish. Wild fish have tails and fins with sharp edges, while farmed fish live so close together that the fins and tails are bitten into shreds. Organically farmed salmon have similar characteristics to wild fish.

Buying and storing Buy only organically farmed fish, or wild salmon, caught in sustainable ways. Eat it on the day it is bought, unless you are curing the fish.

Health benefits Wild salmon are full of healthy fatty acids and lots of minerals. Conventionally farmed fish, which are fed like conventional pigs, are not at all the same. The fats are different and they have dye and

medication in their food. It is not advisable to eat conventionally farmed salmon for health reasons, let alone because the taste is not comparable.

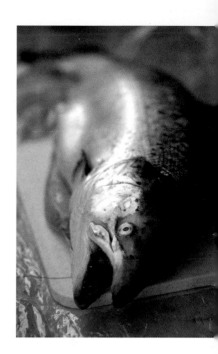

Culinary uses Like all fatty fish, salmon must not be overcooked, though traditionally it often was. We know better now, and bake or fry salmon only long enough for it to become just firm to the touch, and still a little seared in the middle. Cooked for too long, salmon, like other fatty fish, becomes very, very dry. There are several traditional ways of curing and smoking that will make the most of a perfect salmon (page 83).

Salmon pudding

Laxpudding is a Swedish classic. Eat it with rye bread and a green salad, or cucumber salad with dill (page 147).

18oz salmon fillet	4 eggs
2 teaspoons coarse sea salt	1¼ cups heavy cream
3lb 5oz waxy potatoes, thinly sliced	2 cups whole milk
1 onion, chopped	½ teaspoon coarsely ground black pepper
2 bunches of fresh dill, chopped	SERVES 4–5

Slice the salmon fillet as thinly as you can, then pre-salt (page 27) with half the coarse sea salt. Let rest for a couple of hours.

Preheat the oven to 350°F. Layer the potatoes, salmon, onion, and dill in a deep ovenproof dish, beginning and ending with a layer of potatoes.

Whisk the eggs, cream, milk, pepper, and remaining salt together in a bowl and pour over the top. Bake in the oven for about 25 minutes, or until the potatoes are done and the crust is nicely browned.

Sugar-salted salmon with Seville orange

Oranges are extremely popular in winter, especially in Norway, where everybody takes them to snack on when skiing. Their sugar content prevents them from freezing and they are just what you need: thirst-quenching, sweet, and energy-laden, the perfect snack.

Seville oranges, on the other hand, are mostly used for marmalade, but also occasionally in duck and pork dishes, where their bitterness and acidity cuts beautifully through the richness. This dish is not traditional, but it works in a very Nordic way. It is quite simple and is extremely easy to make, unexpectedly delicious, and celebrates the short season of the sour but fragrant Seville oranges in the depths of winter. It is a perfect party dish as it can be prepared in advance and has an elegant feel to it. You can also use other fatty fish, such as trout or mackerel.

18oz–1¼lb raw salmon, preferably a whole fillet, skin on

for the spice rub
2 tablespoons coarse sea salt
1 tablespoon sugar
1 teaspoon ground black pepper
1 teaspoon paprika
1 teaspoon sumac (optional)

for the marinade
Finely grated zest of 1 Seville orange
Juice of 1½–2 Seville oranges
1 tablespoon liquid honey
4 tablespoons extra-virgin olive oil

for the garnish
Thinly pared zest of ½ Seville orange, cut into thin strips

SERVES 5–6 AS A SUBSTANTIAL FIRST COURSE

Dry the fish. If using salmon or trout, you must get rid of the thin, soft nerve bones with tweezers. You can feel them with your fingertips—they are placed at an angle in the front half of the fish. The bones are harmless, but they are irritating as they make it difficult to cut proper pieces from the fish.

Place the fish in a deep dish that accommodates the fillet snugly. Mix together the spice rub ingredients, then gently rub into the fish, being careful not to damage the flesh. Wrap the whole dish in plastic wrap and refrigerate for at least 24 hours, and up to 48 hours.

A couple of hours before you intend to eat it, unwrap the fish and dry the surface of the flesh with paper towels. Cut it into neat, thin, slanting slices.

Mix the marinade ingredients together in a bowl. Dip the fish slices in it, then arrange them beautifully in a dish. Pour over the rest of the marinade, if there's any left. Scatter over the orange zest. Put the fish in a cool place until you are ready to serve, but not in the refrigerator as the flavor will be reduced if the salmon is served too cold.

Any leftovers can be kept for a couple of days in the refrigerator, however.

Eel *Anguilla anguilla*

Eels are mythic creatures, spending their youth in the sea but their adult life in fresh water. As tiny fry (elvers) they take the grand tour of their life, spending three years swimming from the Sargasso Sea off the American coast thousands of miles across the Atlantic, bound for the streams and rivers of Europe and North Africa. They then live their very long adult life in fresh water, before going on the long pilgrimage back to the warm seas of their youth to spawn and die.

These days, wild eel is a threatened creature. This is partly due to overfishing—including, in rather mean ways, using flares to illuminate the water at night, when the eels are most active. However, the most serious threat is the damage to the eels' habitat caused by pollution and intensive drainage. Nowadays, eel farming is big business, and the farmed eels are actually good to eat.

In Scandinavia, eating eel is a male initiation rite, a contest, the proof of manhood being the number of times the bones can reach around the plate, and there is schnapps to go with most of the pieces of eel.

Appearance and taste Eels have small heads and very tough, black skin. They wriggle like a snake and they even taste very much like snake. They are more popular dead than alive—as living creatures, many people find eels nasty, slimy beasts. Wild eels can reach 5ft in length, although specimens this big are rarely seen. Most eels for frying are 12–16in long. Those for smoking need more fat, which comes with age.

Buying and storing Smoked eel must be shiny, firm, and with absolutely no wrinkles. Eel will not keep more than a day, so cook it on the day it is bought; once cooked, eel will keep for several days in the refrigerator.

Culinary uses Eel flesh is rich and robust enough to cope with strong flavorings, including serious spices, vinegar, lemon, beer, horseradish, and/or garlic.

Eel has a great, rough taste and the flesh is fine, very firm, and very, very fatty. When it is smoked the fattiness is a virtue, but if you are boiling or frying it, eel needs special care to get rid of some of the fat, and be as wonderful as it really can be. Broiling is the perfect way to cook fresh eel with the skin on; the fat has time to drip away, leaving succulent meat. If you are pan-frying it, the eel should be skinned. Fry it once until the fat and juices run, then transfer it to a colander and wash it in cold water. Dry the eel, dip it in seasoned flour, then fry again in browned butter.

The traditional accompaniment is creamed potatoes, though honestly this combination is not very easy to survive as the fat content is alarmingly high. It's tasty but devastating. You have to stay in bed for a day to digest it, like a snake that has swallowed a whole goat. There are other delicious ways to eat eel without the health alert: I suggest new potatoes and a vinegary cucumber salad with dill. Or, as in the recipe below, braised in dark beer. Leftovers are beautiful if soused.

Eel braised in beer

The interesting flavor of this dish comes from the dark beer, lots of herbs, and a touch of vinegar, contrasting with the delicious fatty fish. The strange thing about cooking with beer is that the bitterness from the hops diminishes during cooking, leaving an arousing, pleasant complexity. Eat simply with new potatoes.

1lb 12oz eel, cut into large chunks	Generous ¾ cup sweet hard cider
2 tablespoons butter	Coarse sea salt
4 tablespoons cider vinegar	1 teaspoon ground black pepper
A sprig each of fresh tarragon and sage	⅔ cup heavy cream
1 bay leaf	18oz chopped mixed fresh herbs: parsley, dill, chives, chervil, and sorrel
1 teaspoon fresh thyme leaves	
1 cup dark, strong beer	SERVES 4

Fry the eel in butter in a deep, thick-bottomed skillet, browning it lightly all over. Add the vinegar and fry until the liquid has evaporated. Add the sage and tarragon sprigs, bay leaf, thyme leaves, beer, hard cider, salt, and pepper. Leave to braise slowly for 15 minutes until tender. Remove the eel from the pan. Pour in the cream and reduce to a thick sauce over a high heat. Add the chopped fresh herbs, and salt and pepper to taste. Return the eel to the pan and then serve.

Pike *Esox lucius*

Pike are the stuff of nightmares, ugly in a way that scares us on a subconscious level. They are skillful predators, lurking and then attacking their prey at an astonishing speed. In lakes and rivers they feed on larvae, frogs, and river fish, even eating their own species on occasion. When in the brackish waters of the Baltic—for pike do not restrict themselves wholly to fresh water—they even hunt shoals of herrings.

Appearance and taste Pike have a distinctive long snout, and a well-camouflaged, green-gold spotted skin. Their teeth are horrifying, populating a huge set of jaws allegedly big enough to accommodate mini poodles and whole ducks if the pike is fully grown to an impressive 5ft. The males are smaller than the females, and pike grow not only in length, but also get bigger around the waist with age. I have eaten huge pike, and they make very good eating, but their bones keep them on the cheap side in Scandinavia; even a huge one is inexpensive.

The pike's flesh is striking for its unusually firm texture. Pike caught in brackish water are far better to eat than freshwater pike. The taste is meaty, like shark, and delicious.

Pike, contrary to popular belief, do not contain more bones than other fish, nor are they scattered around in the flesh at random. They do, however, have neat rows of nasty Y-shaped bones running at a slant along the front half of the fish's back. These are easy to remove when the fish is raw and are even easier if the pike has been baked whole. You can of course ask the fishmonger to take them out for you.

Culinary uses Pike suffers from the general opinion that it is good only for making quenelles. In fact, it's closer to the truth to say that it is extraordinarily good for fish cakes and quenelles—the pike's gelatinous and firm flesh, exceptional in the fish kingdom, makes it perfect for this purpose.

A perfectly prepared pike is much more juicy and succulent than tuna or shark, which share the same consistency when cooked. It will be inedible if cooked through, but pan-fried it is easy to cook to a perfect doneness. However, baking the whole fish in the oven, as in the recipe on page 27, is perhaps the ultimate way to prepare pike. Pike works well as no scaling is required, and the fish's thick overcoat acts as a self-basting protective layer and also makes it hard for you to overcook it.

Mustard sauces, capers, and horseradish are very good with pike.

Pike rissoles

Whether you are making rissoles or quenelles, the small bones present no problem as they can be ground with the flesh. Eat the rissoles with a heap of steamed, buttered spring vegetables and lemon.

2¼lb finely ground pike	Generous ¾ cup
1 onion, finely chopped	heavy cream
½ cup smoked bacon, finely	2 bunches of herbs, a
chopped	mixture of parsley,
½ cup butter, melted, plus	dill, chervil, chives, thyme,
extra for frying	and tarragon, finely
1 tablespoon all-purpose	chopped
flour	Salt and pepper
1 egg	SERVES 5–6

Mix everything (apart from the butter for frying) in a food mixer or a large bowl. Stir until the creamed fish is forming strands—this is the protein in the fish developing into membranes, which will eventually make the rissoles rise as they cook. With a spoon, make the mixture into oblong rissole shapes.

Heat the extra butter in a skillet until browned, then gently fry the rissoles. Turn them over when they are golden on one side. They are finished when they feel like a foam mattress when you press them gently with your finger.

Alternatively, poach the rissoles in trembling, salted water, and when they rise to the top they are done. Eat as dumplings in a fish soup, or brown them in the oven in a white sauce with Parmesan cheese sprinkled over.

Quenelles

These are classic fish balls, to be eaten in a mock turtle soup, in a tomato sauce, with shrimp and asparagus in a mussel sauce, or in a Nordic fish soup. While pike is the best fish for making quenelles, trout, zander or indeed any reasonably-sized freshwater fish will do.

If you are a fundamentalist quenelle maker, you are not supposed to use any flour, but unadulterated creamed fish is tricky to handle, and it's a harmless precaution to add a little cornstarch. It is wise to cream your fish from really cold ingredients, except for the soft butter. And again, fundamentally it's supposed to be done in a cold bowl, on crushed ice, with a silver spoon. But, born without the silver spoon, you can use a mixer.

5½ cups bread crumbs	2 eggs, plus 2 extra
I cup whole milk	egg yolks
2¼lb finely ground pike	I tablespooon cornstarch
or trout	Fish stock or water,
A pinch of grated nutmeg	for poaching
Salt and pepper	SERVES 4–6
I½ cups soft butter, or	
I cup butter and ½ cup	
finely ground bacon	

Soak the bread crumbs in the milk until soft, then squeeze them relatively dry, saving the milk.

Put the ground fish in a food mixer (or an ice-cold bowl). Add the nutmeg, some salt and pepper and butter, mix for a

More freshwater fish

Arctic char (*Salvelinus alpinus*) This is a huge trout, and the most hardy freshwater fish, able to live even in fresh Arctic waters. It lives near coastal waters and in rivers in the very north of Scandinavia. It is a beautiful, almost neon-red fish with a dark back and dark blotches. The meat is very much like that of other trout, but more tasty.

Zander (*Stizostedion lucioperca*) Also known as pike-perch, zander is very, very good to eat, with dense and fragrant flesh. It is the most exquisite fish to pan-fry in fillets that I know of. Zander usually weigh 2¼lb–4lb 8oz, but a full-grown specimen can be a 33lb beast, and very hard to catch. They are picky eaters, so they don't fall for a fisherman's lure so readily and are therefore considered an accomplishment to catch and land, giving a good fight.

Powan (*Coregonus clupeoides*) A smallish fish in the salmon family, powan is delicious fried, cold-smoked, and gravad. The roes are the famed *løjrom* (page 54).

minute, then add the soaked bread crumbs. Add the eggs a little at a time, then finally stir in the cornstarch. Cover, and leave the mixture in a cool place for at least an hour.

Using two cold, wet tablespoons, shape scoops of the fish mixture into oval quenelles. Poach in trembling fish stock or water—they need only to go firm. Remove with a slotted spoon. Once cooked, they will keep overnight in the refrigerator.

SALTWATER FISH

Buying and storing Fresh fish must be fresh. It is self-evident, but nevertheless true, that the beautiful experience of eating completely fresh fish is in no way comparable to eating not-fresh fish, even if it's still technically edible. If you want to teach your children truly to enjoy fish, stay away from fish packed in a controlled atmosphere, fish imported from far away, and frozen fish, and find a fish market that you can trust. The difference is huge, if elusive, but it can be detected with every sense you have, and especially when you are very young—fresh fish is a joy, not just food.

Sweetness, juiciness, and firmness diminish dramatically and very quickly as fish ages. Eat your fish the day it is bought, and keep it in the refrigerator until ready to prepare. When kept at 32°F it will keep 10 times longer as when kept at 41°F, so get some ice with it, if you can, and go straight home from the fish market.

In the early Middle Ages, the sound between Sweden and Denmark was so full of herrings that the water seemed to boil. When the fish migrated in and out of the Baltic in early spring, and back again in the fall, they were so abundant that they could be caught by hand, and were landed in thousands of tons. Fishing and salting stalls were put up along the shore, and the fish were salted in huge barrels and traded along the Baltic coast for salt, amber, weaponry, and iron.

This "Herring Adventure" and the commerce following it, marked the beginning of Copenhagen as the capital of Denmark, with a resident king. Previously, the king had a moveable feast, going from castle to castle around the country. Even before that, fish was the staple food all along the thousands of miles of coast; fresh for shore-dwellers, dried and salted, or just plain dried, for inlanders. The need to make seasonal fish last during cold and unfishable winter months is the origin of the great northern tradition of preserving fish.

Fish from cold waters have a certain delicacy: they grow slowly and their flesh becomes dense, juicy, and filled with minerals from the abundant plankton, small fish and algae they feed on. Fatty fish such as herrings and mackerel have a perfect balance of essential fatty acids for human stomachs, and like all other naturally fed animals, slow-growing fish are much more flavorsome and easier to make into tasty meals, even if prepared very simply.

Culinary uses The traditions are, in fact, very simple. Fresh fish are simply tossed in rye flour and fried in butter, broiled, boiled in salted water, or baked in the oven. The accompaniments are effective, if not varied: horseradish, capers, mustard, lemon or vinegar, parsley, dill, butter, and potatoes. Delicious if the fish is fresh: the sharp notes set off the mild taste, the butter acts as a sauce, and the herbs add color and a subtle freshness.

Norway haddock *Sebastes* sp.

Norway haddock are actually a number of closely related fish in the rockfish family. Some of these are endangered, some are not. The Nordic species are deepwater fish that gorge on giant Greenland prawns and are caught in large numbers as they follow the shoals of prawns through the deep seas around Greenland. For many years they were considered a pest as they ruin the nets with their ferocious thorns and spikes and cut the hands of the fishermen. They were simply not eaten until some ingenious Greenlander hatched the idea to make them popular as a table fish. This has been a huge success over the past 20 years, as people have realized how delicious Norway haddock is to eat—so much of a success, in fact, that some are now seriously endangered.

Appearance and taste The fish are beautiful creatures, with huge eyes made to catch the sparse light deep in the oceans, a vivid orange body to scare off predators, and spikes that will cut your fingers if you are not careful. The flesh is delicious, dense, and white, and tastes intensely of the prawns they eat. It can be eaten even by people who—like me—are allergic to crustaceans.

Culinary uses Norway haddock is sweet-fleshed, and becomes almost lobster-like and densely flaky if fried on the skin. The skin becomes perfectly crispy and delicious if you fry it (page 28) and eat it with a chervil cream and new potatoes. The huge head and bones should be kept for fish soup.

Norway haddock herbed fish cakes

The Scandinavians love all kinds of fish cakes, often very simply spiced. These are different, however, as they are made more like a burger, using the gelatinous quality of the fish to make the cakes stick together, and including no other ingredients except fresh herbs and salt. Norway haddock, with its shellfish taste, is perfect for the task, but you can also use any member of the cod family, pike, or gray mullet.

Eat the fishcakes hot with herbed butter, potatoes with dill, and lemon wedges, or as a regular burger, with tomato, lettuce, and chervil cream (page 176).

1lb 10oz Norway haddock fillets, skinned and boned	1 teaspoon coarse sea salt
3 large handfuls of fresh herbs, such as parsley, dill, tarragon, chives, and chervil	Butter, for frying
	SERVES 4

Make sure first that the fish contains absolutely no bones.

Chop the fish, herbs, and salt together on a board, using a heavy, wide-bladed knife. No machine can do the job properly. Chop away, but stop while the fish is still coarser than ground meat and is beginning to stick together.

With wet hands, mold the fish into eight burgers. Melt the butter in a skillet until browned, then fry the fish cakes very slowly until they are just set, and browned on one side. Don't push them around the pan as they will disintegrate. Turn them over once and brown on the other side. They will need about 6 minutes altogether: leave them too long and they will become dry.

Cod *Gadinae* sp. *Lotinae* sp.

Cod is both the name of a certain fish, and a roomy expression for a large number of fish that are closely related. The true cod is not really an option at the time of writing, as it is seriously endangered. But all its relatives are usually not and can be cooked in any number of ways: English whiting, pollock (or pollack), coley (or coalfish), tusk, ling, haddock, and hake, to name the species most popular in the north. They all have flaky, tasty, and succulent flesh, and on the whole can be prepared in much the same manner. You could say that we Scandinavians are not particularly imaginative fish eaters. The traditional ways to prepare these fish are certainly not very varied, but they are good all the same, and allow the distinctiveness of each fish to shine.

Appearance and taste Cod are long, smooth-skinned fish, often with dark or greenish stripes along the sides, sporting a small beard, and with mostly white, flaky flesh, even if some species have gray flesh. Most can grow to an impressive size, and are just as good when huge as when they are of the more usual size of 2¼–8lb 12oz. The flesh is mildly salty-sweet and delicious. All cod are most flavorsome in winter.

Culinary uses Cod and its relatives can be made into fish cakes or soup, or baked, fried, boiled, or broiled—in short, they are extremely versatile. We normally eat these fish with the same accompaniments as salt cod, namely horseradish, mustard sauce, melted butter, capers, crispy bacon, pickled beets, hard-boiled eggs, and potatoes—quite a meal, even without the fish! Red hake and English whiting are perfect for soups and fish cakes, and coley's rather glutinous flesh makes perfect, light fish cakes.

Cod with pork fat

This is a simple but delicious recipe, suggested to me by a fisherman's wife from Gilleleje, a small fishing town on the coast of Zealand in Denmark. Lifelong experience in dealing with fish almost every day of the week had taught her that simplicity is best. Her family's all-time favorite happens to be thick slabs of boneless cod, lightly pre-salted, and covered with thin bacon slices. Simply bake in a buttered, deep, ovenproof dish at 400°F until the fish is opaque and the bacon crispy. It's amazing. You can use smoked or unsmoked salted bacon. The recipe also works well with haddock, pollock and halibut.

Cod and sons

Boiled cod is a huge achievement if you are a perfectionist. You can make your life less exhausting by simply baking it. It will be just as you want it to be —perfect flakes of opaque marble. Newly boiled cod's roe, still warm, is a very different thing from cooled; it's creamy, a little gritty, and is so nice with a lemony hollandaise sauce or caper sauce. It has become a luxury, but so has real cod. Other cod fish are just as good prepared this way, and so is halibut.

Serve the dish with a bowl of new potatoes and asparagus or pointed head cabbage with dill, and your preferred sauce.

6 small cod's roes	½ stick butter, cut into
3½lb thick piece of cod on	thin slices
the bone	Salt and pepper
	SERVES 6

Wrap the cod's roes in six small parcels of parchment paper and secure with cotton string. Sink them into a saucepan of boiling salted water. Turn down the heat and let simmer for 5 minutes. Let cool a little in the water.

Arrange the cod in a deep ovenproof dish and place the butter slices on top. Sprinkle with salt and pepper, then cover with aluminum foil. Bake at 350°F and test after 25 minutes. When the fish is still a little bit rosy by the bone, it's done.

Herring *Clupea harengus*

Herrings are the backbone of Scandinavian fish cuisine, and are not endangered at the moment, even if some species, as in the Baltic, are very low. There are several species living in Nordic waters, differing mainly in size and fat content. Most of them are eaten cured in some way. Herrings are admittedly full of thin bones that are very difficult to extract from the soft flesh, but they seem to disappear when the fish are cured. In a fresh herring you must either live with it or eat something else.

Appearance and taste Herrings are beautiful, small, silvery fish, with dark, soft meat, with a special oily flavor. The scales come off when the fish are washed.

Culinary uses Fishing trips are a popular pastime, and sometimes you return with vats of herrings. The classic way to deal with large amounts is to salt them of course, but if you have more modest quantities, there are some delicious traditional recipes using fresh herrings, including the ones described here and on pages 76–7.

Herrings that are absolutely fresh are delicious fried, baked, or broiled and, like other fatty fish, go well with sharp sauces. Even though the bones can be a nuisance, at least the scales come off easily. Like mackerel, herrings should be eaten before the fat turns oily, which pretty much means straight away. Once soused or fried, herrings keep for a couple of days in the refrigerator.

Two ways with fresh herrings

There are two very simple but delicious ways to cook herrings in a deep clay pot or dish. Clay pot herring is very similar to Jansson's temptation (page 87), simply replacing the canned northern anchovies with fresh herring fillets. The fillets should be pre-salted for a couple of hours and then dried with paper towels. Arrange rings of onion, thinly sliced potatoes, and

the fish in your dish, season with salt and pepper, and fill the dish almost to the top with cream. Bake at 350°F until the top is golden and the potatoes are tender and cooked through.

An alternative, but just as good, is *silllåda*. This time there are no potatoes, and each layer is spiced with a little ground allspice and ground ginger, along with some chopped parsley, and the whole dish finished with bread crumbs and generous pieces of butter. Bake in the same way until golden brown.

Mackerel *Scomber scombrus*

Mackerel live in the deep seas in winter, but come to the shores in great numbers in May and again in August. The first season coincides with the ripening gooseberries, and the second with the wealth of herbs, which all go so well with the fish's fine, tasty flesh. Mackerel are not as popular a fresh fish as they deserve to be, but the craving for true Nordic food is putting them back on the menu once again.

Appearance and taste Mackerel is a small tuna fish, with very dark, fatty meat. It's a beauty when alive, clad in an *haute couture* dress of a graphic black pattern on a silvery blue background. It is not severely threatened at the time of writing, even if it is a very popular fish. The flesh is loose when raw, but becomes firm when cooked or smoked.

Buying and storing Like most oily fish, mackerel will develop very high levels of histamine if not kept properly cool, or if too old. Make sure your mackerel is very fresh and is stored at a low temperature, and eat it straight away. If you need to keep the fish overnight, pre-salt it rather heavily and keep it in the refrigerator.

Health benefits Mackerel is always a wild fish, containing large amounts of omega 3 fatty acids, and vitamin B.

Culinary uses Mackerel takes wonderfully to spices, curing, and smoking as the meaty taste can work through anything. Fresh mackerel is perfect for broiling as some of the excess fat drains away. The combination of mackerel and gooseberry sauce, which takes the edge off the fish's fattiness, is legendary. But rhubarb compote or horseradish cream work well too.

In the north, mackerel is mostly hot smoked, and tastes delicious eaten on rye bread with raw egg yolks, radishes, chives, raw onion, and scrambled eggs. But it is also a perfect and very cheap alternative to gravad lax (page 78), or indeed can be soused like herrings (page 84).

Most of the mackerel eaten in Scandinavia is actually canned, in tomato sauce, which makes an extremely popular sandwich filling, with mayonnaise, on rye bread.

Broiled mackerel with gooseberries and elderflowers

The combination of gooseberries and elderflowers is, of course, a classic. So too is the pairing of mackerel and gooseberries, and not only in Scandinavia. I've gone to extremes by combining all three, but the result is pure, Nordic midsummer bliss. Serve with lemon and new potatoes. Pre-salting (see below) the mackerel makes it firmer and tastier.

4 whole mackerel	2 fresh cloves garlic, chopped
4 tablespoons coarse sea salt	1 teaspoon ground black pepper
10 large elderflower heads	Butter, for frying
Grated zest and juice of 1 lemon	**to serve**
1 red chile pepper, seeded and chopped	Gooseberry compote with elderflowers (page 223)
	SERVES 4

Gut the fish, but leave the heads on. Slash each fish three times on both sides with a very sharp knife. Using 3 tablespoons of the coarse sea salt, rub the fish inside and out, then let rest for a couple of hours in a cool place. After that time, clean off the salt under a cold faucet, then dry the fish completely with paper towels.

Cut the white flowers from the green stems of the elderflower heads and mix with the remaining salt, plus the lemon zest, chile pepper, garlic, and black pepper. Fill the fish with this heady mixture. Either fry the fish in hot butter until nicely browned—4 minutes on each side is fine for a small mackerel—or broil them. Turn the fish only once, as they are tender-fleshed. Serve with the compote.

Garfish *Belone belone*

Garfish come to the shores in May, and are a very popular angling fish as they put up a good fight. They are one of the few true seasonal treats, in their short spring season, and again in August, when they return to deeper waters. They're the favorite fish for many Scandinavians, and they're also mine; the flesh is very loose when raw, but becomes meaty and delicious when fried.

Appearance and taste Garfish are wondrous creatures. With their long and slender bodies, which dart through the water like liquid silver, they are hard to mistake for any other fish. The long beak is full of razor-sharp teeth and the bones are eerily green, which has led to much superstition about the garfish's eating habits, but they are quite harmless. They usually reach about 3¼ft in length yet weigh less than 2¼lb. Their meat tastes more like veal than fish.

Buying and storing Garfish are best when they are boned, when the meat can be cut into squares and is easy to handle. But you must ask the fishmonger to do it, as it's rather difficult to do yourself. The alternative is to cut them into chunks and fry them on the bone, like an eel. In Denmark we have special boning machines for garfish, but these probably don't exist anywhere else. One garfish should feed two people.

Culinary uses Garfish come into their own when dusted with fine rye flour and fried in butter until crispy, which takes just a matter of a few minutes. Eat with new potatoes, cucumber and dill salad, and gooseberry compote with elderflowers. They are very good when grilled. Garfish can also be soused like herrings, and this is a clever thing to do with leftover fried garfish.

Monkfish *Lopius piscatorius*

The monkfish must be the ugliest creature on earth. It is a sea dragon that can grow to a scary 6½ft, and is one of our favorite fish.

Appearance and taste With its enormous head and cavernous mouth, the monkfish is unmistakable. The central spine is all the bone there is, sandwiched between two fat fillets of pure meat; the consistency of the flesh is like lobster tail and has much the same taste. Three antennae grow on its forehead, and a waving small flag of skin that resembles a shrimp. The monkfish simply sits on the ocean floor waving the flag to attract smaller and dumber fish into the vicinity of its terrible wide mouth filled with several rows of razor-sharp teeth.

Culinary uses The fish is coated with several layers of strange, slippery skin that has to come off before you cook it—or the fish will end up looking like it's been tied with rubber bands or yanked inside out. When you are lucky enough to find whole monkfish for sale, the enormous head, which constitutes more than half of the weight of the fish, is wonderful for stock, as are the skin and bones.

The boneless fillets are perfect for broiling, roasting, or frying like steaks, or can be just heated through in a soup made from the head and bone (page 31). The cheeks, which are sold separately and are relatively cheap, are delicious little nuggets, fine for broiling on skewers or pan-frying, but you must remove all the membranes or they will look really strange when cooked.

Gray mullet *Chelon abrosus*

A recent introduction in northern waters, the warm waters around the power stations and the general warming of the seas are responsible for having provided breeding ground for this delicious vegetarian fish that eventually grows to a huge size, serving up to 12 people. It has no teeth, just soft kissable lips, as it's a grazer of soft seaweeds. This makes it almost impossible to catch on a rod; where as a net close to the shore is ideal. It can grow to an impressive 2½ft, but most gray mullets are much smaller.

Appearance and taste The fish is covered in huge silver coin scales that need to come off before you cut it open. It's easy to do yourself, or you can have the fishmonger do it for you. The flesh is white, flaky, sweet flavored, and so dense it will stick together even if broiled whole or in fillets. The flesh is fatty and rich in omega 3 fatty acids.

Culinary uses Gray mullet has many of the same qualities as wild salmon, even if it's not quite so fatty, and you can cook it instead of salmon, in every way you wish. It's not farmed, and is a much better choice than farmed conventional salmon.

In its home in southern Europe, gray mullet has been a favorite fish for broiling whole for millennia, but fits naturally into the northern repertoire of serving fish with spiky horseradish, or pickled cucumber salad. The bones and head are very good for fish soup.

The flesh will cook to an almost lobster-like firmness if cut into dice or strips and added at the last moment to the soup. But the preparation that will show off the mullet in all its glory, is when fried crisp on the grill or in a pan. The skin is delicious and so is the flesh underneath.

It's essential that gray mullet is not overcooked, either way you choose to cook it. It is extremely filling and 9oz fish on the bone is enough for one serving. When the flesh is just firm, and it's still a little pink in the middle, or by the bone it's cooked. Longer, and it will dry up, and what a shame that would be.

Gravad with dill, or baked in slices on a plate are also very good ways to eat the fish, and prepared as the Fried Mackerel with Gooseberries, or with a rhubarb compote; new potatoes are perfect with gray mullet. The frying and the butter/olive oil works miracles.

Fried pieces of gray mullet are delicious when soused, like herrings, and if it's served with cucumber salad you can pair the two in a deep dish and eat it for lunch the day after, with toasted rye bread.

Flatfish

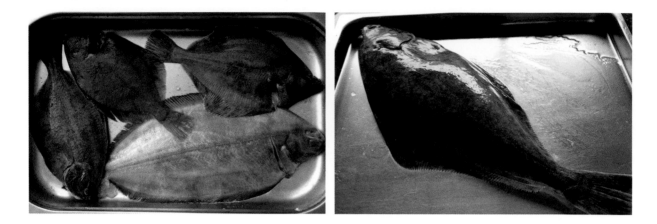

Flatfish are plentiful, and extremely popular. They live all over the north Atlantic and Baltic and are caught in vast numbers, even if the populations of the most popular fish have diminished. Some flatfish, such as sole and turbot, are madly expensive, but the less well-known species, such as flounder and dab, are even cheap.

Flatfish hatch as ordinary-looking swimming fish, with an eye on both sides, and live like this for a long time, until they gradually lose the swim bladder, one of the eyes wanders on to the other side of the fish, and it sinks to live the rest of its life on the bottom of the sea. Some species have both eyes on their left, others on the right, and as some species interbreed, there are lots of exceptions to the rules. Flatfish are almost indistinguishable from the sea bottom, and some have the ability of a chameleon to alter their coloring; when swimming it's not uncommon to step accidentally on a brill or flounder.

Flatfish have beautiful, firm, moist, and sparkling white flesh, except flounder, whose flesh is gray-tinged. They are usually lean, except for Greenland halibut.

Turbot and brill

These luxury fish are stars and need no fancy preparation to take away the attention. Turbot (*Psetta maxima*) is celebrated all over the world, but the turbot from our northern waters is the best. The cold makes the fish grow more slowly, and the brilliant white meat is dense, lobster-like, and flavorful. Its close relative, the brill (*Scopthalmus rhombus*), is almost as good, and at quite a different price.

Don't be put off by a very large brill or turbot: luckily some people believe that they become coarse with age, but this is not true, and it keeps the price of giant turbot at a more accessible level than that of smaller fish. Brill is best in the fall.

Turbot and brill need particularly gentle treatment. Often they are baked in the oven with a piece of butter, until the flesh is almost done. If you cook them too much, the delicateness is gone and they will be dry. Cook them at 400°F until the meat is still pink at the bone. Let them sit on the counter, covered in aluminum foil for a few minutes, and the heat from the pan will cook them gently through. Take away the skin and serve them simply, or with a topping of horseradish or chervil cream, caper or hollandaise sauce, or just plain melted butter and lemon and horseradish.

Halibut

There are two types of halibut, both giants of the north Atlantic. Halibut (*Hippoglossus hippoglossus*) can grow to an impressive table-tennis table size—I once bought one weighing 661lb for my organic restaurant, and it was impossible to get it in through the door. We felt very much like we were on *Candid Camera* working on it, and decided to cut it up spread out on two large tables outside on the quay, in front of the restaurant. The meat was delicious and rich, just as I would expect. Halibut meat is always flaky, but these flakes were large enough to make up a serving each. Usually, though, it's much smaller, and is best eaten in winter.

The Greenland halibut (*Reinhardtius hippoglossoides*) is small by comparison—up to 44lb, but usually weighing 2¼–4lb 8oz. It is not bottom-of-the-sea-bound like other flatfish, so both sides of the fish are usually colored. The flesh is fatty and lends itself beautifully to cold smoking or home smoking (page 83). As with all fatty fish, you need to be very precise when you cook it— too long and it will be bone dry. The fish is fine all year around, but most exquisite in winter.

Plaice

Speckled like a ladybird, with red spots on gray skin, plaice (*Pleuronectes platessa*) is the most loved fish for everyday meals all over Scandinavia. But it is not as plentiful as before and is quite expensive. The flesh has a tender sweetness to it, and is quite firm when cooked. Plaice is often served in the most simple and delicious way, dusted with rye flour and fried whole, on the bone, in butter. The fish is most delicious in late summer and in the fall.

Other flatfish

The flounder is similar in appearance to plaice, but with a knobbed back and no red spots, though the two species interbreed and it can be very difficult to know which is which. Inside, however, the flounder has dark, succulent flesh, with a taste quite different from plaice. The witch (a member of the flounder family) can grow to an impressive size, and is rarely eaten, but delicious. The dab, not unlike a flounder in appearance, is normally what you get if you buy frozen flatfish fillets; it's thin-fleshed and not too interesting. At the other end of the scale, the delicious and expensive soles and lemon soles are mostly eaten in restaurants, and most of the catch is exported; their prices can be prohibitive for private eating.

Culinary uses Flatfish cooked on the bone are much more succulent than fillets, but the latter are much easier to fry, simply coated in rye flour and sizzled in browned butter for a few minutes. Serve them hot on buttered rye bread with lemon and remoulade for a beautiful lunch dish. Other accompaniments might be potatoes and a variety of sweet-and-sour pickled things such as cucumber salad, raw lingonberry jam, and either just melted butter or a parsley sauce; but remember that the smaller flatfish such as plaice and flounder are best in the summer, so don't serve these with anything too substantial. Larger flatfish, such as halibut and turbot, are wonderful if baked whole and served with a chervil cream, butter, and horseradish or a caper sauce.

The bones and heads of all flatfish are pure gold for fish stocks and fish soup. Keep them in the freezer until you have enough for a stock.

Celeriac and apple soup with halibut and shellfish

This soup is not traditional but it tastes wonderful nonetheless. If you want a more traditional Nordic recipe, leave out the apple and celeriac, and simply finish the soup off with more cream. And if you'd prefer a bit more color, you can add thin strips of carrot and leek with the fish. The recipe is not quick, but it's worth it, trust me. You can use chicken stock rather than fish stock if you prefer, or indeed a mixture of the two.

6 conchs
2¼lb mussels
A large piece of butter
14oz apples
14oz celeriac
2 cups whole milk
2 cups heavy cream
A dash of fish sauce
Salt and black pepper
Approx. 9oz halibut fillets (or other firm-fleshed flat fish), in strips
6 oysters

for the fish stock
6lb 8oz halibut heads and bones
3 onions
A large sprig of thyme
4 leeks, green part only
1 carrot
2 celery stalks, or small slice of celeriac
1 tablespoon whole black peppercorns
SERVES 6

Boil the conchs for 3½–4 hours in their shells until they are tender; less than that and they will be like rubber. Take them out of the shells with a pin when they are done, and cut off the upper, brown end. Slice thinly.

Clean the mussels. Steam them at a high heat in a lump of butter until they open. Strain the liquid through a piece of cheesecloth, and reserve. Unopened mussels should be discarded.

Make the stock as on page 31. When it is finished, strain and reduce to 6 cups. Mix with the liquid from the mussels.

Peel the apples and celeriac and dice. Boil them in the stock until very tender. Purée in a food processor or blender. Return to the stock with the milk, cream and a dash of fish sauce. Just before eating, put the turbot, conch slices, and mussels in the warm soup and let them heat through—they should not boil. Put a raw shelled oyster in each soup bowl and pour on the hot soup, which will cook the oyster.

Pan-fried flounder

This is a very basic recipe, useful for all flatfish, and is indeed the most popular way to serve them. The thin edges become crispy, the tiny, bead-like morsels on the edges ready to be savored, and the meat tender and juicy. The accompaniments vary: lingonberry jam in the north, a parsley sauce or just melted butter and lemon further south, and plain boiled potatoes all over.

Pan-frying is an art. The fish is soft-fleshed and scatters easily, but there are a few tricks, and it's easy if you understand the nature of frying. When you put a piece of fish or meat in a skillet with hot fat, the flesh is moist, and there will be a thin water film between the fat and the meat. As long as it's there the meat will stick to the pan; if you push it around, or try to turn it over, the crispy outer skin or coating will come off. If you wait, patiently, until the water has evaporated, it can be moved, turned, and every bit of coating and skin will stay on the meat. So, patience and not too much heat. It is a skill well worth mastering, as fish cooked on the bone is far better than without.

Another word of warning: do not attempt preparing this for more than two to four people unless you have a huge stove and more than two skillets. Choose the recipe for oven-baked fish instead (page 27).

4 huge plaice, the dark	I cup fine rye flour, spiced
upper skin, head, and gut	with salt and pepper
removed	Butter, for frying
	SERVES 4

Dust the fish with the spiced flour and fry in a thick-bottomed skillet in a very generous piece of lightly browned butter. Turn the heat down, and let the fish fry gently until it's easily moved: 5 minutes on each side for a smallish fish, 8 minutes for a big one.

Turn the fish over with two round-bladed knives, and finish on the other side. Test with a pointed knife at the thickest point of the fish; if the meat is white and the bone still slightly pink, it's done. It's important not to hold back on the butter, as it makes all the difference both technically and to the taste when the fish is sizzling in a bubble bath of butter during the whole process. If you are scared of butter, use the recipe for baked fish instead.

Skate/Ray *Raja batis/Raja clavata*

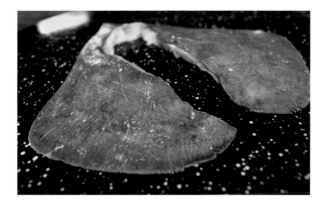

Eating skate is a peculiar and beautiful experience, rather like you might expect it to be if you were eating a dragon steak. You sense that this, like shark, is far older and stranger than any fish, or anything for that matter, that you are likely to eat. A survivor from millions of years ago, the skate is in the same family as sharks, but with a flavor quite different from the shark's meaty taste. There are many species and they are all good.

Culinary uses You eat only the "wings," two wide fins that the fish can move in an unbelievably elegant manner. You understand how when you see the meat, which is made up from long, fibrous strands of muscle, and is very lobster-like, both in consistency and taste.

Under the lizard skin the flesh is white and tender, in long, pearly strands, and is as close to lobster as you can get (apart from monkfish). Allow 9–10½oz per head: there is not much meat, but it is extremely filling. Skate can be fried whole, in butter, or baked, dotted with butter and sprinkled with sea salt, in a pan in the oven. Pour a little water in the bottom, just so it will not burn, and bake for 25 minutes at 400°F. Check the fish with a pointed knife: if the meat is white all the way to the cartilage it's done; otherwise put it back into the oven for a few minutes. It will never become dry, as the jelly will keep it moist.

The skate has thick, inedible skin and several layers of jelly-like connective tissue that must be removed before eating. Cook the skate in whole pieces, and remove the skin after cooking. You eat skate by scraping back the skin, and plucking the meat off. In the middle is a very strong and extremely flexible system of tiny bones and cartilage, like in the fin of a shark, providing the elegance the live skate has as it moves through the water. When you have eaten one side, turn it over and eat the rest.

Eat the fish with a caper sauce or shredded horseradish, browned butter, and lemon. It is best eaten warm, as the meat is easily distinguished from the jelly while warm. Make plenty as the flesh is perfect in a salad for lunch or an appetizer the next day. Moisten, but don't drown the long strands of meat, in a herbed mustard mayonnaise, chervil cream, or herbed vinaigrette. In the fall, combine with diced raw apple, tiny dice of celeriac, and capers and top with crisp bacon and in the spring accompany with new peas, asparagus, and small carrot dice for sweetness. Serve with toasted rye bread.

FISH ROE

Nordic people have a predilection for anything with fish eggs, something that we share with the Russians. We love the roe from lumpfish, cod, and all its relatives, and also from vendace and powans, which are inhabitants of primarily Swedish and Finnish lakes and produce particularly delicious, and expensive, roe. Like the rest of the world, we also enjoy the shiny, orange beads from sea trout and salmon, though while they are lovely as a garnish they are a bit too oily to eat on their own.

Maybe we have become too conservative in our choices, and eating roes from a wider variety of fish certainly makes good sense, given the ongoing problem of overfishing in our seas and oceans. Already some of the most popular roes, including from cod, have moved from an everyday staple to a luxury.

While roes vary in texture and color, they all share a breezy sea taste—in the same way that oysters and mussels do—and a sweet, mineral-rich flavor.

Buying and storing Roes are a seasonal treat, to be eaten fresh in early spring.

They can be bought fresh and unsalted (sometimes in the membrane), salted or smoked, depending on the type. Cod's roe, flatfish roe, and herring roe are usually bought fresh, to be cooked at home, while other types of roe are often bought salted and are eaten raw. Salmon, trout, and lumpfish roes can be bought either salted and cleaned, or come in a whole membrane, to be cleaned and salted at home (page 53). Preserves of roes are not worth the cost and will deprive you of the seasonality and taste of fresh roes.

As with all other food from the sea, roe must smell invitingly fresh. You should generally steer clear of frozen roes, except for those of the vendace and powan—they are so small that they are not really affected by freezing (page 54). Canned roes (of cod or salmon, for example) are not to be recommended; they are too oily and salty, without the fresh sea taste of the real stuff.

Health benefits Fish roe is rich in minerals, vitamins, and omega 3 fatty acids.

Culinary uses Cod's roes, flatfish roes, and herring roes are boiled or fried whole and eaten hot for dinner with a rich sauce and potatoes—if fried alongside, or baked inside, the fish, they have a very different soft and creamy consistency—or eaten cold on an open-face sandwich.

Salted salmon, trout, lumpfish, and vendace roes are never heated, but eaten as a topping on open-face sandwiches, or as a garnish for all kinds of dishes with fish, as a starter with blinis or potato pancakes, lemon, crème fraîche, and red onion. The combination of the salty roes, rich crème fraîche, and sharp sweetness from the onions is just perfect.

Cod's roe

All over Scandinavia, cod's roe—and of the cod's many relatives, often sold as cod's roe—is very popular. It is also versatile, and can be eaten either fresh (boiled or fried) or smoked. But while eating cod's roe used to be an everyday experience, since strict fishing quotas have been imposed it has become very expensive.

Fresh cod's roe is in season in early spring. Try to buy small roes, about the size of two fingers, as they are by far the most delicious, creamy, and sweet; the large cod's roes can be rather coarse and grainy, mainly because the eggs are too mature. The eggs must have intact membranes, or the roe will be impossible to prepare, whether it is to be boiled, fried, or smoked. No cleaning is required.

Boiled whole cod's roe is delicious served plain and hot for dinner, with potatoes and lemon and a rich sauce, such as the egg sauce on page 33 or the hollandaise on page 32. The boiled, cooled roes can also be sliced, fried in butter until crisp, and served with the same accompaniments. Boiled and cooled, cod's roe makes a classic open-face sandwich, sliced on rye bread with a lemony mayonnaise or remoulade, fresh dill, and lemon. This is seasonal food at its very best.

Smoked cod's roes, and roes from many of its relatives often sold as cod's roes, are a delicious topping for open-face sandwiches, either hot or cold smoked. The hot-smoked version is browned on the outside and firm inside, and is easy to make at home (page 83); it is delicious sliced on rye bread with a homemade mayonnaise and lemon. Cold-smoked cod's roe looks like amber and is soft. It's either spread on toast or rye bread as it is, or made into a Nordic version of taramasalata, with crème fraîche and/or mayonnaise, dill, and black pepper, to be eaten, preferably, on crispbread. This is the real thing compared to the ever-popular Nordic industrial spread sold in tubes in every supermarket. This is eaten on crispbread, often with hard-boiled egg and cucumber, and I must confess it is actually rather good, even if purists enjoy disliking it.

Boiled cod's roes

Wrap the roes in separate parcels of parchment paper, making sure the packages are even in size; you can put several small roes together in one parcel. Arrange them tightly in a saucepan and cover with cold salted water (allow 1 generous handful of salt per 8 cups of water). Bring slowly to a boil.

Small roes need to cook for 3 minutes from boiling point, huge ones 10 minutes. Take the pan from the heat and let the roes cool in the water. If you aim to eat them as they are, let them steep in the water for 15 minutes. Remove the outer membrane before eating.

Cod's roes must be boiled the day they are bought; after that, they will keep for 2 days in the refrigerator.

Herring roe

The eggs of herring roe are large, and a little gritty, and must be fried or baked. It was once common to eat herring roe but now very few people do, maybe because many regard fresh herrings with disrespect as poor man's food. As a result, it can be hard to find herring roes, but they are delicious.

Flatfish roe

Personally, I like the creamy, pale roes from flatfish such as sole and turbot; these are usually fried or baked alongside or inside the fish they come from, and are eaten as a bonus with the fish.

How to clean and salt roes

Salmon, trout, and lumpfish roes must be cleaned and salted before use.

Put the whole roe, inside its membrane, in a large bowl with a handful of coarse salt. Add cold water almost to cover. Whisk with a balloon whisk until the non-edible parts cling to the whisk; you may have to clean the whisk several times. Rinse through a fine sieve and clean under the cold faucet, then leave to dry off any excess moisture. Adjust the salt—you want enough to bring out the flavor, but not too much. Eat within 3 days.

Vendace and powan roes

Several fish in the *Coregonus* family, part of the salmon family, yield the most expensive and delicate of all the Scandinavian roes. It is usually called *løjrom*, no matter what the fish. The *Kalix løjrom*, from Sweden, is a protected name, and is always from the *Coregonus albula*, or vendace, a small, silvery fish living in the Baltic. It is eaten as it comes, raw, but salted, in small quantities, like real sturgeon caviar. It's delicious just served on plain toast with a little lemon, dill, and crème fraîche, and onion or chives; as a topping for boiled, baked, or fried fish; or with potato pancakes.

If you buy frozen vendace or powan roes, open the package and let it defrost in the refrigerator, if large; however, very few people can afford a package too large to be thawed on the kitchen counter in an hour. Eat within 3 days, as long as correctly stored in the refrigerator.

Salmon and sea trout roe

You can buy these large beaded beauties fresh when they are in season, in early spring; or you may be lucky enough to buy (or even catch) a whole fish with the eggs inside. Salmon roe can be bought fresh, already cleaned and salted, but it's not difficult to do this yourself, as with lumpfish roe.

Lumpfish roe

Fresh lumpfish roe can look like a weird, glow-in-the-dark toy, the spooky fluorescent sheen caused by unharmful algae. In Scandinavia, roes from the female lumpfish are abundant in spring (the fish itself is extremely ugly and flabby and is not eaten). You can buy them either cleaned (and salted), rather expensively, or not cleaned, very cheaply; or you may be lucky enough to catch or buy a whole fish with the eggs inside. It is not difficult to clean the roe yourself, but it's not a job for the faint-hearted as the giant bag filled with millions of rosy beads looks positively monstrous. When salted, the roes will keep for 3–4 days in the refrigerator.

Lumpfish roe is rosy by nature, and we unfortunately have a bad habit of dying it dark gray, black, or very red (to imitate sturgeon roes) and marketing it as "caviar," sold in glass jars. It's a mess on the plate, is too salty, and has a strange chemical taste. In short, it is disgusting in every way and should be avoided.

Lumpfish roe, or smelt roe if you can't find lumpfish, is eaten like *løjrom*, with blinis or crisp potato pancakes, or just plainly on rye bread or toast. It's often paired with crème fraîche, lemon juice, and red onion.

Potato and Jerusalem artichoke pancakes with *løjrom*

These pancakes work exactly as blinis, and go with all kinds of smoked fish, gravad fish, or fish roe. You can make them without the Jerusalem artichokes and they will be lovely with fried herrings and lingonberry jam, or with fried bacon and more lingonberries. Here, the pancakes are served with *løjrom* (vendace roe) or lumpfish roe, crème fraîche, dill, and red onion.

for the pancakes

12oz potatoes, unpeeled but cleaned
9oz Jerusalem artichokes, unpeeled but cleaned
2 eggs
4 tablespoons all-purpose flour
Salt and pepper
Butter, for frying

for the topping

10½oz lumpfish roe, or as much *løjrom* as your budget will allow
Generous ¾ cup crème fraîche
1 lemon, cut into quarters
1 red onion, finely diced
Fresh dill
SERVES 6 PEOPLE AS
AN APPETIZER, OR
4 AS A MAIN COURSE

Grate the raw potatoes and Jerusalem artichokes coarsely. Put them in a colander and rinse the starch from the potatoes under the cold faucet. Dry them completely on a dish towel. Mix with the rest of the pancake ingredients. The result will not look like a batter, but rest assured that it will be transformed into lovely crispy potato cakes once fried.

Heat a thick-bottomed cast-iron skillet, on a low–medium heat, then heat the butter until browned. Spoon the batter into the pan in blobs, and flatten to ½in thickness. When brown on one side, turn the pancakes over and brown on the other side, until tender. Put them in an ovenproof dish and keep them crispy and warm in the oven while you cook the rest. You will need to remix the batter often, as it separates.

Serve the pancakes with the toppings.

SHELLFISH & MOLLUSKS

The seas around the Nordic countries are full of shellfish, sweet and firm from growing slowly in cold, deep waters: huge black lobsters, spindly and soft-shelled Norway lobsters, quick-witted shore crabs, small sweet-fleshed shrimp, large prawns from the North Atlantic, huge common crabs that sabotage the fisherman's nets, and some of the best round-type oysters in the world. These are all plentiful and eaten as luxuries, though small shrimp and common crabs are very affordable. Crustaceans come in a wide palette of colors, when they are alive—black, bluish, brown, pink, gray, greenish, and green, the red color presenting itself only when they are prepared.

Culinary uses Northern crustaceans (including crabs, lobsters, shrimp, and prawns) and mollusks (including mussels and oysters) have a unique sweetness and succulence if properly prepared, which is coupled with a penetrating aroma and taste and a firm juiciness that lends itself to all kinds of treatment, even if dealt with simply. I believe that because their taste is so fine they do not need many extras from the cook.

So, while you can make delicious shellfish salads with either a herbed vinaigrette or mayonnaise, not much can beat shellfish that is simply broiled or boiled *au naturel* to expose the luscious flesh in all its glory, eaten with a lemony or herby sauce, a simple salad, and some bread. The shells are fine for soups.

The traditional flavoring for crustaceans and shellfish in Scandinavia is fresh dill and, in particular, scented dill flowers. The latter are the most unusual and delicate of northern herbs, and probably unobtainable outside the northern countries if you do not grow your own. They have a deeply complex flavor of dill, fennel, and caraway, and you can substitute a mix of these three herbs if you must. Sugar is often added to the cooking liquid, to bring out the sweetness of the flesh.

Mayonnaises for shellfish

In order to enjoy shellfish at its simplest and best, you must have a good recipe for mayonnaise. In addition to the basic recipe there are three choices of flavorings.

for the basic recipe	1¼ cups extra-virgin
1 egg, plus 1 egg yolk	olive oil
Sea salt, to taste	MAKES 1¾ CUPS

Take care that both the eggs and oil are the same temperature, preferably room temperature.

Mix the eggs in a food processor or mixer, or in a bowl, with the salt. Then, with the motor running (or stirring continuously with a whisk), start to add the olive oil, very slowly at the beginning. Make sure that the oil is amalgamated each time before adding more. Later on, you can progress to a continuous, slow trickle until all the oil is used up. Add your chosen flavorings (finely chopped if you're not using a food processor) and taste. The mayonnaise must be kept in the refrigerator and eaten on the same day it is made.

Dill mayonnaise (good for all shellfish)
Add 1 large bunch of dill, 1 tablespoon of lemon juice, the grated zest of ½ lemon, and 1 tablespoon of cider vinegar to the mayonnaise while it's still in the food processor.

Saffron-garlic mayonnaise
(good for strong-flavored crab and shrimp)
Add 1 slice of crustless sourdough bread, 3 cloves garlic,
2–3 tablespoons of tomato paste, ½ teaspoon of saffron
threads, 1 medium fresh chile pepper (seeded) and
1 tablespoon cider vinegar. Add the bread to the
mayonnaise first, with the motor still running, and add the
rest of the ingredients once it's amalgamated.

Caper mayonnaise
(good for mussels, crabs, langoustines, and lobster)
Add 1 tablespoon of washed, salted capers, 2 cloves garlic,
grated zest of 1 lemon, 1 tablespoon of cider vinegar,
1 tablespoon of lemon juice, leaves from a large sprig of fresh
tarragon, and a large handful of chervil. Add the ingredients
to the mayonnaise while it's still in the food processor, and
run the motor until the flavorings are coarsely chopped.

Herb vinaigrette
A very useful sauce, thick like mayonnaise, but much easier.
It's very good with all shellfish, mollusks, chicken, fish
salads, crudités, boiled potatoes, steamed vegetables, and
baked roots or used as a dipping sauce. The herbs could be

Buying and storing shellfish

Crustaceans and mollusks should be alive when
you buy them, apart from the Norway lobster, or
langoustine, which cannot survive the changes in
pressure when pulled up from the seabed. North
Sea shrimp and king crabs are mostly sold frozen,
and it's best to buy them that way; the ones at the
fish markets have been defrosted for no one knows
how long, so it is better to buy the frozen versions
and defrost them yourself.

If frozen shellfish is the only option, and you
can think of nothing else to eat, defrost them in
the refrigerator overnight, then give them a minute
to warm up in the court-bouillon from page 61.
Remove the shellfish from the court-bouillon and
leave until both are cool, then return them to the
pan to let them bathe in the aromatic stock for a
couple of hours; this really does help the taste along.

With all these creatures there is no optional
storing. When they are raw, keep them in the
refrigerator. They must be prepared the day they
are bought, and preferably eaten the moment
they have cooled a little after cooking. Eating a
fresh, lukewarm lobster, shrimp, crab, or crayfish
is one of the great privileges of inhabiting this
globe, whereas eating a refrigerated creature is
just nice. Even soup containing shellfish is not
good to keep, though it will certainly survive a
night in the refrigerator.

dill, tarragon, lovage, sweet cicely, sorrel, parsley, chervil,
chives, ramsons (wild garlic)… the more the merrier.

1½ **tablespoons dijon mustard**	2 **tablespoons cider vinegar or sherry vinegar**
Generous ⅓ cup extra-virgin olive oil	2 **finely chopped shallots**
	Huge bunch of mixed chopped herbs

Put the mustard in a bowl and add the olive oil in a slow
trickle. Dilute with vinegar to taste, and add the herbs. The
sauce will be creamy and thick, both from the mustard and
the herbs. It will keep for a day in the refrigerator.

Black lobster *Homarus gammarus*

Lobster is the most delicious of all the crustaceans, and the black lobsters living in our cold, northern waters, which reduce the creatures' growth to an incredibly slow pace, are as delicious as they come. They are caught in relatively shallow waters, especially in summer, when they migrate to the North Sea shores.

Small lobsters are the most expensive, but I know from experience that even large lobsters are just as good to eat, as well as much cheaper. As a child, I bought one really scary monster of a lobster in the fishing town of Hvide Sande on the Danish west coast. It measured nearly 3ft from its tail to the tip of the two tremendous claws, each the size of a grown man's hand. It was ridiculously cheap because everybody believed that this creature, which must have been 50 years old, would be tough to eat. My mother had a huge fish poacher, but I still had to cook the lobster in two goes. We ate it simply, with a dill mayonnaise, crusty bread, and lemon, and I have never forgotten it in the past 40 years. We were ten privileged guests and there was more than enough to go round.

Appearance and taste Lobsters are usually a beautiful shiny black, but they can also be greenish, or almost every nuance of dark blue. Once cooked, the lobster will turn scarlet red and, while it should smell of fresh seawater when alive, it should smell spicily shellfishy once boiled. The flesh of a freshly cooked lobster is sweet and dense, almost elastic, and eating it is like taking a deep breath on a summer's day, evoking the smells of a fishing port and a taste of ozone and sex, spiced with a weak whiff of iodine and just-awakened baby.

Buying and storing Lobsters must be very much alive when you buy them. They are sold with a thick rubber band around their fierce claws, and there is a reason for this: the pincers can easily cut your fingers off. Frozen or ready-cooked lobsters are not remotely of the same quality as the ones you cook yourself, and the fact that they're cheap is not a good enough reason to buy them.

For an appetizer, half a lobster per person is fine; for a more substantial dish allow one lobster weighing around 18oz per person. Once boiled in their court-bouillon, lobsters will, in principle, keep in the refrigerator for several days, but the true romance lies in eating them when they have just cooled.

Culinary uses You can create all kinds of flashy dishes with lobster, but unless you are lucky enough to have lobster all the time, the most beautiful way is just to boil it plain, as for crayfish (page 61), and serve it with a flavored mayonnaise (page 56). You need to allow 90 seconds in the court-bouillon for every 3½oz of lobster. Take it out of the pan, let the stock cool to room temperature, then put the lobster back for a flavor-enhancing bath.

Norway lobster *Nephrops norvegicus*

The Norway lobster, more widely known as langoustine, or deep-sea lobster, lives in waters up to 1,640ft deep between Norway, Sweden, and Denmark, in the North Sea, and into the Atlantic, as far north as Iceland and south to Portugal. It is seemingly very fragile, but its thin shell can withstand enormous pressure as it comes up from the bottom of the sea.

Appearance and taste Langoustines have a pink carapace when alive—unlike other crustaceans, they do not need camouflage as they live in tunnels in the seabed. They are sweet, mildly flavored, somewhat like lobster, but not as dense-fleshed. Most of the catch is sold to southern Europe as scampi, which is only the tail.

Buying and storing Langoustines are always dead when you buy them as they cannot survive long after the quick ascent to the surface from thousands of feet below. The smell must be fresh and salty; any whiff of ammonia tells you that they are too old. Their freshness deteriorates quickly, so always buy Norway lobsters the day that you are going to eat them.

Culinary uses They are best when broiled or grilled, but a short ride in a grill pan will also be fine. They need intense heat to bring out their juiciness.

To prepare them for cooking, simply split them in half lengthwise with a very sharp, heavy knife, then remove the thin, dark intestine running along the tail. Brush the raw, split lobsters simply with either melted butter or with olive oil and sprinkle with a little cayenne pepper and garlic; and always a twist of sea salt and black pepper. They need a very short cooking time, just a few minutes, basically until the flesh changes color to white, and not a moment longer. Eat as they are, or with a classic northern accompaniment of lemon, chervil cream, and toast.

You won't find much meat in the claws, but the spent carcasses are wonderful for soup: use the recipe for shore crab bisque (page 65).

Crayfish *Astacus astacus*

Crayfish are protected most of the year, but in August and September the chase is intense in ponds, brooks, and streams all over Scandinavia. Until recently, crayfish were a popular, relatively cheap, and abundant food, to catch yourself in the countless freshwater holes and lakes. But draining, pollution, and a crayfish pest have decimated the population dramatically. Owning a crayfish pond is something to be proud of: what might seem to be just another hole in the ground is jealously protected, and stealing another man's crayfish is an unthinkable crime.

Appearance and taste Crayfish are short, seldom more than 4¾in, resembling a small lobster. They can be greenish, blue, or black when raw, but they all turn a glorious scarlet when cooked. The taste is different from that of all other shellfish, delicate and sweet.

Buying and storing Fresh indigenous crayfish are available in Scandinavia only in August and September, but imports of a different species are available year round. Sadly, Swedes now more often eat imported crayfish from Turkey and eastern Europe, a different species with an inferior taste to that of the native.

You can buy crayfish precooked, and frozen, but these are really not worth buying as they lack the spicy, aromatic saltiness and succulence you get when you prepare them fresh yourself.

When buying live crayfish, ensure that they are very much alive. If they seem lazy, it means the crayfish have been lying around for too long, which drains away the taste and leaves the flesh a flabby, sorry thing to eat. Choose big, broad, fat female crayfish, which contain more meat than the thinner males. One person can easily eat 12 crayfish, even double that. For an appetizer, however, six crayfish per person is fine.

Culinary uses If you have enough crayfish, the best thing is to prepare them in the traditional Swedish manner of the *kräft kalas*, as in the recipe opposite. Even on a normal day, eating crayfish outdoors is a must—a gorgeous, delicious mess, with huge napkins and finger bowls compulsory. For another day, and even if it's not ethnically correct, I suggest you try to make a homemade mayonnaise and eat the crayfish with this, together with some crunchy sourdough bread, lemon, and fresh dill. If you wish, a broiled or home-smoked fish, new potatoes, and a bowl of *rødgrød med fløde* (page 215) will make it an unforgettable and very Nordic meal.

And don't throw away the shells, as they are very good for a shellfish stock.

How to eat a crayfish

You eat a crayfish by twisting off the head and sucking everything possible from it—this is the tastiest part. Crack the claws with nutcrackers, or a special tool designed for the purpose, and extract the fine meat—a lobster fork is the best tool for prying it out. As for the tail, you may be lucky and pull it out in one go; alternatively, you can cut open the underside of the shield protecting the tail. You must remove the intestine, which runs as a thin line along the tail, before eating the flesh in one enjoyable mouthful. You will be glazed with the juices all over—it's deliciously uncivilized.

Crayfish with dill flowers

The court-bouillon in this recipe is good for cooking all kinds of shellfish. If you have no dill flowers, you can use a combination of fresh dill, fennel, and caraway seeds. The quantities given are for four people, for an appetizer, so simply multiply the ingredients to suit your numbers.

24 crayfish
Fresh dill, or dill flowers,
   to garnish
for the court-bouillon
1 bottle of beer (330 ml)
6 large dill flowers

1 tablespoon sugar
2 heaping tablespoons
   coarse sea salt
½ teaspoon black
   peppercorns
SERVES 4

To measure how much water you need for the court-bouillon, put the live crayfish in a big pot and just cover with cold water. Fish them out again with a slotted spoon or, even better, with tongs as the crayfish will bite you if they get the chance, and the tiny claws are surprisingly strong. They will also try to escape if they can—they are well aware that you are not going to keep them as pets.

Add the beer and seasonings to the water and let it come to a rolling boil. Put in the live crayfish and let them simmer for 8–10 minutes, according to size. Then transfer them to a large bowl.

Reduce the court-bouillon a little, then pour it over the crayfish. Leave them to cool in the liquid: they are most succulent if they have at least a 6 hour bath in the stock.

Arrange the crayfish beautifully on a cake stand or dish, and adorn with fresh dill or dill flowers. Eat when just cooled to room temperature.

Crayfish party

The most loved of all Swedish traditions must be the *Kräftskiva*. Lots of Swedes have access to their own or shared crayfish holes, heavily guarded all year long, and the hunt is intense especially in August, even if the ban of fishing before the first week of August is no longer there. Everybody attends at least one *Kräftskiva* in late summer. It's a merry and also very traditional affair. The crayfish are presented in glowing piles of scarlet, adorned with garlands of fresh dill. It's customary to eat shrimps as well. The traditional accompaniment is Swedish cheese, crispbread, and tubs of beer and schnapps. If you follow the Swedes, as is fitting for Vikings, you must drink a toast—with schnapps—for every claw, decimating the number of crayfish needed for the meal, but you can only eat a few before getting very drunk. A schnapps for every other crayfish leaves you able to sing along to the *Snaps visor*, a huge Swedish legacy of songs. The party goes on all night, with colored paper lanterns in the trees, funny hats, and bibs with crayfish images. People are snoring happily in the grass, mosquitoes are buzzing, and the northern summer sun never really sets.

Shrimp *Palaemon adspersus, Pandalus borealis*

There are two very different species of Nordic shrimp: the tiny, sweet-fleshed Baltic shrimp (*Palaemon adspersus*) caught in the fjords and inlets of southern Scandinavia, and the ten-times-bigger North Sea prawn (*Pandalus borealis*), caught in deep northern waters.

Baltic shrimp are caught in low waters; often you can catch them from the beach in big, light nets. It's a favorite pastime on summer evenings for children, and playful parents. Half of the shrimp caught this way are often a different species, the brown shrimp (*Crangon crangon*), which will not turn red on cooking but are delicious just the same, especially if you have caught them yourself. Shrimp must be very much alive, wriggling all their little thin legs, and jumping around in the crate; if they are lazy, they are almost dead and not good to eat. The color is mousy gray, turning to baby pink when cooked.

These Baltic shrimp are traded alive from early summer to September. Freshly boiled, tiny shrimp, still a little bit tepid, are an affordable luxury. If you

cannot get them fresh, the large North Sea prawns are a good choice.

Buying and storing All around the globe, deep-sea prawns live in cool waters, and as they are caught out at sea, they are usually cooked and often frozen in their shells on board. North Sea prawns, on the other hand, are best bought frozen as there is no telling how long they may have been defrosting at the fish market. The quality of these ready-cooked prawns is very good if you defrost them yourself in the refrigerator overnight. Fresh Baltic shrimp are the best. You can also buy them frozen, canned, and in brine, but it's not at all the same thing.

If shrimp are the main course, you should buy at least 18oz for each person; if they're an appetizer, 7oz is enough. North Sea prawns have a higher ratio of flesh to shell, so you don't need more than 10½oz per person; 5½oz is fine for a salad.

Culinary uses Shrimp have a delicate taste, making them best when eaten on their own, with bread and butter. In Denmark we say that pepper on a shrimp is a crime, like putting pepper on a baby.

In Denmark, the shrimp season is the heart of summer. Big bowls brimming with shrimp, new potatoes, asparagus, dill, a simple meat dish, or fish, and strawberries with cream for dessert: it's a well-loved menu for *Sankt Hans,* midsummer evening, celebrated with bonfires and songs, even if it rains on eight out of ten midsummer evenings.

Shrimp should be boiled, like the other crustaceans, in the court-bouillon described on page 61, but here you should use a large bunch of dill weed, which is in season in the summer when the dill flowers are not yet out. Put the shrimp in the boiling court-bouillon, boil vigorously for 1 minute, then let them cool in the liquid. This method makes them easier to peel, while also perfectly firm and salty.

Small Baltic shrimp are really very small, so it takes maybe a hundred of the little pink creatures to make up a proper open-face sandwich. But they are a marvel when piled high on a special sourdough bread made from both wheat and rye, studded with caraway seeds (page 248). You may add a little black pepper, a sprig of dill, and a blob of homemade mayonnaise—but lemon is a dirty word here.

A sandwich like this is worth every effort, but it seems it's becoming less and less popular to spend a summer's evening with friends eating shrimp—we have perhaps grown so accustomed to fast food that people just think it is a waste of time. You can only pity them; the small shrimp are just as good as lobster, and not hard to peel, once you get the knack. Some people, especially men, claim that they are unable to peel shrimp, and let women do it for them. This must be the ultimate proof of true love. It's altogether an interesting study of human behavior, and patience; some people eat them while they peel them, others patiently build up masterpieces of pink-fleshed art and devour the masterpiece at the end.

The shells are very good for a soup, especially if you include a few shrimp still in their shells.

North sea prawns have a strong marine taste and can be used in numerous ways, including in sandwiches and salads, or gently fried in their shells. We usually stick to shrimp salad in Scandinavia, a dish that has appeared in so many inferior versions that you tend to

forget just how exquisite and refined the real thing is. The other possibility is to make a soup (following the recipe for shore crab bisque on page 65) and pile in the huge prawns at the last minute; they can stand up very well to the intensity of the flavors.

Shrimp salad

Peeling small shrimp for a salad, however, requires superhuman patience. It's more realistic to use the larger, easily peeled (and ready-cooked) shrimp like North Sea prawns if you can find them, which will make a shrimp salad miles ahead of any ready-bought version.

It's all about the homemade mayonnaise, and you can use any of the versions on pages 56–57. A large spoonful for each person will do, lightened with the same amount of crème fraîche and turned lightly with a large handful of big shrimp. Pile up on some toast, or toasted rye bread, which has a delicious caramelized flavor, and decorate with fresh dill. Serve with lemon, which tastes good with shrimp.

Common crab *Cancer pagurus*

Common crabs (also known as edible crabs) are very, well, common, and certainly not a fisherman's friend. They destroy nets, eat the fish in them, and their powerful claws can easily cut your fingers off. The claws are the only part of the common crab that's usually eaten in Scandinavia. This practice often means that the fishermen tear off the claws and throw the defenceless creatures back into the sea—enough to put you off eating the crab at all. And, in fact, the whole beast can be eaten, even if it's a bit complicated.

Appearance and taste Common crabs are sold at a mature age. They are huge—8–10in across is not unusual—and have varying colors depending on their habitat. The claws contain fine, thread-like, juicy meat. If you want to eat the crabs whole, female crabs have a broader behind to contain the roe, and are much meatier than the males. Crabmeat generally is more fibrous and has a much more distinct taste than other shellfish.

Buying and storing In Scandinavia, claws are not too expensive, but whole crabs you can buy for almost nothing. You should always try to buy whole crabs, and ones that are not only fresh but alive—beware of the claws, though they should normally be clamped by a rubber band. Ready-boiled claws are always overdone,

and it's hard to know if they are fresh enough. If you detect any whiff of ammonia, the meat is too old.

Culinary uses Crabmeat's strong taste means that it can take heftier spicing—chile works well—or be made into a spicy salad with a saffron-garlic mayonnaise. The easiest and freshest way to dress the whole crab is to mix the edible parts with a little of your preferred mayonnaise, a little diced celery, cucumber, shelled peas, asparagus, or just lettuce. Serve this salad in the shell, so guests can pick at the claws as well as eat the luscious salad—accompanied by some toasted rye bread or sourdough, of course. Alternatively, crab claws can be broiled whole for 10 minutes under a very hot broiler. Eat with a green salad, sourdough bread, lemon, and a mayonnaise (pages 56–57) or chervil cream (page 176).

Crab gratin

This recipe is eminently adaptable however many are eating. Mix the meat from the claws and from inside the crab with chopped dill, parsley, a handful of lightly blanched asparagus, and 3 tablespoons of white sauce. Season with salt, fresh chile to taste, and pepper and return to the shell. Sprinkle with freshly grated Parmesan cheese and place under a hot broiler for 10 minutes, or until browned and bubbly.

Kamchatka king crab

Most of our great shellfish have been here in Scandinavia for hundreds of thousands of years, but a relatively recent introduction, the Kamchatka king crab (*Paralithodes camtschaticus*), is threatening the local shellfish populations. This crab, a native of Kamchatka in the Russian far east, was introduced into the seas near Murmansk in the 1960s to provide a new catch for the Soviet fishing fleet. These gigantic shellfish—measuring 5ft across and weighing up to 17½lb—are a huge biological success, but only to themselves, capable of marching in their hundreds of thousands at an alarming speed; as a result, they have managed to reach as far south as Trondheim on the Norwegian coast, at the expense of most other marine life.

Naturally, in Scandinavia we do not have traditional ways of cooking these enormous creatures—the world's largest edible crab—but they are undeniably tasty and will probably become cheaper to buy in the years to come as their local population increases. The long, scary, spindly legs—each as thick as a baby's arm—are the edible part. King crab is always bought frozen, and is eaten like other crabs.

Shore crab

Scandinavian beaches, especially stony ones, are buzzing with shore crabs (*Carcinus maenas*). They are small (usually less than 4in wide), but big enough to bite your toes and fingers, and make for an exciting hunt. The brave catch them with their fingers, or on a length of string with a piece of meat tied to the end. You can catch as many as your own and your children's patience allows—and if you have enough of both it's possible to end up with a huge bucket teeming with small crabs after a day at the beach. Most parents let them loose, but we are greedy and make them into an intense crab bisque.

How to prepare and eat crab

To boil Crabs can be boiled in the same court bouillon as that used for crayfish (page 61). Whether you are preparing whole crabs or claws only, put them in the boiling liquid, cook for 10 minutes, then remove from the heat and leave to cool in the pan. Remove when they have just cooled and, in the case of the claws, crack them with a hammer—preferably outside!

To eat The claws are relatively straightforward: you simply extract the meat with a lobster fork, or a small pointed knife. When it comes to a whole crab, the fun part is to distinguish the edible from the inedible inside it—it's not difficult but it is messy, which is the reason whole crabs are so cheap.

To begin, pry the top shield off. Stuck inside it is reddish goo, which has a wonderful taste: scrape it into a bowl. The rest of the crab is mostly greenish gills, seemingly made of rock wool, and they must be removed. The rule hereafter is that anything soft and chewable inside the crab is great to eat, including the green, black, and brown stuff.

Crab bisque

This is the recipe I use for home-caught shore crabs, but it works well for all kinds of shellfish. When we eat any type of shellfish at home I greedily collect all the shells and heads and use them to make soup. I often add the court-bouillon in which the shellfish were cooked (page 61), too, bringing with it the predictable dill flavor which I love—but if you don't want it, omit it. The end result tastes great with the saffron-garlic mayonnaise described on page 57 and, of course, toast.

1 large onion, diced	Generous ⅓ cup extra-virgin olive oil
1 fennel bulb, with green fronds, diced	8 cups crabmeat and/or shells
1 red bell pepper, seeded and diced	2¼lb tomatoes, quartered
1 medium chile, seeded	¼ cup dry vermouth or generous ⅓ cup white wine
4 cloves garlic, minced	Coarse sea salt and coarsely ground pepper
A bunch of fresh herbs: chervil, oregano, fennel, tarragon, thyme, or lemon thyme	Sugar, to taste (optional)
1 star anise	Cream, to taste (optional)
A long shred of orange zest	SERVES 6–7

In a large skillet, gently fry the onion, fennel bulb, pepper, chile, garlic, herbs, star anise, and orange zest in the olive oil until golden.

Add the shellfish and let them brown for a good while. They should fry, not burn. Put in the tomatoes and let them fry until the oil separates on the surface. Add the wine and let it bubble for a couple of minutes. Then pour in enough water to cover. Add a small amount of salt and black pepper. Let the soup simmer gently for an hour, then strain.

Whiz the sludge to a purée in a food processor—you can add some liquid to help if necessary. Then press this through a fine sieve, using a rubber spatula: it takes time to work all the good stuff through and leave the rest behind.

Return the soup to the pan to heat through and season with salt, pepper, and maybe a nip of sugar. You can add some cream if you want a milder taste.

TIP

• If you do not have a food processor, and find giant stone mortars too cumbersome, you can still extract maximum shellfish flavor. Go ahead with the recipe as above, but save all the vegetables. Fry the onions, herbs, and other flavorings (excluding the chile) with the shells and shellfish. Add the wine and water and simmer slowly until you have a hefty stock. Pour this through a sieve and press as much of the shellfish through as you can. Then fry the fennel bulb, pepper, and chile until golden, add the tomatoes and reduce. Add the stock and simmer again until you have an intense taste; add cream if you wish, as well as salt and pepper. The result will be more chunky, but just as powerful.

Oyster *Ostrea edulis*

The Nordic oyster is the round-shelled flat oyster, and this is what our oyster shell heaps consist of. Pollution, bad management, and overfishing have reduced the native population, however, so most oysters are imported. Nevertheless, the population of the native oyster is on the rise once again, and as it is much fleshier and in most people's opinion superior to the imported Pacific oyster, it is good to have the choice. There are not many wild oysters to be had, but oysters have been farmed since Roman times.

Appearance and taste A shucked oyster in its prime should have a visible beard and a light brown or grayish color with a white muscle. It should have a good, clean flavor and be firm yet juicy. Oysters contain water, which you either drink, while eating them, or put into any dish with them. The liquid has a refined sea-breeze quality that you don't want to miss.

Native oysters spawn in the summer and are usually not eaten during that time, but other, farmed species are available all year round. There is a great difference in the taste and consistency, depending on whether or not the oysters have spawned: before spawning they are fat and firm, while afterwards, in the fall, they are thin and exhausted—both have their dedicated fans.

How to shuck an oyster

Oysters have a flat and a rounded side. Rest the rounded side in the palm of your glove-clad hand and, using a short, thick-bladed knife, either cut the valve or tweeze the blade between the two shells at the other end, in order to cut the stool (the muscle that keeps the shells together). Remove the flat shell. This operation admittedly takes nerve, patience, practice, and possibly the odd bandage. Put your nose to every oyster: it should smell like a swim in cold salt water; if it doesn't, discard it. Rest your shucked oyster in the deep shell on a bed of crushed ice, or seaweed, so the juices stay in the shell. And continue with the other oysters. Any that are not wet inside should be rejected. Once shucked, the oysters should be eaten as quickly as possible.

Buying and storing With oysters, you must trust your fish market as there is no way of telling how fresh they are, or how long they have been kept out of water. Make sure that they smell fresh and are tightly closed.

Oysters can be stored alive in the refrigerator for a couple of days, in the container they are bought in, though they lose taste and precious water with prolonged waiting.

Culinary uses If eating raw, live creatures seems too much for you, try them in the delicious fish soup with oysters on page 49, or broil them for 3 minutes with a blob of hollandaise and a dusting of bread crumbs. Warm oysters are lovely, and the gentle way to set your mind at ease while getting addicted to them.

To eat raw, serve with butter, good toasted bread, and lemon. Six oysters is plenty per person for an appetizer.

Mussel *Mytilus edulis*

Mussels are regarded with some suspicion by most northerners; their strange, fleshy appearance, paired with ignorance of their sweet juiciness, salty flavorfulness, and relative cheapness keeps far too many from eating them. And maybe, despite countless recipes, you have to know how—it's daunting to attack a bag of mussels if you haven't seen it done.

Stone Age northerners were not such picky eaters; they amassed countless heaps of mollusk shells (the *koekkenmoeddin*), ample proof that we were dependent on marine creatures, and ate just about everything in the animal kingdom.

But those of us who do eat mussels love them. Their flavor is indispensable in fish dishes, soups, and sauces. They are cheap and easy to prepare, and a very sociable thing to eat. You feel a certain togetherness with the other people around the table or campfire, everyone bathed in mussel juices, emptied shells heaping up in a deliciously uncivilized manner.

There are lots of mussels in northern waters, including blue and knife mussels, sweet and fine from the cold waters that reduce the speed of their growth.

We pick wild mussels in tidal waters, from crevices, and poles, where you can gather as many as you can eat in a very short while. Wild mussels must be picked in areas where bathing is considered safe, which means far from sewers and polluting operations, as mussels can't choose what they feed on, and can be full of nasty things.

Knife mussels are abundant in some areas, but they are not gathered commercially. If you can catch them you have to be very quick about it, or they pull themselves deep into the sand, as they sense the vibrations of your feet on the ground.

Appearance and taste Blue mussels are mostly farmed nowadays, attached to ropes where they feed on small larvae and plankton floating in the water. This means that there is no sand in them, and they are a uniform size. They also have thinner shells than the wild mussels. All mussels taste more or less the same —sweet, salty, fleshy, and appetizing.

Buying and storing The good thing is that cultivated mussels are available all year round and are also very safe, with none of the potential health risks of wild ones; being free of sand, they are also much easier to clean.

Mussels must be alive when you buy them, if not necessarily when you eat them. The shells must be smooth, shiny, and whole—cracked mussels are usually dead, and there is no telling for how long. Seaweed and other stuff on the shells does not matter.

Different species have very different shells, but what you must always look for in live mussels are shells that are tightly shut, or shut immediately if you tap them; if they don't, they are not fit for eating and must be thrown away. Cooked mussels that have not opened up are probably filled with mud and must be thrown away.

Prepare mussels on the day that you buy or gather them. (Once cooked, they can keep in the refrigerator for a couple of days.) Wild mussels need a good scrub, and you'll need to cut off all the cumbersome little threads (beards) that they use to cling to the rocks. Cultivated or line mussels just need a quick wash in a bowl of cold water. Check that every every single mussel is tightly closed before you cook them.

Avoid frozen mussels as they are always rubbery.

Culinary uses Mussels have two missions in the kitchen: the succulent flesh (well, succulent if not cooked for too long) and the juices. The latter, when boiled to a dishwater-colored essence, taste like a vacation at the seaside and are pure gold in any soup, risotto, stew, or sauce containing any kind of marine creature. If it's the juices you are after, you might have to surrender the mussels themselves, and boil them for too long to make good eating, in order to extract most of the taste.

Raw mussels are easy to hot smoke (page 83), and this is a lovely way to spend a summer evening on the beach. Or simply bake them on a bed of seaweed in a bonfire on the sand. Remember to bring a lemon.

Northern mussel soup

All mussels are cooked in the same way in the north, beginning with mussels to eat, and a lovely buttery herbed soup to finish; knife mussels just need a lot longer cooking time to tenderize. Two and a quarter pounds of mussels is enough to feed two for a main course.

Prepare a big pot with a handful of chopped shallots, a sprig of thyme, a bottle of beer (or 1¼ cups white wine or hard cider) and some black pepper. When it boils, put in the mussels and place a lid on. Boil at a high heat, while shaking the pan vigorously every now and then, until the shells open. Remove the mussels from the pot using a slotted spoon. Test the bottom of the pot with a spoon: if there is sand at the bottom, you need to strain the soup through a sieve lined with fine cheesecloth; if not, don't.

Whisk in a generous piece of butter and lots of finely chopped herbs, preferably a mixture of parsley, dill, chervil, tarragon, ramsons (wild garlic), and chives. Pour over the mussels in huge serving bowls and serve with lemon and crusty bread, for mopping up the juices. Eat them with your fingers, using the shells for soup spoons.

TIP
- For mussel stock, you can follow the above recipe, only this time doubling the amount of cooking liquid, and boil the mussels gently in it for 30 minutes. While you will have to throw away the mussels at the end of it, you will be left with a most delicious stock. A handful of mussels will also greatly improve any fish stock.

Mussel salad

If you have too many boiled mussels because you need the liquid for soup, and they are boiled just until they open up, they make a delicious salad with classic herbs such as parsley, dill, chervil, tarragon, ramsons (wild garlic) or chives, raw red onion, lettuce, and a herbed mayonnaise dressing.

Mussels and Jerusalem artichokes

Mussels are wonderful paired with Jerusalem artichokes; they share a lot of flavors, and combine beautifully. Marinate boiled Jerusalem artichokes and the mussels themselves in a dressing made from mussel liquid, olive oil, herbs, and chopped shallots, or put quartered warm Jerusalem artichokes in with the mussel soup above. Alternatively, make the mussel liquid into a creamed soup with Jerusalem artichokes and cream, then serve with mussels and croûtons.

Fish has been a vital source of food on the long Scandinavian coastline since man first inhabited the north after the last Ice Age. Fish were plentiful in the past and migratory fish were easy to catch, even without boats. The need to preserve this seasonal abundance to survive long months of cold and unfishable waters, with primitive means, is the basis of the enormous heritage of all manner of preserved fish in Scandinavia. Drying fish in the cold, dry winter air has been a necessity for as long as man has lived in the north. Fishing waters in the lakes and rivers freeze solid for a large part of the winter, or storms make fishing at sea impossible, so the preservation of fish caught in the summer has long been a means of survival. It's the mastery of skills such as smoking, drying, and vinegar pickling that has kept us alive—the Vikings would not have been able to launch multiple and ambitious adventures abroad without their reliable supply of salted, smoked, and dried fish.

Early preservation methods were simple, and before salt was available at an affordable price, drying and smoking were the only methods used. As trade improved, salt became another means of preserving, either on its own, or combined with drying, smoking, and fermentation. Lactic acid fermentation and lime curing are relatively new methods but are still at least a thousand years old. Over time and through human ingenuity, the skills of salting, smoking, and pickling have developed and survived the advent of modern refrigeration. Preserved fish is still an important part of the economy of fishing communities all over the north, transformed from an age-old necessity into something refined and delectable in its own right.

preserved fish

Dried fish

Dry, salty air that contains almost no bacteria comes naturally in northern Scandinavia, and makes drying fish, even huge whole, split fish, fairly easy. As with many of our ancient necessities, the product has been refined over time and is now a delicacy sold at a high price.

Norway has been trading dried fish, caught as far away as Newfoundland, with the Catholic countries of southern Europe since before the Reformation. In the Catholic fasting tradition, you are allowed to eat only fish for a large part of the spring. And although Portuguese and Spanish fishermen were catching and drying fish in the same waters, the huge demand exceeded the supply. Stockfish and salt fish, made from a variety of fish in the cod family, are very good travellers and keep for years. Even if preservation is no longer a necessity, the taste of these foods is more than enough reason for people all over southern Europe to demand an ongoing supply, even now and whatever the price. Most salt cod sold in Spain and the rest of Europe

is still sourced in Norway and Iceland, though nowadays most of the fish is salted and dried industrially. Confusingly, while stockfish and salt fish are two rather different products, Scandinavian recipes are not usually specific, which means you can use either: as long as you know what you are dealing with, it is not a problem. The term *klipfisk* (*klippe* means cliff, after the cliffs originally used for drying the fish) is used loosely for both types, as well as for the dishes made from them.

Stockfish *(tørfisk)*

This is the oldest and most basic form of dried fish. It is not salted, and as it is extremely dry takes several days to reconstitute in fresh water. Stockfish is made by dipping the whole, gutted, split, and flattened fish in seawater and then hanging it up to dry in the icy wind—being practically free from bacteria, the cold, dry air allows the fish to dry out without it going bad. The famous wooden racks often featured in pictures of northern Norway are not used much any more. Once dried hard, stockfish keeps for years. During drying, the fish ferments slightly, giving it a delicious taste not present in salt fish. While stockfish is still produced, it is rare and very expensive. The flesh of a dried stockfish keeps magically fresh and, once soaked, can be restored to a salty, lightly fermented glory. Some people say it's an acquired taste, but I don't agree: if you love fresh fish, you will love this. If you are lucky enough to come across stockfish, the flesh is dry and cream-colored rather than white.

Salt fish *(klipfisk)*

Made from several species of fish in the cod family, which are caught way out at sea, gutted and salted straight away, then dried after landing either in the open or in huge drying sheds, salt cod is much more common than stockfish. It has also been made for thousands of years, beginning with the Phoenicians, but it only gradually became common in the north. Nowadays, salt cod is made all over Scandinavia, but mostly in Norway.

Salt cod flesh is extremely salty, but not very dry, and reconstituting it is only a matter of drawing out the salt in several changes of cold water. The flesh should be white—yellow flesh indicates old age or poor quality and, while edible, is not as delicious.

Buying and storing You can buy both kinds of dried fish at good fish markets, or at West Indian, Spanish or Portuguese shops. Always look for a good color and avoid dark pieces. The best quality is from the thick, meaty middle part of the fillet. This is also the easiest to handle as it contains fewer bones, fins, and skin, which means more flesh to the pound. Thinner pieces tend to be drier and saltier, with more wastage. Needless to say, the best pieces are more expensive. Pieces with a high ratio of bone and mucilage should be cheaper. Dried fish keeps indefinitely if stored in a container in the refrigerator. Soaked fish keeps maybe a little better than fresh fish, but should be eaten within a day or two.

Culinary uses You can't do a thing with salt cod or stockfish until it has been soaked in clean water to soften the flesh and, in the case of salt cod, to remove most of the salt. Salt cod should be soaked for about 12 hours, with 3–4 changes of water, though you should adapt the soaking time to suit the thickness of the fish and how salty you want it. Be warned, though, that if the fish becomes completely devoid of salt, it's actually a little bland. Stockfish, on the other hand, needs around 48 hours if it's a thick piece. When it resembles fresh fish it's ready to use, and the saltiness will be gone.

We are not too adventurous up north, and almost all dried fish is eaten in much the same way, maybe because it's so good. Strong spicing is necessary to stand up to the fish's flavor, and a rich sauce and floury potatoes to mop up the sauce. Horseradish, mustard, vinegar, and capers are all traditional accompaniments, as are pickled beets and bacon.

Along Denmark's west coast there is a traditional specialty known as *tørrede jyder*, meaning "dried people from Jutland." This consists simply of dried fish which are soaked for a day, fried in butter, and served with potatoes and raw sugared lingonberries.

Lutefisk

This unique treatment of dried fish often gets put on to lists of "the world's weirdest foods." Originating in Norway during the Middle Ages, *lutefisk* is a relatively new invention. Traditionally it was served on Christmas Eve, but now a rising number of Norwegians—and Swedes, too, these days—eat *lutefisk* not so much on that particular evening, but during the winter in general. This is part of a growing awareness and pride in northern specialties and food culture. Interestingly, more *lutefisk* is eaten by North Americans of Nordic ancestry than by native Scandinavians themselves.

To make *lutefisk*, stockfish or salt cod is soaked in water for several days to swell, and then treated with lye (*lut*): historically, this was generally in the form of birch ashes, but nowadays caustic soda (leached from wood ash) is normally used. This breaks down the proteins in the fish and gives it a particular, jelly-like consistency. Then it is soaked for several days to bring down the pH to neutral, and finally prepared very simply: baked in its own juices for a very short time, sealed in with a lid or aluminum foil. The odor is strong but the taste is surprisingly mild. The fish is mostly eaten with a white sauce, buttered peas, bashed neeps (mashed rutabaga), and potatoes.

Prepare all the trimmings first and put in bowls for serving. Put the potatoes on to cook.

Place the soaked fish in a shallow saucepan with the bay leaf, peppercorns, and thyme. Pour in enough cold water to cover, bring to a boil, and skim off any scum. Lower the heat and let simmer for about 5 minutes. Leave the fish to cool slightly in the water until it's just cooked through. The cooking time can vary a lot depending on the thickness of the fish. If you are using fresh fish, this can be cooked in the same way.

Meanwhile make the mustard sauce.

Serve the fish with all the trimmings and the mustard sauce in a sauceboat.

Salted cod mousse

Like other civilized nations who love salted fish, Scandinavians also make salted/dried fish into a delicious chewy mousse to be eaten on rye bread, as an open-faced sandwich, or as an appetizer with a seasonal salad. For an appetizer, 5½oz dry fish for each person will be sufficient. Soak the fish, as on page 73, cover with plenty of unsalted water, and bring to a boil. Turn off the heat and let the fish cool in the water. Remove the skin, bones, and mucilage and stir the fish with as much mashed potato as there is fish. The result should be a somewhat coarse, stringy, soft mousse. Soften with milk, and spice with black pepper, lots of chopped ramsons (wild garlic, or garlic), and maybe salt if the soaking was too successful. If in season, it will be even more delicious mixed with chopped fresh morels fried in butter.

Klipfisk with lots of trimmings

This is our unadventurous but classic and delicious way to eat dried or salted fish. The sharp trimmings and mustard sauce provide the perfect contrast to the mild fish and bland potatoes, and the whole dish works wonderfully. The same trimmings can be eaten with fresh cod and its relatives.

2¼lb salt cod or stockfish, soaked (page 73)
1 bay leaf
1 teaspoon black peppercorns
1 sprig of thyme
Mustard sauce as for gravad fish (page 78)
for the trimmings
½pt jar of pickled beets
2in piece of fresh horseradish, in thin shavings
4 tablespoons salted capers, soaked
1 cup smoked bacon, diced and fried until crispy
⅓ cup butter, melted
1 bunch of parsley, chopped
2 hard-boiled eggs, chopped
2¼–3lb 5oz potatoes, boiled

Serves 4

Salted fish

Salting is a method of preserving in its own right. The salt, by drawing out water, prevents bacteria from spoiling the food, and adds a new taste in the process: salting is usually followed by fermentation, changing the aromas of the food to something even more inviting. Salting is what comes first in all the different and delicious fish preserves from the north. Some fish, like the famous gravlax, is eaten as it is, but most salted fish is treated further.

Salting fish at home

The home-salting of fish can be anything from a slight scattering of coarse salt grains on a piece of fish you are about to eat, to "green salting," which is the perfect method of draining excess liquid from filleted fish in order to make it tastier and easier to fry and, especially, broil. Broiling loose-fleshed fish in one piece can be very tricky, and green salting results in less watery, plump, juicy, and perfectly firm fish. Scatter a teaspoon of coarse salt over every fillet, let sit in a cool place for a couple of hours, then dry with paper towels; the fish is then ready to be cooked.

This method is for every day. Hard-core salting to keep fish fresh during winter is quite another matter. To be truthful, we do not usually make our own salted herrings, but when you are far away from home, or find yourself with a glut of home-caught fish, it's worth trying to make your own.

How to salt herrings

It's easy to salt herrings, even if you have to be meticulous about hygiene, but a word of warning that I do hope is not off-putting. In the past, when everything was made at home, food rules were carved into the mind of every housewife. This no longer exists since most foods are ready-made and full of preservatives. But it is of paramount importance that every single step of the way the utensils are absolutely clean and hygienic, since the smallest trace of dirt can turn your tasty herrings into a bubbling hell-hole of botulism.

Also, there are no two ways about it, salted herrings stink: herring oil is not exactly perfume, except maybe to polar bears. When you salt your own herrings, the oil will seep out. The smell will go in the process of desalting and curing, but this part you do not experience when you buy the herrings ready-made.

If you want to try to make your own salted herrings, you must buy or, even better, catch very fresh, fat, and large herrings. It's a firm tradition in many Scandinavian families to go on fishing trips at sea to catch their own fish, mostly cod and herrings. Alternatively, the fish can be bought directly in the fishing harbors. Have the fish gutted, or do this yourself. You will need coarse salt and a deep earthenware crock or plastic container suitable for food, and a heavy plate that you can use as a lid.

Wash the prepared fish and place them head to tail, side by side, on a ½in-thick layer of salt in the crock or container. Then add enough coarse salt to cover, followed by another layer of fish, until the container is full. Finally, add a thick layer of salt to cover. Place the heavy plate, which must be sterilized, and maybe a completely clean stone, on top. Cover with plastic wrap, then put in a cool place and wait. The salt will draw liquid from the fish to form a brine. After 2–3 months the fish is ready to be used in recipes.

Salted herrings

Before refrigeration, salted herrings were the starting point for all herring products. The exquisite herring dishes from the north are made with fall-caught herrings, which are salted and lightly fermented to give flavor and everlasting life. Gutted, but otherwise whole, the herrings are layered with salt in huge barrels for many months.

Appearance and taste The best and fattest are known as "Iceland Diamonds," which come in two forms: plain salted herrings or spiced salted herrings, the latter red-hued from sandalwood, cloves, pepper, and allspice. Which you initially choose is mostly a matter of taste. They are both sold as whole (to be gutted and filleted at home) or sometimes filleted fish, in brine, and are the starting point for a wealth of herring recipes.

Either way, the fish must be soaked in cold water, to remove excess salt, and then anointed in a marinade, often consisting just of vinegar, sugar, spices, and onions, and left to macerate for a day before eating. But the tradition is huge, and we have literally hundreds of local marinated herring recipes including flavorings from mustard and dill to curry, tomato, and sherry.

To confuse matters more, salted herrings, both spiced and plain, can be bought desalted and already in a variety of marinades, and ready to eat. There are so many to choose from that it can seem bewildering. The taste in herrings differs throughout Scandinavia, with countless local specialties, and also particular herrings for different seasons—it's an inexhaustible wealth of variation. Most people these days buy ready-marinated herrings, which can be as good as the homemade version, but many families still have special traditional herring recipes, mostly made for Christmas.

Matjes herrings are a special Swedish way with salted marinated herrings, and they are delicious. They are sold ready to eat in oblong cans, as whole fillets.

Buying and storing Buy salted herrings in quantities to suit immediate use as the fat in the fish goes rancid when kept out of the brine. Once home-marinated, the shelf life of the fish depends on the marinade. Marinated herrings sold in cans or jars keep for a long time, though some are semi-preserved and must be kept cool.

Culinary uses All marinated herrings taste good more or less served in the same way, which is very simple: on rye bread, with egg, onion, cold boiled potatoes, chives, and sliced apples, plus a blob of crème fraîche for herrings that are not already in a creamy marinade. This must be the ultimate Scandinavian open-face sandwich, and the ultimate lunch: you can serve one type of herring on a ready-made open-face sandwich, or put a variety on a plate to put on the bread yourself. Or you can serve them as a summer dinner or lunch dish with new boiled potatoes, crème fraîche or butter, dill, and chives.

Red herring salad

A homemade herring salad is a necessity on a well-laid Christmas lunch table in Scandinavia, and this recipe is a particular favorite. Most northern homes would have all the necessary ingredients to hand, but none of them are hard to come by. The salad is eaten as a topping on rye bread, decorated with the eggs. It comes as part of an assortment of herrings.

8 spiced, marinated herring fillets or *matjes* herring fillets	1 tablespoon Dijon mustard
4 hand-eating apples	Pickling liquid from the beets
2 medium pickled beets	Salt and pepper
2 large pickled cucumbers	**for the garnish**
A thick slab of raw celeriac	4 hard-boiled eggs, halved
for the cream dressing	2 tablespoons chopped capers
1 cup crème fraîche	SERVES 8

Cut the herring fillets into ¾in biased slices. Cut the apples (with their skin on), and vegetables into ½in dice.

To make the dressing, blend the crème fraîche and mustard to a consistency that will coat the salad ingredients, adding a little of the beet liquid to thin it. Season with salt and pepper if necessary, though it's probably not.

Mix all the salad ingredients with the dressing and arrange in a dish. Garnish with the egg halves and capers.

Herring with onions, apples, and crème fraîche

This is a favorite way of enjoying marinated herrings of almost any sort. First rye bread, then a thin layer of rendered pork fat, followed by the herrings, raw apple slices (with the peel on), rings of red onion, and a blob of crème fraîche. You can add a few rinsed salted capers on top if you wish. If the apple and onion are abundant, this is a lunch in itself. If you suit the ingredients to your taste, and put them in a pretty dish, this is an obvious choice for Christmas lunch.

Fried salted herring with caramelized onions

Most people soak whole salted herring before they eat them, but on the island of Bornholm in the Baltic they have a delicious way of frying the herring as they are—countless beers are required to quench the following thirst! The sweetness from the caramelized onions and the beets and spice from the mustard sauce work wonders with the salty crisp fish.

8 plain salted herrings
Butter, for frying
for the caramelized onions
18oz onions, sliced into rings
⅓ cup salted butter
1 tablespoon sugar
1 teaspoon coarse sea salt
½ teaspoon ground black pepper
A sprig of fresh thyme
4 tablespoons cider vinegar
to serve
Mustard sauce as for gravad fish (page 78)
½pt jar of pickled beets
Rye bread and butter
SERVES 4

Buy filleted salted herrings, or buy them whole and fillet them yourself. It's dead easy with a long, sharp knife. Just cut along each side of the backbone, following the inner bones, until the fillet comes off. Keep the skin on, and maybe soak the fish in plenty of cold water for 3–4 hours—if you are not a native, you'll probably want to reduce the salt a little. Pat dry.

About 30 minutes before you are ready to eat, put all the ingredients for the onions into a heavy skillet and allow to caramelize slowly until the onions are browned and caramelized, and the vinegar evaporated.

At the last minute, fry the fish in plenty of browned butter for 2 minutes on the skin side, 1 minute on the other.

Serve with the sauce, beets, onions, bread, and butter.

TIP
• The caramelized onions are also the classic accompaniment for steaks, beef patties, and smørrebrød.

absolutely essential to use very fresh fish. The mustard sauce, along with rye bread, cold butter, and lots of fresh dill, are perfect accompaniments, but you can also try it with new potatoes, butter, and yet more dill. You will also need a small rocky Swedish island, a keg of beer, and a bottle of schnapps.

2lb 12oz fatty fish fillets of your choice (skin on)

for the spice rub
4 tablespoons coarse
   sea salt
2 tablespoons sugar
2 teaspoons ground
   black pepper
6 cups finely chopped dill

for the mustard sauce
½ cup Dijon mustard
4 tablespoons muscovado
   sugar
¼ cup heavy cream
1 cup chopped dill
1 tablespoon cider vinegar
SERVES 6–8

Wash and dry the fish. Mix together the spice rub ingredients. Choose a deep, non-reactive dish and sprinkle a third of the spice mixture over the bottom. Place half the fillets skin-side down on top, then sprinkle over another third of the spice rub, and follow with the rest of the fillets, this time flesh-side down. Finish with another layer of the spice mixture.

Gravad fish

This classic Scandinavian dish works perfectly with all kinds of fatty fish, including salmon, herrings, mackerel, white fish, and Greenland halibut. It is always generously flavored with dill. If possible, use whole fish with just the head and bones removed; the skin must be left on. You can have your fishmonger do this, or give it a try yourself. The important thing in filleting fish is a sharp knife, and patience; work slowly, using the tip of the blade as a finger, feeling your way though the flesh.

Gravad means a light salting, drawing moisture from flesh with a mixture of salt and sugar. The salting is not meant to preserve the fish for long, but long enough to allow a slight fermentation and add a depth of flavor.

The dill is not optional—it's the only flavoring and it's wonderful. The dill must be thoroughly cleaned in a large tub of cold water as the only risk of eating this lovely dish is from botulism bacteria from dirt. Keep all utensils absolutely clean and work with rubber gloves as this fish is eaten raw. It is of course, as with sushi,

Wrap the whole thing in plastic wrap, then put a heavy board that fits neatly inside the dish on top. Place in the refrigerator.

After 12 hours, unwrap and dismantle and turn the fish over so the top becomes the bottom. Replace the plastic wrap and board and let it sit for another 12 hours. While a total of 24 hours is sufficient for small fish, a large salmon will take 48 hours to cure, and needs to be turned over twice.

Eat very thinly sliced, within 3 days. The mustard sauce involves nothing more complicated than simply mixing everything together.

Rimmad lax

Rimmad lax is basically the same as gravad fish: fish cured with the same rub of sugar and salt. However, the fish is cured for a shorter time and tastes more like fresh fish. It is eaten as a main course with dill creamed potatoes.

It's often cured with a splash of flavored schnapps— a small glass for a whole fillet of salmon, and it's delicious.

The dill creamed potatoes can be varied with creamed mushrooms in season, also flavored with

massive amounts of dill, and this is delicious even without the fish. Alternatively you can serve the fish with plain potatoes and a horseradish cream.

Both rimmad and gravad lax, and other fish can be cured with other herbs as well, with a different, but fine result. Tarragon, basil, and chervil are all perfect.

Try the methods above with gray mullet, or mackerel too—it is just as good.

Surströmming

This Swedish specialty is made from a Baltic strain of small herring, called *strömming*, which is fermented in cans (*sur* means "soured"). Eating it is not for the faint-hearted, though in Scandinavia it has a large and eager following. The taste is acid, cheesy, intoxicating and redolent of rotten eggs for those who have acquired the taste.

The herrings are fermented with lactic acid first, then lightly salted in huge barrels, and then canned. The fermentation continues in the can, turning it into a football shape in a matter of months. The can virtually explodes when opened, which is why this is generally done out of doors, far from human habitation. British and other airlines have forbidden taking these cans on board, so you'd better try this particular specialty in situ.

This treatment of the *strömming* dates back at least

5,000 years and is known throughout the north and Russia, too. The Romans used an almost identical process to make their famed spice sauce, *garum*, which they used to flavor almost anything. The process was invented at a time when salt was scarce, and you used only as much salt as is necessary to prevent putrefaction —thus leaving room for unharmful, preserving bacteria and yeasts to take hold. This fermentation process is similar to that used in producing all sorts of foods, but particularly cheese—hence the strong, rather cheesy taste.

The Norwegians produce a specialty similar to *surströmming*, called *rakefisk*, which is made from trout and fermented in closed jars. In Norway it's widely eaten as a Christmas dish, and is easier for the uninitiated to eat as it is milder and less cheesy.

Both *surströmming* and *rakefisk* are eaten on soft crispbread, with onion and sour cream, or with new potatoes and the same accompaniments as a main dish.

Smoked fish

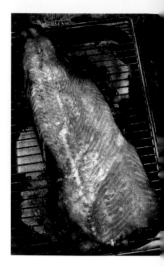

Hot-smoked fish

This method of smoking is easy to do at home without much fuss (page 83). It's simply a means of cooking, in which you smoke the fish while baking it, imbibing it with a discreet smokiness at the same time. In the process, the flesh becomes meltingly tender, foamy, and aromatic, with a sweet and salty juiciness. This style of smoking, however, does not dramatically prolong the fish's keeping qualities. The traditional fish for hot smoking vary from place to place, but herrings, mackerel, eels, trout, and large sea trout are all smoked in great quantities; as is the lumpsucker, or lumpfish, an unfortunately ugly fish which provides wonderful pink fish roe in winter (page 54) but with otherwise no obvious virtues. Its jelly-like, flabby, fatty flesh is inedible when fresh, but hot smoked it takes on a beauty you would not imagine.

Cold-smoked fish

Cold smoking is the more demanding of the two methods, in terms of both the equipment and the process, and is not nearly as easy to replicate at home; for one thing, you need to build a special smoking cabinet or even a dedicated smokehouse. As with hot smoking, the fish must be lightly salted first. Then it is transferred to the smokehouse, where the temperature never goes above 80.6°F. The smoke generated by the burning wood (deciduous wood of various kinds is used) is cooled on its journey through long pipes before coming into contact with the fish. For obvious practical reasons, cold smoking is often done on an industrial scale, but has its keen followers who produce some amazing smoked fish in their homemade smokehouses. The Sami, or indigenous, people of Scandinavia have traditional smoking huts (see opposite).

The process of cold smoking leaves the flesh transparent as in a raw fish, but firm enough that it can be easily cut into thin slices. Salmon and halibut are usually cold smoked. Nordic smoked salmon is less salty and smoked for a shorter time than its American equivalent.

Smoked fish in the Nordic countries is an exceptionally well-loved part of our culinary heritage, from the luxurious, thinly cut, cold-smoked wild salmon to more unassuming treats such as newly hot-smoked herrings for a summer lunch. I, for one, love the gastronomic virtue inherent in the simple alliance of smoked fish and all things Nordic—potatoes, rye bread, our favorite herbs, and fresh spring vegetables and greens.

Smoking fish is no longer a necessity. In the past, however, fresh fish were first salted and then hung up to smoke until bone dry in the chimneys: an easy but essential means of preservation. Nowadays, we smoke fish for the sheer joy of it and, of course, for the deliciousness. While vast quantities of fish are smoked on an industrial scale, Scandinavians love to smoke their own fish at home. This is mostly done in primitive fashion —using a battered old pot, a small smoking box, and a bonfire. All it takes is heat, sawdust, and a closed container.

Fish can be either cold or hot smoked.

Buying and storing There is no comparison between freshly smoked and store-bought smoked fish with an expiration date. Buy or make your own just before you are going to need it.

All smoked fish must look wonderfully oily and fatty. If cold smoked, the fish must be firm-fleshed and smell intoxicatingly of sea, tar, and wood smoke. Hot-smoked fish is soft-fleshed and must be absolutely freshly smoked. Steer clear of dry and skinny-looking fish, and avoid eating smoked fish that's obviously been lying around too long as it can develop severe quantities of histamine over time.

A properly cold-smoked fish will keep for a week or two in the refrigerator. Hot-smoked fish is not really preserved, and will keep for just a day or two.

Culinary uses Smoked salmon must be eaten as simply as possible. Its delicate taste must not be overwhelmed, and comes into its own when eaten on *sigtebrød* (page 248), a bread made from both rye and wheat, or toasted rye bread. Give it a dusting of ground black pepper, lots of dill, and chervil cream, but absolutely no lemon. Smoked salmon and horseradish cream is another match made in heaven: the cream can be simply spread directly onto a plate, and covered with thin slices of salmon; otherwise, combine as a topping for an open-face sandwich.

The best alternative accompaniment is creamy scrambled eggs, perhaps with chervil cream and fresh dill, too. For a more elegant dish, simply slice the fish and serve with delicate vegetables such as asparagus, pointed head cabbage, fresh peas, or creamed spinach. Smoked halibut and other smoked species from the salmon family can all be eaten in the same way.

Hot-smoked fish is eaten as simply as possible, mostly on buttered rye bread or crispbread, with chives or dill. It tastes heavenly with new potatoes, dill, and butter; in a green salad sharp with vinegar and mustard and with abundant herbs; or on rye bread with scrambled eggs and chives.

The sweetness of baked beets is perfect with smoked fish, if balanced with lemon and horseradish and a dusting of coarsely ground black pepper. For the more adventurous, a Nordic pesto made with lovage or chervil (page 177) is delicious.

Smoked eel is best bought on the bone with the skin on. It's easy to peel off the rubbery skin from the eel, then slice off the two fat fillets on either side of the central bone. Eat it on buttered rye bread with a topping of scrambled eggs, chives, and black pepper.

Sun over Gudhjem

Gudhjem, meaning "God's home," is a small fishing village on the east coast of Bornholm, Denmark's only rocky island in the Baltic. It has long been famous for its lovely old smokehouses and its amazing smoked herrings. You buy them directly from the huge, sooty chimneys, where the golden fish hang side by side in their thousands. They are a real delicacy, and well worth the detour if you are in Scandinavia.

Assemble a sandwich on rye bread, with a whole peeled smoked herring (or a large piece of smoked mackerel), a few rings of red onion , a couple of sliced radishes, lots of finely cut chives, and on top, as a rising sun, a raw egg yolk. Add coarse sea salt, black pepper, a cold beer, and a sea view to the Baltic and you will not find anything more authentically Nordic than this.

Hot smoking your own fish

Freshly smoked fish is overwhelmingly good, with meltingly tender flesh and a juicy, sweet saltiness that's a pleasure money just cannot buy. Aside from its inevitable lack of freshness, most commercially hot-smoked fish is also overdone, so home smoking is definitely a skill worth mastering.

The smoking can be done indoors if the extractor hood of your stove is working, as the process naturally produces a lot of smoke. Usually, however, it is best as an outdoor pursuit—which, once you have practiced a little, can become one of the pleasures of summer, while also providing everyone with a welcome break from charred meat cooked on the grill.

You can hot smoke any type of fish, but fatty fish is by far the best. If lean fish is all you have, simply smoke it for a slightly shorter time to prevent the flesh drying out too much. To begin with, use fillets, whole small fish, or a double fillet, with the bone removed but the head still on. Later you can move on to whole big fish.

As a rule, hot-smoked fish should always be a little underdone—fattiness is no guarantee against dry fish if it's cooked for too long. Whether fish is being smoked or plain baked, it should be cooked only until it's just heated through, as the flesh denaturizes at 149°F, and that's all you're after. Salmon and tuna must not be completely done, remaining raw in the middle—it simply tastes better that way.

The gear Make sure you have everything ready before you start. You will need an oven pan and a metal rack or mesh of equal size that will fit into your oven; neither will ever be the same again, so hopefully your first smoking experiment will not be your last. You can also smoke the fish in a spherical or other closed grill. You will also need aluminum foil, good thick oven mitts, tongs, and 7–10½oz sawdust from untreated deciduous wood. Some people are positively religious when it comes to which wood to smoke with, but I am not part of any congregation as I don't believe it's crucial. There is very little time for the fish to absorb flavors from the wood during home smoking; it's much more important when you cold smoke, as the smoke can permeate the fish for days with interesting flavors. Even so, you can choose to spice up your wood with dry twigs from aromatic wood, herbs, and leaves if you wish.

Salting and spicing The fish will have a better flavor if it is prepared in salt and a smaller amount of sugar beforehand: 80 percent salt to 20 percent sugar is fine. Dark, unrefined sugar such as muscovado adds a lovely caramel taste. The Nordic and elderflower herb salts (pages 186 and 183) are perfect for this purpose, adding a gorgeous flavor. You will need 3 tablespoons of the salt-and-sugar mixture for one whole salmon fillet, less for smaller fish. Just sprinkle it over the surface and rest for 4–8 hours or overnight.

The smoking Dry the salted fish with paper towels, then lay it skin-side down on the rack. You can fill the whole space up with fish, as long as there is room between each piece to allow the smoke to circulate freely. You also need to leave room to place a cup or glass, upside down, at either end to prevent the foil from clinging to the fish.

Now heat the oven pan either over a fire, a grill, or on the stove. When it's very, very hot, throw in the sawdust. When it smokes, but before it catches fire, lay two or three layers of aluminum foil over the fish and quickly make a tight package. With your mitts on, squeeze the foil tight around the edges and make sure no smoke escapes. Turn down the heat to very low, and proceed to smoke the fish. Herring takes just 10 minutes to smoke, mackerel 15 minutes, and a large whole fillet of salmon 25–30 minutes (depending on its size). When the fish is golden, firm, but still slightly undercooked in the center, it's finished.

The newly smoked fish is overwhelmingly good, with a juicy sweet saltiness that's almost naughty. It's a pleasure that money cannot buy. Cooled and eaten the day after, it's very fresh and still so much better than the bought stuff. It will keep in the refrigerator for 2–3 days.

If you develop a (healthy) smoking habit, you can smoke all sorts of things, including tender cuts of meat that will need only a short cooking time, as well as potatoes, salt, chiles, garlic, bell peppers, chicken, duck, homemade sausages, fresh cheese… probably just about anything edible.

Cured fish

Herrings and other fish are often salted before curing, but there is also a wealth of cured fish recipes, prepared with freshly caught fish, without initial salting. These herrings are delicious and the same marinades can be used as for soaked, salted, and spiced herrings, if you keep an eye on the salt. You can use any other fresh, fatty fish in these recipes, such as mackerel.

Soused herrings with mustard and herbs

This is easy to make. The herrings will keep for a week, if you omit the herbs and put them on just before eating; in fact, they will get better and better.

Rye flour, for coating
Salt and pepper
10 double herring fillets
5 tablespoons coarse-grain
  Dijon mustard
Lots of butter, for frying
2 large red onions, sliced
  into rings
2 handfuls of herbs:
  a mixture of dill, chervil,
  parsley, chives, and
  tarragon, chopped

1¼in piece of horseradish,
  grated into long strands
  (optional)
for the pickle
Generous ¾ cup cider
  vinegar
½ cup sugar
1 tablespoon coarse sea salt
1 teaspoon ground
  black pepper
SERVES 4–5

Season the flour with salt and pepper, then use to coat the fillets. Spread the inside of each double fillet with a tablespoon of mustard and fold it in half.

Heat the butter in a skillet and, when it is golden brown, add the fillets and fry until crispy; this takes only a few minutes on each side. Place them in a deep dish.

Put all the ingredients for the pickle in a saucepan and bring to the boil. Set aside to cool a little, then pour over the fish when both the fillets and pickle liquid are lukewarm. Cover with the onion rings and a serious layer of chopped herbs (make sure these are washed thoroughly), along with some horseradish if you'd like an extra kick.

The herrings can be eaten straightaway or at any temperature, besides cold from the refrigerator. You can reheat them in the souse, if you prefer. More simply, serve the fillets on buttered rye bread, with more onion rings.

Leftover herrings should be kept in a cool place, but not the refrigerator, as this will stiffen the fish, and the butter.

TIP
- As an alternative to the above recipe, you can sandwich the fillets around an apple-horseradish sauce and spice them with cider vinegar instead of the pickle. You can eat them while they are still hot, with rye bread on the side, of course.

Mustard gravad herrings

Sweetly mustardy, these are delicious on rye bread, maybe with sliced new potatoes and a mountain of fresh dill. Mackerel can be treated in the same way, with a delicious result. The first pickle is to extract moisture from the fish, and make them firm, the next is for spicing and a delicious creamy sauce to eat with the fish. You can also use salted herring, in which case you should desalt the fillets and then jump directly to the mustard pickle.

2¼lb small herring fillets
for the pickle
2 cups water
1¼ cups cider vinegar
1 teaspoon coarse sea salt

for the mustard pickle
5 tablespoons Dijon
  mustard
3 tablespoons coarse-grain
  Dijon mustard
3 tablespoons sugar
2 teaspoons coarse sea salt

A little white pepper
4 tablespoons cider vinegar
3 cups water
Generous ⅓ cup
   vegetable oil

2 bunches dill, leaves picked
   off and meticulously
   washed

SERVES 8 AS PART
OF LUNCH

Wash the herring fillets, making sure that you clean all the blood away. Lay them in a deep dish and pour over the first pickle, made simply by mixing the water, vinegar, and salt. Leave the fish to macerate for 4–6 hours.

Mix together the ingredients to make the (cold) mustard pickle.

Remove the fish from the first pickle and dry with paper towels. Cut into slanting 1¼in-thick slices and submerge them in the mustard pickle, cover and place in the fridge until the next day. Turn them over a couple of times.

Eat on rye bread, with dill and maybe sliced potatoes. They will keep for a week.

Scania spiced herrings

This is a traditional, spicy version of fresh, pickled herrings from the southern province of Sweden. If you want to make it from salted herring fillets (desalted), you just need to omit all the salt, then stick to the rest of the recipe, and add ⅓ cup + 2 tablespoons of cider vinegar and 2 tablespoons of neutral oil to the spices while the fish is marinating.

Serve it on rye bread, with dill, a raw egg yolk, and onion, or with new potatoes, sour cream, and dill.

2lb 12oz fresh herring
   fillets, washed
for the pickle
6 cups water
2¾ cups cider vinegar
2 tablespoons coarse
   sea salt
for the spice mix
1 tablespoon white
   peppercorns
3 tablespoons whole allspice

2 tablespoons cloves
1 teaspoon ground ginger
1 teaspoon powdered
   sandalwood
5 bay leaves
1 tablespoon long pepper
   (*Piper longum*)
1 small/medium dried chile
4 tablespoons coarse sea salt
1¾ cups sugar
SERVES 8

Mix the ingredients for the pickle and use it to macerate the fish for 24 hours, covered. Dry the fish with paper towels. Reserve the pickle.

Scrub the jar or jars you intend to use. You will need one 5¼ quart jar or several smaller ones. Make sure that all your equipment is sterilized, and wear thin rubber gloves.

To make the spice mix, crush the peppercorns, allspice, and cloves very lightly in a mortar—just so that the flavors are released more rapidly. The bay leaves, long pepper, and chile are kept whole. Blend together until well mixed.

Put 4 tablespoons of the spice mix into the bottom of the jar, then proceed to alternate herring fillets and layers of spice mix until you reach the top, finishing off with a spice layer. Press the fish together in the jar while you work. Add enough of the reserved pickle to cover. Finish with a scalded plate (small enough to fit inside the top of the jar) and a heavy weight on top. Close the jar with a lid or plastic wrap.

Let the fish steep in the refrigerator for 2–3 weeks. During this time, it's important to keep the fish submerged in the pickle. The herrings will keep for a month, as long as you remember to remove the fillets each time with a clean fork.

Northern anchovy *Sprattus sprattus*

These tiny salted and fermented fish may be the cause of some really odd dishes, made from Nordic cookbooks, by people wanting to cook a really Scandinavian meal at home. They have also created much agony in northern kitchens, where people are trying to reproduce beloved Italian dishes with "anchovies." The fact of the matter is that Scandinavian anchovies are very different from anchovies in the rest of the world, as they are not made from true anchovies (*Engraulis encrasicholus*), but from a variety of small fish in the herring family (*Sprattus sprattus*). They are even cured quite differently.

True anchovies are gutted and immediately packed in barrels between thick layers of sea salt. Here they ferment and are then either sold as whole salted anchovies, or filleted and drowned in olive oil. These are the ones needed in pizzas, *bagna cauda*, and all other southern European dishes with anchovies. The northern anchovies (*ansjovis*), on the other hand, are preserved

whole in spiced, sweetened brine. You buy them in cans and fillet them yourself. The raw fish are also eaten in a number of other ways: for example canned like sardines or eaten fresh.

Appearance and taste Northern anchovies taste much the same as sweet varieties of spiced pickled herrings, and especially the Swedish matjes herrings (*matjessild*), though they have a quite different consistency, virtually melting in your mouth. They are spiced with cardamom, pepper, sandalwood, cinnamon, and oregano.

Buying and storing The best anchovies are from Norway. The fish are caught in late summer and are then left to mature in cans to be sold predominantly at Christmas, for delicacies such as Jansson's temptation.

The anchovies keep almost indefinitely in the can, though they must be stored in the refrigerator. Once the can has been opened, transfer the fish in their brine to a non-reactive container, where they will keep for ages. Since the fish are whole, you fillet them yourself (see below), though you can also buy them filleted and ready-to-eat in cans or small jars (but these do not keep for very long once opened).

Culinary uses Northern anchovies are eaten on open-face sandwiches much like other herrings, and taste divine eaten on crisp, or rye bread, with hard-boiled eggs and chives, or with cold sliced potatoes with raw onion and chives. They have other uses too, as a spice in potato gratins and liver paste. But try putting them on your pizza and you'll regret it.

To fillet an anchovy, put the fish on a board, cut off the head, then flatten it a bit from the back to loosen the spine and turn it over. The spine is removed by pulling it from the head end toward the tail, along with the gut, after which the two fillets are easily pulled off the skin.

Sunny eye sandwich

Known as *sölöga*, this is a favorite open-face sandwich in Sweden, very simple and very effective. It consists simply of buttered rye bread topped with chopped pickled beets, chopped red onion, capers, and filleted anchovies criss-crossed on the top. It's finished off with a golden raw egg yolk, dill, and chives. It makes a beautiful appetizer or lunch dish.

Jansson's temptation

There is something thoroughly Nordic about this classic Swedish dish, whose simple ingredients—potatoes, onions, cream, and fish—are available even in the depths of our cold winter. The combined taste is the epitome of Scandinavian food: buttery, salty, sweet, filling, nourishing, and still a little elegant, as the salt fish creates small explosions of umami sensations in your mouth. Originally, the potatoes were steeped in cold water to draw out the starch, but I solve the problem by using waxy salad potatoes.

The classic accompaniments are toasted crispbread, beer, and schnapps. But I suggest a huge green salad as well.

18oz firm red or new potatoes
2 onions, cut into rings
½ stick salted butter
Ground black pepper
3½oz anchovy fillets
Generous ⅓ cup brine from the anchovies
Approx. ¾ cup heavy cream
SERVES 4

Preheat the oven to 350°F.

Cut a few of the potatoes into thin slices and the rest into thick matchsticks. Butter an ovenproof dish well, then cover the bottom and sides with the potato slices.

Fry the onions in the butter until pale golden. Mix with the potato sticks and black pepper to taste. Put half of the onion-potato mixture in the dish, cover with the anchovies, and then fill with the rest of the onion/potato mixture. Pour the anchovy brine and cream over the top, and bake until the potatoes are very tender and the dish has achieved an inviting, golden crust. If the dish appears to be drying out you can pour in a little more cream, and maybe a little water.

Scandinavians are great meat eaters. The surviving recipes from the past were mostly recorded in wealthier households, as they ate much more meat that the poorer majority who survived on a diet of hot oatmeal, and later bread and potatoes, with the occasional piece of meat. In the 1960s, we generally became wealthier very fast, and meat consumption rocketed, especially chicken and beef. Cheap meat like offal was rarely eaten, and the general idea about meat as food changed. Most still regard vegetables as an accompaniment to meat, and not the other way round.

So our heritage is made up from different periods; very old ways of roasting big cuts of meat and game, and festive pork and mutton recipes. More recently we've seen bourgeois stews and more intricate dishes inspired by France and England, and relatively new dishes from ground meat. Before the meat grinder was invented in the mid-19th century, ground meat was a rare and expensive treat, and sausages were a delicacy. The home meat-grinder immediately became immensely popular, because it meant that large parts of the animal could be used for immediate consumption, and a whole new array of Scandinavian dishes became everyday, cheap fare. Meatballs, fresh sausages, meat loaf, hamburgers, and meat dumplings became a possibility, and extremely popular, and these dishes are still the favorite everyday food of the majority of the population.

Another part of our legacy are the salted, boiled meats that have a much older ancestry, as salting, drying, and smoking were the only way to preserve meat 150 years ago.

poultry, meat, game, & offal

Chicken

The chicken's route from being a springtime delicacy to junk food has been fast. In just 30 years, chickens have become too cheap and too off-puttingly insipid to be considered good food. The chicken cooking traditions in Scandinavia make this an even bigger problem. Our northern recipes rely solely on tasty and succulent poultry, with mellow spicing that cannot—and should not—make up for lousy modern quality.

Fortunately, there is a growing number of Scandinavians willing to pay for the luxury of eating a chicken bred in the traditional manner, and the reward is a bird that can be cooked simply and delicately and given to children and young people who have never had anything so inviting and delicious to eat. Old people, who had believed that their taste buds had tired, discover the taste of food they have not enjoyed for decades.

Chicken-keeping on a small scale has long been popular among Scandinavians, and as in other countries the passion for home chicken-keeping, including in towns and cities, is currently on the increase. This is in part a reaction to the trend for the mass-production of poor-quality chickens with next to no taste, and certainly no quality of life.

Habitat and appearance Chickens were first introduced to Scandinavia during the Bronze Age. These were sturdy little birds, very much like the wildfowl originating in Asia. They evolved in time into what are now called *landrace* chickens, beautiful birds that easily withstand temperatures of -40°F, and lay more than 200 eggs a year. The plumage of the *landrace* hen is mottled brown, like that of a hen pheasant (perfect camouflage for hiding in woodland), while the cocks are brightly colored in brown, black, and white. They are agile birds and fairly good flyers and will stay in tall trees overnight if you let them.

Landrace chickens can still be found all over Scandinavia, where they are loved for their beauty, hardiness, and friendly nature. On smallholdings they are often left to roam freely, and find most of their food themselves. They are also popular among home chicken keepers, even in cities. The eggs are small, but the yolk is as large as that of a big hen's egg, and they are delicious.

In the past 200 years, the original *landrace* chicken has been interbred with hundreds of other breeds

(many of them British ones) to improve meatiness, size, egg size, egg-laying capacity, and fast growth. It is part of man's nature to keep developing and improving both animals and plants, and it has had beautiful consequences in many cases. With chicken breeding, however, it has just gone too far. Chickens now grow so fast that their legs cannot carry them. Egg layers are so effective, laying an egg every single day, that they are little more than skeletons when slaughtered, and not worth eating.

There is, however, a fast-growing counter-offensive of conscientious chicken farmers who are producing fine, large, slow-grown organic chickens, though at a much higher price. Fortunately there are more and more of us prepared to pay for the luxury of eating a bird that goes a long way, and which has all the taste you rightly expect from a chicken.

Buying and storing It is simple. If you want to succeed with northern recipes, you must invest in prime-quality, large, organic chickens that have been raised slowly. Anything else will be a disappointment. If you rub it with a little salt inside and out, a fresh chicken can be kept in the refrigerator for a couple of days.

Culinary uses Scandinavian recipes for chicken are relatively few—chicken has been a luxury for centuries, a spring treat you did not want to take chances with—but they are certainly delicious. Furthermore, there is a solid logic to the way our chicken recipes have evolved: Soups were made from old and worn egg layers, fattened to make a beautiful broth, while spring chickens were filled with parsley and roasted slowly in butter and served with a delicious curdled sauce, fresh peas, cucumber salad, and new potatoes. Leftovers were used for stews, salads, and our beloved chicken tartlets (*tarteletter*). White asparagus is a classic feature of some of our favorite chicken dishes, as are the creamy flavorings of parsley and tarragon.

Chicken soup with dumplings

A huge pot of steaming chicken soup is food for friends and family for several days, and the essence of home cooking. It is always made with a piece of beef, preferably a fatty cut, which will cook to melting tenderness in a couple of hours. The soup may take some time to prepare, but you can serve it for several days in a row, the chicken first, with sauce and steamed cabbage, and the beef the day after with leeks. The soup can be served plain, or with dumplings and small dice of parsley root and sliced leeks. (The dumplings can be made several days in advance and stored in a closed container in the refrigerator.)

for the soup

1 large chicken (approx. 6lb 8oz), or 2 smaller chickens
4lb 8oz beef neck, on bone
3 onions, quartered
5 carrots
1 parsley root or parsnip
½ celeriac or ½ head of celery
8 small leeks
1 small bunch of fresh thyme
2 bay leaves
1 tablespoon black peppercorns
4 cloves garlic
1 clove
1 bunch of parsley
3 tablespoons coarse sea salt

for the sauce

2½ cups stock
2 tablespoons white wine or cider vinegar
4 tablespoons sugar
2 tablespoons cornstarch
Generous ¼ cup heavy cream
6 tablespoons freshly grated horseradish
⅓ cup currants
3 tablespoons coarse sea salt

for the dumplings

½ cup butter
1 cup all-purpose flour
1 teaspoon sea salt
1 cup water or stock
4–5 eggs

Serves 14–16

Put the chicken and beef in a pot that's big enough to hold everything comfortably. Cover with cold water and bring slowly to a boil, then lower the heat to a simmer. Remove any scum frequently.

Meanwhile, rinse all the vegetables and cut into chunks; the green parts of the leeks go into the pot at this stage, but reserve the white parts for later. When there's no scum on the surface of the soup, throw in the vegetables, herbs, and spices, including the parsley, stalks and all (reserve a little parsley to chop as a garnish). Remove any scum again and,

when it is gone, season with the salt.

When the thighs can be easily loosened from the carcass, the chicken's done. Lift it from the pot with two slotted spoons and leave until the bird is cool enough to handle. Remove the skin and cut the breast meat from the carcass, then remove the thighs and cut them in two; remove the two nuggets of meat from the back, and the upper part of the wings. Save all this meat, and return the carcass and skin to the pot.

Test the beef and remove from the pot when really tender. Taste the soup. It may need reducing, and it may need salt: you're after an intensely flavored soup, but be careful not to oversalt it if the stock still needs reducing. When you're happy, put the soup through a sieve. Cool a little and remove the fat from the surface with a spoon. Reserve 2½ cups for the sauce, and put the rest in the refrigerator unless you are going to eat it the same day.

For the sauce, put the stock, vinegar, and sugar in a saucepan and reduce to half. Blend the cornstarch and cream. Whisk this into the sauce and let it boil for 5 minutes until the floury taste has gone, then remove from the heat. Add the horseradish and currants, and adjust the salt. Add more horseradish if you wish: the sauce must be hot, slightly sweet, and a little sour.

To make the dumplings, mix the butter, flour, salt, and water (or stock) in a saucepan, and stir continuously until the batter is glossy, and comes away from the sides of the pan. Cool a little. When it is lukewarm, beat in the eggs one at a time, and stop when the batter is thick (you may not need the fifth egg). Bring a saucepan of water to a boil, then drop marble-sized blobs of batter into the simmering water —you can use a plastic food bag, with a corner cut off, or a proper pastry bag to do this. When the dumplings rise to the top they are done.

Serve the soup first, with the dumplings and the white parts of the leeks. Heat the meat gently in a little of the soup (this can be done in a slow oven), dust the meat with parsley, and serve with an assortment of steamed vegetables, potatoes, and the delicious sauce.

Chicken and asparagus stew

This is as classic a Nordic chicken dish as it gets, whose natural place is on a high pedestal in any European kitchen. Its origins lie in nothing more complicated than the fact that chicken and white asparagus traditionally coincided in late spring and the combination of two such exquisite ingredients made this creamy stew a trophy on the Sunday lunch table. Only the best chicken and the freshest, fattest white asparagus will do, but I have to confess that good-quality canned asparagus will make a fine, though not an unforgettable, dish. Serve with plenty of white, crusty bread to absorb the sauce.

2¼lb fresh white asparagus	2 tablespoons coarse sea salt
1 bunch of chervil	1 bay leaf
1 bunch of parsley	1 sprig of thyme
2 bunches of scallions	3 cloves garlic
2 carrots	2 teaspoons black
4 celery stalks or 1 thick	peppercorns
slice of celeriac	1 tablespoon cornstarch
3 leeks, green parts only	Generous ¾ cup
2 onions	heavy cream
1 large chicken (at least 4lb	A little sugar
8oz)	SERVES AT LEAST 6

Peel the asparagus spears from the heads down, and snap off the woody ends. Save the ends and peel for the stock. Pick the leaves from the chervil and parsley, reserving them for the garnish, and save the stalks for the stock. Clean the vegetables and cut into chunks.

Put the chicken in a large stockpot, along with the vegetables, odds and ends from the asparagus, and the salt. Cover with water, and bring slowly to a boil. Remove the scum and add the bay leaf, thyme, garlic, and peppercorns, plus the reserved parsley and chervil stalks. Continue to remove the scum frequently. Simmer slowly until the chicken is tender, then remove and let the stock simmer on. As soon as the chicken is cool enough to handle, remove the skin and pick the breast meat off the carcass, and then the meat from the thighs, and the thickest part of the wings. Cut the meat into large bite-size pieces.

Put the carcass, skin, and upper wings back into the stock and simmer until there is only about 4 cups of liquid left. Put this through a sieve, and let all the good stock drip from it. Mix the cornstarch and cream and whisk into the stock, warming it through in a saucepan for 5 minutes.

Cut the peeled asparagus spears into bite-size pieces, and put the heads to one side. Add the asparagus and chicken pieces to the sauce and let them simmer in a pan for 3 minutes, then add the asparagus heads and heat through for 3 minutes more. Adjust the seasoning with sugar and salt, and serve scattered with a thick layer of chervil and parsley leaves.

Tartlets with chicken stew

Tartlets have been sadly out of fashion, but are lately experiencing a very welcome revival. Delicious tartlets made with chicken and asparagus stew have been one of our favorite festive meal appetizers for decades, and are very popular with children too. They are often made with leftover stew, but I make mine from scratch, just for this. The tartlet shells can be bought ready-made (you have to be a grade 1 housewife to make your own), but small puff pastry shells will do instead.

The chicken pieces in the stew will be too large to go in the tartlets, so remove these from the sauce and shred them. Meanwhile, lightly steam 1¼ cups fresh green peas or very young fava beans, and 2 diced carrots, and warm the tartlets shells (24 for 12 people) in the oven according the package instructions.

Return the chicken to the sauce and warm through, then add the carrots and peas just before serving. Fill the warmed tartlet shells with the stew at the last minute, otherwise they will be soggy. Garnish with lots of chopped herbs (parsley, chervil, dill, and chives) and serve while still very warm.

Chicken salad

This is a superb chicken salad, to eat as it is, or for a topping on toast or toasted rye bread. There is just enough mayonnaise to cast a veil of creaminess around the chicken, sharpened with mustard so your taste buds won't fall asleep, while the salted capers make wonders happen in your mouth. No wonder chicken salad is crowned as one of the most loved *smørrebrød* (open-face sandwiches) in Scandinavia. It is a perfect picnic dish, a beautiful summer lunch, topped with plenty of fresh herbs and served in scallops of butterhead lettuce. It's worth preparing an extra chicken, or perhaps simply a larger one, while you are making your chicken dinner, just to have enough for this dish.

1 cup diced celeriac	parsley, or dill, chopped
Generous ⅓ cup white wine vinegar	1 tablespoon salted capers, washed and chopped
¼ cup chopped smoked bacon	Salt and pepper
½ boiled or roasted large chicken, or 1 smaller chicken	2 butterhead lettuces
	for the mayonnaise
2 bunches of herbs, e.g. chervil, chives, tarragon,	1 egg, plus 1 egg yolk
	1 teaspoon sea salt
	1 tablespoon grated lemon zest

1 tablespoon Dijon mustard	Approx. 2 tablespoons white wine vinegar
1¼ cups extra-virgin olive oil	
2 tablespoons crème fraîche	Serves 6 as an appetizer, or 4 for lunch

Heat the celeriac in a saucepan with the vinegar and stir over a high heat until the vinegar has evaporated. Fry the bacon in a skillet until crisp, then set aside.

Pluck the meat off the chicken carcass into fine shreds.

For the mayonnaise, the trick is to make sure that all the ingredients are at the same temperature, preferably room temperature. Mix the egg and extra yolk, the salt, lemon zest, and mustard in a bowl or food processor, and gradually drip in the oil until it is used up. If the mayonnaise separates, try adding a small amount of cold water and stirring vigorously. Dilute the mayonnaise with the crème fraîche and a little vinegar, then mix with the celeriac, herbs, half of the capers, and chicken; reserve a few of the herbs to decorate. Season if necessary.

Serve the salad on a bed of lettuce, garnished with the bacon and chopped herbs and capers. As the mayonnaise is fresh, you should eat the salad the day it's made.

Goose & duck

Scandinavian geese—both wild and domesticated—have been immortalized in the famous book *The Wonderful Adventures of Nils*, written by Swedish author and Nobel Prize laureate Selma Lagerlöf and published in 1906. It tells the story of a naughty boy called Nils, who is turned into a *Tomte*—a small man with magical powers, guarding livestock and farm life—for the way he mistreats the farm animals and for involuntarily riding the farm goose and following a flock of wild geese migrating to Lapland. Lagerlöf's descriptions of the Swedish landscapes and customs featured in the book are the most precise and beautiful descriptions of Scandinavia ever written.

We have kept both geese and ducks for millennia, and both have always been extensively farmed. They are able to thrive mostly on grass, so it was normal for every farm to have a few, either to eat or to sell for a good price at market. In communities untouched by agricultural-supporting laws and money, geese and ducks (which do not compete with human needs for grain) are far cheaper to keep than chickens, which basically eat the same as humans. In our over-supported farming communities, the picture is askew, and these birds cost a fortune.

Geese and ducks are certainly not everyday fare in Scandinavia. In general, both are eaten only on festive occasions, even if some people hold on to the delicious way of eating salted duck with horseradish sauce as a summer dish. And twice a year the consumption of both rockets: at Christmas and on St. Martin's Eve on the November 10.

Appearance and taste We have several special Nordic breeds of both geese and ducks. In recent years, we have tended to buy more of the meaty Barbary ducks, though many people stick with the old breeds, which have more intramuscular fat and lack the gamy taste of the Barbary.

Geese and ducks must be raised on abundant grass and with plenty of fresh air if they are to end up as the truly wonderful meal they can be. And the best are raised organically, slowly, and eating nothing but fresh grass and grains. This gives a taste, and lots of intramuscular fat, that you won't find in conventionally farmed birds. The latter are so intensively reared that meat and fat are mostly separated in the body, with far too much fat under the skin and in the belly. Organic birds are easier to prepare to the succulence you want. Conventionally raised and fed animals tend to leave a small, dry bird in a pool of fat.

Buying and storing Geese and ducks must look as though they are made of marzipan: firm to the touch, the breast arched and covered with light yellow or white skin (according to the feed). The skin must be without holes, and untorn, or it will never be crispy; if it has purplish spots or blemishes, you should not buy it. There will always be feathers and stubble left, as well as pieces of peeling wax, but if it looks too furry buy another one—it's quite a job to pluck a large bird clean with tweezers, and you need to get all the feathers off as they stink when roasted. Remember to check that the giblets are inside the bird as you will need these for the sauce/gravy.

Most ducks for eating weigh around 6lb 8oz, but you can find monster ducks weighing up to 10lb. The bigger, the better, since a duck's carcass is huge compared to its size: the carcass of a 6lb 8oz duck is much the same size as that of a heavier bird, so the extra weight is pure meat. Ducks weighing less than 6lb 8oz are too young and have too little taste. A large duck will feed five to seven people. A 6lb 8oz duck is not really enough for four.

A goose weighs 11–15½lb, and again the bigger ones are much better value. While not as monstrously sized as a turkey, a goose can certainly feed quite a gathering: a large one is enough for 10–12 people.

Most birds are sold frozen, and must thaw slowly in the refrigerator for 2–3 days. A fresh one will keep in the refrigerator for 3–4 days.

Culinary uses Both duck and goose are fat, juicy birds, and they can become meltingly tender if slow roasted. They have dark, hefty meat, standing up to the traditional spiced, vinegary trimmings.

In Denmark and parts of Norway, ducks and geese are eaten on Christmas Eve, and are always prepared in more or less the same manner: roasted with an apple and prune stuffing, pickled red cabbage, caramelized potatoes, and gravy. Trimmings vary, but might include lingonberries, applesauce spiced with horseradish, halved apples with jelly, or baked apples. It's usually the same for St. Martin's Eve, though some people try to be more innovative, as the pressure of tradition on that occasion is less severe.

The summery way of cooking, in which the bird is salted and slowly poached, is more elegant and served with creamy horseradish, new potatoes, and creamed spinach. The salting dyes the meat an appetizing pink, and makes it even juicier. Anyone who tastes this dish will never forget it.

Compared with turkey, goose and duck meat is very rarely dry, and leftovers are a treat to eat. At Christmas few things beat rye bread topped with some cold jellied gravy, duck or goose meat and pickled red cabbage.

The third traditional way to prepare goose is with *gule ærter*, a filling and delicious yellow split pea soup, served with sausages, vegetables, and salted pork. In more well-to-do homes, it is traditionally made with salted goose also, and it's wonderful, even if it has been diluted to poorer versions over time and heads the list of dishes that Nordic people really hate to eat.

The bird's carcass, bones, and neck, as well as leftovers from the roasted bird, can be made into a wonderfully flavored stock with the addition of a few onions, carrots, and herbs such as sage, thyme, and bay leaf, and maybe a glass of dark beer. Cover with water and simmer for a couple of hours, strain and use for sauce or soup.

St. Martin's Day

St. Martin of Tours, a French bishop living in the 3rd century and founder of the monastery of Marmoutiers, definitely did not want to be a bishop. When the election committee came to bring him the news that he was elected, he hid with the geese, penned to be fattened for Christmas.

Geese are as capable watch keepers as dogs, and squawked so loud that the poor man was found by the clergymen. In fact, he turned out to be a very capable bishop.

St. Martin installed November 11 as the official slaughtering day for geese, followed by 40 days of fasting. Why we in Scandinavia—where we have not been Catholic since Luther—eat goose must be a somewhat delayed revenge. The truth is that nowadays the goose is usually replaced by totally innocent ducks, as families tend to be smaller, and their festive meal requirements more duck-size.

And what can I say about the duck or goose fat, other than that it is pure liquid gold in your kitchen? Nothing beats potatoes or root vegetables sizzled in this fat, or pâtés and liver paste made with it. And rendered duck or goose fat is heaven on rye bread, just sprinkled with salt; and it's the traditional spread to use with herrings, sausages, and most meat toppings on open-face sandwiches. It can be used on its own, or melted with pork fat, which is solid at room temperature, to give it a higher melting point.

How to roast a duck or goose

Roasting a duck or goose for the first time is a major, daunting and challenging operation, which is why it is explained in some detail. For the inexperienced Nordic cook it's the culinary challenge of the year. There are high expectations on Christmas Eve, and many choose to have a dress rehearsal on St. Martin's Eve in November.

The first thing you need to do is pluck off every feather and every piece of wax. Apart from real feathers, both geese and ducks have some thin, hair-like feathers, which must be burned away with a lighter, or over a naked flame, and then rubbed off.

Right inside the cavity, attached to the body, are two lumps of solid fat which should be torn out. This is the finest fat in the whole bird and you should save it for frying all kinds of vegetables. Remove the giblets and place in a bowl. Cut off the neck at a joint close to the body and save it for the sauce. Cut off the outer joint of the wings for the sauce as well.

Dry the bird with paper towels then weigh it (before you stuff it). Goose and duck must be roasted for 35 minutes per 2¼lb at 325°F. If you have a convection oven,

reduce the overall time by half an hour. It is important that this calculation is accurate.

Rub the bird with coarse sea salt, inside and out; use 1 large tablespoon for a duck, even more for a goose. Stuff it with the stuffing described on page 97 then lay the bird breast down on a roasting rack set over a deep roasting pan. If you have planned ahead, this is where you let the bird sit quietly, overnight, in a cool place, completely naked and unwrapped, to dry. It will work wonders for the crispness.

When you are ready to roast the bird, pour ⅕in cold water into the roasting pan, then place the bird in the preheated oven. Roast the bird breast-side down for the first third of the cooking time. Turn it breast-side up for the remaining time. Keep an eye on the liquid in the pan, as it must not dry out. All the scrumptious fat and juices will drip into the pan, but if it's pure fat it will burn, and the lovely pan juices will be ruined. Keep it moistened by pouring off some of the fat two or three times during roasting and replenishing with a little water. Don't add too much, though, as you want the pan juices, which will end up in the gravy, to be as tasty as possible.

When the cooking time is almost up, the skin should be browned and crisp, but this is not always the case. To be sure, take the bird out of the oven 20 minutes before the cooking time is up and scrape every last tasty morsel and bit of browned goo from the roasting pan into your gravy pan. Cover the bottom of the oven with aluminum foil, turn the heat up to maximum and put the bird back in. You must watch it closely, as in a few minutes the skin will blister and crackle and produce a lovely crispness, and in a few more minutes it will be cremated. Leave the bird to rest on the counter, uncovered, for 20 minutes while you get everything else ready.

The giblets

Giblets are miracle workers in your gravy. Together with the neck and wings, these spare parts are the cornerstones of your sauce. If the giblets are missing, you can always buy chicken hearts, duck livers, and duck legs separately.

It is important to examine the giblets thoroughly, and clean them where necessary. First, remove the liver and check it over carefully. If it has green-yellow spots, this means that some of the bile has seeped out of the gall bladder; if only part of the liver is spotty, you can just cut this bit off, but if the whole liver is soaked in bile you must throw it away. Even a small piece of tainted liver can give an extremely bitter taste.

The gizzard (the thick-walled part of the bird's stomach) can be a whole lump, in which case you cut it open and remove the stones and hard leathery inner lining. When cleaned it's ready to use, and will eventually be the most tasty morsel of the whole meal. The heart must be cleaned of blood.

(The liver does not go into the sauce, but can either go into the stuffing, or be turned into a delicious pâté. For this, simply fry the liver lightly in butter, with onion and thyme, then lift it out and pour a glass of wine into the pan and reduce to a syrup. Process this with the liver and a very generous piece of butter to a smooth purée in the food processor. Eat cold on toasted rye bread, with gherkins or pickled beets.)

The stuffing

A large lump of fat from inside the bird	3 tablespoons sugar
1 large onion, chopped	1 cup large prunes, preferably Agen, with stones
1 teaspoon fresh thyme leaves	
The whole liver(s) from the bird(s)	1 tablespoon sea salt
2¼lb hand-eating apples, peeled, cored and chopped	1 teaspoon ground black pepper
	MAKES ENOUGH FOR 2 DUCKS OR 1 GOOSE

Melt the fat in a heavy skillet. When it is sizzling hot, fry the onion and thyme to a golden mass. Add the liver(s) and fry quickly, then remove to a bowl. Fry the apples and sugar in the same pan until golden. Add to the bowl, along with the prunes, salt, and pepper. Mix it all together well and then use to stuff the birds.

The gravy

This gravy is nothing less than divine. It's a very successful fusion of Nordic and French traditions, maybe a little more spiced than your mother's gravy—depending on who your mother is, of course. The sauce is easy to make but it needs time for the flavors to flow, so start the minute your bird (or birds) go into the oven.

If you like, you can use red wine instead of the hard cider, which will make the gravy less sweet, and definitely more French, but I love the slight sweetness.

A lump of fat from inside the cavity	4 cloves garlic
2 large onions, chopped	Giblets, wings, and necks
1 small carrot, diced	4 tablespoons cider vinegar
1 smallish piece of celeriac or 1 celery stalk, chopped	4 cups hard cider, or ½ bottle red wine
1 fresh bay leaf	1 tablespoon coarse sea salt
1 large sprig of thyme	2 tablespoons tamari (Japanese soy sauce)
4 juniper berries	
2 whole allspice	1 tablespoon cornstarch
½ tablespoon black peppercorns	Generous ¾ cup heavy cream, or to taste
	MAKES ENOUGH FOR 2 DUCKS OR 1 GOOSE

Melt the fat in a large saucepan. Fry the vegetables, spices, herbs, and garlic slowly to a golden mass. Remove from the pan with a slotted spoon and set aside. Now fry the giblets in the fat until thoroughly browned. Return the vegetable mixture to the pan, then add the vinegar and hard cider or wine and reduce the liquid to a syrup at the bottom of the pan. Add the salt and enough water to cover.

Bring to a boil, then put a lid on askew and let the gravy simmer gently for 3–4 hours, while the birds roast. Add the pan juices and fat from the birds, when these threaten to overflow during roasting. By the time the birds are done you will have a very good, concentrated gravy.

Put the gravy through a fine sieve, pressing down well to extract all the good stuff. Skim most of the fat from the surface, but do leave ¼in or so floating on top as there's loads of taste in there. Save both the giblets and the fat: the giblets are so nice to pick at later in the evening, while the fat is good for almost any frying task.

Flavor the gravy with tamari, which is a wonder liquid, able to salt in a mellowing way. Mix the cornstarch with a little cream and whisk into the gravy, along with the rest of the cream. Boil for a few minutes and then it's ready to serve.

Poached and salted goose or duck

This is a beautiful summer dish, sufficiently elegant for a formal dinner, and geese and ducks can be quite cheap out of season. The salting imbues the meat with an intense flavor as well as firmness. However, it's not worth doing if the birds are not of the highest quality, or they will be dry and insipid. The only problem with this recipe is finding a pot large enough to fit the bird into.

Serve the meat with seasonal fresh greens, asparagus, new potatoes, pointed head cabbage, peas, spinach, steamed with butter, and cold, creamed horseradish.

1 goose or duck

for the brine
1½ cups coarse sea salt
1 cup sugar
10½pt water

for the flavorings
1–2 fresh bay leaves
1 teaspoon black
   peppercorns
1 sprig of thyme
½ garlic bulb
3 onions, quartered
4 carrots, sliced
3 celery sticks

for the creamed horseradish
1¼ cups heavy cream
2in fat, fresh horseradish,
   finely grated
1 teaspoon cider vinegar
1 teaspoon sugar
Salt and crushed
   black pepper

Put the salt, sugar, and water for the brine into a large pot and bring it to a boil. Remove any scum, then leave the brine to cool completely.

Meanwhile, wash the bird inside and out in cold water, and remove any feathers and peeling wax with tweezers. Put the bird in the cold brine, either in a large container or in a double plastic food bag, then place in the refrigerator. A duck will need 12 hours', a goose 18 hours' salting.

Once it's salted, transfer the bird from the brine to your appropriately sized pot. Add enough cold water to cover the bird and bring to a boil very slowly. Remove any scum. When the water is boiling, add all the flavoring ingredients to the pot.

Let the bird simmer very gently until the meat is tender. Try to pull gently at the leg after 45 minutes; if it is loose, it's done. Remove the bird from the pot, carve, and serve.

To make the creamed horseradish to go with it, just whip the cream and add the other ingredients, seasoning to taste. This can be served as it is at room temperature, chilled, or even slightly frozen.

Now or later, you can reduce the stock in which the bird was cooked; which is very nice for green pea, asparagus, fava bean, or chervil soup, or for a northern-style risotto with asparagus, dill, and chervil.

Yellow split pea soup with salted goose

This soup is divine, and very, very filling. You can combine the salted goose or duck with salted pork —and unsmoked sausages—any way you want. The *medisterpølse* (page 106) are a traditional addition.

The soup is undoubtedly quite a challenge to make, but it's lengthy rather than difficult. For this reason you might as well prepare a large amount while you are at it, especially as it freezes very well. The soup tastes far better on the second day, so prepare it a day ahead if you can manage to.

1 salted goose, or two
   salted ducks
3 cups yellow split peas
3lb 5oz large chunks of
   cleaned root vegetables,

such as carrots, parsley
   root, or parsnips
4lb 8oz piece of salted pork
   belly
3 large onions, quartered

2¼lb unsmoked, coarse
   sausages, such as
   medisterpølse
8 large leeks, white part
   only, chopped
3lb 5oz new potatoes,
   peeled and diced
Salt and pepper
A few sprigs of thyme
A bunch of parsley, chopped
Dijon mustard, to serve

for the stock
2 fresh bay leaves
3 cloves garlic
3 sprigs of thyme
1 sprig of sage
1 sprig of oregano
   or marjoram
4 juniper berries
5 whole allspice
1 tablespoon black
   peppercorns
8 large leeks, green part only

SERVES 12 HUNGRY PEOPLE

Day 1 In the morning, prepare the brine for the goose as in the recipe opposite, and leave the bird to soak for 18 hours. In the evening, rinse the split peas, cover with lots of cold water, and put in the refrigerator to swell for 12 hours.

Day 2 Clean all the root vegetables. Remove the goose from the brine. Cut off the thighs, wings, and breasts, and cut the carcass in two, so you're left with 8 pieces. Bring 10½pt

of water to a boil in a large pot. Put in the goose and the pork. Add more water if the meat is not covered. Bring slowly to a boil and remove any scum.

Add the herbs, spices, and leek greens to the stock. Simmer gently until the meat is tender; the breasts should take 30–40 minutes (at which point, take them out), the rest will take longer.

When the meat is done, remove, then strain the stock thorough a fine sieve. Reserve 6 cups for later. Put the rest back on the heat with the split peas, onions, and root vegetables, and let them simmer until completely tender. Whiz to a smooth purée in a blender or food processor.

Put the goose and pork in a roasting pan, cover, and heat slowly in the oven at 225°F until warm. Meanwhile, poach the sausages in the reserved stock. When these are cooked, remove, and add the leeks and potatoes. When they are tender, strain and add the cooking liquid to the soup. Season and add water if necessary.

Serve the soup in a tureen, or the pot, scattered with fresh thyme leaves. Serve the meats and vegetables on a separate dish, sprinkled with chopped parsley. Eat the soup and meat together, with hot Dijon mustard.

Pork

In centuries past, pork was a rare household delicacy. Each farm had a pig or two, carefully fattened and butchered before Christmas, and this was a true feast, as it was the only time of the year when fresh pork could be had. The blood was carefully collected, the intestines rinsed, and used for fresh sausages, blood puddings, and blood sausages. Most of the offal was eaten straight away. The rest of the pig was salted, dried, and smoked for winter storage.

This means that pork is a revered part of our culinary heritage, and traditional, festive dishes with pork are numerous and very, very good. We also have a rich heritage of recipes for preserved meats, primarily eaten at Christmas. With the advent of mass production, Scandinavians have long since lost faith in conventional pork as a food worth celebrating, and it is regarded by those who eat it as a cheap and everyday commodity. However, the interest in organic and free-range flavorful and healthy pork is growing, and this has meant a recent revival of traditional and inventive pork cuisine.

History The domesticated pig has been with us in Scandinavia since the Stone Age. For many centuries, pigs were reared on a very small scale. Each family had only the number of pigs they could look after in a sustainable way, feeding them on scraps. In winter the pigs were kept indoors, while in summer and fall they lived in the woods, foraging and growing fat on beech nuts and acorns. (The woods all belonged to the local kings, and huge taxes were paid for the privilege of using these areas as feeding grounds.) This practice meant that the pigs could breed freely with wild boar, and the distinction between the two was not always clear. You can only imagine how delicious the meat

from these animals must have been. This is how it still is in less developed parts of the world.

In the latter part of the 19th century, a time of great political change, farmers and workers in the cities began to unite in a widespread cooperative movement, most of which still exists today. An important part of this was the establishment of hundreds of local dairies, which were an immense success. A dairy produces huge amounts of buttermilk and whey, so this was returned, in part, to the farmers, but as production boomed they could not use up the whey, and pig farms were established in connection with the dairies, feeding the pigs on the surplus.

From these beginnings grew Denmark's phenomenal export venture in pork and dairy products. As there were strict regulations for imports in the rest of Europe, the first national system of veterinary control was established, reassuring the primarily English consumers of pork and bacon that the meat and butter they were buying was safe and healthy.

Having a wide genetic background, with the spread of pig farming the pigs were bred into a common Danish landrace, a meaty, relatively lean, long porker, designed for bacon production. They even succeeded in lengthening the pig's body with an extra pair of ribs, for even more bacon, an achievement that saw the landrace pig spread worldwide. Denmark still has an absurdly large population of pigs, in the region of 20 million (annually)—about four times the number of humans. The pig populations are more modest in the rest of Scandinavia, where pigs are reared mostly for local consumption. The level of Danish pig production is not in any way sustainable, causing immense pollution, and the quality of this industrial meat is so bad that it has led to many people not wanting to eat pork at all.

Appearance and taste Organically reared pigs taste the best as they are left to roam, and use their incredible snout for foraging in the ground. They are fed organic food, and this amounts to happy pigs, with a superior taste and cooking qualities. Conventional pork is watery, chewy, far too lean, and without the intense pork flavor that you are after.

Buying and storing Good pork is a luxury, even if it's an affordable one, that you have to seek out. Always choose organic or at least free-range meat. Traditional recipes were created for pigs reared in a natural way, with all the beautiful flavor this meat has, and they will only work perfectly if made with perfect pork.

It must be said that the Danish bacon available in other countries is a very different product from that sold in Denmark, where bacon is made from the fatty part of the ribs. This must be taken into account in the many recipes that include bacon.

Fresh pork has a relatively short storage life.

Culinary uses Pork is extremely versatile and lends itself beautifully to every kind of preserving, as well as spicing. Pork is rarely made into stews, but is used ground in a great variety of ways, including as our beloved meatballs; pork chops and roasts are also popular.

Every part of the pig is used: the bones are boiled for stock, and the fat is rendered and spiced, and used as a spread for open-face sandwiches. Meaty ribs are fried slowly in a brown sauce and eaten with mashed potatoes. The belly of the pig is made into bacon, or into rolled, salted sausages, the hind legs into ham, and the head into delicious headcheese. Odds and ends are usually made into sausages, fresh like *medisterpølse*, or cured, smoked and/or dried.

Modern pork is free from trichinella, a parasite formerly a threat when eating omnivores like pigs. This means that you do not have to roast pork beyond recognition. You can bake, fry, or roast it until tender and pale pink, and retain the juiciness, which is so important when cooking pork.

Jellied stock

This meat jelly is a must for open-face sandwiches, traditionally eaten on liver paste, fried pork, or matured cheese.

The essential starting point is a deliciously rich pork stock, made from browned meaty pork bones and flavored with port or sherry. All you need to do is put the stock in a large pot with a trotter (to make it set) and some pot herbs, and let simmer gently for hours. When it's ready, strain the stock and leave it

to cool. The fat will rise to the surface and can be removed, together with all the debris collecting just below the fat. Reheat the stock and pour into a container to set in the fridge. Serve it sliced or cubed.

Scandinavian meatballs

This is the ultimate Scandinavian dish, eaten everywhere and every day. As with all recipes for popular dishes, we each have our own favorite, and believe everything else to be heresy. As I cannot possibly please everybody, I have simply chosen my own favorite.

The shape and size of the meatballs vary in different parts of Scandinavia, and so do the accompaniments. In Sweden these are inevitably mashed potatoes and lingonberries, while in Denmark it's pickled red cabbage in winter, and creamed kale or creamed summer cabbage with potatoes and pickled beets for the rest of the year. Norwegians eat their *kjøttkaker* with potatoes, lingonberries, and creamed cabbage or mashed rutabaga.

You can use dry, day-old bread as in the recipe, bread crumbs or all-purpose flour to keep the meatballs together, but I prefer bread. The best meatballs are made from a mixture of veal and pork.

2¼lb ground mixed veal
   and pork
1 large onion, grated
1 tablespoon coarse sea salt
2–3 eggs
2 large slices wheat bread,
   without crust, soaked
   in milk
1 teaspoon fresh
   thyme leaves

¼ teaspoon ground ginger
¼ teaspoon ground nutmeg
1 teaspoon coarsely ground
   black pepper
½ bay leaf, finely ground
Approx. ¾ cup milk
Butter, for frying
SERVES 5

TIP
• Leftover meatballs are perfect for open-face sandwiches
  on rye bread, with pickled red cabbage or beets on top.

Mix everything, except the milk and butter, in an electric
mixer or bowl. It's important to mix for a long time to form
a spongy "dough," able to retain moisture and expand when
fried. Add enough milk to make it soft but manageable. Let
the finished mixture rest for an hour, or longer, then shape
into balls with wet hands.

Fry the meatballs slowly in browned butter until
they feel spongy. You can cook the meatballs in different
ways and thus influence their shape. Danish *frikadeller*
are largish, each a very large tablespoonful, and often
triangular as you turn them three times instead of twice.
Norwegian *kjøttkaker* are flat, while Swedish *köttbullar*
are small and round, and rolled over in the pan to keep
them that shape.

Perfect roast pork

A huge roast of pork is the traditional dish for
Christmas Eve, when you are not eating *lutefisk*,
pinnekött, ham, goose, or duck. The Danes roast just
the back, either the fillet, which is considered the
finest, or the neck, which is cheaper, juicier, and does
not dry out as easily as the fillet. Alternatively, you can,
like the Norwegians, roast the leanest part of the ribs,
which will give a rather fatty but delicious roast.

All three cuts are roasted throughout Scandinavia,
and not only for Christmas. Roast pork is a Sunday
dish, and leftovers are wonderful for open-face
sandwiches on rye bread, spread with jellied sauce, and
topped with pickled red cabbage or cucumbers. The
only difference is really that the Danes spice the pork
with bay leaves and the Norwegians use mustard, while
the Swedish stud the meat with prunes and spice it with
ginger and black pepper. The accompaniments are
much the same all over Scandinavia: potatoes, maybe
caramelized (page 153), pickled red cabbage, a sweet-and-
sour cucumber salad, lingonberries, baked whole apples,
or apple compote with horseradish.

It's the crackling that matters—a pork roast with
gummy skin is a disaster. Any part of the pig with the
skin on can be roasted, with a crisp crackling if you
follow a few simple rules.

Score the skin with a very sharp knife, and only down to
the white tissue separating the fat from the flesh. If you cut
through this, juices from the roasting meat will seep into the
skin and make it impossible to crisp. You can make a lattice
or thin stripes, just as you fancy. The skin must be absolutely
dry before you put the meat in the oven. The trick is to
score, spice, and finish the meat in a roasting pan, and let it
sit, uncovered, at room temperature, for 3–6 hours to dry.

The spices should be rubbed into the meat on the
meaty side, and coarse salt must be rubbed between the
cracklings, not on top. If you fold the meat back, the cavities
are easier to fill with salt. Bay leaves can be stuck between
the cracklings, too.

Mock duck

We have a lot of mock animal dishes in Scandinavia, made from cheaper ingredients than the original. The recipe is simple, children love it, and I do not feel the least sorry for the mock duck—a pork tenderloin filled with prunes in winter, parsley in summer. As with all extremely simple dishes, the ingredients have to be perfect: juicy Agen prunes, organic pork, and a really good hard cider. You can substitute the hard cider with beer and have a more grown-up, less sweet sauce. Serve the "duck" with potatoes and a celery and apple salad in winter, new potatoes and rhubarb compote in summer.

12 Agen prunes (pits in) or 1 large bunch of parsley
¾ cup + 2 tablespoons hard cider
1 large apple (suitable cooking variety)
1 large pork tenderloin, or 2 smaller ones
1 tablespoon fresh thyme leaves
Coarse sea salt and black pepper
½ stick butter, for frying
¾ cup + 2 tablespoons heavy cream
2 tablespoons tamari (Japanese soy sauce)
3 tablespoons chopped parsley, to serve

SERVES 4

Cuts obviously vary in size, but when it comes to roasting pork a useful rule is to allow one hour per 2¼lb at 325–340°F (if you have a convection oven, reduce the temperature by approx. 70°F). This is a good, low temperature: while ribs are fatty and will not dry out, other cuts need long, slow cooking to retain their juiciness.

Place the meat skin-side down in a roasting pan. Pour in enough water to cover the skin but no more. Roast this way for 20 minutes, then turn it over and roast for a further hour. Make sure that the pan does not dry out; add some white wine, hard cider, or more water if needed. After the hour is up, turn the heat up to 425°F and roast to crisp the crackling for another 20 minutes. Remove the meat to a board, and let sit, uncovered, for 20 minutes before serving.

The sauce is made from the nice brown goo in the pan. Scrape every little bit of it into a saucepan while the meat is resting, and add some white wine or hard cider, a little soy sauce if not too salty, and cream. Boil vigorously to thicken. This will be extremely concentrated and lovely.

Soak the prunes in the hard cider for 6–8 hours, then remove the pits. Cut the apple up, remove the core, then slice with the peel on.

Make a deep incision lengthwise along the tenderloin, and flatten the meat on a board, with the inside up. Arrange the prunes (or parsley), apple pieces, and thyme along the middle, and reserve the cider. Season, then tie up the meat with cotton string to form a fat sausage. Rub the meat with black pepper on the outside as well.

Melt the butter in a skillet and brown the meat on all sides, before turning down the heat to a simmer. After 15 minutes, pour in the hard cider and cream and reduce for the next 5 minutes. Season with the tamari and the "duck" is ready. Serve it sliced, scattered with the parsley.

TIP
• You can rub the meat with garlic as well as black pepper if you wish.

Ham

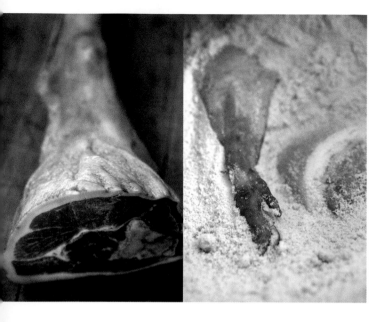

There are several traditional hams in Scandinavia, all salted and smoked, but not dried. It is possible of course to dry ham in the northern climate, as we do fish, but for some reason it has just never been done. Considering the quantity of pigs reared in Scandinavia, the number of gourmet preparations is surprisingly small, and a really good ham is hard to come by. Actually a lot of salted and dried Italian hams are of Danish origin.

Should you feel the urge to make your own salted and air-dried ham it's not difficult, if you live in a country where the winters are cold. I make mine from my organic pigs, and it rivals any from Italy or Spain.

Smoked salted hams are nearly always boiled or baked. The Swedish *julskinka*, served for Christmas Eve, is prepared with a delicious layer of mustard, bread crumbs and brown sugar. Boiled and sliced ham is a favorite topping for open-face sandwiches, often topped with Italian salad (page 144) and cress.

A whole ham is a daunting hunk of meat, but for a great big party it's easy to prepare and there are no last-minute jobs to attend to, once it's boiled and baked. You can prepare smaller family-size cuts in the same way.

It's far too easy to overcook ham, so the safest way for a 2¼lb piece is to put it on the stovetop in a pot with herbs on the bottom and then plenty of cold water. Bring to a boil and turn off the heat. Let the ham steep until the water is cool and it will be perfect.

Home-salted hams

I must stress that for this you need a very special ham from a pig that you know has had a varied diet, and has lived a totally free-range existence, as this affects not just the quality but also the fatty acids that the fat is composed of—the quality of the fat is vital to the keeping quality and, of course, to the taste.

You must salt ham in the cold season, which coincides with the traditional pig-slaughtering in November. Frost does not matter, it just slows down the process. All you need is a large, non-reactive container or box, preferably made of wood, with holes in the bottom for the brine to run out. This is for the initial salting.

Rub the leg with coarse salt all over, making sure that you rub it in close to the bone, as this is the most difficult part to keep clean. You can also rub in spices and herbs, such as pepper, sage, thyme, and rosemary, if you wish.

Cover the bottom of your box with coarse salt, and place the ham on it. Now cover the leg completely with salt, and wait. Once a week you scrape off the salt, turn the leg over, and rub in salt around the bone again. When the meat feels firm, the salting is finished. If it is still wobbly, it's not. For a large ham this may take two months.

Now take the ham out of the box and hang it up to dry in a well-ventilated, cool place out of the sun: an airy attic or porch is fine. Before doing so, wrap the ham in several layers of thin gauze, or a clean sack made from a natural fiber. This is to keep off fleas and other insects, which are the only real threat to your ham.

After a couple of months your ham will be ready for sampling. But it can dry for a whole year if the conditions are cool and airy, and will only improve. Once you have cut it open, rub the cut surface with more salt and hang it to dry again.

Swedish Christmas ham with mustard crust

This festive ham (*julskinka*) should be served, alongside the yummy pan juices, with creamed kale, rye bread, potatoes or caramelized potatoes, beer, and schnapps.

3lb 5oz piece of smoked, salted ham
1 cup muscovado sugar
¾ cup Dijon or homemade mustard (see right)
1 tablespoon ground ginger
1 handful of dried bread crumbs
10 cloves
SERVES 6–8

Put the ham in a large pot with plenty of cold, unsalted water. Bring slowly to a boil, simmer for 10 minutes, then remove from the heat and leave to cool in the water.

Preheat the oven to 400°F.

Remove the skin from the ham and make a crisscross pattern in the fat with a sharp knife. Mix the sugar, mustard, and ginger. Place the ham in an ovenproof dish and spread the mixture over the surface. Dust with the bread crumbs there should be only a thin layer—and stud with the cloves.

Bake in the oven until golden and warm all the way through; this should take around 25 minutes.

Christmas mustard

This is the taste of the Middle Ages   similar mustard has been made ever since. It's very hot and spicy, and perfect for all the pork, sausages, and cold cuts eaten at Christmas in Scandinavia. The starting point is powdered yellow mustard seeds. It will keep for many months if stored in a sterilized jar in the refrigerator.

Generous ¾ cup yellow mustard powder
Generous ⅓ cup cider vinegar
8 tablespoons sugar
1¼ cups heavy cream
1 teaspoon ground ginger
1 large star anise, ground
1 tablespoon ground turmeric

Mix everything well in a food mixer or bowl until smooth and let rest overnight.

Taste, and season with a little more sugar and vinegar if needed, and maybe dilute with some cold water until smooth and spreadable. The taste will mature for another couple of days, and it will eventually mellow, so adjust the seasoning again after a day or two.

Sausages

Scandinavia has a huge variety of sausages, some for slicing like salami, smoked sausages meant for cooking with cabbage or dried peas, and wiener/frankfurter-type sausages. Many store-bought sausages are industrial ones brimming with fat and preservatives that almost glow in the dark from the pinkish-red coloring, and do not even contain regular meat. However, there is also a growing number of small-scale butchers and sausage-makers producing beautiful charcuterie, though it's not always easy to find. Farm stores, farmers' markets, and specialty stores in the cities are the best sources of delectable sausages and other charcuterie.

Store-bought *medisterpølse* are not generally to be trusted (it is too tempting for the industrial sausage-makers to tamper with the basic recipe), so they should be bought from a good butcher. You can also buy smoked *medisterpølse*, which is often fried in slices to eat with mashed potatoes, or used as a topping for open-face sandwiches.

Most traditional charcuterie is not easily replicable at home, as it needs cold smoking, but the two sausage recipes here are easy to make at home and well worth the trouble.

Medisterpølse

This thick, spicy sausage is eaten in varying ways all over Scandinavia. It is a classic part of yellow split pea soup (page 98) and is often just fried in plenty of butter, as a dinner dish, and eaten with pickled red cabbage, pickled beets, and either creamed cabbage or creamed kale, mustard, and potatoes. Leftovers are also very good on rye bread with pickled red cabbage and mustard.

This is my own recipe, admittedly more spiced and interesting than is traditional, but not so much that the sausages aren't recognizable. I make them every year for my farm store at Christmas, and they are immensely popular. The natural sausage skins are made from the animal's intestines, which are salted, and your butcher will supply them, if given proper notice.

for the brine

6 cups water
½ cup sugar
¾ cup coarse sea salt
2 bay leaves
1 tablespoon whole
   coriander seeds
1 tablespoon black
   peppercorns
10 whole allspice
3 cloves
Walnut-size piece of fresh
   ginger
2 tablespoons fresh thyme
   leaves

for the sausages

6lb 8oz fatty cut of pork
   (belly, neck, and/or rib),
   cut into 1½in cubes
9oz onions, quartered
½ garlic bulb
Spices from the brine
6–7 tablespoons potato
   starch
Water or pork stock
   (made from bones)
Butter, for frying
Salt and pepper
Natural sausage skins,
   preserved in salt
MAKES ABOUT 9LB

To make the brine, boil up the water, sugar, and salt in a saucepan. Remove the scum until no more appears. Add the spices and herbs and let brine simmer for 30 minutes. Let cool completely.

Add the meat, onions, and garlic to the cooled brine. Let salt for at least 8 hours, but no more than 12. Drain the spices, meat, and onions from the brine using a colander, and discard the liquid. Wash the meat briefly with cold water while it's still in the colander, then spread it onto a clean dish towel to dry.

Grind the meat, onions, and spices in an old-fashioned or electric grinder; if the holes are very big, grind it twice, though the meat must not be finely ground. Mix the forcemeat with the potato starch and sufficient water or stock to make a soft but shapeable "dough." The more you mix it, the juicier the sausages will be. When you think it's finished, fry a small patty in butter. Adjust the seasoning.

Wash the sausage skins on the outside by soaking them in cold water, and rid them of salt on the inside by folding the skin onto the cold water faucet, and then turn on the water to flush out the inside. It may look funny but it works.

Put the forcemeat through the meat-grinder with the sausage appliance attached, but be careful not to stuff the sausages too tightly or they will burst when you fry them. You can make portion-sized sausages, or 3¼ft lengths to fill a skillet, when coiled up.

These sausages are made of fresh meat, and must be eaten within a few days, or frozen.

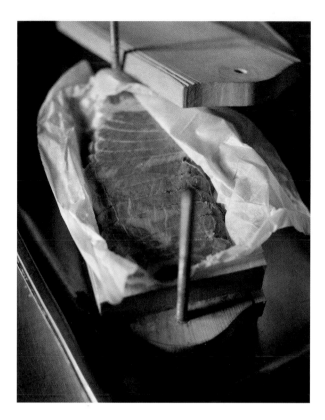

Rullepølse

This is a delicate, lightly spiced, and somehow luxurious sausage. It is usually made with pork belly (the thin flap of meat below the ribs, with no bones) but works just as well with breast of lamb. In the lamb version, a layer of blanched parsley is rolled in with the spices. The sausages need to be pressed after cooking, and in Scandinavia we have special wooden presses for the purpose, but a bread box plus a slightly smaller box/container (that can be weighed down with something heavy on top to fit into the first box) will do.

Rullepølse is served very thinly sliced on rye or wheat bread, and it's delicious on crispbread with cress, mustard, raw onion, and jellied stock (page 101).

Put the belly in a sealable plastic bag with the brine and place in the fridge for 12 hours, then dry it with paper towels and spread on a board. Using a very sharp knife, remove any excess fat without piercing the outer layer of lean flesh. Patch it up, cut, and repair to achieve an almost square piece of meat.

Scatter the onion and spices for the filling over the meat and rub them in. Cut the gelatin with scissors into strips and distribute over the meat. Roll up the meat like a jelly roll and tie around with cotton string, as tightly and evenly as possible.

Boil slowly for 2 hours in water, taking care to find a pot that is big enough but without using too much water. Let the sausage cool a little in the water, then place in a press—or a bread box lined with plastic wrap; cover the sausage with the cooking liquid and place another container on top, with a board or heavy book pressing down on it. Don't make the whole lot too large as it has to go in the refrigerator.

If you do not press it, the sausage cannot be carved. This is quite a large quantity, but you simply cannot make less. Freeze some of the sausage as soon as it has been pressed if you do not expect to eat it within a week. The sausage does not keep for very long, as it is basically just boiled meat.

1 whole slab of pork belly (approx. 2lb 12oz) or 2 pieces of breast of lamb	**for the filling/stuffing**
	1 large onion, grated
½ quantity spiced brine (page 106)	2 ground allspice
	2 ground cloves
	2 tablespoons coarsely ground black pepper
	4 gelatin sheets

Lamb & mutton

Sheep were the first domestic animals in the north, and are still of great importance in areas where the land is not arable—in the mountains and in wet regions. Sheep can live on very sparse vegetation, even on bad, stony ground or heathland, and thrive on a varied diet of weeds, grass, and leaves. Formerly they were fed on dried young branches in winter, cut from fields with grass and trees grown to harvest the new growth. This tradition is the reason for the famed landscapes of the middle of Sweden, now almost extinct. So sheep have always been the food of the poor, as anybody could keep a few animals on whatever land they happened to have. For this very reason, lamb and mutton have been held in generally low esteem, and have fetched very bad prices.

Appearance and taste While the taste and texture of lamb meat varies with each breed, it also has a unique way of reflecting the land and vegetation on which the sheep have fed. For example, the sparser and drier the vegetation, the leaner and spicier the meat will be: so, meat from mountain and heath lambs has a unique spiciness, while grass-fed lamb is mild tasting. Lamb from the Nordic islands and Greenland is very sought after as it has a distinctive taste of its own.

The Scandinavians have been breeding sheep since the Iron Age, and there are several robust Nordic breeds of short-tail sheep. The best-known Nordic breeds include the immensely hardy Spelsau (*sau* means sheep in Norwegian), which are found all over the north, including in Iceland and the Faroe islands. They have a layered fleece intended to keep the sheep warm in very bad weather; the distinctive long covering hairs were once used in the making of sails for Viking boats.

Black-faced Gotland sheep, also short-tailed, are skinnier than their Spelsau cousins, with very good lean meat. Some of the offspring are horned, some even having two pairs of horns. Their beautiful and extremely thick wool is made into carpets and whole sheepskin rugs.

In southern Scandinavia we have marsh lambs, whose meat has a special salinity because the flat marshland is sprayed with salt water from the sea, and this gives the meat a notable flavor, juiciness, and color.

Many older people believe that lambs have a terrible taste, like chewing on a wet woollen glove. This view stems from a time when the meat was often from old ewes, which does admittedly have a distinct woolly taste. Mutton is very rare nowadays, and hard to come by, even if you want it—outside Norway, that is—as it is mostly made into sausages. Mutton is fattier than lamb, with a pronounced gamy taste.

Culinary uses November is traditionally the month in which lambs and older ewes are butchered and the meat then prepared to last during the winter. *Pinnekött* (see opposite) and *fenalår* are two Norwegian methods of preserving the meat for winter. *Fenalår* is a salted (and sometimes smoked), then dried leg of mutton that can last for several winters. Other than these old ways, lamb is prepared pretty much like it is in the rest of Europe—roasted as whole legs or chops, or made into light stews, often with dill (page 170–1).

Salted leg of lamb cooked with capers and lemon

This recipe for a home-cured and baked leg of lamb is an Easter specialty in northern Scandinavia. It is easy to make, as long as you remember to salt the meat 24 hours before it's needed. The meat becomes extremely juicy from the salting, and is delicious.

Serve the lamb with chervil cream, potatoes, and maybe spring cabbage and asparagus, or with a green pea mash with horseradish.

5lb leg of lamb, upper bone removed, and tied together with cotton string

for the brine

2½ cups coarse sea salt

1 cup sugar

10½pt water

1 handful of fresh bay leaves

TIP

- A whole leg of lamb is often fairly expensive, but it's usually a little cheaper if you ask for the front leg or shoulder, even if it has a large, awkward bone in the middle (you can ask the butcher to take the bone out). The shoulder meat is actually tenderer than that of a leg, and will need only 12 hours in the brine rather than 24.

Pinnekött

The name of this recipe literally means "stick meat" in Norwegian. It is easy to understand why as it consists of whole racks of lamb that are salted, dried, soaked, and boiled for a very long time on a bed of birch twigs, and finally broiled until crisp. The dish is extremely old, dating from a time when salting and drying were the only ways to make meat keep. Birch is a handy flavoring, with a fresh, sap-like aroma even when the ground is covered with snow, and it also acts as both flavoring and support for the meat as it steams. It is certainly quite a job to make this dish, but is delicious if made properly. Serve the lamb with potatoes, mashed rutabaga, and mustard.

1 tablespoon whole black
  peppercorns
Pared zest of 3–4 lemons
2 tablespoons salted
  capers, washed

for the sauce
½ stick butter
A little lemon juice
SERVES 8

6lb 8oz rack of lamb, with
  breast meat attached
for the brine
10½pt water
3¼ cups coarse sea salt

1½ cups brown sugar
A handful of birch twigs,
  bark removed
SERVES 10

Put the salt, sugar, and water for the brine in a large saucepan and bring to a boil. Skim off any grayish scum until no more is forming. Add the bay leaves, peppercorns, and zest and continue boiling for 5 minutes, then cool.

Submerge the meat in the brine, either in a non-reactive container, or in a large sealable plastic bag. Leave the meat to salt in the brine for 24 hours. (If using a whole leg, with the bone, it will need 48 hours in the brine). When it's ready, remove the meat, zest, and spices and then discard the brine.

Preheat the oven to 350°F. Wrap the meat in several layers of aluminum foil, with the capers and reserved zest and spices. Place in a roasting pan and cook for 2 hours.

Take the meat out of the oven and let rest for 30 minutes before carving. Meanwhile, tip all the spices and juices into a saucepan and whisk in the butter and a little lemon juice. Strain into a pitcher and serve with the meat.

Boil the brine ingredients together in a large saucepan, removing any gray scum, then let cool.

Submerge the meat in the brine—you can use a non-reactive container but I find it easier to use a sealable plastic bag—and leave it to soak in the refrigerator for 48 hours. Drain the meat (discarding the brine), then dry on a rack in a very cool place for 3 days—not the refrigerator, but somewhere cold and preferably windy. At this stage, the meat will keep for a week or more. Cut the meat into long-handled chops and soak in cold water overnight.

Arrange the birch twigs in a lattice in the bottom of a large saucepan and lay the meat on top. Cover the twigs with water and let the meat steam, covered, for about 2 hours—more if it is from an old ewe. Then grill the meat straight away or broil until crisp.

Beef & veal

Beautiful, grass-fed, tender, fat-marbled beef is much sought after in Scandinavia and is the reason for all the lovely, rich stews that are a cherished part of our cultural heritage. But you can only buy this beef at markets, on farms, and special dedicated butchers as good beef is not easy to get. So at the moment, Scandinavians eat beef mostly as steaks and ground meat, and the long-simmered stews are not as popular as they should be. When you do find good beef, however, the potential of these lovely dishes is evident.

I have to be truthful about the reasons for the decline in beef eating in Scandinavia. Perhaps this is partly due to the fact that we don't take the science of hanging meat very seriously; most Scandinavian beef is hung for 10 days, which is much less than is usual in the rest of Europe, and is not enough time to allow enzymes and lactic acid in the meat to work their magic. Another reason is that people who are concerned with organic issues, and animal welfare, rarely eat meat, and even if they do, it's not beef; so there is not a large body of people campaigning for better treatment for cows, more access to grazing, and so on, which surprisingly are not issues that most Scandinavians are much concerned about. As a result, the demand for high-quality beef remains small.

Large parts of Norway and Sweden are too difficult to farm, and cattle are still kept in semi-wild areas, giving beautiful, richly marbled, and tasty meat. Southern Scandinavia is dairy country, and here the quality of the beef is not so interesting. This may very well be because somehow we never got round to producing really prime-quality beef in our milk-producing regions. Most of the beef is from milking cows or young steers, which are too old to be used for veal, and far too young to have the rich, deep mineral flavor of beef. However, there is small-scale production of beef cattle where the land is suited to permanent grass, and their meat is prized by people who know what they can expect from really good beef.

Veal used to be a much sought-after meat; the very young calves were always tender, and the meat a lovely pale color, with a milk and grass flavor. True, good-quality veal is very difficult to find nowadays, mainly because we are not willing to pay the price for it.

History Cattle have been very important to the Scandinavian economy since the early Middle Ages, when the population was dramatically decimated by the plague. There were so few hands left to farm that wheat and other grains became extremely expensive, whereas cattle herding was relatively easy to manage; most herding was done by children, which left the surviving men free to work at other tasks. For a century or more the population ate more beef than at any other time in history.

Before effective refrigeration, cattle were slaughtered only in winter, when they could safely hang in cool conditions. With the invention of cooling, butchers could slaughter animals all year round, and tenderize the meat by hanging it for several weeks, making big roasts a possibility. Even so, most of the meat was tough, and suited only for salting, stews, and soups. As a result, we have a large and very old tradition of these dishes, which is well worth preserving.

Habitat The cow has played a major role in creating what we now see as typical and unique Scandinavian landscapes. The high pastures in northern Scandinavia are kept lush and green by grazing cattle, and in the past grazing was the only way to prevent large areas being taken over by trees. In centuries gone by, it was common to keep the cattle in woods, where their grazing would keep down new trees, thereby creating beautiful low-grown meadows both around and in the woods.

Lovely hay fields, studded with deciduous trees, provided winter fodder, and later the cattle were let loose to graze both the grass and the trees.

Buying and storing You will have to trust your butcher, who should know about meat, and ask him which cuts he finds suitable for the dish you are going to make. The meat will have to be hung for at least three weeks to have the taste you are after, and it will be worth eating only if it's grass fed and has had access to year-round exercise.

Cuts of meat vary too much around the world to be precise, but as a general rule you will need dark, fat-marbled cuts from the front part of the animal, breast and neck, for stews. These take time to cook, and are comfortably cheap compared to the back cuts that are more tender, and much more expensive. The marbling will ensure that the meat will be amazingly tender and juicy, after long hours simmering in the pot.

If it's veal you're after, you will also have to know and trust your butcher. You must buy proper veal, which comes from young calves that are no more than 10 months old, slaughtered just before their meat develops into a nondescript beefy flavor, and has been hung for two weeks. Choose organic veal that will have the right, slightly acidic taste from wind-blown sun, warmed grass, and milk, and nothing else. What you don't want is veal raised under cruel conditions, fed on milk only, and slaughtered just before the animals' legs collapse. The flesh may seem nice and pale, but it will leave a foul taste in your mouth.

Culinary uses Our traditional beef dishes tend to be spicy and tender stews that need long, slow simmering. The slowness of the cooking means that these recipes are not particularly popular at the moment, but the tide appears to be turning; young people are starting to realize the beauty of food that takes more care to cook, but is richly rewarding and cheaper—much cheaper—than the steaks and roasts that are easy to make, but cost a fortune if you want proper meat.

Beef and potato stew

This beef and potato stew (known as *labskovs*) is a favorite slow food, a one-pot meal. Everything amalgamates into a thick stew, heavily flavored with bay leaves, and with small, pungent surprises as you bite into a softened peppercorn along the way. The final touches of butter, parsley, chives, and pickled beets are essential. If you include a piece of diced bacon the stew becomes slightly smoky and changes its name to *skipper labskovs* (captain's stew).

You will need a marbled piece of beef (neck or shank is fine), and the right kind of potato, that will be able to hold together somewhat during the long, slow cooking (white boiling potatoes are ideal). The stew will only improve with waiting around for a day or two, so it's a good party dish to prepare ahead for people who care about taste more than good looks.

1lb 10oz beef, such as shank
3lb 5oz firm potatoes
1 tablespoon butter
2 large onions, sliced
8 fresh bay leaves
1 tablespoon black peppercorns
A large sprig of fresh thyme

Coarse sea salt
to serve
½ stick butter
Chopped parsley and chives
Pickled, sliced beets
SERVES 5–6 HUNGRY PEOPLE

Cut the meat into 1¼in dice. Peel the potatoes and cut into thick slices.

Brown the meat in the butter in a saucepan big enough to hold everything. Add the rest of the stew ingredients, and water to cover the bottom half of them. Put on the lowest possible heat and let simmer until the meat is absolutely tender. Season with salt and serve in soup plates, with the accompaniments in separate dishes, so everyone can put them on top as they prefer.

Beef *lindström*

These beef patties are a Swedish classic, but with a twist as they are more like hamburgers and less meatball-ish than usual, to good effect. Serve them with fried diced potatoes, and nothing else. Usually the beets are pickled as in the recipe on page 151, but in this recipe I have substituted raw beets, quick-pickled in a saucepan.

1lb 10oz ground beef	**for the pickle**
2 tablespoons whole salted capers, washed	2 tablespoons salted butter
	⅔ cup finely diced raw beets
2 tablespoons tomato ketchup	⅔ cup finely chopped onion
	2 tablespoons cider vinegar
1 tablespoon Dijon mustard	1 tablespoon sugar
Salt and coarsely ground black pepper	1 teaspoon coarse salt
	SERVES 4
Butter, for frying	

For the pickle, melt the butter in a skillet, add the beets and onion and fry for 5 minutes without coloring. Add the vinegar, sugar, and salt, and reduce at a high heat until syrupy. Cool.

Mix the beef, capers, ketchup, mustard, and seasoning until they stick together; it's easiest done with your hands. Shape into four patties and fry in browned butter until

brown on one side. Turn over, and when the red juice comes seeping out on the surface, they are done.

Roast veal with curdled sauce and kidneys

This is a summer dish of great, old-fashioned charm. It's not famed for its good looks, but the taste is universally delicious, and children love it too. It was once the grand roast, served for important formal dinners—at baptisms, confirmations, and weddings—half a century ago. It was a dish you had only a few times during your life: partly because of the price of veal, and partly because a whole piece of veal rack on the bone feeds at least 15 people.

Incomprehensible veterinary laws have banned selling kidneys attached to the carcass, but you can buy them separately, encased in their fat, and add them yourself. They are essential to the sauce. Serve the veal with new potatoes, lettuce with a cream dressing, rhubarb compote, and a sweet-and-sour cucumber salad.

7¾lb veal rack, neck end, on the bone	9oz pork fat, in extremely thin slices
Coarse sea salt and coarsely ground black pepper	2 veal kidneys, preferably still in their fat casings
	8–10 cups whole milk
	SERVES 10

Rub the meat all over with salt and pepper. Wrap in the pork fat slices, leaving the bone uncovered, and tie it with cotton string. Place the kidneys (still in their fat casings), with the meat on top, on a rack over a deep roasting pan. The meat must be at room temperature before cooking, otherwise increase the total roasting time by 15 minutes.

Brown the roast at 425°F. When it has browned, pour 4 cups of the milk over the meat, and lower the heat to 350°F. Make sure the roast is in the center of the oven. Every 15 minutes, pour the excess juices from the pan, and gradually pour the rest of the milk over the meat. Roast for 1½ hours, but try to poke a skewer into the meat, all the way to the bone, after 1¼ hours; if the juice runs red, the veal is not done, if the juice is rosy, it is.

Place the meat on a wooden board and wrap it in aluminum foil and a clean thick towel. Let rest for 30 minutes.

Leave the sauce in the roasting pan, in the oven. If it needs to be reduced, you can turn up the oven to 400°F. If not, just keep it warm; do not stir it as the curdled consistency is very, very good.

Remove the fat from the kidneys and slice the kidneys thinly before serving with the veal and the sauce.

Salted breast of veal with caper sauce

This is a truly old-fashioned and incredibly tasty dish; frankly it's not too pretty, but the taste..! Serve it with new potatoes and summer cabbage.

1 quantity spiced brine,
   page 106
2lb 12oz breast of veal,
   with ribs
for the stock
2 onions, unpeeled
2 carrots
2 celery stalks
2 sprigs of parsley

for the caper sauce
1 handful of salted capers
1 teaspoon cornstarch
1¼ cups reduced stock
3 tablespoons white
   wine vinegar
2 tablespoons sugar
⅔ cup heavy cream
SERVES 4

Boil the brine, and cool. Cut the meat into four equal pieces. Combine with the brine in a sealable plastic bag and place in the refrigerator for 12 hours. Strain and reserve the spices. Discard the brine.

For the stock, wash the vegetables and cut into chunks, then put into a large pot with the parsley, the meat, and the spices from the brine. Fill with cold water to cover the meat. Do not add salt. Bring slowly to a boil and remove any scum. Simmer for maybe 2 hours or more until the meat is extremely tender. Remove the meat and reduce the stock until intensely flavored. Strain and discard the vegetables and spices.

When you are ready to eat, reheat the meat if it has cooled by adding a little of the stock, covering with aluminum foil, and placing in a warm oven.

For the sauce, wash the capers in lots of cold water to remove most of the salt. Cream the cornstarch with a little stock and whisk into the rest of the sauce ingredients in a saucepan. Bring to a boil and simmer for 5 minutes until the starchy taste has gone. Adjust the seasoning and serve with the meat.

GAME

Good game is difficult to come by if you are not from a family of hunters, but many are, as hunting is a very popular sport all over Scandinavia. Wild meats have always been enjoyed as the flesh is rich-tasting and the difference from farmed animals is evident; the variety of their feed can be tasted in any wild animal. Venison is very lean compared to farmed meats, and free of pesticides as deer usually graze in the wild. In populated areas, the animals seem to prefer organic fields—and gardens.

The hunting itself is a matter for debate, and what species to hunt is another. As hunting is no longer a means of survival, the ethos of it is a mystery to a growing number of people. The issue is hot, especially in the north, where wolves and bears are once again able to move freely over countries' borders after the fall of the Iron Curtain. These species are indigenous to Scandinavia, but have been extinct or extremely rare for centuries, and are now coming back, scaring people and threatening livestock.

Political battles are fought over the right to shoot them. The same controversy surrounds the shooting of wild boar, which are returning to Denmark from the south after an absence of 200 years. Farmers see them as a safety risk to their domesticated pigs, while others want to safeguard the returning population. But wild boar are numerous in southern Sweden, and are hunted there in great numbers.

There are numerous wild mammals and birds in Scandinavia, most of them hunted and eaten locally, and many can be hunted for private consumption, but not for sale.

These species must be enjoyed when living in or visiting Scandinavia. Some of the species are globally endangered, but are allowed to be hunted by the communities that have lived with them, and hunted them for centuries, as an acknowledgement of their traditional lifestyle.

Buying and storing Good-quality game is not easy to find. If you don't know the hunter personally, you must trust your butcher to know his game: for example, how old the animal was (there is a big difference between a young animal of 1–3 years and an old one of 4–12 years). Venison should be stored like all other mammal meats.

Culinary uses Young venison can be treated like domestic meats, which means that it can be fried, skewered, and roasted, according to the cut, with beautiful results. Older meat should be ground or made into stews. As an everyday option, ground venison is actually very cheap and makes fabulous hamburgers. *Frikadeller* and meatballs are also very good made with ground venison, served with the classic accompaniments for venison.

Venison is often smoked, salted, and dried to keep the summer and fall glut of fresh meat for winter. The Sami *suovas*, a piece of reindeer that is salted, smoked, and dried (see opposite), is the most renowned. There are several kinds, some very dry and salty, others more mildly cured. Norrland *tjälknöl*, another preserved meat, or one that makes use of the freezing climate, consists of a frozen leg of venison that is gently baked for 12 hours, then brined.

The traditional Scandinavian way to serve game is with a thick creamed sauce, potatoes, and a flavorsome, sweet accompaniment such as lingonberry jam and crab apple jelly, or rowanberry jelly. Other accompaniments that work well are sweet-and-sour salads, such as the celery, apple, and walnut salad on pages 193–4, or the apple, celeriac, and beet salad on page 158. Baked whole apples are good with it, too. This whole arrangement is lovely, if heavy, and there are many, especially with hunting relatives, who grow tired of all the hullaballoo and simply serve venison as you would domesticated meats.

Deer

Roe deer

In Denmark, deer are primarily roe deer, the size of a small sheep, which have inhabited Scandinavia for at least 8,000 years. They exist in vast numbers and as many as 100,000 are shot every year, most of them consumed by hunters' families and restaurants. Their meat is dark and has a pleasant, intensely gamy taste. They can be treated as other game, or lamb.

Fallow deer

This deer, about the size of a llama, is not indigenous to the Nordic countries, but was imported for hunting game in the Middle Ages and has spread all over southern Scandinavia. The meat has a very mild taste, much like veal. It can be successfully farmed and most of the fallow deer meat today is farmed. It does not have as much flavor as wild deer, but is still a pleasant change from other domestic meats.

Red deer

The red deer is larger, similar to a small cow in size, and has been in Scandinavia since the last Ice Age. A red deer stag is an impressive sight, and the calves are lovely, if you are lucky enough to see such shy animals. The red deer has been threatened in the past, but the numbers are again on the rise so they can now be hunted legally. The meat is like gamy beef, very lean and tasty.

Reindeer

In northern Scandinavia the reindeer reigns, roaming over the low-growing Arctic tundra, finding food where there seems to be none. Reindeers are charming, relatively small animals, with spreading hooves designed to work like snow shoes, and a rather strange but very fast stride.

All reindeer have their particular owner, who keeps an eye on them and protects them from wolverines and other predators, but basically they are wild animals. They are not hunted, but butchered in special abattoirs.

Reindeer are more than a livelihood. They are part of a culture much older than the farm culture of the rest of Scandinavia. The Sami now have the exclusive right to reindeer herding in most of the vast area occupied by this ancient people. The Sami live in an expanse stretching across Norway, Sweden, Finland, and Russia—an area as big as Sweden, known as Sapmi. Their traditional culture is flourishing, now finally being supported by the governments after centuries of conflict and ill treatment comparable to apartheid in South Africa. Reindeer have been herded by Sami since the Middle Ages; before that they were hunted along with other game. Reindeer travel great distances, moving from the lower forests in the winter to the mountains in summer, and back again. The Sami once lived a nomadic existence as they followed the herds, but nowadays reindeer herding is done by helicopter, snowmobile, and four-wheel drive; and the Sami are no longer nomads, though some choose to camp with the herd in the mountains in summer.

Reindeer meat is like no other, being extremely tender and with a sweet taste rather like a mildly gamy veal. Many of the various forms of preserved reindeer meat, and many traditional dishes, have their origins in the foods eaten by the Sami shepherds on the long seasonal migrations. Every imaginable part of the reindeer is used: you get salted and smoked reindeer tongues, smoked hearts, and sausages in great variety, both smoked and fresh.

Suovas

The best-known of the dried reindeer meats, *suovas* (meaning "lightly smoked"), has been dry-salted, smoked, and then normally dried. The smoking is traditionally done in a special smoking hut, in the form of a small Sami tent (called a *kåte*) placed on the ground with a smoking bonfire in the middle; the meat is simply hung up to smoke over the fire. The delicacy comes in different forms, some very dry and salty, others more mildly cured. The best cuts of leg are used. When not excessively dried, *suovas* can be eaten like fresh meat, and is often cut thinly and eaten like other cold cuts, or cubed and skewered as a kebab. The drier forms of *suovas* are eaten with soft flatbread and a topping of pickled mushrooms and lingonberries —it's simply delicious.

Renskav

This is thinly sliced, dried, or frozen reindeer meat; as it's shaved so thinly, it's a way of using the less tender parts of the animal. Usually, it's pan-fried with onions and mushrooms and served with mashed potatoes and lingonberries. It is also used for the homely *pytt i panna*, a much-loved dish often made with leftovers of roast meat, but raised to something beautiful and celebrated when made with fresh *renskav*: the meat, onions, and potatoes are fried separately and then mixed, and often finished with a little cream. It's served with pickled mushrooms and the ubiquitous lingonberries.

Tjälknöl

This traditional dish, properly known as Norrland *tjälknöl*, was created by people living in a country frozen solid for most months of the year. It is essentially a frozen leg of venison that is gently cooked for 12 hours, then brined. The method of salting the meat after it's cooked is unusual, but it works wonderfully well. By the end, the meat has a silky softness to it and is absolutely lovely. Use it in sandwiches, or as an alternative to a roast. It can be made with any kind of venison, lamb, or veal. If you are not quite sure that the temperature in your oven is accurate, you must test it with a thermometer before trying this dish. The temperature has to be exact.

5lb 8oz frozen leg of reindeer (or other venison) or lamb
3 handfuls of herbs, such as fresh bay leaves, rosemary, sage, basil, and/or lovage

for the brine
10 cups water
Generous ¾ cup coarse sea salt

1 tablespoon black peppercorns
1 whole garlic bulb, cloves separated, peeled, and cut into thin slivers
1 large handful of lovage leaves
1 large sprig of fresh oregano

SERVES 8–10

Preheat the oven to 167°F. Wrap the frozen meat and herbs in some aluminum foil, wrapping it twice so that no juice can leak out. Place the package in an ovenproof dish on the middle rack of the oven and cook for 12 hours.

While the meat is slowly cooking away, boil up the brine, removing any gray scum, and cool until needed.

When the meat is done, reheat the brine, unwrap the meat, and put it in. The brine should cover the meat, so put it in a snug container made of plastic, stoneware, or stainless steel, to fit. If you do not have such a container, you can put the whole thing in a plastic food bag, once the brine has cooled a little, and close it tightly.

Leave the meat to soak in the brine for 3–5 hours. When it is ready, lift the meat out, dry it off, and then slice it thinly. You can eat it tepid or cooled, but it's most delicious when it has not been in the refrigerator at all. You could, of course, heat the meat gently, wrapped in foil, but it is not supposed to be eaten hot. Any leftovers can be kept in the refrigerator for up to 4 days. It is delicious in sandwiches.

Roast leg of venison

A whole leg of venison is an impressive thing to serve, and easy too if you have many mouths to feed. It's perfect for a large party. Alternatively, you could make *tjälknöl* (see above) or the salted leg of lamb on page 108, which is even easier.

Traditionally, venison was roasted until absolutely gray, but it's not a tradition worth maintaining—venison is best if roasted slowly until still pink in the middle. The roasting time for a whole leg varies depending on its size and also the age of the animal, but a good rule is 35 minutes per 2¼lb at 325°F. If you are used to roasting lamb, this will not be difficult.

Precise measures for the marinade are difficult to specify, but the quantities given below are enough for a large leg of fallow deer.

Serve the venison with plain potatoes, raw sugared lingonberries or jelly, and maybe whole baked apples or a sweet-and-sour salad, such as apple and walnut salad.

I large leg of venison	I tablespoon fresh
A little cream (optional)	rosemary, chopped
for the marinade	I very large onion, grated
¾ cup extra-virgin olive oil	3 cloves garlic, minced
¾ cup hard cider	I tablespoon fresh
I tablespoon coarse sea salt	thyme leaves
Grated zest and juice of	I teaspoon coarsely ground
I lemon	black pepper

Mix together the marinade ingredients and brush the meat with the mixture. Let marinate covered in a dish, or in a sealed plastic food bag. If you have a cool place to put the meat, it's not necessary to fill up the refrigerator with it. Let marinate for 2–3 days if you have the time.

Roast the meat in the marinade, calculating the time as explained above and adding more hard cider or water to the pan as needed to avoid burning. When the time is up, insert a skewer all the way to the bone. If the juice runs red, it will need more time; if pale pink, the meat is done. Leave the venison to rest on the counter, covered in a clean dish towel, for 25 minutes in order for the juices to settle in the meat.

While the venison is resting, reduce the roasting-pan juices in a saucepan, season, and perhaps add a splash of cream. Pour into a gravy boat and serve with the meat.

Grilled venison

In summer, roe deer bucks can be shot, fat from spring grazing, and their meat is gorgeous, and tenderer than in winter. They can be prepared as you would lamb, or simply grilled. Any cut from the leg, a boned front leg or cutlets should be tender enough to put on a grill.

The venison's taste is less pronounced when the meat is grilled, and you can pair it with anything you fancy, but an asparagus and potato salad and chervil cream would be nice.

To keep the meat moist, wrap it in bacon, secured with toothpicks, and grill it slowly until just tender and still pink in the middle. The easiest way to determine if it's done is to poke the meat with a finger: if it feels like jelly inside, it's not done; if it feels like a mattress, it is.

Alternatively, you could make kebabs. The marinade from the roasted leg of venison recipe opposite would be perfect for these, though you would need to marinate the meat for only 6–12 hours. Be sure to cut the meat into large chunks so that they can grill long enough to get a good crisp crust, and still be pink inside.

Elk

In Sweden, and also in Norway and Finland, elk hunting is a passion, as well as an important contribution to both the personal and national economy. The elk had already been hunted to extinction in Denmark in the Stone Age, though once in a while a young elk desperately looking for a mate swims across the sound between Sweden and Denmark.

The elk population is controlled in order to keep the population healthy, and to protect the deciduous woods. Elk hunting in Sweden is a much-regulated affair, usually taken care of by hunting parties, which then share the meat as dictated by a very strict set of rules. According to official figures, hunters kill about 100,000 elk each year in Sweden alone, though the actual figure is probably much higher. Elk meat represents a substantial portion of the meat eaten in Sweden.

Appearance and taste The elk is a giant deer, about the size of a very large horse, big enough to give you 551lb of meat to eat, and big enough to do serious damage to your car if you collide with one (a relatively common occurrence in Sweden).

The elk is an awkward-looking animal, rather like a wildebeest, which has the appearance of being made up from the spare parts of several animals. The elk's neck is too short to reach the ground, so it feeds mainly on the young shoots and leaves of deciduous trees. To eat grass it has to squat down on the ground – a very funny sight, but elks are surprisingly agile swimmers, and they often dive to feed off the vegetation to be found in lakes and streams.

Elk meat is extremely dark and very lean, and tastes like gamy beef. Elk offal is much sought after, the liver being a particular delicacy.

Culinary uses Elk can be bought in northern Scandinavia from butchers and supermarkets, but it is quite expensive. Also, you will have no way of knowing how old it is, nor usually which cut of meat you're buying. The safe way to use this meat is in a stew.

Elk meat can be cooked like beef, but take care not to overcook it as it is much leaner than beef. Elk meat takes well to a marinade, and it's very good in kebabs, patties, hamburgers and whole roasts. The recipe for a whole leg of venison on page 116 is useful.

Dark elk stew with chocolate

This dark, velvety stew is irresistible, and works with elk, venison, or wild boar meat. Serve with mashed or roast potatoes, apple and celeriac salad, and sugared raw lingonberries. Sweet-and-sour sauce is traditionally used for all game in Scandinavia, but the addition of chocolate is new.

for the stock
2 onions, unpeeled, quartered
Bones from the elk, cut into smaller pieces to fit in the pan
2 fresh bay leaves
1 sprig of fresh thyme
8 juniper berries
10 black peppercorns
1 tablespoon extra-virgin olive oil
2¾ cups red wine
Salt

for the stew
3lb 5oz elk meat (leg or neck), cut into 1¼in cubes, bones reserved for the stock
2 tablespoons extra-virgin olive oil
Generous ⅓ Madeira
Generous ⅓ red wine
6 juniper berries
⅛ cup (just over 1oz) chopped bittersweet chocolate
1 tablespoon dark brown sugar
⅔ cup heavy cream
1oz blue cheese
Salt and pepper
SERVES 6

For the stock, fry the onions, bones, herbs, and spices in olive oil in a large, heavy-bottomed pot. Brown well, at a low heat. When everything is golden, add the wine and reduce until it has almost evaporated. Pour in 10 cups water, add some salt, and let boil slowly until reduced to about 4 cups. Remove any scum from the surface. Strain and cool.

Don't wash the pot; just add the olive oil for the stew and brown the meat on all sides over a high heat. Add the Madeira and red wine and reduce to almost nothing, then add the stock and juniper berries. Let come to a boil, remove any scum, then lower the heat to a slow simmer.

When the meat is tender, almost melting, reduce the liquid to a rich, extremely hefty sauce. Take the pot from the heat and stir in the chocolate, sugar, cream, and cheese. After this the sauce must not boil. Adjust the seasoning and serve.

Wild boar

Wild boar are sought after both as a treasured bounty for hunters (as they are really difficult to hunt) and for their meat. For many, hunting wild boar is motivated primarily by a desire to protect land and livestock: these animals are uncomfortably intelligent (like all pigs) and a grown male boar, with its giant tusks, is downright dangerous, and can wreak havoc on crops.

Appearance and taste Wild boar piglets must be the cutest creatures in the world, with their fuzzy fur and finely striped backs in brown and black, but they grow into rather less pretty and extremely powerful creatures. With its curved tusks, a boar's snout is an amazing instrument which it inserts into the ground like a plough to search for food, with disastrous results for both farmers and gardeners. One boar let loose in your garden will eat everything and turn your topsoil for you, and a herd of boar can wreck a whole field in a matter of hours. (Mind you, the same goes for the domesticated pig, which will turn any field into mud in a very short time.)

True wild boar is delicious, a tastier forefather to the domesticated pig, with dark, juicy meat, and a spicy flavor from foraging in the wild. Wild boar are omnivores and will eat anything, including roots, small animals, worms, and wild greens. The meat that you usually buy is from farmed wild boar, which are often crossed with domesticated pigs to make them fleshier (and also to give them a more docile temperament). The flesh is nice, but naturally lacks the unique flavor of the wild version.

Culinary uses You can cook wild boar pretty much any way that you would pork or venison; while boar meat is leaner than pork, it shares the same qualities in cooking. It will also taste perfect if you use the elk stew recipe opposite.

Wild boar braised in beer

This recipe highlights the virtues of wild boar, but can be used with pork as well. It's eaten Viking-style, directly off the bone, without cutlery, and you will be a mess by the end of the meal, but the meat between the bones is delicious and well worth it. If you prefer a more civilized meal, choose a couple of huge knuckles or a piece of neck instead as these can be eaten with a knife and fork. Serve with mashed potatoes and a beet salad with caraway, or any salad with sweetness in it.

2 whole garlic bulbs
A handful of sprigs each of fresh rosemary, thyme, and sage
3lb 5oz wild boar rib, with bones
Coarse sea salt
Coarsely ground black pepper
3 cups dark ale or stout
1 tablespoon muscovado sugar
1 teaspoon cornstarch (optional)
SERVES 4–5

Preheat the oven to 300°F. Cut the garlic in half crosswise, wash the herbs (leaving them as whole sprigs), then place in the bottom of a deep, ovenproof dish, or a *römertopf* if you have one. Rub the meat with plenty of salt and pepper and place in the dish on top of the herbs. Pour in the beer (top up with water if it does not cover the meat).

Cook the boar very slowly in the oven until the meat is meltingly tender. Depending on the age of the animal, and the cut, this may take 3–4 hours. Remove the lid after 2 hours if using a *römertopf*; if the sauce has reduced dramatically and is in danger of burning, add more water. There should be about 1¾ cups left when the meat is cooked.

When the meat is done, remove it and put the sauce and garlic through a fine sieve to extract all the garlic mush into the sauce. Season with salt, pepper and sugar, depending on the bitterness of the beer.

If you wish, dissolve some cornstarch in a little water and whisk it into the sauce to thicken it (letting it boil to remove the starchy taste), though this is not really necessary.

Wildfowl

Hundreds of species of wild birds migrate every year to northern Scandinavia from Africa and southern Europe. Every year in March you can watch migrating birds far overhead, and wonder how they find their way, and how they get the strength to travel thousands of miles twice every year. The fascination with this is beautifully described in Selma Lagerlöf's famous story *The Wonderful Adventures of Nils Holgerson*, which recounts a boy's journey with the wild geese to the very northern part of Norrland in Sweden.

Many species are shot and eaten, mostly ducks and geese, but some are protected and can be eaten only locally. There are numerous different ducks and geese, mostly just marketed as wild duck, and if you want a specific duck you must know the hunter. Eider and coot are plentiful and available. In the mountains and on the moors there are grouse, black grouse, and ptarmigans, and in the south mostly pheasants; the last, which were originally imported for hunting from Asia, are bred intensively to offer shooting possibilities for trigger-happy city dwellers. Partridges are becoming rare, and so are the delicious snipe. Some sea birds, such as puffins, are hunted locally when the bird population permits, but are not sold commercially.

The common eider duck is a beautiful sight, the male having strikingly beautiful black-and-white plumage. As with all ducks, the female has mottled brown plumage so it can remain undetected on the nest.

The eider is the source of luxurious eiderdown, collected in the wild after the ducklings have left the nest; it's an exciting thing to find, and one nest is enough to stuff a pillow. The nests, filled with regurgitated fish and bird excrement, look unappetizing but are in fact easy to clean. The tiny down feathers, which the female eider plucks from her breast, are barbed and stick together even in the strongest gale, so you can bash the whole nest against the rocks, and every piece of dirt will blow away, leaving only unbelievably soft and warm down.

Buying and storing With wildfowl, you must be happy with what you can get. The recipe opposite is suitable for all wild birds and can be used for whatever species you can lay your hands on, wherever you are.

Young birds have bendable beaks and tender feet—a young duck's webbed feet can easily be torn with your fingers, which is impossible with old bird's leathery feet. It would take up far too much space here to give advice on hanging, plucking, and cleaning wildfowl. Your hunter friend or butcher can tell you how.

Culinary uses Wildfowl are generally lean birds and can be cooked like chicken, domesticated duck or goose, though the leaner flesh must be compensated for in terms of fat, and cooked in a sauce to prevent it from drying out. The recipe for old-fashioned chicken on page 91 is perfect for wildfowl. Many wild birds have a huge breast and almost no other meat, and this can be cut off and broiled or fried as you would a duck breast.

All wildfowl are prepared in much the same manner throughout Scandinavia.

All fish- and mollusk-eating birds need a 24-hour soak in buttermilk to take away any fishy taste; after this they can be prepared like other wildfowl. The fishy taste is in the bone and tissue and seldom in the meat itself. The older the bird is, the fishier it becomes. Wildfowl that do not eat fish will not need the soak.

When dealing with coots, there is not much meat apart from the breast, so you can simply cut off the breast meat and fry it like a steak, or braise it as you would other wildfowl, except for a shorter time as there is no bone.

Pheasants must be cut up as they are very lean, and the breast will need only a short time to cook, whereas the thighs will need a long time to be tender. The thighs have numerous thin, needle-like bones, so take care when eating them, or simply take them out with tweezers before serving. Ducks do not need to be cut up, as the thighs and breasts both become tender in a very short while.

Braised wildfowl

This is a wonderful dish to make, and it works with any kind of wildfowl, though the cooking time varies with the species, size, and age of the bird; older birds take much longer to cook. Serve it with sugared raw lingonberries or jelly and plain boiled potatoes to soak up the wonderful sauce. Provide huge napkins, as you will have to eat the meat with your fingers, or the best parts will go to waste.

4 wild ducks, coots, or eiders	1 teaspoon coarsely ground black pepper
Buttermilk, for soaking	1¼ cups red wine or hard cider
¼ stick butter	
Fresh thyme, bay leaf, and parsley	1–2 teaspoons coarse sea salt
6 juniper berries	1¼ cups heavy cream
2 whole allspice	1 teaspoon cornstarch (optional)

SERVES 4

First pluck all the remaining feathers, and any residues of the peeling wax used for extracting the feathers. Soak the birds in buttermilk, or another sour milk product, for 12 hours. Rinse the birds under the cold faucet, and dry with paper towels.

Brown them all over in the butter in a large, heavy-bottomed skillet. This takes time, so be patient. When they are golden all over, add the herbs and spices, the wine, salt and a little water. Simmer with a lid on for 20 minutes, turning the birds over continuously in the sauce. After 20 minutes, check regularly to see if the birds are done—when the thigh is easily loosened from the body, they are ready.

Remove the birds from the pan and keep them warm. Add the cream to the sauce and let bubble away to reduce. You can thicken it with a little cornstarch if you like, but a reduced creamy sauce is better as the starch will always take away a lot of the taste.

Pigeons (Squab)

Woodpigeons are wild birds, and can be cooked like other wildfowl. Tame pigeons are smaller, and one bird for each person is not quite enough, so there must be an appetizer as well. They make the loveliest sauce of all, and must be cooked for just 25 minutes. You can use the recipe for wildfowl, or for old-fashioned chicken with curdled sauce (page 173). They are a summer delicacy and very hard to find. You must know someone devoted to raising plump young birds; they are best when they have never flown.

OFFAL

Scandinavians have an old and beautiful tradition of using every imaginable part of the animals we eat. In times before refrigeration, offal was considered the best and most nutritious part of the animal and was eaten fresh, or made into headcheese, sausages, and long-simmered, flavorful stews.

It is part of the ethics of good animal husbandry to eat up, letting nothing go to waste, and was considered a way of showing respect for the animals in question. But this is admittedly not so any more. Offal is regarded as extremely old-fashioned, and eating it is not remotely fashionable or usual with anybody under 60. So cooking offal is largely a forgotten skill these days, though young chefs are discovering the virtues and rich, distinct taste of all the best parts of the animals.

Traditionally, most of the specialties made from offal were eaten at Christmas, as the pigs were slaughtered in November. And this is still the time of year when blood sausages, liver sausages, headcheese, and fresh sausages are eaten, with all the Christmas specialties still made from the regular meat.

Buying and storing Offal must be bought very fresh, as its keeping quality is not as good as that of regular meat. As several of the organs have a huge blood content, and serve a cleaning purpose in the body, it is vital that they come from naturally reared, non-medicated animals.

Liver

In most homes, liver is only ever eaten as liver paste, which is a standby in every household in Scandinavia. When liver is eaten in its natural state, it is mostly plainly fried in butter and served with caramelized onions, crispy bacon, potatoes, and a pickle.

Liver paste is more or less the same everywhere, namely a fine-grained, spreadable pâté, gently spiced with thyme, onion, allspice, and black pepper. Originally, though, it was spiced with northern anchovies (pages 86–7), which added a kick to it, and most people who bake their own liver paste still make it in this way. There is absolutely no comparison between a homemade liver paste and the convenient, store-bought version which can be found in every store across Scandinavia.

Liver paste is spread on rye bread or crispbread and topped with sweet-and-sour pickle in winter or fresh cucumber slices in summer. When served for lunch at home, or at Christmas, it's served warm, topped with crispy bacon and fried mushrooms.

Liver paste with duck fat and anchovies

Liver paste can be made from either pig's or calf's liver or, better still, from a mixture of the two; the calf's liver has a beautiful taste, while the pig's liver adds a nice rosy color. Pork fat is traditional in liver paste, but rendered fat from a duck or goose, or a mixture of pork fat and one of the two, is even better. These quantities make 3lb 5oz liver paste, which can be baked either in one large terrine or several smaller ones.

for the ground meat
18oz calf's liver, chopped
7oz pig's liver (or duck or goose liver), chopped
1 large onion, grated
5 northern anchovy fillets, chopped
4 tablespoons anchovy brine
1 teaspoon fresh thyme leaves
4 whole allspice, crushed
1 teaspoon coarsely ground black pepper

Salt, to taste
for the white sauce
½ stick butter
½ cup all-purpose flour
1¾ cups whole milk
2 eggs
7oz pork fat, chopped
3½oz duck or goose fat
to finish
4 fresh bay leaves and a few bacon slices
MAKES 3LB 5OZ

Have the butcher chop the livers for you, or do it yourself. Mix the livers with the rest of the ingredients for the ground meat, apart from the salt.

For the sauce, melt the butter then stir in the flour, followed by the milk, a little at a time. Simmer until thick, stirring often. Stir in the two fats, and simmer until melted. Cool a little, then mix with the ground meat and eggs. Add salt to taste, which means that you will either have to taste the mixture as it is, which is quite pleasant actually, or fry a little patty of it in a skillet and then taste.

Pour the paste into one large or several smaller molds, preferably pretty ceramic ones that can be put directly on

the table. Garnish with the bacon and bay leaves.

Put the mold or molds in a deep pan in the oven at 325°F and fill the pan with cold water. Bake until done, which is when the paste is no longer raw in the middle. If the water evaporates, top it up with more (boiling) water; if it dries up completely, the fat will melt from the liver paste.

The paste can be frozen either baked or raw.

Sweetbreads

Sweetbreads are the pancreas and the two glands from the throat of young mammals, which help to digest milk and play an important role in the immune system; they disappear with age. They are neither easy to come by, nor cheap. The ones available are usually from calves or, if you are lucky, lambs.

Sweetbreads are a delicacy, with a taste and consistency all their own. They are a little lengthy, but immensely rewarding, to cook, especially when fried until crispy. They have a creamy consistency and a mild, rich taste that is best when not overwhelmed by the accompaniments. A crisp salad with lots of herbs, or creamed spring vegetables such as asparagus, are lovely with sweetbreads.

They are also very good served as *tarteletter* (page 92), the pre-cooked sweetbreads replacing or supplementing the chicken stew. The cooking liquid from the sweetbreads also makes a fine stock for a vegetable soup.

Fried sweetbreads

These deliciously crispy morsels should be served with one of the accompaniments described above.

18oz sweetbreads
for the cooking liquid
4 cups water
1 carrot, sliced
½ onion, sliced
1 sprig of fresh thyme
1 fresh bay leaf
1 scant teaspoon black peppercorns
1 tablespoon coarse sea salt

¼ cup hard cider or white wine vinegar
to finish
4 tablespoons all-purpose flour
¼ stick butter
Coarse sea salt
Coarsely ground black pepper
Lemon juice
SERVES 4

First, soak the sweetbreads in cold water for a couple of hours to draw out any blood.

Boil up the cooking-liquid ingredients, and add the sweetbreads. Lower the heat and simmer for 15 minutes, removing any scum regularly. When the sweetbreads are firm, usually after 15 minutes, they are done. Remove the saucepan from the heat and let the sweetbreads cool a little in the liquid. When they are cool enough to handle, put the sweetbreads on a board and remove the membranes on the outside, as best you can; if you are too efficient, the sweetbreads will crumble.

Place the sweetbreads in a deep square dish where they will just fit, and fill with the cooking liquid. Wrap the dish in plastic wrap, place a heavy board on top and cool completely in the refrigerator. They will keep in the refrigerator for 2 days.

Cut the sweetbreads into ⅓in slices, dust with flour and fry until crispy in the butter. Season with salt and pepper, sprinkle with lemon juice, and serve.

Hearts

The hearts of pigs, calves, and lambs are eaten with more appreciation than other pieces of offal. The meat is more like proper meat, even if it takes an eternity to cook. But when it is tender, heart tastes lovely in a comforting and richly flavored way that is popular with almost everyone.

The traditional way to serve heart is like game, in a cream sauce, with mashed potatoes and lingonberries. This dish will inevitably give you a tummy ache, as you cannot stop eating before it's too late. Hearts can also be cooked like old-fashioned chicken, stuffed with parsley and simmered for a couple of hours, with the same accompaniments—cucumber salad, new potatoes, and a lettuce salad with a cream dressing.

Hearts share a peculiarity with squid, in that you can cook them either very briefly, or for a very long time, and both ways they will be tender and delicious; anywhere in between and they will be chewy and inedible. Cooked fast, skewered, and broiled, the hearts will be crispy on the outside, and rosy on the inside.

Hearts are usually bought whole, but opened, and you can choose to cook them whole, or slice them up lengthwise into french-fry-sized bites. Either way, they must be cleaned of blood and you must remove fat, gristle, and anything that does not look like meat.

Hearts braised with apples and prunes

This is a wintry dish, sweet and sour from the fall apples and onions. Serve with mashed potatoes, baked root vegetables, and lingonberries.

1 cup prunes, with pits	3 sweet eating apples,
3lb 5oz hearts, from calf, pig,	quartered and cored
or lamb	4 cups apple juice, unfiltered
½ stick butter	Salt and ground black
2 large onions, quartered	pepper
1 teaspoon coriander seeds	⅔ cup heavy cream
1 sprig of fresh thyme	2 tablespoons tamari
3 tablespoons cider vinegar	(Japanese soy sauce)

Serves 6

Soak the prunes in cold water.

Clean the hearts, removing all the sinews, gristle, and solid fat. Cut calf's or pig's hearts into long, wide strips and quarter any lamb's hearts. Wash in cold water and dry with a clean dish towel.

Melt the butter in a wide, heavy-bottomed skillet large enough to hold everything. When it is golden, fry the onions, coriander seeds, and thyme for 15 minutes at a low heat, then remove. Brown the hearts in several batches. Add the vinegar to the hearts in the pan and fry until reduced to almost nothing. Add the onions, apples, apple juice, and enough water to half-cover the meat. Add salt and pepper, but not too much salt, as the sauce will reduce, and you will also add tamari later. Let simmer for 2–3 hours at a very low heat until the hearts are very tender and the sauce reduced, mushy, chunky, and delicious.

Pit the prunes, when soft, and add to the pan along with the cream. Heat through, then adjust the seasoning with tamari, and maybe a little more cream if very acidic.

Blood

Blood from pigs is an age-old specialty, valued for its taste and its immense nutritional value. The blood is collected at the moment of slaughter, and stirred non-stop until it has cooled, to prevent it from coagulating. It is eaten in several forms, as pudding or sausages, but they are very similar. The cooled blood is stirred with

grains, often barley or oats, diced pork fat, raisins or currants, spiced with cinnamon, pepper, salt, and thyme, and cooked in wide sausage skins or a mold. The heat coagulates the blood, making a moist and delicious, bread-like pâté.

Blood can even be made into spicy, almost black bread by adding rye flour, salt, and spices. Store-bought blood sausage can be very good, and is found mostly at Christmas. It's eaten sliced and fried, with cinnamon, dark syrup, and apple compote. It's essential on Christmas lunch tables, and in many families is eaten for dinner during December, often followed by rice pudding. For four people you will need 1lb 10oz blood sausage and apple compote from 2¼lb apples.

Fat

Northern people—Scandinavians, Inuit, Sami, and the countless tribes of the Arctic Circle—have always valued fat as a perfect source of energy, necessary for survival in an extremely cold environment. Even in southern Scandinavia, physical work has been hard and fat has been an invaluable part of everyday fare, to an extent that we find hard to understand nowadays. And while fat was necessary for bare survival, it has, through the ages, become an integral part of so many of our best traditions in food. Almost all festive food, sausages, and toppings for open-face sandwiches have fat as an important part of their taste, consistency, and looks. The typical tastes of Scandinavian food are simply not possible without animal fat.

Of course, the amount of fat consumed can be reduced, and it must be, as traditions that are not compatible with modern, centrally heated life in front of the computer are bound to die out. Nevertheless, a number of dishes would lose their meaning if not fatty, and a lot of dishes will just stop being good to eat if scrutinized by low-fat addicts. Such a tradition is the love of rendered pork fat, instead of butter, on a large number of open-face sandwiches. Sausages, herrings, and cold cuts are all eaten on rye bread spread with a thin, delicious layer of spiced pork fat.

We often use fat for frying. Vegetables, potatoes, and roots are all so good if fried or baked with tasty fat, and fat from cooking a pork roast is saved and used for both sandwiches and cooking.

Goose and duck fat is even better for these purposes, and leftover fat from the Christmas goose or duck is put to innumerable uses, in liver paste, frying, and especially for roast potatoes.

Spiced pork fat

This delicious fat can be eaten spread under open-face sandwich toppings, or on its own on rye bread, scattered with salt. The rendered fat can be made from pure pork fat, or a mixture of duck/goose and pork fat. The rendering process supplies another delicious specialty: the little morsels of fat tissue that will not melt, but crisp up, during frying. They are traditionally eaten like crispy bacon, on liver paste or smoked sausage sandwiches, or on plain rye bread. Pork crackling is almost an obsession, especially in Denmark, where it can be bought in any store, lovingly named "pig candy."

18oz pork fat (from inside the belly is considered superior)
3 cups thinly sliced onions
3 hand-eating apples, cored and diced

2 tablespoons fresh thyme leaves
1 tablespoon ground black pepper

Grind the fat in a meat-grinder. Put in a heavy-bottomed skillet on a low heat and let it simmer gently until it has melted. Take out the tiny, unmelted morsels with a slotted spoon and place on paper towels to absorb the excess fat. When these are cool, scatter with coarse sea salt and enjoy.

Add the onions and apples to the fat and simmer on, as the onions slowly crisp and the apples are cooked. When this stage has been reached, take the pan from the heat and stir in the thyme leaves and black pepper. Cool, stirring a little while it is cooling to distribute the flavor.

Tongue

The tongues of veal calves, cows, pigs, and lambs are eaten, but veal tongue is considered the best. Tongues are always salted before boiling in Scandinavia, as all fatty meats are improved with salting, and it adds to the keeping quality.

Tongue is eaten as a dinner dish, often with a horseradish sauce, or a caper sauce. In summer it's delicious with a lovage pesto (page 177), or a plain horseradish cream (page 179). Tongue is simmered slowly, until a skewer will go right through it with ease. Cool a little and then peel off the outer, leathery layer—quite a pleasurable task. Leftovers are eaten, thinly sliced, on rye bread with horseradish and mustard.

Salted veal tongue with caper sauce

If you want to prepare this truly delicious old-fashioned dish, proceed exactly as in the recipe for salted veal with caper sauce on page 113. The tongue must soak in the brine for 72 hours. One veal tongue will feed four to six people, according to size. You can alternatively serve the tongue with the horseradish sauce made to accompany the boiled chicken on page 91.

Heads and tails

In a time when nobody could afford to let edible things go to waste, a wide array of delicious and time-consuming dishes were invented to use absolutely every part of the animal. Cooking odds and ends of animals, however, is not just an economically virtuous way of cooking; the results are wonderful if you take the time and care. All meat close to the bone has lots of intramuscular fat, and a certain mucilaginous quality that is simply delicious.

Mock turtle

This recipe traditionally uses a halved calf's head, cooked for hours with Madeira, tomatoes, spices, herbs, and onions until absolutely tender. You pick the meat from the bones and serve it in the delicious sauce with small fish cakes, fish dumplings, meat rissoles, meat dumplings, brain dumplings, brined tongue, and a dash more Madeira. It's filling and laborious, and has been the finest of all fine dishes to serve at special occasions for centuries. It is a dish for the accomplished cook; any lack of experience and you are bound for disaster. But if you make this dish, your guests will never forget it.

A calf's head can be hard to find, but if you succeed, use it instead of the other meat in the recipe below and the dish will be wonderful. Without a head, the dish will still be outstanding as the taste and gelatinous quality are much the same in shanks and tails.

The mixture of sea and land creatures in the dish mimics the taste of real turtle, and I am old enough to have tasted the real thing, in a time when it was not considered politically incorrect. This recipe omits the fish and meat dumplings, but if you want them (as I am sure you do), use the recipes for quenelles and meatballs on pages 39 and 101 respectively. If you use 2¼lb of each, both made into half-boiled dumplings and half-fried patties, there will be more than enough for 20 people.

2¼lb langoustines
5lb 8oz calf's shanks (*osso buco*), sliced, or calf's tails, cut into joints
¼ stick butter

2 large onions, chopped
4lb vegetables, such as carrots, celeriac, parsley root, and leeks, chopped (prepared weight)

Generous ⅓ cup
   concentrated tomato
   paste
1 bouquet garni: 10 large
   sprigs each fresh thyme
   and tarragon, 1 small
   bunch of fresh basil,
   4 fresh sage leaves, and the
   green part of the leeks,
   tied with cotton string
1 whole garlic bulb, halved

2½ cups red wine
¾ cup Madeira or Marsala
Salt
1 tablespoon black
   peppercorns

to serve
Fresh basil
6 hard-boiled eggs,
   peeled and halved
Crusty bread
SERVES 10–12

Yank the tails from the langoustines. Peel the tails from the shells and remove the long, thin gut. Save all the shells and heads.

Cut the outer rim of the shank slices eight times each to stop them from curling up. Brown all the meat well in the butter in a heavy-bottomed pot large enough to hold all the ingredients. Remove the meat, then brown the onions, half of the vegetables, and the lobster shells and heads in the same fat. The browning of these ingredients is paramount to the taste. It will take time, but it's well spent.

Add the tomato paste, herbs, and garlic and fry for a while, then add the wines and let them evaporate while stirring. Add water to cover all the ingredients, and season with salt and pepper. Leave to simmer for 2 hours.

Strain everything through a sieve. The part in the sieve is then whizzed in the food processor. Put this delicious mush through a fine sieve, and save it for later. The liquid part is put back in the pot with the browned meat and simmered slowly for at least 2 hours more, until the meat is meltingly tender. During this process, the sieved ingredients are gradually added to the meat. The thicker the contents of the pot become, the more likely they are to burn, so keep a close eye and stir frequently. Twenty minutes before the dish is finished add the remaining vegetables. (While the meat is cooking, you can make and prepare the meat and fish dumplings, if you wish to serve them too.)

When you are ready to eat, bake the lobster tails, brushed with melted butter, in a small dish in the oven at 425°F. As soon as they turn from translucent to white-fleshed, they are done. Pour the meat and sauce into a tureen, and arrange the dumplings and patties, if serving, lobster tails, and eggs on top. Scatter with basil and serve with crusty bread.

Scandinavian headcheese

This dish is extremely old, as old as pig-keeping in Scandinavia, and it was—and still is—an extremely fatty dish. But not this one. Any tradition can be improved and changed over time, and conditions have changed dramatically in the past 50 years—both our need for calories (as we rarely work hard outdoors for days any more) and our taste in food.

A headcheese will never be lean, but this version is a far cry from times when absolutely everything from the pig's head, except the bones, was put in the headcheese, simply because it was too good to waste; even gums and eyes are evidently edible. My version is made with meat only, suspended in a extremely flavorful jelly, crowned by a thin layer of fat. If you feel the urge for a more substantial headcheese, you can include as much of the fat as you wish, with the meat.

Headcheese is served on rye bread, with pickled beets and mustard. It's a traditional Christmas dish, always on the Christmas lunch table.

½ a pig's head
2 pork shanks, with trotters
Extra pork bones
4 large onions, quartered
1 bouquet garni: 1 large
   sprig of fresh thyme,
   1 large sprig of fresh
   marjoram, 10 fresh sage
   leaves, 2 bay leaves,
   parsley stalks, and
   1 celery stalk

1 whole garlic bulb, halved
   horizontally
2 tablespoons black
   peppercorns
1 teaspoon juniper berries
1 teaspoon whole allspice
A walnut-sized piece of
   fresh ginger
6 tablespoons coarse
   sea salt

SERVES 6–10 PEOPLE AS
PART OF A LUNCH

Put the meat, bones, and onions in a large pot and cover with cold water. Bring slowly to a boil. Once it's boiling, remove all the scum at regular intervals, until no more gray scum is forming. Add the herbs, spices, and salt, and simmer slowly until the meat is very tender. Remove the meat with a slotted spoon and cool slightly.

While the meat is still very warm, extract all the regular meat from the head and shanks. Be very thorough as the meat is buried in fat in the shanks, and in the cheek, and it's

nice to have a little of the fat in the headcheese as well. Cut the meat into dice.

Return everything except the meat to the pot and simmer for a couple of hours until the stock is very intense. There will be only a little more than 4 cups left by the end. Adjust the salt—headcheese is supposed to be a little more salty than soup.

Strain the stock through a piece of cheesecloth, or a clean dish towel, and remove the layer of fat on top and reserve. Arrange the meat in one large, or a couple of smaller, pretty earthenware molds and pour over the hot stock. Pour in a ⅛in-thick layer of the reserved fat; this will float to the top and must cover the meat completely. Pack in plastic wrap and cool immediately.

To serve, turn the headcheese on to a board, cut into thick slices, and eat on rye bread with pickled beets and lots of mustard. The headcheese will keep for a week or more, if not opened, but it does not freeze well.

TIP
• Any leftover stock is perfect in pea soup, and in sauces for duck and pork. Leftover fat can be used for frying.

Scandinavia is not a world leader in vegetable cooking. Our traditional diet is based on that of the peasant and fishing societies and, in the north, some hunters and former nomads, which together made up our society for thousands of years. Many still regard vegetables as inferior food, fit only for women and rabbits. Even more cosmopolitan city people eat a very limited range of vegetables. Nevertheless, this is changing fast and most young people today eat a greater variety of vegetables, and are adventurous with the ways they cook them.

We have had kale, and other leafy cabbages since the Viking age, but we have eaten onions, dried peas, parsnips and other roots, garlic, ramsons (wild garlic), angelica, and fava beans for much longer, and people have been gathering wild greens since the first hunter-gatherers came back to Scandinavia after the last Ice Age 15,000 years ago.

Before the age of the deep freeze, a very large proportion of our vegetables were canned, pickled, or fermented, and these preparations are still a useful part of our diet: pickled red cabbage, beets, and cucumbers are everyday commodities, eaten both for lunch and dinner, with almost all traditional Scandinavian dishes.

vegetables

Cabbage & kale

Cabbage is one of the oldest Nordic vegetables, and is considered as one of the most important. It has been grown in some form or other for thousands of years in Scandinavia. In the Viking age, it was the only vegetable grown, and kitchen gardens around the houses were simply called kale-yards. Cabbages and kale are perfect winter food even in extreme climates. Historically, cabbage was eaten in unbelievable quantities, and its wholesome, vitamin-packed leaves have been a means of survival during many winters, long before the potato reached our shores.

After the arrival of the potato, it became a winter staple alongside cabbage. The total amount of vegetables eaten was much larger then, even though these were mainly cabbages and potatoes. This is evident in the variety and abundance of recipes for these vegetables, and in the use of cabbage as an accompaniment to everything, except fish. There are countless regional recipes for kale and white cabbage, and some are worth preserving, though others are too fatty or labor intensive to make except at Christmas, when old traditions are still kept very much alive.

Cabbage has always been cheap, and this simple fact made the vegetable increasingly unpopular among the bourgeoisie in the 19th century, who considered it far too low and common for their dinner tables. This meant that they introduced and grew a lot of new vegetables, and there was a decline in cabbage-eating, except by country dwellers and the very poor. Cabbage-eating was considered as unthinkable as wearing diamonds in the morning; the very smell of boiling cabbage became the smell of poverty, and nobody ate cabbage if they did not have to up to the 1950s–70s. As new leafy and imported vegetables have become popular, the total amount of vegetables eaten has declined dramatically, so we eat a far greater variety of vegetables now, but far fewer of them. The heavy cabbage has been replaced by much less lettuce and other salad greens.

The health food movement and growing environmental concerns have brought a change in attitudes over the past 20 or 30 years. Young cooks eager for indigenous originality, health nuts and foodies have rediscovered kale, cabbage, and other brassicas. Small farms are growing interesting cultivars again, and an increasing number of Scandinavians are tiring of tasteless imports, and are sourcing local, seasonal foods. There has been a small revolution in cabbage-eating. Cabbage is once again becoming all the rage, and is seen as far too good not to eat every day; at the same time it is one of the cheapest ways of making sure your family is well fed.

How it grows Kale is extremely hardy, and well suited to the harsh growing conditions in the north. Kale and Brussels sprouts are not usually all harvested at once, but left in the ground to be gathered when needed. Kale leaves sticking out of the snow in private gardens, even in deepest winter, are a familiar sight. Headed cabbages are not nearly as hardy, and must be harvested and stored before the first severe frosts.

All brassicas are greedy and need a great deal of watering and nurturing to grow to the enormous size they can accomplish. Kale, for winter, and leafy summer cabbages for eating straight away should be in every kitchen garden. Winter cabbages, on the other hand, can be bought at ridiculously low prices, and only if you have lots of space are they worth growing and storing.

Appearance and taste All the varied and strange cabbages we now grow stem from a single wild biennial cabbage, *Brassica oleracea*, which still grows all over southern Europe. Through the ages, expert gardeners have domesticated and selected cabbages so that we now have a huge amount of choice. Every part of the plant has been carefully selected, by watchful plant breeders over time, until flower heads, unfurled shoots, stems, and leaves have become new cultivars in their own right, such as cauliflower, Brussels sprouts, and kohlrabi.

Wild cabbages, consisting mostly of large green leaves, have been selected for their beauty, coloring, growing habit, and taste to create all the different types of kale we now grow. Kale (also known as borecole) is the oldest form of domesticated cabbage, very close to its wild ancestor, but an enormous improvement on the inedibly coarse and bitter original. These cabbages have been with us since the Romans efficiently spread them all over Europe.

The cultivation of round and pointed red, green, and white cabbages is not nearly so old. There are such a number of forms that they probably evolved in several places at once, but white cabbage is believed to have originated in Germany during the Middle Ages. Savoy cabbages are a couple of centuries younger.

The origins of cabbages chosen for their enlarged flowers, such as cauliflower, are not clear, but cauliflower was probably selected in the Arab world during the Middle Ages. It spread very fast, reaching Europe in only a hundred years, and was grown in northern Europe by the 17th century. Cauliflower has always been considered a fine thing, even by the rich.

Calabrese, broccoli, and sprouting broccoli come from Italy and have been known to the rest of the world only for some 200 years. Brussels sprouts are essentially cabbages whose unopened new buds along the stem are what's eaten. They were first cultivated in Belgium (not surprisingly) only 200 years ago.

Eating habits have spread slowly, throughout history, and it's fair to conclude that the region in which the plant is most prolifically grown and consumed is likely to be where it first originated. There is something awe-inspiring about a plant that bears in it the possibilities of such enormous variation, and about the tremendous amount of human insight and labor which goes into making this variation happen.

Buying and storing Kale can be bought as a whole beautiful uprooted plant; it will be very decorative for weeks in a bucket of water by your front door. Or you can buy the washed leaves, in plastic bags, or chopped and frozen. Winter cabbages are easy to store, as long as you choose a cold place, not necessarily the refrigerator. Leafy cabbages must be very fresh and juicy; if they are limp, with yellowing leaves, they are past their prime. When buying green summer cabbages, check that they are well filled and not just green leaves surrounding emptiness. You can eat the tenderest of the outer leaves, but the inner ones are best.

Health benefits Green brassicas are bursting with beta-carotenes, the red cultivars with anthocyan, both powerful antioxidants, and some B vitamins which are not readily obtainable in other foods. They also contain lots of calcium, phosphorus, iron, and a considerable amount of vitamin C. In other words, brassicas in some form should be eaten every day.

Culinary uses We have many lovely cabbage dishes, some more and some less traditional, in which meat, cabbage, and onions synthesize in melting ways. Some, such as creamed kale and pickled red cabbage, are indispensable for a traditional Christmas, while some dishes are pure comfort food: creamed cabbage for *frikadeller*, or creamy cabbage soup topped with crispy bacon and mace, which will make you feel like a child again, even if you are actually still a child.

Sea kale

Sea kale (*Crambe maritima*), a huge, white-flowering perennial with giant, glaucous leaves and billions of fawn seeds in the fall, is a different species from cabbage. It is protected wherever it grows, and you cannot pick the leaves or even the seeds, as it is endangered. Sea kale was grown as a luxurious spring vegetable in Victorian times, cut and blanched in early spring. I grow sea kale in my kitchen garden, and it's beautiful. You can buy seeds for a white and a purple-tinged cultivar.

Other dishes are for every day, but must be cooked in large quantities to make any sense: for example, slow-cooked caramelized brown cabbage with pork ribs, or *får i kål*, a Norwegian favorite originally made with mutton, but more palatable for touchy modern taste buds if made with lamb. Winter cabbage salads are also popular, such as red cabbage and fruit, kale with sour cream, or Brussels sprout salad with nuts.

In summer, we eat fine young pointed cabbages barely cooked with dill or bacon, perfect with smoked fish and light meats. We eat cauliflower as a velvet soup (prepared exactly like asparagus soup), or lightly steamed and dressed with small shrimp, dill, and melted butter.

Cabbage is infamous for the smelly fumes it emits while cooking, and for the uncompromising way it makes you pass gas. Many cabbage recipes include caraway seeds, both for their taste and because they keep the flatulence to a minimum. It is a matter of habit, however, and if you eat cabbage frequently your bowels get used to it.

Kale is bitter, and also rather tough, which is not a problem if it is cooked; it just needs a long time in the pot to cook to perfect tender creaminess. If used as a salad, kale must be cut into very fine strips.

Kale salad with lemon dressing

This salad is very satisfying, the sweetness of the dressing balancing the bitterness of the leaves, and the lemon adding extra interest. This is the way to make children eat fresh kale. It goes with anything fried—fish, pork, lamb, *frikadeller*, or smoked meats and fish.

10½oz kale	of 1 lemon
Generous ¾ cup	2 tablespoons sugar
heavy cream	1 teaspoon coarse sea salt
Finely grated zest and juice	Serves 4

Wash the kale and remove the ribs. Stack the leaves, roll into a tight package, then cut into ⅛in wide strips. Mix together the remaining ingredients to make the dressing and blend with the shredded kale; the dressing will eventually thicken. It may need more salt and sugar. The salad is best the day it is made, but will keep in the refrigerator for another day.

Creamed kale

Creamed kale is loved by everyone, if it's made properly. The name must be taken seriously and the cream must not be replaced with milk and flour, even if it may look the same. It is eaten with *frikadeller, medisterpølse* (sausage), smoked meats, ham, and *julskinka* (Christmas ham) and is absolutely essential for Christmas lunch. It is usually served with caramelized potatoes—a very good match. The best creamed kale is made by boiling the leaves in some kind of stock, which need not be any more ambitious than the liquid from the meat you intend to eat with it; this is the method used here.

1 whole stem of kale, or 2lb 2oz kale leaves	1 teaspoon coarsely ground black pepper
8 cups cooking liquid from salted or smoked meat	1 tablespoon cornstarch
½ teaspoon ground mace	1¾–2 cups heavy cream
1 tablespoon coarse sea salt	3–5 tablespoons sugar
	SERVES 6

Remove the coarse ribs from the leaves, then blanch in a large saucepan of boiling water until tender; about 5 minutes. Drain well in a large colander. Stack the leaves and chop them coarsely.

Place the chopped kale in a saucepan with the stock, mace, salt, and pepper, though if the cooking liquid is very salty, omit the salt. Simmer without a lid until the kale is very soft. This will take longer than you expect, maybe even 45 minutes. Stir often.

Tip into a colander and reserve the liquid. Put the kale back in the pan. Mix the cornstarch with a little of the cream, then add to the pan along with the sugar and the rest of the cream, stirring vigorously. You may want to add some of the cooking liquid too. Stir until the floury taste is gone. Adjust the seasoning and also the creaminess, adding more of the cooking liquid if it is too dry. Eat the kale while piping hot. It will keep in the refrigerator for 3–4 days.

TIP
• If you don't have any meat stock to hand, simply boil the kale in water until very tender, and then chop and finish with the cream, as above.

Brussels sprout salad with apple

A very simple, delicious salad, making the best of the sweetness of raw sprouts. The salad is good with fish, pork, venison, and poultry. You can add smoked fresh cheese, mild blue cheese, or use toasted pumpkin seeds or hazelnuts instead of the walnuts. With the cheese it's substantial enough for a starter.

12–18 large Brussels sprouts	2 tablespoons canola or walnut oil
1 large apple	3 tablespoons cider vinegar
1 teaspoon sugar	2 tablespoons walnut kernels, toasted
1 teaspoon coarse sea salt	SERVES 4
2 tablespoons olive oil	

Cut the sprouts and apple into very thin slices, leaving the apple peel on, but discarding the core. Mix with the rest of the ingredients and leave to steep for a couple of hours.

Leftovers are fine the next day.

Pickled red cabbage

As with any popular dish, there are countless ways of making this traditional accompaniment for the Christmas goose, duck, or pork. Any version other than the one from your childhood is doomed from the beginning. The principle is simple: slowly cooked shredded red cabbage, smothered in something vinegary and something red, dark, and juicy, and seasoned with salt, pepper, bay leaves, and thyme. The exact ingredients are open to all manner of variations and combinations. For example, the vinegar could be cider, sherry, or raspberry, or you could even use red wine, maybe enriched with some balsamic vinegar. The juice could be cranberry, lingonberry, black- or red currant, or could be replaced by a good berry jam. The cabbage also tastes lovely with juniper, allspice, or caraway seeds, and finely sliced apples are a good addition.

The aim of all this mixing and experimenting, is to create a perfect balance of sweet and sour, fruit and spice. The result should be a rich and satisfying dish that can be combined in countless ways with meat and potatoes. It even tastes great cold on open-face sandwiches.

I don't believe in giving a proper recipe for this dish. Follow your own taste buds and your cabbage will be the better for it. However, if this is the first time you've cooked red cabbage, the instructions below will lead you in the right direction.

1 large red cabbage, finely shredded	1 teaspoon caraway seeds
Generous ⅓ cup vinegar	2 juniper berries
Generous ¾ cup red fruit juice or jam	2 whole allspice
	1 scant tbsp coarse sea salt
2 apples, peel on, cored and cut into chunks	1 bay leaf
	1 sprig of fresh thyme

Put all the ingredients into a large pot and leave to simmer at a low heat for a couple of hours. Take care that it does not dry out, and add a little water if it starts to. Taste the cabbage after an hour, and add more of this and that as you like. When the cabbage is meltingly tender, jammy, and tasty, it's finished. Add a spoonful of duck, goose, or pork fat when you heat it up for dinner and it will be shiny, too.

This dish will keep for weeks in an airtight glass or plastic container in the fridge, and improve in the process, so you can cook it well ahead of when you want to serve it.

Red cabbage salad with caraway seeds

This salad is very good for any bleak day in winter, and works well as an alternative to the traditional pickled red cabbage (see above) served as part of Christmas dinner. The initial salting and the hot apple syrup make a perfectly balanced semi-pickled salad to suit all cold cuts, venison, pork, or duck. You can happily make a large portion as it keeps for weeks in the refrigerator.

1 small red cabbage	½ cup sugar
Scant ¼ cup very coarse sea salt	1½ tablespooons caraway seeds
4 cups unfiltered apple juice	SERVES 6

Cut the cabbage into quarters, remove and discard the stem, then cut into very fine strips. Place in a large bowl and scatter over the salt. Now squeeze the cabbage with your hands until it releases some of its water—which is actually quite fun. Transfer the cabbage to a large colander and let sit in the sink for an hour. (The cabbage will go limp, but will still be crunchy), then rinse with cold water to remove excess salt. Let the cabbage start to dry on a clean dish towel for 30 minutes, then pat dry.

Meanwhile, reduce the apple juice to a syrup with the sugar. Turn the cabbage in the syrup in a large bowl, while the syrup is still hot. Toast the caraway seeds in a dry skillet until they wriggle like jumping beans.

Scatter the seeds over the cabbage and serve.

Caramelized white cabbage

This dish is as traditional as it gets and very macho—which, in a Nordic context, means that it is extremely filling, not too pretty and usually makes you pass gas. Nevertheless, it's delicious and children love it, too. It's bittersweet from the caramel, and melts in your mouth in a very satisfying way. It can be eaten either as an accompaniment for all kinds of pork, or as a hearty dish in its own right—in either case, the pork is the thing: simmering the cabbage with a salted, and maybe smoked, piece of pork, a handful of fresh or smoked sausages, or a dinosaur-sized heap of spare ribs creates a sublime and very Nordic unity. Even so, you can omit the meat if you want to, and still enjoy the dish.

It makes no sense to prepare this dish for just one meal, which is why I suggest making such a huge quantity. The cabbage itself keeps for a week in the refrigerator and it also freezes well. The meat can be frozen separately, or you can simmer a fresh batch of meat in the cabbage when the time comes. Serve the dish with steamed vegetables, mashed potatoes, strong mustard, beer, and schnapps.

1 cup sugar
⅓ cup butter
2 medium white cabbages, shredded
2 bay leaves
1 sprig of fresh thyme
3 whole allspice, bashed

4 tablespoons coarse sea salt
2 teaspoons black peppercorns
6lb 8oz piece of fatty, salted, and/or smoked pork or 5lb 8oz sausages
2 cups water
SERVES 10

Melt the sugar and ½ stick of the butter to a light caramel in a heavy-bottomed saucepan that is large enough to hold everything eventually. Stir in the shredded cabbage, herbs, and spices, and mix well to coat evenly.

Let the cabbage sweat gently, stirring frequently, until the juices run. Remove the cabbage to a bowl while you brown the meat in the remaining butter. Return the cabbage to the pan and pour in the water. Season with salt to taste and let simmer very gently for several hours until all the water has evaporated. Remove the meat when it's done.

TIP
• If you use sausages, such as *medisterpølse* or a Swedish *Prins korv*, brown them in a separate pan and add to the cabbage about 25 minutes before the end of cooking, otherwise they will be dry.

Cabbage rolls

The Swedish dish *kåldolmar* is actually Turkish in origin. It was brought north by the Swedish warrior King Charles XII, who fled to the Ottoman empire after he lost the battle of Poltava, in the Ukraine, against the Russians in 1709. He befriended the Sultan, grew fond of Ottoman food—who wouldn't?—and brought the dolma home with him. This, in time, evolved into our beloved meat-filled parcels wrapped in white cabbage leaves rather than the Turkish vine leaves.

The best accompaniments are lingonberry jam and boiled potatoes. The recipe makes a large amount, but you can either eat it over two days, or freeze half of it (when half-baked).

2 well-filled pointed head cabbages or Savoy cabbages

for the meat filling

4 slices dry sourdough bread, crust removed

Generous ¾ cup whole milk

2¼lb ground mixed pork and veal

2 tablespoons coarse sea salt

4 eggs

1¼ cups heavy cream

1 onion, chopped

Grated zest of 1 lemon

1 tablespoon chopped fresh thyme

1 tablespoon chopped fresh marjoram

3 cloves garlic, chopped

1 teaspoon coarsely ground black pepper

4 tablespoons tomato ketchup

2 tablespoons Dijon mustard

for the braise

18oz mixed roots (e.g. celeriac, carrots, and parsley root), chopped

2 onions, chopped

1 cup stock (veal, chicken, or vegetable)

1 cup hard cider

Juice of 1 lemon

3 tablespoons tamari (Japanese soy sauce)

1 tablespoon liquid honey

⅓ cup butter

SERVES 4

For the filling, soften the bread in the milk, then combine all the filling ingredients in a food mixer or large bowl. The longer you mix, the lighter and juicier the filling will be.

Remove any very tough outer leaves from the cabbage, then peel off 20 beautiful leaves, more if you can; if the ribs are tough, cut them out with a V-shaped incision. Place the leaves in a large bowl and pour over 6¼pt of boiling water. Let steep until very pliable, then dry on a clean dish towel.

Put 2–3 spoonfuls of the filling on each leaf, fold in the sides, and roll it up, like a little closed parcel. If the leaves are too small, use two at a time. Repeat until all the filling has been used up.

Mix the vegetables for the braise and arrange in one deep ovenproof dish, large enough also to hold all the parcels, or in two smaller dishes. Place the stuffed leaves on top and wiggle them down between the vegetables. Pour over the stock, cider, and lemon juice, then drizzle on the tamari and honey and dot with ¼ stick of the butter.

Bake at 350°F for about 45 minutes. Baste the rolls with stock every 15 minutes to keep them moist.

When the dolma and vegetables are all cooked, pour off the stock from the dish, into a saucepan, and reduce at a high heat. When it is syrupy, remove from the heat and whisk in the remaining butter. Pour over the rolls and serve immediately.

Cabbage soup with crispy bacon and thyme

Wintery and soothing, this is a simple and cheap soup for cold nights. For the best results, use the cooking liquid from a piece of salted, smoked meat for the stock.

1 small white cabbage

14oz floury potatoes

2 large leeks

½ stick butter

Scant ¼ cup cider vinegar

4 cups stock (ham, pork, chicken, beef… whatever you have)

1 sprig of fresh thyme, plus extra leaves to garnish

7oz smoked bacon, in one piece

3 walnut-size pieces of fresh
 ginger, chopped
Generous ¾ cup heavy cream

Salt and pepper
Sugar, to taste
SERVES 6

Cut the cabbage, potatoes, and leeks into relatively large pieces. Melt generous ¼ stick of butter in a saucepan which can hold everything and sweat the vegetables for 15 minutes without browning them. Add the vinegar and let it reduce to nothing. Add the thyme sprig, stock, bacon, and ginger and let simmer for 30 minutes, or until the vegetables are very tender.

Remove the bacon, rinse it under cold water, then cut into small pieces. Fry these until golden and crispy in the remaining butter.

Remove and discard the thyme sprig and then blend the soup, with the cream, in a food processor or blender until smooth. Season with salt, pepper, and sugar, to taste, adding a little more vinegar if you wish. Serve the soup very hot, topped with the bacon and thyme leaves.

Pointed head cabbage with dill

Summer cabbages need very little treatment.
Eat with smoked or fried fish, *frikadeller*, or lamb.

2 pointed head
 cabbages, halved
¼ stick butter

1 bunch of dill, chopped
Salt and pepper
SERVES 4

Steam the cabbages in a saucepan with the butter and very little water. This will take only a few minutes. Once the cabbages become bright green and the second they no longer taste raw, remove them from the heat. Mix in the dill, add salt and pepper to taste, and serve.

TIP
• As an alternative to the above recipe, you can add generous ¾ cup smoked fresh cheese (page 16) to the cabbage in large blobs. Eat as an appetizer with toasted rye bread and maybe a piece of smoked fish.

Asparagus

Asparagus has always been an expensive treat, a vegetable for the rich, who could afford either to grow or to buy it. The average Scandinavian was too hard-working to have the time to cultivate asparagus, a slow and labor-intensive business. Green asparagus has been popular in Scandinavia for only 20 years or so, which is why all traditional recipes use the white version. White asparagus spears are the pale, fat queens of May and June, with a consistency so beautiful and a taste so refined that they must be truly unique among vegetables.

Appearance and taste Green asparagus tastes very much like a long, tender green pea. It has a delicious, fresh, and distinctly "green" taste. White asparagus, on the other hand, has a definite sweetness, paired with a slight bitterness, and a pervading flavor that spreads its loveliness over other foods that come into close contact: add it to a salad or stew and the dish will taste as though it consists of nothing else, a quality the white asparagus shares with artichokes.

How it grows The spears of wild asparagus, which can be found growing in sandy soils in southern Scandinavia, are very thin, and are even tastier than cultivated asparagus. White asparagus is grown widely in areas of sandy loam, though this is not easy. Asparagus is extremely time-consuming to grow, and a huge investment if you grow more than a few. The crowns must grow undisturbed for three to four years before they can be harvested, and after that you work from first light until noon for three months during the harvest in April, May, and June.

The paleness of white asparagus is achieved by excluding all light, which is done by piling up soil over the plants as they grow. All weeding must be done by hand, so as not to damage the still-invisible spears growing underground. When they are ready to harvest you venture into your asparagus patch very early in the morning with a sharp, long-handled tool to cut the spears before the sun's rays turn them green. It must be inserted at ground level, and you work blind, as only the very upper tip of the asparagus is poking through the soil.

Green asparagus is grown in flat fields and can be cut at any time of day, as long as it's every day because the spears grow at an alarming rate and are short and tender for only a day or two. If you miss the moment, they will be very long and tough.

Buying and storing Asparagus is pricey, but not irresponsibly so considering its growing conditions. You can buy relatively cheap white asparagus, which is too cumbersome to peel but perfect as a base for soup, and even big fat spears for much less than a mediocre, small piece of meat. The thickness of green asparagus is not important, but the white needs serious peeling, and if the spears are too thin there will be nothing left. Thin white asparagus tempts you to slack off when it comes to the peeling, and that is not a good idea. They can be used as they are for stock and are a good buy for that purpose, as thin spears are much cheaper.

When buying asparagus, the most important thing is to check for freshness. Begin by checking the bottoms (which are often wrapped) as the spears dry out from the bottom up. They must be freshly cut, and the whole stalk must be juicy and firm, without signs of wrinkled old age; and the heads should be tight and not beginning to stretch. If the spears are not fresh, don't buy them, even if they are cheap, as the taste alters with age and they will disappoint you. My advice is to limit yourself to buying asparagus only during their brief season in May and June, when you can gorge on them at their best and then long for them until the next season.

Asparagus can be stored wrapped in a clean damp dish towel in the refrigerator for no more than two days. If you are not going to use the peels straight away, they can be frozen and used for stock later.

Culinary uses Both types of asparagus are beautiful in stews, salads, or simply steamed and eaten with fish, as an appetizer, or veal, chicken, or smoked and salted meats. Remember always to add a little sugar to balance the bitterness of white asparagus.

Before you even consider cooking your white asparagus, the spears must be peeled. Rest them in your hand and peel from the head down. When you think you are done, try to bend the asparagus a little, and any traces of peel will show as long, shiny strands. It's heart-breaking to watch your asparagus shrink, but any trace of peel will be a nasty experience. Asparagus are extremely fibrous, and in the past you were forced to eat asparagus when you had swallowed a sharp item as the vegetable's fibers curl themselves around anything in your stomach, guiding it safely on its way out. (Nowadays, they give you cotton to eat instead.)

The woody ends and peel from white asparagus can do magic in the kitchen, in stocks, sauces, and vegetable stews: if you boil the peels in water, then add the cooking liquid to your dish, you will find a satisfying asparagus flavor that suits anything. The woody ends of green asparagus are also useful in stocks and soups.

Green asparagus can be eaten raw, but a fast blanching will make its flavor much more intense.

White asparagus must be cooked, but not for a second longer than necessary. A few minutes in the pot are enough. If you want to eat the asparagus whole, boil them in a wide, shallow saucepan with a little water, and the lid on, rather than in a huge pot of boiling water.

Asparagus soup

Asparagus soup used to be a Sunday special, and was often served as an appetizer at confirmations and weddings coinciding with the asparagus season. Serve with crusty sourdough bread.

18oz thin white asparagus	1 bay leaf
2 celery stalks	1 tablespoon coarse sea salt
1 bunch of new onions with the green tops	1 tablespoon black peppercorns
1 sprig of tarragon	1 tablespoon sugar
1 small bunch of chervil	Generous ¾ cup heavy cream
1 small bunch of parsley	1 small bunch of chives, chopped
Generous ¾ cup white wine	SERVES 4–5
4 cloves garlic, or a small bunch of ramsons (wild garlic)	

Rinse the asparagus and cut off the tips. Save the latter and chop the rest into small pieces. Rinse and chop the celery and onions, including the green part. Pick the leaves off the herbs and save for later.

Put the wine, garlic, bay leaf, salt, pepper, and sugar in a saucepan along with the vegetables and herb stalks. Boil slowly until the vegetables are very soft. Fish out the bay leaf, then purée the soup in a food processor until smooth. Push through a fine sieve, making sure that only inedible fiber is left in the sieve.

Reheat the soup with the cream and reserved asparagus tips, and adjust the seasoning. Serve with the reserved herb leaves and the chopped chives on top.

Asparagus salad with new potatoes

This salad makes fat white asparagus go a long way. The combination of chives and chervil is pure magic with asparagus. Serve lukewarm or cooled.

1lb 10oz white asparagus

18oz small new potatoes

2 bunches of chives

1 bunch of chervil

4–5 tablespoons sherry vinegar

6 tablespoons olive oil

1 tablespoon coarse sea salt

1 tablespoon sugar

½ teaspoon ground black pepper

4 eggs, boiled for 5 minutes, peeled (optional)

SERVES 4–5

Rinse and peel the asparagus, cut off the tips, and slice the rest into ¾in pieces. Rinse the potatoes and boil in salted water until just tender. Remove with a slotted spoon and set aside, then place the asparagus into the water. Boil for 2 minutes, then remove (saving the water to make a vegetable soup).

Chop the herbs finely and save half for the garnish. Mix the rest of the herbs with the vinegar, oil, salt, sugar, and pepper, then fold into the warm vegetables; adjust the seasoning, if necessary. Halve the eggs and decorate the salad with them (if you like), along with the reserved herbs.

Peas

Peas, a delicacy loved by everyone, have always had a special place in our culinary hearts. Arguably, this is no longer the case with the advent of frozen peas: these are almost as good, but not quite, so it's hard to get excited over the small, but important, difference. But when you do find the perfect fresh pea, that is the moment you realize the small difference, which makes the time-consuming task of shelling peas very much worthwhile. Fresh peas, simply prepared, have the most exquisite taste—maybe it's the rare taste of human effort.

History Peas are one of the most ancient crops that man has grown: 10,000 years is an almost incomprehensibly vast span of time. Cultivation began in the fertile crescent of the Middle East, as with so many other crops, including barley, wheat, lentils, and garbanzo beans. Dried peas are good travelers, and hardier than other legumes, and we know

that peas had reached Scandinavia by the late Stone Age and have been grown here ever since.

The first peas were meant for drying, and they are still part of northern tradition. Any pea can be dried and we have ancient cultivars that are not very good to eat as they are: immature, bitter, and mealy, as in most of the Old World, but are perfect for drying. The oldest peas, found in tombs, are much the same as the field peas, meant for fodder, that we grow now. There is no evidence that peas were eaten fresh, but children probably ate fresh peas from the pod, just as they do now, scraping them from the shells with their teeth. Peas are perfect partners for wheat: when combined, they provide almost the complete protein, and man must have known then that you could survive on this, if meat was scarce. During the 17th century, pea cultivars were gradually improved, to become the large-podded and large-seeded shelling cultivars we grow today; they were, and are, a colossal improvement.

Appearance and taste Dried peas last almost indefinitely. The only difference is that old peas, from previous growing seasons, take longer to cook than more recently dried ones. Yellow split peas and green split peas are what you are after, in the Scandinavian context. Very similar versions can be found in Indian shops.

Fresh green peas are a different matter; their high sugar content is their reason for being, and this is converted into starch as they mature. Just 24 hours after picking, most of the sugar has gone. If you want fresh, sweet, tender green peas, you must grow your own or buy them at farmers' markets, freshly picked.

Culinary uses While our stock of recipes that feature peas is relatively small, the ones that we have are simple, good, and satisfying. Tender, fresh peas are best simply heated in butter until they turn frog green, then seasoned with salt, pepper, and garlic; in the right season, adding handfuls of chopped ramsons (wild garlic) instead of clove garlic is very good. Peas are important in *tarteletter* (page 144), and in our so-called Italian salad. Older peas can be fine for cooking, too, as in the recipe for chicken with peas, on page 174. Dried peas are the basis of winter soups, or are simply mashed with butter and thyme.

Mashed peas with goat cheese and horseradish

This recipe makes use of peas that are not quite as sweet as they could be. It tastes delicious with fish of any kind, or salted lamb.

3½ cups shelled peas	Black pepper
½ stick salted butter	A little lemon juice
⅓ cup goat cheese	2in piece of fresh
3 cloves garlic	horseradish, shredded
1 tablespoon coarse sea salt	SERVES 4

Heat the peas with a little water until they turn bright green; if the peas are tough, you may need to boil them for longer. Drain them, then mash in a food processor with the butter, garlic, and goat cheese, until they turn into a creamy mash. Season with salt, pepper, and lemon juice, to taste. Serve hot with a heap of finely shredded horseradish on top.

Italian salad

The name of this recipe probably comes from the green peas, reddish carrots, and white asparagus, but in Italy the same salad is called *insalata russa*... Names aside, it's extremely popular and, if homemade, it's delicious. We eat it with ham, tongue, and other salted meats, as a topping on open-face sandwiches.

1 bundle of green or	Lemon juice
white asparagus	Salt and freshly ground
4 baby carrots	black pepper
1½ cups freshly shelled peas	A little sugar
Generous ⅓ cup cider vinegar	1 handful of cress or
Generous ⅓ cup crème fraîche	nasturtium flowers
1 tablespoon Dijon mustard	SERVES 4

Snap off the woody bottom part of the asparagus and cut the rest into ¾in pieces. If using white asparagus, they must be peeled. Peel the carrots and cut into small dice. Steam all the vegetables in the vinegar and generous ¾ cup boiling water for 2 minutes. Drain and cool.

Mix the crème fraîche, mustard, and lemon juice to a smooth sauce and season to taste with the salt, pepper, and sugar. Mix with the vegetables and decorate with the cress or nasturtiums before serving.

Winter pea soup with bacon

This is a denser, more filling, and creamier winter soup than the recipe opposite. You can expand the concept by serving the soup with a plate of sausage or ham, and a batch of steamed vegetables; this will make an easier version of *gule ærter*, the classic yellow split pea soup.

2 cups dried split yellow	5 cloves garlic
or green peas	1 small bunch of fresh
2¼lb mixed vegetables, e.g.	thyme
carrots, celeriac, leek, and	2 bay leaves
parsnip	1 sprig of fresh marjoram
6–8 cups water	Generous ¾ cup cream
2 cups vegetable, pork,	Scant 1½ cups shelled fresh
or chicken stock, or the	or frozen green peas
cooking liquid from a	2 tablespoons butter
piece of salted and/or	Salt and pepper
smoked meat	Chives, to garnish
7oz bacon, in one piece	SERVES 10

Soak the dried peas in water for at least 8 hours, then drain. Rinse and peel the vegetables and cut into chunks.

In a large saucepan, simmer the dried peas in the water

and stock with the vegetables, bacon, and herbs until tender. Take out the bacon, rinse it under the cold faucet and cut into small dice, then fry in its own fat until golden and crispy. Purée the rest of the cooked ingredients in a food processor with the cream until smooth, and return to the pan.

Heat the fresh peas in the butter until very green—they must not cook, or they will turn brown. Purée until smooth in the food processor, then mix into the soup. If it is very thick, you can add some whole milk or more stock. Season with salt and pepper

Serve with the crispy bacon and chives on top.

Summer pea soup with horseradish cream

The horseradish cream adds a bit of bite, necessary for the otherwise very sweet peas. Serve with crusty bread.

2 new onions (with the green tops)
2 cloves garlic
Scant tablespoon coarse sea salt
1 teaspoon black peppercorns
1 sprig of thyme
1 sprig of mint
¼ stick butter
2 cups strong chicken, fish, or vegetable stock, or

the cooking liquid from a piece of salted meat
2¾ cups shelled green peas
A little lemon juice
for the horseradish cream
4 tablespoons grated fresh horseradish
4 tablespoons crème fraîche
SERVES 4

Rinse the onions and cut into large pieces. Over a low heat, let the onions, garlic, salt, pepper, and herbs sweat in the butter, in a large saucepan, until translucent; do not let the onions brown. Add the stock and let simmer until the onions are very tender. Add the peas and bring to a boil. Remove the thyme and purée the soup in a food processor until smooth.

While the soup is cooking, you can mix the horseradish and crème fraîche, and season with salt and pepper. Let rest for a while, and adjust the seasoning; you may need to add more horseradish.

Season the soup with salt, pepper, and enough lemon juice to balance the sweetness of the peas. Serve the soup with a blob of the horseradish cream.

Cucumber

Culinary uses There are not many ways to prepare cucumber. It's a favorite topping for liver paste on rye bread or is used in salads, often with dill. It can also be pickled in different ways, with more dill, and a few slices of horseradish, making the most of both the sharp taste and amazing preserving qualities of horseradish.

Sweet-and-sour cucumber salad

Preserved in a vinegary marinade, this salad will keep for several weeks in the refrigerator. Eat it on open-face sandwiches, with chicken, *frikadeller* or sausages.

Generous ⅓ cup water
Generous ⅓ cup cider vinegar
4 tablespoons sugar
I tablespoon coarse sea salt

I teaspoon coarsely ground
   black pepper
2 small cucumbers
SERVES 4

Put the water, vinegar, and seasonings in a saucepan and bring to a boil. Meanwhile, slice the cucumbers finely (with the peel on), then place in a bowl. Pour over the boiling marinade and let cool before serving.

Pickled asiers with dill flowers

In their pickled form, asiers are eaten with just about every kind of meat, and in open-face sandwiches, particularly in combination with liver paste. Their popularity dates from a time when pickled vegetables were all you had in winter, apart from kale and potatoes, so you simply ate them, or beets, with every meal. The asier's long-lasting place in northern folks' affections stems from its crunchiness and refreshing taste.

Of course, if you don't have access to asiers proper, you can use ordinary overgrown cucumbers, preferably the prickly outdoor cultivars, or very large pickling cucumbers. This recipe makes a large quantity, designed for old-school households; if you don't want to keep it all for yourself, the jars of pickled cucumbers make a lovely present.

Until about 40 years ago, cucumbers were eaten only in late spring and summer. The arrival of the first cucumbers was awaited with eagerness, a feeling now reserved only for the very first new potatoes. The watery cucumbers that we buy in their plastic sarcophagi all year round cannot be compared to the freshly picked summer cucumbers that are sweet, heavy, and crisp, with a much lower water content and much more taste. Cucumbers have been known and grown in the north for a very long time, and have found their place both fresh as salad greens and pickled. They match the favorite herbs dill and horseradish, whichever way you choose to prepare them.

How it grows Most cucumbers in Scandinavia are grown in greenhouses, and many people grow their own.

Appearance and taste Most of our cultivars are the same as in the rest of the world, except for the asier, a Nordic cultivar which is a very large, thick, fleshy, and thick-skinned cucumber. It is filled with inedible hard seeds, and is used only for pickling, while still green. If it is successfully pickled it will be extremely crisp, and is used in the same way as pickled gherkins and cucumbers.

11lb asiers, or other large cucumbers
1½ cups coarse sea salt
3 tablespoons yellow mustard seeds
10 small dried chiles
6 bay leaves
10 fresh dill flowers
1¼lb pickling onions, peeled
3oz fresh horseradish, peeled and thinly sliced
10 cups sugar
8½pt cider vinegar

Peel, halve, and core the cucumbers, preferably using a silver spoon for the coring as it helps the cucumbers' preservation qualities. Put them in a large bowl and sprinkle over the salt. Let sit overnight.

In the morning, discard the salt/brine and dry the cucumbers with a cloth. Thinly slice and layer in sterilized earthenware or glass jars along with the spices, dill flowers, onions, and horseradish. Boil the sugar and vinegar together until the sugar is dissolved, then pour it over the cucumbers while still piping hot. Close the jars, using a small sterilized plate to keep the cucumbers submerged. Then cover with plastic wrap, or use old-fashioned waxed paper and string. Leave for 1 week, then eat, but always use a sterilized fork to take the cucumbers out of the jar.

Mustard-dill-cucumber pickle

A spicy but fresh and long-lasting pickle to make when the cucumbers are abundant in summer. It's perfect with sausages, roast pork, on open-face sandwiches and with fish and fish patties.

The long peppers are a traditional ingredient in all kinds of pickled stuff —they have a delicious aroma.

6lb 8oz fresh, green ridge cucumbers
2¼lb onions
1 large bunch of fresh dill
for the pickle
7oz yellow mustard seeds
4½ cups sugar
3¼ cups cider vinegar
⅓ cup coarse salt
1 tablespoon black
peppercorns
1 star anise
1 teaspoon juniper berries
1 dried red chile
10 long peppers *Piper longum* (optional)
2 fresh bay leaves
1 tablespoon coriander seeds, preferably fresh
MAKES 8 JARS

Boil the mustard seeds in plenty of water for 5 minutes, drain in a fine sieve, and then wash in cold water.

Bring all the ingredients for the pickle to a boil, simmer for 5 minutes, and cool.

Wash the cucumbers and grate rather coarsely with the peel on, unless it's unusually tough. Grate the onions. Let vegetables drain in a colander. Pluck the leaves from the dill and chop the stalks medium-fine. Combine the vegetables with the pickle and dill. Put into sterilized jars, seal, and store in a cool place.

Beets

The color alone is enough to make you want to eat beets—the tint of pure health and wholesomeness. It's the how that keeps us from using them more, because they are not part of the daily diet in Scandinavia, unless pickled. The pleasure of eating well-prepared fresh beets comes as a surprise to most people, particularly if they are used only to the pickled kind. Sweet, juicy, new beets are becoming more popular—and increasingly available to buy.

But maybe it's best that the vegetable remains an occasional pleasure. Overuse of beets can make you tired of them; the best thing is to make not quite enough, so you are not faced with overwhelming amounts of beets to work your way through. Eat them once in a while, as you would Jerusalem artichokes or parsnips, to keep it special.

History Beets (and later sugar beet) were, according to common Latin, selected by the Romans from the wild beet that still grows on shores all over northern Europe. They selected them for root size, and the beets that resulted came in an impressive array of colors—anything but blue. They were mainly used for their medicinal qualities, not for food, until they reached northern Europe and Russia in the 1600s. But some evidence suggests that they were in fact developed by the ancient Egyptians, and I think this is true as they grow marvelous beets in Egypt—soccer ball-size but tender,

and they have the deepest coloring of all. And the Egyptians have a lively tradition of eating them, as do the people that they were in contact with in antiquity.

How it grows Smallholders and gardeners grow beets because they must be one of the least demanding crops: they grow quickly, grow well in cool conditions, and can tolerate any soil. Furthermore, given the confetti-like range of colors now available, they are simply too much fun not to grow—or eat for that matter. Beet plants look good wherever you put them, and the red-leaved varieties are wonderfully ornamental in a border.

Appearance and taste Beets have an intense, metallic, and earthy flavor, very sweet and satisfying. The taste varies according to the variety and color, and round beets are much less stringy than the oblong varieties. All sorts of less common varieties are now available as seed and at good food stores: white beets that look—and taste—more like turnips; the Italian *barbietole di Chioggia*, with internal candy stripes as fresh that turn orange when cooked; the yellow-fleshed varieties that actually taste more like corn kernels, or the flat, extremely dark Egyptian versions with a deep carmine color. The more colored, the more intense the taste. The leaves can be used like spinach, and young people enjoy cooking both the leaves and roots a lot more than older generations.

Heath benefits The color of red-fleshed beets is brimming with betanine, a water-soluble coloring that colors your urine blood-red, which can be a real scare for the unsuspecting beet-eater. Natural coloring boosts your immune system, and beets are full of antioxidants, minerals, trace elements, different B vitamins, and iron.

Culinary uses There are some delicious ways to eat beets. From Russia and Germany we have inherited the tradition of pairing beets with dill, crème fraîche, horseradish, and vinegar. The northern touch is to use fresh smoked cheese (page 150) and caraway seeds, both of which give the roots an extra kick.

Beets' sweetness are their great strength, and also their weak point; you have to work with beets to make them really good, to pair them with something acidic, sharp, or hot to match the sweetness, and something creamy to balance its earthy solidity. If you have sweet and juicy young beets, eat them simply, turned in butter and lemon juice, or with grated horseradish and sour cream.

Beets' cooking time depends on the freshness and the cultivar.

Beet terrine with horseradish

This terrine is a beautiful thing in all its trembling, deep purple glory, and a more challenging alternative to a simple beet salad. Its sweetness is a perfect match for soused fish, smoked meat or fish, or salted fish roes. Using the liquid from boiling smoked or salted meats gives the terrine a lightly smoky flavor, but it can live without it. You can even make the terrine with a vegetable stock, as long as it's intensely flavored. The terrine is good in a sandwich with thin slices of smoked meat or fish. However you eat it, it tastes great with a dollop of horseradish cream (page 179).

3 bunches of new beets (approx. 2lb 12oz)
8 cups liquid from boiling smoked, or salted meat, or stock
4 sprigs of fresh thyme
4 shallots
10 leaves of gelatin
Salt and pepper
2 tablespoons cider vinegar
2 bunches of dill, chopped
2¼in piece of fresh horseradish, to garnish

SERVES 10–12

To make this recipe you will need a loaf pan measuring 3x3x8in, and also some plastic wrap.

Rinse the beets, and set aside three. Bake the rest at 325°F until tender. The time depends on the freshness and the variety. Once they have cooled, peel and cut into ½in slices.

Meanwhile, bring the stock to a boil with the thyme and shallots, and let the liquid reduce by half, removing any scum that rises to the surface. Strain through a piece of cheesecloth, or clean dish cloth, and let cool. Remove any fat from the surface.

Juice the raw beets, either in a juicer, or by grating them finely and then wringing in a dish cloth (which will be a lovely deep purplish color forever after).

Line the loaf pan with plastic wrap, allowing a surplus of 4in all around, hanging over the edges. Soak the gelatin in cold water for 5 minutes, then melt in a little of the stock in a small saucepan, before whisking it into the rest of the stock. Mix with the fresh beet juice. Season with salt, pepper, and a little vinegar to sharpen.

Place a layer of beet slices as tightly as possible in the bottom of the loaf pan, scatter over a little dill, and repeat the same layers until the pan is full. Pour over the liquid to cover, bang the pan against the counter to remove any air pockets, and fold the plastic wrap over the top. Cool overnight to set.

There will probably be surplus liquid, in which case you can put it in a plastic wrap-covered dish to set. This jelly can be chopped and used to decorate the terrine.

Beet salad with fresh smoked cheese

This salad is a beautiful thing to serve with fish, fish roes, smoked meats, or as part of a buffet. If the smoked cheese is not available, a very good and very fresh sheep's milk ricotta will do, or alternatively a homemade, drained junket (page 21).

4 medium beets	1 tablespoon cider vinegar
1 bunch of dill	2 cloves garlic, minced
for the cream	1 tablesoon sugar
5½oz fresh smoked cheese	Salt and pepper
½ cup Greek yogurt	
3 tablespoons mayonnaise	SERVES 4

Clean the beets well, then bake at 325°F until tender. Let cool. Meanwhile, mix together the ingredients for the cream, seasoning to taste.

Peel the beets and grate them coarsely, then mix with the cream. Serve, garnished with dill.

TIP
• An alternative method to make this salad is to slice the beets very thinly rather than grate them. Spread the slices in a thin layer on a large dish, then drizzle over a marinade made of 3 tablespoons olive oil, ½ teaspoon coarse sea salt and 2 tablespoons cider vinegar. Spoon the cream on top and decorate with dill.

Pickled beets
with cardamom

6lb 8oz beets

for the pickle

3 tablespoons coarse
   sea salt

8 cups cider vinegar

4 cups sugar

1 tablespoon whole green
   cardamom pods

1 cinnamon stick

1 tablespoon whole allspice

3 bay leaves

4 tablespoons mustard
   seeds

2 tablespoons black
   peppercorns

1 sprig of fresh thyme

to finish

4in horseradish, cut in
   thin slices

Boil the beets in plenty of water until almost tender.
Rub off the skins, and cut into chunks or slices. Put into
sterilized jars.

   Boil the pickle ingredients and pour over the beets.
Take care to distribute the spices evenly in the jars. If there
is not enough pickle to cover the beets, fill up the jars with
boiling water. Distribute the horseradish on top, then put
the lids on.

   The beets can be eaten straight away, but will improve in
a couple of days. The pickle will keep for 3 months.

Beet salad with apple
and caraway seeds

The salad is extremely good, interesting from the spices,
and nice with pork, wild boar, fish, or as an appetizer
with bread and a slice of cold smoked fish.

1¼lb beets

2 hand-eating apples, not
   too sweet

1 tablespoon caraway seeds

Plenty of flat-leaf parsley,
   chopped

for the dressing

5 tablespoons extra-virgin
   olive oil

Scant ¼ cup apple gastric
   (see Tip)

2 tablespoons cider vinegar

1 tablespoon coarse sea
   salt, maybe more

Rinse the beets and boil until tender, then peel and cut into
medium-size dice. Core, but do not peel, the apples, and cut
into similar-size dice.

Combine the dressing ingredients and mix with the beet
and apple. Toast the caraway seeds in a dry skillet until they
jump, then grind to a fine powder. Scatter this and the
chopped parsley over the salad and serve.

TIP
- Apple gastric is a very useful concoction, intended to give
flavor and sweet acidity to any dish that needs it. To make
it, you simply boil together 2 cups unfiltered apple juice
with 1¼ cups cider vinegar until syrupy; pour it into a small
bottle, add a sprig of fresh rosemary and keep it handy on
your kitchen counter.

Potatoes

Potatoes are the soul of Nordic cooking. They are eaten with almost every meal, and accompany anything traditional. You would think that, given such culinary success, they have been here for ages, but in fact potatoes have been eaten in Scandinavia for only 200 years. Before that, they were known but regarded with great suspicion: potatoes are a member of the nightshade family, and it was hard for the authorities to convince the public that they were edible. When finally people were convinced, everybody grew and ate them; as well as being a crop that protected people against famine, potatoes were relatively easy to grow on the extremely stony ground of much of Scandinavia.

Most importantly perhaps, people soon realized that potatoes fitted beautifully with all the core elements of Nordic cooking—fish, butter, cream, herbs, apples, and onions. Everything tasted much nicer with potatoes than with the hot oatmeal, hard bread, pea mash, and parsnips that were eaten before the potato became the staple.

Nowhere is the potato cherished as much as it is in the north, where the year's new potatoes are awaited with great excitement. The first new potatoes of the year are auctioned at sky-high prices and the event is even published in the papers. Local people hunt the potatoes down from numerous road stalls with rickety signs or from the stores—supplies frequently run out by noon, despite the often ridiculous prices.

Appearance and taste Many Scandinavians grow potatoes in their gardens just to enjoy the exquisite taste of very young, new potatoes. Freshly dug new potatoes are a national passion. Mothers teach their children the only truthful indication that potatoes have been newly dug: when you rub your fingers against the flaky skin it must come off in one stroke, revealing a moist, mother-of-pearl sheen to the flesh.

We have many Nordic cultivars; some are in constant use, while others are kept in the Nordic gene bank, from where anyone can order a few spuds and help to keep the regional potato heritage alive. (This gene bank, which administers seeds of 30,000 Nordic plants and cultivars, is kept both in southern Sweden and in a secure storage bank on the Arctic islands of Svalbard.)

There are specific cultivars for new potatoes, and potatoes for winter use. New potatoes have a much higher water content and are best boiled. Starchy winter potatoes have numerous uses, as mash, baked, fried, or oven-cooked wedges, making use of their starchiness. Special, waxy salad potatoes are also available. In reality, you must love what you can get as the number of cultivars available in the stores is very few. If you want to eat old, tasty cultivars, or potatoes for a specific use, you must grow your own, or go to a farmers' market.

Buying and storing New potatoes are supposed to be bought fresh every day, while old potatoes can be stored, as long as they are kept cool and out of the light. The refrigerator is not ideal as it is much too humid. Instead, use a crock with a lid kept in a cool, frost-free place. In spring, all potatoes tend to sprout, sending out long pale shoots if kept in the dark. As long as the sprouts are small and the potato is not too wrinkled, it is fine to eat. A partial sprinkling of black spots on the skin are harmless scabs which you can remove with a good scrub.

Damaged, green (or partly green) potatoes should not be eaten. The green could indicate that the level of toxic solanine is high, even if this is not always the case. It's not good enough to cut off the green patches. Potatoes provide plenty of starch, relatively high levels of vitamins, and also good protein.

Culinary uses It's important to remember the different qualities of seasonal potatoes and the variations of how to serve potatoes year round reflect this.

In Scandinavia, when new potatoes are in season they are the most important part of the everyday meal.

Roles are reversed for a short time, meat and fish becoming the accompaniments to the potatoes, temporarily the stars of the dinner show. A salty-sweet *matjes* herring, chives, and dill, and a blob of crème fraîche, or a few slices of bacon, butter, and dill, are all you need for dinner until the new potatoes become old news, by which time the magic is gone, and potatoes assume their traditional, accompanying role.

Even though pasta and rice are becoming the everyday starch in many northern families, potatoes remain a vital part of Scandinavian cooking. Many open-face sandwiches are unthinkable without potatoes. Maybe the most popular *smørrebrød* is a piece of buttered rye bread, boiled, sliced new or even old potatoes, chives, homemade lemony mayonnaise, and perhaps a slice of bacon. And then of course there's the eternal classic—rye bread with potatoes, various herrings, dill, and onion.

Caramelized potatoes

These potatoes are a truly Scandinavian specialty. They accompany the traditional Christmas dinner, and are also very good with many cabbage and pork dishes, including creamed kale and fried sausages. Caramelized potatoes were originally prepared by poor people in the 19th century, in an attempt to copy the roasted chestnuts eaten by the bourgeoisie. And a very good copy they are, too—delicious and very easy to prepare. Often they are served with a similar portion of plain boiled potatoes, to suit everybody.

2lb 12oz small, round, red or new potatoes, unpeeled	8 tablespoons sugar
	⅔ cup water
	¼ stick salted butter
1 tablespoon coarse sea salt	SERVES 4–5

Boil the potatoes in heavily salted water until they are almost done; they must still be a little hard in the middle. Cool a little, then peel, and set aside.

Melt the sugar in a heavy-bottomed saucepan large enough to accommodate the potatoes in a single layer. Take care not to burn the sugar. When you have a light caramel, pour in the water and take even more care as it will splutter.

The sugar will harden to begin with, but after a while will dissolve. At this point add in the potatoes and butter and leave to simmer, turning the potatoes in the caramel from time to time. When the water has evaporated, the potatoes will be beautifully covered with caramel. The potatoes must be eaten while warm; reheating them is not a good idea.

Burning love

How this dish ever got its name, I have no idea. It's far too filling to get you in the mood, but it's very satisfying in other ways, and a cheap, comforting dish in its own right.

1 quantity caramelized onions (page 77)	**for the mashed potatoes**
for the baked apples	3lb 5oz russet potatoes
4 hand-eating apples	⅓ cup butter
4 tablespoons sugar	Generous ¾ cup whole milk
20 slices of bacon	Salt and pepper
	SERVES 4–6

Quarter the apples and remove the core, then arrange in an ovenproof dish. Sprinkle the sugar on top and turn the apples to coat. Arrange the bacon slices on top. Bake in the oven at 400°F until the apples are tender and the bacon is crispy.

Rinse and peel the potatoes; if they are large, cut into slices. Boil in unsalted water until completely tender, then drain, keeping some of the water. Mash the potatoes with the butter, milk, and black pepper, using a balloon whisk. If the mash is too dense, add some of the cooking water. Salt at the last moment, to avoid glueyness.

Heap up the mashed potato on a pretty dish to form a Norwegian mountain, then arrange the apples, bacon, and onions around the base, and let a piece of butter melt down the peak.

Dill creamed potatoes

This is a very Swedish summer dish, the traditional accompaniment for rimmad lax, which is like gravad lax but without the dill (which is included in the potatoes instead). With potatoes rather than bread as the accompaniment, the salmon is turned into a more substantial dinner or lunch dish. A green salad is good with it. The dill potatoes are also perfect for other fish, for all kinds of salted or cured pork, and for sausage.

2¼lb small new potatoes
Salt and pepper
Generous ¾ cup heavy cream
1 large bunch of dill, chopped
SERVES 4

Scrub the flaky skin off the potatoes with a handful of coarse salt—the easiest way to get most of the skin off new potatoes. Put them in the sink, and rub the wet potatoes until most of the peel is gone, then wash. They don't have to be totally free of peel.

Boil in salted water until half done. Drain. Put the potatoes in a wide saucepan with the cream, salt, and pepper, and let simmer until the cream has reduced and the potatoes are done. Add the dill at the last moment.

Warm potato salad

This salad used to be a weekly treat, and now it seems to be extinct. It's in need of a revival, because for all its simplicity it's one of the most delicious and comforting potato dishes. It tastes good with anything you would eat with mustard.

1¼lb small new or red
  potatoes
Salt and freshly ground
  black pepper
1 onion, chopped
½ stick butter

1 tablespoon sugar
4 tablespoons cider vinegar
1 small bunch of parsley
  and/or chives, chopped
SERVES 4

Boil the potatoes in salted water until almost done. Peel them while warm, then cut into halves or thick slices, according to size.

Sweat the onion in the butter in a heavy-bottomed saucepan, until transparent. Add the sugar and vinegar and let simmer until most of the vinegar has evaporated. Put in the potatoes and heat through, turning them over so that they absorb the vinegar and butter, but not too much—they must not break up. Scatter with the herbs and serve.

Rutabaga

This large, round root, a subspecies of the cabbage family, is known as swede in England, and neep in Scotland. It's called *kålrabi* or *kålrot* in much of Scandinavia, which is confusing to foreigners because it sounds similar to kohlrabi, the name for German turnip, which is a very different vegetable, with swollen root stems. The name swede is an abbreviation of "Swedish turnip," the name indicating this root's origins.

Rutabaga is one of the hardiest of all root crops and is the perfect winter vegetable for the cool climates of northern Scandinavia, where it is immensely popular and widely grown. Traditionally, it has less of a following in southern Scandinavia, though with the growing demand for local, seasonal vegetables its popularity is on the rise.

How it grows Rutabaga are easy and undemanding to grow, like huge beets, and mature in October.

Appearance and taste A rutabaga can be up to 8in in diameter, and is usually a purple-green color on the outside and yellow-fleshed inside. Basically, the rutabaga is a large turnip, though it tastes very different. The sweet, nondescript flavor, somewhere between cabbage and potato, is nothing like the taste of the crisp-fleshed, spring-grown turnip. As a vehicle for butter, the rutabaga is perfect, and its soft texture and mildness are inviting in a comfortable, undemanding way, particularly for kids.

Culinary uses Rutabaga is often prepared with potatoes as a mash, thick soup, or gratin, but is versatile enough to be included in any dish calling for mixed root vegetables; mixing it with mashed celeriac and potatoes makes a nice change. As with all sweet-fleshed roots, you need to balance the rutabaga's bland sweetness: salt, chile, lemon, horseradish, herbs, vinegar, ginger, and butter are all good additions. A plain dish of "bashed neeps" (mashed rutabaga) with mace and butter goes well with any succulent Scandinavian stew.

Bashed neeps

Bashed neeps are a traditional accompaniment to the Norwegian *pinneköt*—salted and smoked ribs of mutton served at Christmas—but work well with any meat. This is a big quantity, but you might as well make it while you are at it, and turn leftovers into a crispy gratin, dusted with Parmesan or *Västerbottenost*, bread crumbs, and butter, the next day.

2¼lb rutabaga	1 teaspoon ground mace
2¼lb russet or Idaho potatoes	1½ tablespoons coarse sea salt
2 cups warm milk	1 teaspoon ground black pepper
Scant ½ cup salted butter	

Peel and dice the vegetables, then boil separately in plenty of unsalted water. Mash the potatoes and rutabaga together, with the milk, butter, mace, and pepper. Reserve the salt for when the roots are all mashed, as it will make the consistency gluey if added at the beginning.

Root cellars

Storing was a great concern for all our forefathers; to keep food for many winter months without it decaying, safe from rodents and scavengers and, further north, from frosts. It was ingeniously done for centuries in beautiful root cellars, dug into the ground, often into a hillside, so you would not have to dig so deep, and to facilitate entering. They could be anything from a hole in the ground to a walk-in "cupboard" lined with stones like a burial chamber, with shelves and boxes of all you needed to take your family safely through to the next summer.

Root vegetables, cabbages, and apples were stored so deep in the ground that frosts could not reach them, and the natural humidity of the soil would keep them fresh until the new crops of vegetables were ready to eat. It was a perfect, energy-saving system, which the modern food industry tries to copy using loads of unnecessary energy.

Salsify & scorzonera

Salsify and scorzonera and are not very much in use today, but were formerly an important part of bourgeois cooking. They have a special buttery texture and a pleasant taste reminiscent of mache. Found wild, as escapees from cultivation, they are not indigenous to Scandinavia. They belong to a huge genus, and other plants from it are eaten in similar ways elsewhere.

How it grows Salsify has beautiful purple blooms, opening in the morning and closing by noon; scorzonera is similar, but with bright yellow flowers. They are generally grown as annuals, for their roots, but can be grown on as perennials, just for the leaves. It's an art to grow the fine roots to perfection, as their extremely long, fragile roots need a very deep loam. They are, however, extremely hardy, and can even be harvested the spring after they are sown; or you can choose to use the young tuft of leaves and shoots for a salad.

Appearance and taste Scorzonera can be 3¼ft long, and up to ¾in thick, with a pitch-black, strangely dry skin. Salsify is paler and only 10in long. Both have a high content of inulin, a sugar that will trick your taste buds into believing that anything you eat and drink with them is extremely sweet. The taste is very different from other roots, as they are not sweet, and seldom mealy, but retain their shape, and certain juiciness when cooked. They have a deliciousness not found in other roots, which is done justice by the recipe opposite. The roots'

taste is a little like a day at the beach, and in fact salsify is sometimes known as oyster plant. Actually, the oyster taste is much more prominent in young borage leaves, hence its inclusion in the oystered vegetables.

Buying and storing Both must be freshly dug, with no soft spots, and must not be bendable. They can, however, be restored in cold water. They keep for a long time wrapped in wet newspaper in the refrigerator.

Culinary uses Both go well in soups, pies, salads, baked, in a gratin, or marinated, but they are not good raw, or boiled and mashed.

Both salsify and scorzonera secrete a white rubbery substance, which will turn red and taint anything it touches. Handle them with gloves, and put the roots in a bowl of cold water with a drop of lemon juice, the second you have peeled them.

Oystered vegetables

If you like the idea of eating mollusks, but do not dare to eat them raw, this will be a gentle way of introducing them. Six oysters will go a long way, their intense sea flavor spreading over a seabed of vegetables.

2¼lb mussels	**for the cooking liquid**
1lb 10oz scorzonera or salsify (cleaned weight)	2 cups hard cider
Salt	2 tablespoons sherry or cider vinegar
6 oysters	1 large sprig of thyme
Scant ½ cup butter	4–5 red onions, quartered
1 bunch of very young borage leaves, chopped	4–5 cloves garlic, sliced
1 bunch of flat-leaf parsley, chopped	1 teaspooon black peppercorns
	SERVES 6 AS AN APPETIZER

Boil the cooking liquid for 5 minutes in a large saucepan.

Rinse the mussels and discard any that will not close, or are broken. Put them into the pan and steam until they open, which will take just a few minutes. Lift them out with a slotted spoon, together with the onions, and set aside, discarding any which are still closed. Remove half of the shell of each mussel if you have the time.

Try scraping the bottom of the pan. If it feels like there is sand in it, pour off the liquid, very gently, leaving the sand behind. Wash the pan, then pour the liquid back in and continue. Bring the liquid back to a boil and reduce to almost nothing. Peel the roots and cut into bite-size pieces. Boil until almost tender in salted water, then keep warm.

Shuck the oysters with a blunt knife, wearing thick gloves. Save every drop of the juice inside them. Chop the oysters. Whisk the butter into the sauce, and stir in the roots, mussels, oysters, and juice from the oysters. Season with salt if necessary. Serve with the chopped herbs.

Celeriac

Celeriac has been known in Scandinavia for centuries, but has been used sparingly, mostly as a flavoring for soups and stews. The root is not widely eaten anywhere else, except in France.

Celeriac is too strong-flavored to become a universal favorite, and it is rarely eaten on its own, but for those of us who love it, celeriac is a marvel, and we do not mind if it is served as the main vegetable. However, many don't love it, particularly children. Adults share childhood memories of how clear soup with all the unbelievably nasty pieces of celeriac floating among the diced carrots and leeks was the scare of the week. The carrot and leek were acceptable, and edible, but the celeriac was considered nothing but a punishment. Even worse were the celeriac "steaks," a slab of boiled, breaded, and fried celeriac that health-conscious housewives believed to be good for you.

How it grows In other parts of the world, a similar taste is achieved by celery, or the herb parsley-celery, or par-cel, which is actually the ancestor of them both.

They are all biennials, and umbellifers, like carrots, and will flower in their second year. The celeriac has been selected for its swollen roots, over millennia, and looks very much like celery when growing, except that part of the root grows above ground and most growers will mulch the roots to keep them pale. The leaves of celeriac taste like celery, only much stronger, and are very useful as a pot herb, or chopped like parsley and scattered over winter dishes.

Celeriac is a greedy feeder, and must be sown indoors in February, as it grows extremely slowly.

Appearance and taste The taste of celeriac is so overwhelming that it is often used more like a herb than a root. Its flavor a cross between that of celery and a parsley root, with overtones of parsley leaves and lovage. The root can be used in any size, from tennis-ball to monumental soccerball; like other roots, a very young, small celeriac is the most delicate and tender. The roots have a tendency to become spongy in the middle, due to a lack of minerals while growing, so choose one that is very firm and heavy, with no soft spots. They keep forever wrapped in plastic in the refrigerator.

Culinary uses Celeriac is used as a flavoring in stews, soups, and braises; celery adds a similar, but milder flavor, though celery is seldom used in Scandinavia. Celeriac can also be mashed and made into fries and gratins, because of its starchy nature. Try a 50:50 potato-celeriac mash, or include it as part of a mixed root bake.

When raw, celeriac has a delicate, nutty taste and, if very finely diced, it's beautiful in a salad. Even children seem to like it raw, or made into chips as an alternative to the more usual potato. These will never become crisp, but the frying brings out the sweetness and a caramelized melting quality that children love. They are very good with game.

Coarsely grated, raw celeriac, coated in a vinegary homemade mayonnaise or crème fraîche, spiked with mustard, is a delicious accompaniment for venison, and very good in sandwiches with all kinds of cold cuts. When very young, in late summer, and only the size of a tennis ball, celeriacs can be braised whole in butter, or simmered in stock and served as a very interesting accompaniment for fish and beef, or on their own as an appetizer. A whole large celeriac is difficult to handle and clean. The roots make up a tangle at the bottom, and if you cut them all off, there is not always much left. The easiest way to clean a celeriac is to cut it into thick slices and peel the slices individually.

First, whip the cream for the topping in a bowl. Press the juice from the grated ginger by wringing it through a handkerchief; add this with the other seasonings to the cream, which will thicken and be soured by the seasonings. Set aside.

Grind the cardamom seeds to a fine powder.

Rinse the celeriac and leeks and cut into large chunks. Fry the leeks and garlic gently, without browning, in the butter; when they become translucent and fragrant, add the curry powder and cardamom, and fry a little more. Add the celeriac and stock, and season sparingly with salt and pepper. Add water just to cover the vegetables, if necessary. Simmer until the vegetables are very tender.

Purée in a food processor until smooth. Adjust the seasoning, then eat while really hot, with the cream on top.

Celeriac, apple, and beet salad

This beautiful-looking salad is very good with both dark meat and fish.

3 hand-eating apples	3 cloves garlic, crushed
2 beets	1 tablespoon coarse sea salt
1¼in slice of celeriac, peeled	½ teaspoon ground black pepper
for the dressing	1 bunch of flat-leaf parsley, chopped
⅔ cup extra-virgin olive oil	
Scant ¼ cup cider vinegar	SERVES 4

Core the apples, but do not peel off the skin; peel the beet, and rinse the celeriac. Cut all into ¼in dice—no bigger or you will not find the salad as satisfying to eat.

Mix together all the dressing ingredients, saving some parsley for garnishing. Toss the apples, beet, and celeriac with the dressing. The salad will turn every hue of shocking pink to purple, and will look superb once scattered with bright green spots of parsley.

Celeriac soup with cardamom

In this soup you get the full advantage of celeriac's spectacular taste. The topping makes a good spicy contrast to the velvety soup.

1 teaspoon cardamom seeds, picked from whole green pods	Salt and coarsely ground black pepper
2 medium celeriac	**for the topping**
2 leeks	Generous ¾ cup heavy cream
2 cloves garlic	½ cup fresh ginger, finely grated
1 tablespoon butter	Finely grated zest of 1 orange
3 heaped tablespoons Madras curry powder	Juice of 1 lime
4 cups very strong chicken or fish stock	SERVES 6

Root vegetables with elderflower and lemon

A medley of baked root vegetables, often with potatoes, is an extremely popular winter dish all over Scandinavia, either on its own, or accompanied by meat or fish. The dish is dead easy to prepare, and transforms the root vegetables from the rather ordinary to something delicious and fragrant. You might think that more sugar is not what the roots need, but this is perfectly balanced with the lemon and vinegar, which add two very different forms of acidity—and you need them both.

2¼lb mixed root vegetables, e.g. swede, celeriac, carrots, parsnip, and parsley root
18oz onions and leeks
Generous ¾ cup elderflower cordial (undiluted)
Juice and grated zest of 2 large lemons

4 tablespoons cider vinegar
A handful of fresh bay leaves
A sprig of lemon thyme
2 tablespoons coarse salt
1 teaspoon ground black pepper
⅓ cup butter
SERVES 4

Preheat the oven to 350°F.

Rinse and peel all the roots and cut into large chunks. Peel and quarter the onions, and clean the leeks and cut (including the tenderest part of the green top) into 1½in pieces. Put all the vegetables in a roasting pan large enough to hold everything in a single layer. Add the rest of the ingredients and mix together well. Bake until tender and caramelized.

Root chips

This is a new and delicious snack, and quite easy to prepare. The roots can be fried in oil, but this is much easier, and just as good. They are beautiful and delicious as they are, or served with chervil cream (page 176) as a dip.

18oz mixed root vegetables
5 tablespoons vegetable oil or canola oil
SERVES 10

Slice the roots into very thin slices; you will need a mandolin for this. Spread them out on parchment paper on a baking sheet and brush with the oil. Bake at 325°F until crispy. You must watch closely, as they will burn if baked for too long. They will not stay crisp for long so eat immediately.

Northern Scandinavians have an obsession with mushrooms, a passion shared with the Russians. In times of famine, they have made up a significant part of the diet in northern Scandinavia—many species picked and used are not even considered good to eat in other parts of the world—and by means of salting, pickling, and drying, mushrooms can even be preserved through the winter. In southern Scandinavia mushrooming is not so popular, maybe because there are not so many woods to pick them in.

Mushrooming is a national pastime in the fall, every family having its secret places, which they do not share. It's quite fun if you meet someone in the woods in the mushroom-picking season as they might pretend they are not there at all, and they will try to escape or hide behind trees; or, if an encounter is unavoidable, they are definitely not out to pick mushrooms, just walking the dog.

A lot more mushrooms than you might think are edible, and quite tasty at that, but only a few are really delicious. Mushrooms are as much about consistency as they are taste. Many have a lovely flavor, but are too slippery or gummy to be good when roasted.

When you pick a variety, the less good ones can be made into a very tasty soup, while the best should be eaten on their own, in all their glory.

mushrooms

You must also remember that mushrooms vary, and the following descriptions apply strictly to those found in Scandinavia: mushrooms described as safe are safe in Scandinavia; in other parts of the world there may be very similar-looking mushrooms which are poisonous.

Mushrooms can be found everywhere, even on old, withering elders by the sea and in apparently barren landscapes, but the majority are found in woods in the fall; the morel is a delicious exception, which shows itself in spring and early summer. Chanterelles can already be found from late June, if it has been raining, and ceps from early August. The season ends with oyster mushrooms, growing by the pound on broken-down beech logs on the forest floor.

Habitat is very important when determining the identity of mushrooms. A few grow almost anywhere, but the majority live with certain trees, and in certain habitats, which makes it easier to identify them correctly.

Chanterelles

It is safe to pick the abundant chanterelle (*Cantharellus cibarius*), which I consider to be the best mushroom to eat. It is entirely orange, darker when growing under pine or spruce, lighter when found in oak and beech woods. It grows in huge colonies in both deciduous and coniferous woods.

Its close relative, the horn of plenty or trumpet of death (*Craterellus cornucopioides*), is an easily recognized and delicious mushroom. It is black, with a gray bloom, and completely hollow. The folds of very thin flesh look like scalloped leaves about to be drawn into the ground by earthworms; only the color betrays them. The name "trumpet of death" refers only to the black color, not to anything more sinister.

Another chanterelle, the yellow-foot (*Craterellus tubaeformis*), pictured right, is hard to find as its cap has the color of rotting leaves, but when you do come across it, you will find enough not just for soups and stews but for drying and pickling as well.

The huge northern woods are home to hundreds of edible mushrooms, and a few deadly ones, if you do not have an experienced mushroom picker or book at your side, it is a dangerous business.

Finns and Swedes are taught from childhood what to pick, and what not. Some species are easy to find and identify, but, even then, you must take a comprehensive mushroom book with you. I am absolutely not saying this to put anyone off the experience—it's greatly rewarding—but just to remind you to play it safe.

The small but pretty mushrooms form virtual carpets with their bright yellow, twisted stems and pale gills resembling fine lace.

All three types of chanterelle are firm and dry-fleshed, and have a delicious, chewy consistency when cooked. They are also perfect for drying.

Milk-caps

The different varieties of milk-cap in the Lactarius genus are recognizable for the fact that they all bleed "milk" when cut. The "milk," actually latex, is often white at first but changes color to various shades of yellow-orange and red. There are many, many types of milk-cap and the best way to determine if they are edible is to taste the milk—if it's bitter, don't pick them (though the Finnish and Russians eat most of them). Because of the mushroom's natural bitterness, milk-caps are often salted in brine, which draws out the bitter juices.

Russulas

There are hundreds of types of mushroom in the Russula (meaning "reddish") genus. In Scandinavia, russulas are everywhere, their beautiful caps strewn across the ground like brightly colored toys. Despite the genus name, they can be pretty much any color except bright blue: pink, red, burgundy, canary yellow, pistachio green, dark green, black-gray, or violet. The gills and stems are usually white, and the fleshy stems have a certain cheesy consistency, with no rings attached, and with no detectable fiber. They are good to eat if they have a mild taste; bitter or sharp, peppery ones are not good to eat, or can even be slightly toxic.

Picking mushrooms

When you pick your own mushrooms, just pull them out of the ground. The very bottom of the stalk can be the only way to determine a deadly mushroom, as it often carries the remnants of the membrane that covers the entire mushroom when it is young. Clean them straight away, with a small knife and a soft brush. If you wait, the dirt will settle and be very difficult to remove. Place the mushrooms in a basket, not a plastic bag, because the spores can then blow away while you walk through the forest (and initiate new colonies of fungi), and also because they can lie separately in a dry basket, rather than sweating together in plastic.

Don't mix mushrooms you know to be safe with other interesting mushrooms of an unknown species that you want to check out or sample—collect them in a separate basket. If you actually collect a deadly mushroom, even a small piece will make you very sick. Once at home, go through the unidentified mushrooms with a book or an experienced collector by your side.

Try not to wash the mushrooms; if you have cleaned them while picking, they won't need it. If you must, however, fill a bowl with cold water and wash them very quickly (don't leave them to soak), then dry them on paper towels. Mushrooms should be eaten the day they are collected, though you can fry them in butter and then freeze them.

Boletus

Boletus mushrooms, pictured top left, are visually very different from other varieties. There are no gills, but a spongy layer on the underside of the cap, made up of tiny tubes, which is easy to recognize. Many Boletus mushrooms are particularly good to eat. There are, however, a couple of toxic species (albeit rare) and two extremely bitter ones. The bitter ones are not poisonous, but will ruin the rest of your mushrooms if you cook them together. So take your mushroom book with you on your hunt.

The best-known is *Boletus edulis*, the giant cep or porcini, and the king of mushrooms. It grows to an impressive 12in in height, and one, fully grown, is enough to feed a whole family. The top is the color and size of a lightly burnt bun, the stalk thick and cream-colored. When young, the mushroom resembles Humpty Dumpty, the cap folded over the fat stem, and this is when it's at its best. Later, it can still be wonderful, as long as it's firm-fleshed.

Boletus edulis is abundant in Scandinavia and very much sought after. It is delicious however you cook it, and is the only mushroom besides the button mushroom that you can eat raw. If you want to fry it, do so in plenty of very hot olive oil or unsalted butter, as any salt in the frying will make it soggy. Fry at a high heat, until barely tender and season with salt, pepper, garlic, and plenty of chopped parsley. It's beautiful on toast, or as an accompaniment to almost anything.

Morels

Mushrooms in the Morchella genus are often found where wood has been cut, even in strange places where you do not expect them, like among wood shavings used for ground cover in private gardens and public parks.

There are two common species, as well as a so-called false morel, in Scandinavia. They are all hollow inside. The black morel (*Morchella conica*) has the characteristic deeply grooved cap, resembling honeycomb, in the shape of a pointed goblin's hat. It comes in many shades, from whitish gray to pitch black.

The common or yellow morel (*Morchella esculenta*) is another species, much larger, with yellowish, rounded heads. There is a fairly good chance of finding them from April to June in beech woods, especially where white and yellow anemones grow together, though the wood shavings that they also grow on can be found anywhere they are spread by man. Yellow morels are not quite as intensely flavored as the black ones, but you are bound to find many of them, and this will more than make up for any disappointment in flavor.

Both these species are poisonous when raw, and will make you sick unless they are thoroughly cooked.

The false morel (*Gyromitra esculenta*) is not a true morel, and it is poisonous. The toxins are not destroyed completely by either drying or cooking. Its cap looks like a twisted brown brain, and it is found in coniferous woods from March to June.

Buying and storing The range of mushrooms that can be cultivated successfully is extremely small, which is why such a limited variety is available in the stores, often restricted to button, portobello, or cremini mushrooms, all versions of *Agaricus bisporus*. However, all the recipes here can be made using bought mushrooms.

Bought mushrooms must be very fresh, unblemished, and clean. Fresh, young mushrooms can be kept in the refrigerator—on a dish covered with a clean dish towel and not in a plastic container—for a few days. The reason for being so careful is that other fungi, or mold, can grow on them, and this can be slightly poisonous, or can just ruin the original mushrooms.

Culinary uses Mushrooms all have the strange ability to add a meaty flavor to other ingredients, and are good in almost all stocks, soups, and vegetable mixtures. We have some lovely mushroom soups in Scandinavia, and these are the best way to use nondescript common mushrooms. Only ceps and button mushrooms can be eaten raw, and they make a lovely salad, carpaccio-style.

Firm mushrooms can be turned into a versatile pickle, which is good with cold cuts, fried meats, venison, and game. They are lovely on a plain green salad when pickled in vinegar with spices and kept in olive oil.

Dried mushrooms have been a staple for millennia: for centuries, drying was the only way to keep mushrooms through the winter, long before salting and pickling. They were often dried over an open fire, giving them a smoky flavor which matched the mushrooms' meatiness perfectly. Dried mushrooms have a strange, alien beauty, and will keep for years if stored in closed jars. They can be crumbled into a stew or used whole.

Both dried and fresh mushrooms are perfect with game and venison, being at their peak season at the same time.

Creamed mushrooms on toast

This is a classic wherever people pick mushrooms, and always tastes lovely if prepared carefully. You can use chanterelles, button mushrooms, or other firm mushrooms, but it does not work well with ceps. If you should ever tire of this traditional recipe, you can always spice it up by adding wine, onion or garlic.

4–4¾ cups button
   mushrooms or
   chanterelles, cleaned
¼ stick butter
1 cup heavy cream
Coarse sea salt and freshly
   ground pepper

½ teaspoon lemon juice
Lots of finely chopped
   parsley
4 slices sourdough bread,
   toasted
SERVES 4

Quarter the mushrooms, then fry in the butter, in a heavy-bottomed skillet at a high heat. Fry until the juices have run and then evaporated, and the mushrooms are golden.

Pour in the cream and season with salt, pepper, and a little lemon juice, then reduce until the cream is a thick coating on the mushrooms. If this goes too far, and the sauce separates, you can put it back together with a little cold water.

Pile on the toast, top with parsley, and eat immediately.

A little lemon juice
   (optional)
1 small bunch of basil

2 tablespoons cep powder
   (optional)
SERVES 4–6

Mushroom soup with baked garlic

Mushroom soup is a perfect end to a day of foraging. If you bring home a basket full of mushrooms, save the chanterelles for creaming, on toast, and fine ceps for a raw salad, and use the less distinctive mushrooms for this lovely soup.

2 whole garlic bulbs
A little extra-virgin olive oil
8 cups mixed mushrooms
3 large onions
1 slice of celeriac
Butter, for frying
1 teaspoon coarsely ground
   black pepper
1 whole allspice

1 large sprig of fresh thyme
1 bay leaf
8 cups chicken, veal,
   or vegetable stock
Generous ¾ cup hard cider
   or white wine
Generous ¾ cup heavy cream
3 tablespoons tamari
   (Japanese soy sauce)

Cut the garlic bulbs in half horizontally, brush with olive oil and bake at 350°F for 30 minutes. Clean the mushrooms, but don't wash them if possible. Leave a few whole, and chop the rest. Chop the onions and celeriac.

Melt some butter in a large saucepan, then add the onions, celeriac, spices, and herbs and sweat, very slowly, to form a golden, scented mush. Add the chopped mushrooms and fry them, letting them release their juices. Scoop out the tender cloves of garlic from their husks, and stir them in. Add the stock, cider or wine, and cream, and simmer for 30 minutes.

Fry the reserved whole mushrooms at a high heat in some butter, then set aside. Pour a little of the soup into their cooking juices, to incorporate every bit of taste, then return it to the pan. You can cream the soup in a food processor, or let it be—personally, I prefer it chunky. Season with tamari, and maybe a drop of lemon juice. Garnish with the fried mushrooms and sprinkle with cep powder, if you have it, and basil. Serve the soup piping hot with toast.

Hang the mushrooms to dry in a windy place (the temperature is not so important), either suspended on netting, in open baskets, or threaded on a piece of string. If it's very humid, you might want to dry them in a very slow oven, at no more than 95°F, or just with the fan on. The mushrooms must be absolutely dry and brittle, after which they can be stored in airtight containers.

Salted mushrooms

Common, store-bought mushrooms are fine for this recipe, but make sure they are fresh, clean, and unblemished. Once salted, they will keep almost indefinitely. The salted mushrooms are delicious in soups; they are traditionally used in beet soup and in pies.

8 cups mushrooms	1 bay leaf
for the brine	1 sprig of thyme
¾ cup coarse sea salt	2 onions, quartered
8 cups water	2 cloves garlic

Boil together the brine ingredients until the salt has dissolved, then pour over the mushrooms in a large (or two smaller) sterilized jar(s) and put the lid(s) on. Leave them to salt for a couple of months, then they are ready to eat.

When using them, remember that the mushrooms are very salty. You can remove some of the salt by soaking them in cold water for a couple of hours.

Mushrooms pickled in vinegar and olive oil

This pickle is just so very delicious and beautiful. It tastes good with cold cuts, fried meats, game, or simply on a plain green salad. All kinds of mushrooms are fine for it, including store-bought ones, ideally firm in texture. The mushrooms will keep for a year as long as they are submerged in oil. You can do exactly the same thing with beans, cauliflower, carrots, artichokes, and asparagus, which can be pickled together or separately.

Dried mushrooms

Drying mushrooms is easy, and maybe a more satisfying thing to do with a glut of mushrooms than frying and freezing them. They can be powdered, and used as a thickening agent for soups and stews, or you can use them as a fine dusting on vegetables, broiled meat and mushroom soups. If you plan on using the powder raw, take care only to use ceps and button mushrooms; but if used for stews, it can be made from any mushroom. Alternatively, dried mushrooms can be used whole, either added at the beginning of cooking, to absorb liquid as they cook, or plumped up in whatever liquid you are using and added later (the soaking water also goes in the dish).

Thin-fleshed mushrooms dry the best, but even big ceps can be dried, if they are young and firm-fleshed. Large, meaty mushrooms must be sliced before drying, while small, firm ones can be left whole.

Raw mushroom salad

This is a Nordic take on the carpaccio theme. *Västerbottenost* is a Swedish cheese with a rich, crumbly texture, and the same virtues as Parmesan. Serve the salad with crusty bread, or as part of a buffet.

4 cups ceps or button mushrooms, in very thin slices
2 handfuls of chopped herbs, a mixture of tarragon, dill, basil, ramsons (wild garlic), and parsley
1 red onion, very finely sliced
½ cup *Västerbottenost*, or other firm, matured cheese, thinly shaved

for the marinade
1 teaspoon coarse sea salt
½ teaspoon coarsely ground black pepper
Juice of ½ lemon
Scant ¼ cup extra virgin olive oil

SERVES 4

First, prepare the mushrooms, herbs, onion, and cheese. Mix the marinade ingredients together.

On a pretty dish, arrange the mushrooms, herbs, onion, and cheese in alternate layers, then pour over the marinade. Adjust the seasoning and leave to macerate for a couple of hours.

Generous ¾ cup cider vinegar
3¼ cups water
2 tablespoons coarse sea salt
8–12 cups mushrooms
5 fresh bay leaves
3–4 dried chiles

½ cup black olives, with the pits in (optional)
1 whole garlic bulb, cloves separated and peeled
1 tablespoon black peppercorns
Extra-virgin olive oil, to cover

Bring the vinegar, water, and salt to a boil, then add the mushrooms and boil until they have shrunk to half their normal size. (If using a variety of vegetables, cook each type separately until just barely tender.) Let cool, then strain the mushrooms (reserving the pickling liquid) and put into a large (or two smaller) sterilized jar(s).

Tuck the bay leaves, chiles, olives (if using), and garlic cloves down between the mushrooms. Reduce the pickling liquid to approx. ¾ cup, then pour over the mushrooms. Add enough olive oil to cover the mushrooms completely and put on the lid(s).

The pickle is ready to eat straight away, but improves with age. The mixed oil and pickle in the jar makes an exquisite dressing for salads, baked roots, and potatoes once the mushrooms are eaten. Over time, the garlic may turn an eerie blue, but it only adds to the fun—it is perfectly safe. Make sure you pick from the pickle with a sterilized fork.

Herbs are the essence of the soil, the climate, and the tradition of any given culinary tradition. The Nordic kitchen is very much influenced by Russian cooking and its use of horseradish and dill. The other herbs that infuse our dishes are used all over the world, although the subtle flavors of chervil, tarragon and parsley, wild thyme, sorrel, and wood sorrel are used in mild Nordic ways, particular to our habits of eating delicately flavored food, with the ingredients as the key note.

Herbs have been gathered from the wild since the Stone Age, and more than now. The necessary common knowledge of herbs has more or less vanished, although cooks and foodies are regaining know-how and adding new-old local herbs to the table once more. Ramsons (wild garlic), nettles, woodruff, and angelica are new to us, but can be found in all old Nordic cookbooks. There is no clear distinction between herbs and edible leaves except that herbs are more pungent, not being a considerable part of the dish, but a leafy flavoring nonetheless.

herbs

Dill

Dill is the ultimate Nordic herb, adding a special, fresh, and typically northern taste to almost every dish made with fish, shellfish, lamb, and vegetables. It cannot be replaced with anything else. If you must, you can try a mix of fennel, parsley, and tarragon, but it will not be the same, though still good. Dill seeds are not a successful substitute as they are more like caraway.

How it grows Dill is an annual and a very easy herb to grow, particularly in partial shade. Sow it in a shallow drill from April onward, water well, then thin to 2in. You can pick the soft leaves, or wait for the flowers, lime green and lovely, which are a herb in their own right, with a stronger, more caraway-like taste.

Culinary uses Dill is a prolific umbellifer, used for pickles, pickled fish, gravad fish, in mild spring stews with veal or lamb, and served with all kinds of fresh fish. It is perfect for boiling fish and shellfish and for marinating all kinds of vegetables. Spring or summer cabbage is lovely with dill (page 139).

Lamb stew with loads of dill

In this recipe, the dill penetrates the whole dish with a wonderfully fresh, green taste that Scandinavians love. You can add delicate spring vegetables, such as peas, spring cabbage, new carrots, or asparagus, but it's better to eat the vegetables on the side. In winter, you could add a root vegetable such as scorzonera or salsify, parsley root or parsnip, or even celery.

If you ask your butcher to bone the lamb for you, make sure you ask to keep the bones.

1 neck of lamb or large shoulder or leg, boned (approx. weight 3lb 5oz, including the bone)
1 large onion, sliced
2 cloves garlic
1 bouquet garni, consisting of the green parts of 1 leek, 2 celery stalks, the stalks from the dill (see right) and 1 sprig of fresh thyme

Butter, for frying
Salt and 1 teaspoon whole black peppercorns
Generous ¾ cup white wine or hard cider
All-purpose flour, for coating

to finish
Generous ¾ cup heavy cream
1 tablespoon cornstarch
2 large bunches of dill, chopped
SERVES 4

Begin by cutting the lamb into large cubes, if the butcher hasn't already done this for you.

Fry the onion, garlic, and the bouquet garni in a piece of butter and add the lamb bones. Leave to sweat for a while, then add the salt, pepper, and wine or cider. Simmer without a lid until almost all the liquid has evaporated, then add enough water to cover. Let simmer gently for an hour, skimming off any surface scum at regular intervals. Strain the stock and throw away the remains in the sieve. Wipe the pan with paper towels, though it's not necessary to clean it thoroughly.

Shake the cubed meat in a sealable plastic bag with a little flour to coat, then brown gently in a piece of butter in the pan. Pour on the stock and simmer very gently for an hour, or until tender. You can prepare the dish up to this point a couple of days before eating.

When you are ready to eat, gently warm the sauce, without the meat, and pour in the cream, mixed with the cornstarch. Let bubble until the taste of the cornstarch has gone, then add the meat. Add the chopped dill at the last moment.

Cucumber salad with dill

This fresh and delicate spring salad makes a great side dish for fish, lamb, veal, chicken, or smoked meat. The combination of cucumber and dill is hardly new, but it's very, very good.

4 cucumbers
1 large bunch of dill
4 tablespoons sherry vinegar
1 tablespoon sugar
2 teaspoons coarse sea salt
1 teaspoon coarsely ground black pepper
SERVES 6

Peel the cucumbers, halve lengthwise and scrape out the seeds. Cut into ¼in slanted slices. Chop the dill, including the stems, until medium fine. Mix all the ingredients together, then let rest for a minimum of 2 hours before serving.

Parsley

it available almost all year round. Parsley sauces are served with crisp pork and fried fish, and pigeons (squabs) and chickens are stuffed with the herb.

Traditionally, curly parsley is used in Scandinavia, but I prefer the flat-leaf variety. Use whichever you prefer; the flavor is in fact indistinguishable.

Crisp pork slices with parsley sauce and new potatoes

Traditional parsley sauce is a wonderful thing, if it's not too thick, and is emerald green from the inclusion of much more parsley than usual. We love tradition if it's not too stuffy, and parsley sauce is just so good.

Parsley is an over-used, familiar herb—the garnish and everyday provider of a healthy-looking, green finish to many dishes. But it has virtues too, its reliable good looks and leafy green taste making it wonderfully versatile. Furthermore, parsley is packed with minerals including iron, and is definitely good for you, especially in larger quantities than a mere sprinkling.

How it grows Parsley can be a little tricky to grow. It takes an eternity to sprout, up to eight weeks; in the Middle Ages it was believed that the seedling had to travel to the devil and back seven times before it came up. I usually sow the seeds in trays, and plant the seedlings out in neat rows when they're looking good and healthy. It's a hardy biennial, flowering and then dying in its second year, but is usually grown as an annual. With some clever planning, you can have a good supply all year round.

Culinary uses Parsley can be added as a sprinkling to many dishes, but it is used as a major flavoring in a number of typical Nordic dishes, as its hardiness makes

2¼lb pork belly, sliced into ½in slices, with the rind on
1 heaped tablespoon coarse salt
2¼lb tiny new potatoes
for the parsley sauce
1 tablespoon butter

2½ tablespoons all-purpose flour
Salt and freshly ground black pepper
2½ whole milk
2 large bunches of parsley, finely chopped
SERVES 4

Arrange the pork slices in an ovenproof dish, in one layer, then sprinkle with the salt. Let sit on the counter for 2–3 hours, turning the meat over once or twice.

Pat the meat dry and roast in the oven at 350°F until lovely and crisp.

Meanwhile, put the new potatoes on to boil and make the sauce. Melt the butter in a deep saucepan, then whisk in the flour and cook for a couple of minutes. Add salt and plenty of coarsely ground pepper. Whisk in the milk, a little at a time, making sure the sauce is smooth before adding more. Once the milk is used up, the sauce should be shiny and have a nice pourable consistency. Let it simmer slowly until the floury taste has gone.

While the meat cooks in the oven, it will provide a lot of lovely, browned, tasty fat, which you can whisk into the sauce a little at a time—all of it! It is grotesquely fattening, but it makes a superb taste. When everything else is ready, stir in the parsley; there must be enough to make the sauce thick with the herb, and totally green-freckled.

Do not consider reheating this sauce; any leftovers must be thrown away.

Chicken with parsley and curdled sauce

This traditional chicken dish—a recipe from an era when chicken and cucumbers were a summertime treat eaten only on a balmy June evening—makes tears come to our northern eyes. The chicken is crammed full with parsley, the flavor seeping slowly into the sauce while the bird is pot roasted for an eternity. New potatoes, cucumber salad, and maybe rhubarb compote, plus a side dish of creamy-leaved, yellowish lettuce in a cream-lemon dressing are all you need with this. Enthusiasts like me eat the parsley, others don't. Domesticated pigeons are cooked in the same way, but only for 25 minutes.

The flavoring is not overwhelming, so the chicken itself is the central focus of the dish, and it must be fresh, huge, and organic, as the muscle and taste that come from freedom and foraging are needed. The dish is a good example of the very traditional and seasonal: the first chickens; just big enough to eat, the cow's milk,

creamy after a month on fresh grass, the first cucumbers, swelling in the cold greenhouse, the first new potatoes, and the last of the overwintering parsley, just before it comes into bloom, paired with rhubarb or gooseberries, the only fruity thing anyone had, before the strawberry season, and tiny butterhead lettuces. All made into one, memorable meal, always eaten on Sundays.

Even now, when seasonality is only slowly returning, a meal like this can be recreated, if you take the trouble to source the right ingredients.

The preparation is very simple: just follow the recipe for pot roasting the chicken on page 174 cramming it full of parsley and omitting the lemon and tarragon.

Tarragon

Tarragon has to be one of the great culinary herbs, though people who grow Russian tarragon never understand the love that growers of the true French tarragon have for this herb. No wonder, as they are two very different plants. The Russian variety (*Artemisia dracunculoides*) is a tall, bullying perennial, totally hardy, with a sometimes brutish bitterness and none of the aromatic elegance or tenderness of its less hardy, French cousin (*Artemisia dracunculus*).

How it grows Unfortunately, French tarragon cannot be grown from seed and is much trickier to grow than the Russian version. If buying plants to grow at home, make sure you buy the right kind as few commercial growers sell the French type. Plant tarragon in a hot, sunny, and dry spot and don't overwater.

Appearance and taste Tarragon has slim, tender leaves on a tough stalk. French tarragon has a powerful but glorious and elegant aniseed taste.

Culinary uses Tarragon is well worth growing as the soft tips are magical in every dish with eggs, tomatoes, chicken, shellfish, and also in pickles and marinades. Its complex anise flavor is related to the anise in dill, chervil, and basil, and you can both mix and replace them all with each other. Try it instead of dill in gravad fish; chervil cream is also lovely made with tarragon.

Slow-roast chicken with tarragon and peas

Tarragon has a very special affinity with chicken. This spring/summer recipe is a new take on an old theme and is well loved by all. New potatoes are the only side needed.

I chicken, weighing at least 3lb 5oz	**for the peas**
I lemon	¾ cup bacon, diced
I large bunch of French tarragon, leaves separated from stalks	5½oz shallots, peeled but left whole
Salt and pepper	1¼ cups hard cider
Piece of butter	2¾ cups fresh shelled peas (frozen if necessary)
Generous ¾ cup heavy cream	4 Little Gem lettuces, quartered
Generous ¾ cup water	Salt and pepper
	SERVES 4–5

Preheat the oven to 325°F.

Cut the lemon in half. Pare the zest and extract the juice from one half (reserving both the zest and the juice), and put the other half in the cavity of the chicken. Put the tarragon stalks inside the chicken with the lemon and salt and pepper.

Rub the surface of the chicken with the butter, salt, and pepper. Put it in a tight-fitting ovenproof pot, preferably clay, and scatter over the tarragon leaves and lemon zest. Pour on the cream and water, and put the lid on.

Put the chicken in the oven and let roast for 1¼ hours. The cooking time can vary, so keep an eye on it: when a thigh is easily pulled off, it is done. The sauce should be reduced to a thick glaze in the pot; if it has separated, take out the chicken and add a little cold water. Season with the reserved lemon juice and more salt and pepper.

While the chicken roasts, prepare the peas. Fry the bacon in a heavy-based skillet at a low heat so the fat runs off. Add the shallots and let fry slowly until soft and lightly golden. Pour in the cider and let reduce by half.

When the chicken is done, and while you are making the sauce, add the peas and lettuces to the bacon and shallots, put a lid on and leave the vegetables to heat through until the lettuces have wilted—this should take about 10 minutes. Season with salt and pepper.

Serve the vegetables in the pan with the chicken, nicely carved, on top. The sauce should be served separately.

Chervil

Chervil is a very old herb in Nordic cuisine, but almost impossible to buy. People who love it and know how to use it are almost gone, and young cooks have yet to discover its virtues—so even in Scandinavia you have to grow your own.

How it grows Chervil is a winter annual, so it can be sown in the fall and be the first plentiful herb to appear in spring. Sow it again in early spring and you can enjoy a supply of chervil all summer long.

Appearance and taste Chervil has light green, fern-like leaves that are not dissimilar to parsley in appearance, and clusters of tiny, white flowers from spring to summer. The leaves are the subtlest of the aniseed-flavored herbs; their mild anise flavor is never overwhelming, as tarragon, for example, can be.

Culinary uses The classic use of chervil is with eggs, and it goes perfectly with ramsons (wild garlic) in an omelette (page 180). Alternatively, try mixing it with almonds, new garlic, olive oil, salt, and lemon juice to make an unusual pesto to go with fish, salted meats or new vegetables.

Sweet cicely (an easily grown and beautiful perennial herb) is a good alternative to chervil, even if it's not quite as delicate.

Chervil cream

The easiest and most versatile sauce of all, chervil cream will add a spring-like lightheartedness to all fried, broiled, and baked fish, shellfish and new vegetables.

1 large bunch of chervil
1 cup crème fraîche
Salt and pepper
SERVES 6

Simply chop the chervil very finely, almost to a mush, and then mix with the crème fraîche. Season with some salt and a little pepper, to taste. The result is an incredibly flavorful, light green cream sauce.

Chervil soup with poached eggs and asparagus

This is my favorite spring soup, a recipe from another generation. It must be very green, and the chicken stock a homemade one—any store-bought stock will overwhelm the delicate anise flavor. If chervil is unobtainable, you can use sweet cicely.

Approx. 18oz thick white asparagus	1 handful of fresh spinach or blanched fine, new nettles
2 leeks	
4 cups chicken stock	Salt and pepper
⅔ cup heavy cream	A pinch of sugar
4 medium russet or Idaho potatoes, sliced	4 eggs, poached or boiled
1 large bunch of chervil	1 bunch of chives, very finely chopped
	SERVES 4

Peel the asparagus spears, then bend each one in order to snap off the stringy bottom part. Put both the peel and the bottom bits of the asparagus, as well as the green part of the leeks, in a saucepan with the stock. Simmer for an hour, then strain. Cut off the tips of the asparagus and reserve. Simmer the stock with the cream, potatoes, white part of the leeks, and asparagus spears until the vegetables are very tender.

Wash the chervil and spinach. Blend the boiled vegetables and raw chervil and spinach with a little of the stock in a food processor until smooth. Pour this mixture into the remaining stock through a fine sieve. Add the asparagus tips.

Take the pan off the stove—the soup must not be heated now, as the fresh green color will turn into gray-brown if overheated. Season with salt, pepper, and a little sugar. Serve each bowl with a poached or a halved boiled egg and a scattering of chives.

Lovage

Lovage, although originally a Mediterranean plant, grows wild all over the north. It is a classic example of an old herb that has fallen into disuse among home cooks, though it is often the main flavor used in bouillon cubes. Lovage is not easy to buy, so your best option is to grow it.

How it grows Lovage, a huge umbellifer, is a hardy perennial, though short-lived. It can grow up to 6½ft in height, so plan its position in the garden carefully, ideally at the back of a border. Lovage prefers a rich, well-drained soil, but generally needs very little encouragement to grow whether in full sun or partial shade. It dies right back in winter.

Appearance and taste With its hollow stems, lovage bears a passing resemblance to celery, and its flavor is certainly similar, though perhaps celery on speed is the best way to describe its penetrating, slightly citrussy taste. The leaf and very young stalks are the parts used.

Culinary uses Lovage is a herb that all good old sensible kitchen literature tells us should be used sparingly, as it makes hostile takeovers on all other aromas. This is not true, it takes its place nicely beside the other flavors, but it

does not hide itself. The taste is slightly bitter, meaty, and herby. It's lovely if you put a leaf in the water for boiling potatoes, use it with other herbs for soup, or go all the way and make it into a powerful, northern pesto.

Lovage pesto

This pesto is perfect as a dressing for new potatoes, as a sauce for broiled meat and fish, or on rye bread with sliced new potatoes—just top with a blob of pesto and scatter with salt flakes.

A handful of lovage leaves
1 cup walnuts, toasted
1 tablespoon lemon juice
Generous ⅓ cup extra-
   virgin olive oil
Salt and pepper

A pinch of sugar
½ smallish new garlic bulb
1 tablespoon capers
1 tablespoon cider vinegar
2 cups bread crumbs, toasted
SERVES 6

Process everything except the bread crumbs in a food processor, but not too much as you want a coarse, chunky consistency; alternatively, you can chop everything up by hand on a board. Simply mix with the crisp crumbs and it's ready to use.

Horseradish

Horseradish is to the northern kitchens what chile is to the south and east. Its hot flavor, high vitamin content, and very potent anti-inflammatory effect have probably done more to keep us alive than any other food in the north during cold or wet winter months when there are few other greens to choose from.

How it grows Horseradish is a perennial that grows wild all over the northern hemisphere in fertile soil. It is a handsome, big-leaved plant to cultivate in a wild corner of the garden. It spreads vigorously by seed, but the young plants are easy to remove—and eat. Both the fragrant, white flowers and the roots are edible. The only problem when growing it is harvesting the roots if you want them whole. The taproots are up to 23½in long, and you may have to settle for smaller bits of it, unless you grow it as the professionals do: at a sharp angle, almost lying down, in extremely loose soil. But less will do—a short piece of horseradish root is enough for paper-thin shavings for a whole family. There are no cultivars available, but even wild plants show huge variation.

Appearance and taste Horseradish, as a spice, is primarily a huge root, and the fresher it is, the more powerful the flavor. Grating horseradish can make you weep as the volatile oils are very pungent. The one growing in your garden or gathered from the wild is bound to be more flavorsome than industrially grown horseradish. The outer layers of the root are generally milder, the core more pungent.

Health benefits This hot and spicy vegetable contains lots of vitamins and a very potent anti-inflammatory. In fact, it kills germs so effectively that it's always included in pickles, doing the job perfectly while adding pungency and flavor.

Buying and storing Fresh horseradish can be very difficult to find in stores, but beware of the convenient, ready-grated kind. This has absolutely no flavor, which is not so convenient after all. Fresh roots will keep for weeks in a sealable plastic bag in the fridge.

Culinary uses Horseradish is either grated very finely to go in a cream or sauce, or shaved extremely thinly to top sandwiches, fish, or meats, or to make a relish. The shavings tend to be sweeter and more flavorsome the finer the root is grated. As with chile, you have to wait a while after adding it to a dish to taste the full effect, especially in cold sauces such as the classic horseradish cream for smoked fish. It may be mild to start with, but given half an hour the flavor will develop.

Horseradish is cherished as an accompaniment for plain baked or boiled lean fish with butter sauce. It is served with all kinds of cold cuts, with smoked meat and fish, for steak tartare, and for the lovely traditional sweet-sour horseradish sauce eaten with the boiled meats from the festive soup, *hønsekødsuppe*.

Horseradish is also the classic dance partner for all kinds of beet preparations; in salads, relishes, and with pickled beets, the earthy sweetness of the beet is perfectly balanced by spiky horseradish.

Horseradish has only one flaw: its taste and effects do not stand up to high temperatures. Therefore it should be added at the very last moment to a sauce or dish, or simply shaved on top—otherwise the taste will vanish, leaving drenched and bitter wood-like shavings.

Smoked salmon with horseradish cream

Generous ¾ cup crème fraîche
4 tablespoons finely grated horseradish
A pinch of sea salt
A pinch of sugar
8 slices cold-smoked salmon (preferably wild)
1 bunch of fresh dill
4 slices sourdough bread
SERVES 4

Mix together the crème fraîche, grated horseradish, salt, and sugar. Ideally, let the sauce sit for half an hour to bring out the flavor.

You can serve this dish in two ways. Either spread the horseradish cream directly on to four plates, put the slices of salmon on top, and decorate with dill, serving the bread on the side. Or spread some of the cream on the bread, arrange the salmon on top, and put another blob of the horseradish cream on top, followed by a sprinkling of dill

Pickled beets with horseradish

This is the everyday pickle to eat with all kinds of pork, *frikadeller*, charcuterie, on liver paste, with smoked fish or boiled cod, at almost every meal. This version is more interestingly spiced than most, the horseradish keeping the pickle fresh, and adding exactly what sweet, bland beets needs, namely spiciness and sex.

6lb 8oz beets
4in piece of horseradish root, thinly sliced
for the pickle
3 tablespoons coarse sea salt
8 cups cider vinegar
4 cups sugar
1 tablespoon whole allspice
3 bay leaves
4 tablespoons mustard seeds
2 tablespoons black peppercorns
1 sprig of thyme
5–6 dill flowers
MAKES A LOT

Boil the beets in salted water until just tender. Cool a little, then rub off the skins—a pleasurable task.

Put all the ingredients for the pickle in a saucepan. Bring to a boil and boil for 10 minutes.

Dice or slice the beets and cram into sterilized pickling jars. Pour the boiling pickle over the beets to cover. Top with the sliced horseradish, then seal the jars.

This pickle can be eaten immediately, but is best after a couple of days. It keeps for up to 6 months.

Ramsons (wild garlic)

In spring, ramsons (or wild garlic) cover the floors of deciduous forests in Scandinavia. They can be detected from miles away, their permeating garlic smell pungent in the warm May air. Collect and eat them while you can, as the darkening canopies of beech leaves will soon make them wither. You can grow ramsons yourself in a woodland area of your garden, but beware—they must be planted where they can be allowed to follow their rampant nature. The North American cousin is called ramps, which is a good substitute in the following recipes.

Appearance and taste The bulbs themselves, the broad, soft leaves, and the white, starry flowers are very much edible. Perhaps surprisingly, the flowers tend to have a stronger flavor than the mildly garlicky leaves.

Culinary uses Ramsons are so abundant in spring that they can be eaten and cooked like spinach, in soups, omelettes, as an accompaniment for everything nice and light, for a pesto, or in salads. The mild garlicky taste and softness of the leaves mean that they lend themselves to anything that you might associate with spinach and garlic.

Omelette with ramsons and other herbs

There are several secrets behind making a good omelette—as is often the case when cooking very simple seeming dishes. Firstly, add no salt before the omelette is finished. Also, omelettes need a very hot skillet, with lots of butter or olive oil to make the eggs fluff up. And always use very fresh eggs, from decently raised and fed birds. You do not need to consider all the lore about expensive omelette pans washed by mermaids in the moonlight. A heavy skillet, preferably iron or copper, is fine (Tefal pans do not work very well at high temperatures). Mozzarella is not, admittedly, very Nordic, but the consistency amidst the soft eggs is beautiful. Eat the omelette with rye bread, and maybe a tomato salad. Leftovers taste lovely in a sandwich, especially with smoked fish—ideally as part of a picnic.

Generous ⅓ cup extra-virgin olive oil

4 cups fresh herbs, finely chopped: choose from ramsons (wild garlic), sorrel, chervil, tarragon, chives, dill, parsley, and blanched nettles

8 large organic eggs

1 buffalo mozzarella, cut into thin slices

Salt and pepper

SERVES 4 FOR LUNCH

Heat a heavy skillet until very hot, then pour in the oil, and heat again. Meanwhile, whisk the herbs into the eggs.

Pour the eggs into the hot pan and let them fluff up wildly into a bubbly, light, thick omelette. Add the mozzarella slices.

As soon as the eggs are solid around the edge, lift with a round-bladed knife and tilt the pan so that more uncooked egg runs underneath. When the omelette is no longer fluid, but still very soft in the middle, remove it from the heat. Scatter with salt and pepper, and fold into a half moon.

Nettles

The long, thin fibers of the stinging nettle have been used for centuries to make the finest, shiny, durable, and soft materials for dresses and bed linen, finer even than flax-linen, rotted and woven in the same way. Nettle cloth was even discovered in a Danish grave of the later Bronze Age, wrapped around cremated bones.

Nettles are not overwhelmingly flavorful, but are fine as a spring-time, vaguely spinach-like treat. They have a distinct foxy smell—which comes from all the little glass-hard needles that contain the poison that creates the sting and irritates the skin—but you can easily blanch this away.

How it grows Nettles grow everywhere, particularly on deep, rich soil in disturbed habitats, and can reach an impressive 6½ft high in the summer, dying down to the ground in winter. They appear from March onward and are best picked early. It's the soft, young tips of the plant that you're after, and don't forget to wear gloves.

Health benefits For hundreds of years, nettles have been used to treat a whole range of ailments, even to stimulate hair growth! They are rich in minerals and vitamins (particularly A and C), and are relatively high in protein for a leafy green vegetable.

Culinary uses Put the cleaned nettles in a colander, pour over a kettleful of boiling water, and drain. After this initial blanching, the nettles can be used in all kinds of ways as you would use spinach: in soups, omelettes, dressed with olive oil and lemon, creamed. You could also try them in the chervil soup on page 176.

Nettle waffles

You can use these thick waffles as wraps to fill with dried or salted meats, smoked fish, or fish eggs, or simply topped with chervil cream and smoked salmon.

5 cups fresh herbs, including blanched nettles, spinach, parsley, dill, tarragon, and/or sorrel
3 eggs
Scant ⅓ cup beer
⅔ cup whole milk
1½ cups all-purpose flour
½ cup butter, melted
Salt and pepper
MAKES 10

Chop the herbs finely. Blend the eggs, beer, milk, and flour together in a bowl. Add the melted butter and continue mixing until it forms a shiny batter. Season with salt and pepper. Add the herbs.

Bake the waffles in a waffle iron (there is no need to grease it) in the usual way. The waffles are crisp when freshly baked; once cold, they can be restored to their former glory in a warm oven.

Elderflower

Elderflower is a marvellous herb, draping its aromatic veil over anything it comes into contact with. The elder tree is found all over Scandinavia; in the US, it's called elderberry. Steeped in myth and magic, the elder was long regarded as sacred, and people would plant it near their house to ward off witches and evil spirits. It is said that if you fall asleep under a flowering elder you should be able to dream of your future—and the smell is certainly intoxicating if you stay long enough.

How it grows Common elder (*Sambucus nigra*) grows wild, self-seeded, in every country garden and in ditches and clearings everywhere. There are flowers enough for everyone in late May and June. In the fall, the elder tree bears small, round, purple berries, that are good for cordials (page 230).

Appearance and taste The cream flowers are used when young, but not while unopened. The smell is very complex and intoxicating: musky, heady, and even foxy if you smell long enough. Choose freshly opened flowers, and leave those whose petals start to drop when you pick them. Don't wash them as they will lose their perfume. Instead, simply shake off any insects.

Culinary uses The elderflower's muscat-grape aroma permeates and blends well with lemon and green herbs, butter and sugar, berries, and fruit. It works well in teas, syrups, and, of course, in cordials. Elderflower cordial captures the flavor so well that it effectively allows you to replace the flowers when the season is over.

Elderflower doesn't have to be used exclusively in sweet dishes: it works well as a filling in mackerel, and is a beautiful ingredient in herb or spiced salts. The flowers' affinity with gooseberries is legendary, both as a sauce for fish, in compote, and in jam (page 223).

Elderflower cordial

This is a very strong cordial, and should keep well, but it's important that everything that comes into contact with it is sterilized in boiling water first, including the bottles, corks, and even the cheesecloth.

50 elderflower heads	8 cups boiling water
Juice and thinly pared zest	3½ oz tartaric acid
of 6 lemons	MAKES 8½PT
15 cups brown sugar	

Remove the coarsest stalks, as well as any little bugs, from the elderflowers, then put everything in a large, non-corrosive bowl. Stir in the remaining ingredients and cover with a clean cloth. Let the mixture steep for 5 days, mixing occasionally, until the sugar has dissolved.

Strain through a scalded piece of cheesecloth, then bottle. Store in a cool, dark place. Once opened, the cordial should be kept in the refrigerator and drunk within a week. There will be a layer or clouds of pollen in the drink, but this is harmless.

Spiced elderflower salt

This spiced salt has a very special Nordic feel to it. With a jar of this in your larder, you will never have to worry about what to do with your chicken, pork chop, leg of lamb, grilled meats, baked vegetables, or fish. You can, naturally, add other, less Nordic ingredients if you like, such as lemon thyme, cardamom, cumin, or fenugreek leaves, but this basic version is very useful as it is.

The idea is to blend the salt and herbs and spices while they are fresh so that the juices and volatile oils

penetrate the salt, and the oils stay there instead of vaporizing. If you can use Guérande sea salt from France or Trapani salt from Sicily, so much the better.

2 cups elderflowers, stalks removed
2 or more medium red chiles, seeded
⅔ cup very coarse unrefined salt
2 whole new garlic bulbs, quartered
Thinly pared zest and peel of 2 lemons
MAKES 9OZ

Gently shake and pluck the white flowers from the elderflower stalks. Set aside half of the flowers, and put the rest with the remaining ingredients in a food processor; pulse to a coarse consistency; it's best if the chiles and lemon peel are still in discernible shreds.

Stir in the reserved flowers, then spread the mixture out on a tray to dry. Put the tray in a windy place, preferably in the sun. The salt itself will absorb the juices, and will never dry out completely. But leave the tray until the rest of the ingredients have dried out, which will take time.

The salt can be used fresh. Once in a jar, it will keep for years—if you let it.

Elderflower gelatin

Gelatin is an old-fashioned dessert, with a severely bad reputation. And it's a crying shame. A soft, wobbly, and tasty jello, without too much gelatin, is a beauty. Too much gelatin gives a chewy result, and it's horrible. Proper gelatin must melt immediately in your mouth. This elderflower gelatin is a perfect foil for ripe strawberries, or even raspberries.

Juice of 1 lemon
Scant ¼ cup dark rum
5 sheets of leaf gelatin

1 cup undiluted elderflower
    cordial
18oz ripe strawberries
Elderflowers, to decorate

Mix the lemon juice and rum and add enough water to make the liquid up to 1 cup.

Soften the gelatin in cold water, then melt in a little of the lemon-rum liquid. Mix with the cordial and the rest of the rum mixture.

Slice the strawberries into tall glasses, and cover with the gelatin. Cool until set. Decorate with elderflowers before serving.

Veal scaloppini with elderflowers

New potatoes and butterhead lettuce with a cream dressing go well with this dish.

1lb 10oz very tender cut of
    veal, in approx. ¼in slices
10 elderflowers
Thinly pared zest and juice
    of 2 lemons
½ stick butter, plus ¼ stick
    for the sauce

Generous ⅓ cup
    elderflower cordial
    (undiluted)
1 fresh clove garlic, sliced
Generous ⅓ cup white wine
Salt and pepper
SERVES 4

Bash the slices of veal between two pieces of waxed paper until very thin. Wrap each slice around some elderflowers and a piece of lemon zest. Roll up and secure with a toothpick. Fry gently in butter until browned all over.

To make the sauce, boil together the lemon juice, elderflower cordial, garlic, and white wine at a high heat until you have a syrup—it's a matter of minutes. Whisk in the remaining cold butter and season with salt and pepper.

Put the scaloppini back in the pan, scatter a few elderflowers over them and serve.

More herbs

Angelica

This is a truly northern species. It grows wild all over the northern countries, thriving in damp, cool conditions. It is said to be the only plant grown for food by the white settlers on Greenland in the early Middle Ages, and was a common plant in Viking-age gardens. However, it's hard to believe that angelica was ever eaten in massive quantities—its taste would forbid it. But the herb definitely has its uses.

An even bigger plant than lovage, angelica grows to an impressive 10ft, with huge, lime green flower heads. The young stalks can be candied, while the tender, young shoots, thinly sliced and in small quantities, can give an extraordinarily exquisite taste to anything with rhubarb. The root and stalk lend flavor to schnapps.

Rhubarb soup with angelica

This cold soup is delicious served with cardamom or vanilla ice cream, and a dusting of cinnamon. You can substitute six rose geranium leaves or a small bunch lemon verbena if you can't get hold of angelica.

If you are at the beginning of the strawberry season, you can add some sliced strawberries just before serving.

2 bunches of rhubarb (approx 14 stalks)	4 cups water
4in piece of angelica	Juice and thinly pared zest of 1 lemon
for the syrup	1 vanilla bean, split
3 cups sugar	SERVES 6–8

Cut the rhubarb into in thin, slanted slices, or thin matchsticks. Be sure to use the bottom part of the stalks; these are often discarded, which is a shame. Cut the angelica into very thin slivers.

Boil together the syrup ingredients until the sugar has dissolved. Pour over the rhubarb and angelica in a bowl. The heat will tenderize the fruit sufficiently, leaving the rhubarb a little chewy and delicious. Let cool and the soup is ready to serve.

Buying and storing herbs

In Scandinavia, the essential herbs are all fresh, and are used abundantly during the summer months, or during the short spring season in the case of wild herbs. The rest of the year, cultivated herbs can be bought fresh. Dried herbs are just not an option, as the texture and taste are altered too much to be an alternative, the only exception being thyme, which is used both fresh and dried.

Fresh herbs will keep for a couple of days in a sealable plastic bag in the refrigerator. Some of the herbs are hard to obtain outside Scandinavia, but I recommend that you grow your own.

Sweet woodruff

Galium odoratum is a small, fine-leaved plant, which covers vast areas of dry, shady acid woodland in Scandinavia. You can collect it in the wild or grow it yourself in a shady area in your garden.

Dried woodruff has an aroma of newly mown grass. It is traditionally used for small garlands and wreaths, and is given to people moving into a new house to sweeten their future, along with bread and salt as an omen that they will never be in short supply.

Use dried woodruff for teas and for flavoring sweet things, and fresh in cordials and fruit punch (as you would mint). It can also be used to flavor sausages and is a favorite flavoring for schnapps.

Chives

Chives are a penennial bulbous plant, easy to grow, with hollow leaves and lovely, purple, edible flowers in spring. Cut the stalks back and they will come again several times in a season. Chives are one of the first herbs of substance in the spring, and are eaten on all types of spring food, often together with chervil. They go naturally with smoked fish, potatoes, eggs, herrings, and asparagus. Chives have a mild onion flavor, with no sweetness, and are impossible to overuse.

Wood sorrel

Wood sorrel can be gathered in the wild, often in deciduous forests. It is a lovely little plant with edible, heart-shaped leaves and edible, pink-striped white flowers. Its acid taste is mild and lemony and it's used in omelettes, fish, salads, or simply as a garnish.

Dandelion greens

Dandelion greens are edible and sweet as long as they are not yet green. You can blanch them under a pot, or simply pick them while they look like a strange octopus resting on the ground, furry and dark reddish-bluish. The whole plant with a little bit of the roots can be picked, washed well, and eaten with a honeyed marinade.

Sweet grass

Sweet grass (*Hierochloe odorata*), a native grass of most of the northern hemisphere, has a lovely flavor of vanilla and sweet woodruff, very much like that of Asian pandan leaves. It is the grass used to make Poland's famous bison grass vodka. It is used for teas, and as a spice for sweet dishes. In northern Finland and Sweden it is collected by the Sami people, who braid it into decorative, fragrant, thick braids that keep their scent for years. Other indigenous people and most of the northern tribes of American Indians consider it a sacred plant, and have numerous uses for it.

Sweet grass is easy to grow and extremely hardy, but not drought tolerant. It is happy in sun or partial shade. The flavor is extracted in water, and is sweet, summery, and enchanting in all manners of desserts, ice cream, cocktails, and in sauces for fish.

Salad of Nordic herbs and ancient grains

Ancient wheats are delicious; the extra nutrients are very much detectable in the rich, summery taste, evident in breads, and certainly when used as you would rice, bulgur, or couscous. You can buy the grains polished, and this reduces the cooking time to about 30 minutes, or you can buy whole untreated grains of kamut, spelt, or ølands wheat. These will need a soak, like beans, and then boiling in plenty of salted water till soft and chewy.

Precise cooking time is hard to predict, as it has too many variables, but a 12-hour soak and 1–2 hours' cooking is probably fine. The huge, swollen grains are tastier than rice, and do not become sticky or gluey. They soak up a marinade, and combine beautifully with Nordic herbs like chervil, dill, tarragon, parsley, and mint.

1 cup whole grains of spelt or other ancient wheat	Juice and grated zest of ½ lemon
for the dressing	2 tablespoons cider vinegar
1 fresh red onion, thinly sliced	3 handful chopped mixed herbs: ramsons, parsley,
2 cloves garlic, finely chopped	dill, chervil, scallions, tarragon
1 teaspoon salt	SERVES 4
4 tablespoons olive or canola oil	

Soak and boil the grains, as above, until soft, then drain, reserving the cooking water. Mix together all the dressing ingredients, adding enough of the reserved cooking water to moisten the grain when dressed (the remaining water, which has a meaty taste, can be used in soups). Blend the dressing with the hot grains. Cool and stir in the herbs. Eat this salad with any fish, chicken, or roast meat.

Nordic herb salt

This herb salt is good for flavoring fish, pork, *frikadeller* (meatballs), butters, sauces, and all kinds of vegetables. The recipe is very similar to the elderflower spiced salt (page 183), the main difference being the substitution of an abundant amount of herbs for the chiles, lemon and garlic. Herbs to choose from include elderflowers, dill, dill flowers, fennel flowers, parsley, chervil, thyme, lemon thyme, and chives; caraway seeds taste good too.

4 cups mixed Nordic herbs
⅔ cup very coarse unrefined salt

Blend the herbs finely in a food processor with half the salt, but be sure not to reduce it to a complete sludge. Mix with the rest of the salt, then spread the mixture out on a tray. Leave it to dry as described on page 183. The salt will absorb the liquid of the herbs and become very wet. It does not have to dry out completely, but enough so that the herbs become dry and the salt is still a little sticky.

Fruit can be grown all over Scandinavia—apples and rhubarb almost up to the very north, and pears, plums, and cherries in almost all of it. The gulf stream makes it possible to grow fruit much farther north than in similar latitudes in America.

There has been much research into finding and developing hardy cultivars and rootstocks of fruit to suit even the harshest climates, and the worst situations, and people grow fruit in almost every garden across Scandinavia. This is necessary if you want a more locally flavored fruit as most of the fruit in the stores is imported.

Fruit grown in cool summers, with daylight almost till midnight, and even longer in the far north, has a special sweetness, a very thin, crisp skin, and lots of taste. It's very different from fruit grown in warmer climates. There is a rising interest in growing—and eating—old tasty cultivars, and awareness after many years of bland imported fruit, to take care of it, preserve the cultivars, and support the growers by gorging on it when it is in season. Local fruit can now be found with little effort in markets, and good supermarkets, and the trees can be found in special nurseries to grow yourself.

Scandinavians love fruit, especially in cakes and desserts, but also in main course dishes. We share a love of eating apples, cherries, plums, and rhubarb with meat and fish; we stuff the roast for Christmas with apples and prunes, and serve fruit preserves and compotes with fried fish, chicken, game, and venison. Fruit is preserved in a multitude of ways: dried, pickled, jellied, jammed—and all the nice things in between.

fruit

Apple

Apples are the most loved, most widely grown, and varied fruit crop in the Nordic countries. There are thousands of original cultivars, but few of them are known outside the region, despite the fact that apples grown in our northern soils are tastier and crisper than those from warmer, sunnier climates.

Such qualities are being appreciated by a rapidly growing number of people in Scandinavia, who are rejuvenating the fruit-tree trade, grafting at home, planting small orchards, saving aged fruit trees, and demanding old cultivars with more taste in the stores. This comes after decades during which imported apples, such as Golden Delicious and Granny Smith, have dominated the scene. It's high time that we discovered these national treasures, a much too good and interesting heritage to let disappear. It is time that we taught our children that there's more to apples than sweetness.

Cultivars There are thousands of original cultivars, some of them known worldwide, such as Gravenstein. Gråsten is the original Danish name, after the royal castle in Gråsten, where a very old tree of this cultivar (if not the original tree) still exists.

The Swedish apple Aroma has also achieved worldwide recognition, a lovely dark red hand-eating apple with a waxy bloom. The Pigeon apple is another very special variety of old ancestry; it is probably even able to reproduce itself true to seed. It's a pretty, small, dark red apple with a unique almond flavor. Traditionally picked in October, it is left to ripen and develop its intense color. Pigeons are eaten at Christmas, and even used to decorate the Christmas tree. They are delicious in salads and dipped in caramel.

Every country has its own cultivars, and many are kept alive in the national arboretums and local *pomets* (tree museums), where you can see the trees and taste the apples. Naturally, many more have vanished, but some can still be found, unnamed, in old gardens and orchards. These multitudes of cultivars are mostly chance seedlings, revealing themselves on compost heaps and wherever somebody threw an apple core. The vast majority are worthless, but are a perfect example of serendipity at work: people have stumbled upon them, tried them, and a few have been recognized and grown on for generations, in the neighborhood, long before there was any trade in fruit trees. Vicarages once played a large part in spreading both know-how and planting material of both useful and ornamental plants to their parishes, and before the Reformation the monasteries did the same.

Having religion paving the way was a very useful method of spreading the know-how to stubborn peasants, who did not want to use precious land for dainty fruit trees or berry bushes. But it caught on, the women probably realizing first that collecting wild apples of doubtful taste was not as good as growing your own grafted trees that were more prolific, with sweeter, juicier, and more useful fruit. Sweetness was precious in old times, before sugar was accessible, when many fruits were dried for winter—and the sweeter the apples were, the better they were as dried.

Appearance and taste The cold climate in Nordic countries means that apples grow at a slow pace, allowing the fruit to take up more minerals and other nutrients, which deepen the taste. Also, when the sun is not so scorching, the apples do not need to grow such thick skins to stop the fruit from drying out.

Perfection in an apple is far from enough to secure a good fruit. You must know your cultivars, for example, and their uses. There is a huge difference between hand-eating apples and apples for cooking. Hand-eating apples have more acid and sometimes more sugar, keeping them firm while cooking. Apples suitable for cooking are lower in both, cooking to a pulp—it's nice to know the difference if you plan on an apple pie or baked apple. Furthermore, how the apples are grown is important. Organic apples have been shown to have more taste (as well as more nutrients) than conventionally grown fruit. Modern consumers often refuse to buy imperfect-looking apples with spots,

fungi, or blemishes, considering looks more important than taste or origin.

Buying and storing If you just buy a bag of apples for immediate consumption, it's easy—the fruit should be fragrant, firm, and without rotten spots. Home-grown apples that you wish to store must be picked off the tree and put into wooden crates very carefully, as the slightest pressure will influence their durability. Store very cool and frost free. The apples should keep all winter—depending on the cultivar, of course. Apples collected from the ground must be used within a few days. Keep cool, but not necessarily in the refrigerator.

Health benefits Apples are very good for you, particularly if you choose organic fruit, which have a higher and more varied content of minerals, micronutrients, and vitamins than conventionally grown varieties. All apples contain serotonin, which helps to keep us happy.

There are a couple of important facts to be aware of. Firstly, modern cultivars are too sweet—actually so sweet that dentists advise us to consider them more like confectionary than fruit. Secondly, if you don't choose to eat organic apples, you are exposing your body to the residues of pesticides found both on the skin and in the flesh of the fruit. The content may be below a level that is considered harmful, but even small doses are definitely not good for you or your children.

Culinary uses Apples must be the most versatile fruit in the kitchen. They are eaten raw, in salads, or cooked, whether as a sauce, baked, stuffed, or fried. As a dessert, in a cake, trifle, or simply baked, apples are of course a classic. But they are as useful in main course dishes as in sweet cooking—and in Scandinavia there is a thriving tradition in both.

In main courses, apples are often paired with fish and pork. The tradition of combining them with meat and fish is celebrated particularly at Christmas, when they are stuffed into the Christmas goose or duck along with prunes and thyme, and on the Christmas lunch table there is apple with the crisp roast pork, the herrings, and the herring salad.

Apple and horseradish compote

This concoction is a most useful and versatile member of the pickle-sauce-relish family. It keeps for ages, because of the horseradish, which is naturally anti-bacterial. It's also perfect for fighting off winter colds, and is magic served with either fried fish or all manner of roast meats, or indeed open-face sandwiches made with any of these. It's simply a basic apple compote, like the previous recipe, but spiced with fresh horseradish.

Scrape the peel off the horseradish and grate finely. It will make you cry your heart out, and strangely, when you cry, it actually makes you feel sad, but the sauce will make you happy again. Stir the horseradish into the apple compote a little at a time, as it can be very hot. Keep tasting: you want a hot apple sauce, but one you can eat several spoonfuls of without bursting into tears.

Apple syrup

This syrup is very useful in all sorts of desserts, or poured over ice cream, cereals, hot oatmeal, or fresh fruit. It can be used to flavor stews, marinades, dressings, and sauces that need a little extra something.

4 cups unfiltered apple juice
1 cup sugar

Simply boil the juice and sugar in a saucepan to a rich syrup. Stored in a sterilized jar or bottle, this will keep for years.

Apple compote

Apple compote is a very basic commodity, and extremely versatile. We eat it on hot oatmeal, with blackberries and cream, make it into old-fashioned apple cakes, use it as a topping for pork sandwiches, or eat it just as a snack. It makes sense to prepare a large quantity, which you can dust with granulated sugar and keep in the refrigerator; it will disappear in a few days.

5lb apples suitable for cooking, peeled and cored
2½ cups sugar, or to taste

Put the apples in a non-reactive saucepan, add ¼ cup water, and put it on the heat with a lid on. The apples will disintegrate into a fluffy, white cloud. Check once in a while and stir with a spoon until the last of the apples has softened. But small chunks are no problem.

Cool a little, then add the sugar, stirring until it is dissolved. Taste, and add more sugar if needed; note that the compote will taste a little less sweet when cold. If you are going to eat the compote with cream and berries, you must leave room for a sprinkling of sugar on top.

Braised pork with apples

This is the perfect take on the age-old marriage of pork and apples—ideal for Christmas, or a buffet. Once in the oven, it takes care of itself. Serve with potatoes.

4lb 8oz pork neck, in one
  piece, with rind
Coarse sea salt and pepper
4 fresh bay leaves
3lb 5oz hand-eating apples
1 whole garlic bulb
2¼lb onions, peeled and
  quartered

2 cinnamon sticks
1 large sprig of fresh thyme
Generous ⅓ cup cider
  vinegar
6 cups unfiltered apple juice
  (not from concentrate)
SERVES 10

Preheat the oven to 300°F.

Using a sharp knife, make slashes in the rind of the pork, then rub the meat generously with salt and pepper; make sure you rub plenty of salt into the cuts in the rind. Stick the bay leaves into the cuts.

Core and quarter the apples, but do not peel. Divide the garlic bulb into cloves, but do not necessarily peel. Arrange the apples, garlic, onions, cinnamon, and thyme in a deep ovenproof dish. This must be big enough to host the meat and vegetables in a layer about 1½in deep. Squeeze the meat into the middle. Pour the vinegar and juice over the vegetables.

Bake in the oven for approximately 2 hours, turning the vegetables over once in a while to coat with the pan juices. The meat is done when the juices run a pinkish brown and the crackling is crispy. If it is not crispy, put the meat on a rack and roast for a few minutes at 475°F, while you watch.

Let the meat rest for 20 minutes before carving. Mash the garlic in with the vegetables before serving.

Crisp pork slices with caramelized onions and apples

This is a classic Christmas dish in Scandinavia, served with rye bread or new potatoes, or as part of a buffet.

2¼lb fresh unsalted belly of pork	½ cup sugar
1 tablespoon coarse sea salt	Black pepper
4lb 8oz hand-eating apples	**to serve**
1 large sprig of fresh thyme, leaves stripped	Caramelized onions (page 77)
1 fresh bay leaf	SERVES 4

Cut the meat into slices roughly ½in thick, then arrange on a rack that fits over a large ovenproof dish you will need for the apples. Sprinkle over the salt, then let the meat rest for a couple of hours, turning the pork slices over once or twice.

Preheat the oven to 350°F.

Quarter and core the apples, but leave the peel on. Place in the large ovenproof dish, in a double layer. Sprinkle over the thyme leaves, bay leaf, and sugar, and some salt and

pepper. Place the meat-filled rack on top and bake in the oven until the pork is crispy.

The fat from the pork will drip deliciously onto the apples as the meat cooks. Take out of the oven once during cooking in order to turn the apples over. If they are tender and beautifully roasted before the meat is ready, take the apples out altogether; you don't want them to go mushy.

Serve the pork and apples together with the caramelized onions.

Celery, apple, and walnut salad

Crisp and slightly sweet, this makes a perfect salad for venison, game, goose, and duck, and for roasts in general.

1 celery heart	Scant ¼ cup extra-virgin olive oil
5–6 hand-eating apples (preferably a spicy cultivar)	5 tablespoons cider vinegar
2 handfuls of walnuts	Salt and coarsely ground pepper
1 medium bunch of seedless grapes, preferably Muscat, halved	1 tablespoon liquid honey
	SERVES 4–6

Apple cake with a potato crust and cranberries

The potato crust on this cake is seriously old-fashioned, stemming from a date when leftovers were always used up. The potatoes give an unexpectedly delicious texture. Eat it for tea, or as a lukewarm dessert with vanilla ice cream.

3 cups sweet, dryish apple
   compote (page 192)
2 cups plain flour
1 cup + ¼ stick butter
9oz boiled potatoes
   (unsalted)
½ cup sugar

⅓ cup dried cranberries,
   or raisins
1 egg, for glazing
2 tablespoons superfine
   sugar, for dusting
SERVES 8

Preheat the oven to 325°F. If your apple compote is watery, put it in a fine sieve and let the excess liquid drain off while you make the dough.

Mix the flour and butter to a fine crumble on the counter. Mash the potatoes with the sugar then add to the dough and knead with your hands.

Cut the celery and apples into nice bite-size pieces, reserving the pale yellowish leaves from the celery. Mix the celery and apples with the rest of the ingredients, except for the salt. Leave the salad to macerate for a while, then taste and season with salt and maybe a little more honey. Coarsley chop some of the reserved celery leaves and scatter on top, and it's ready.

Leftovers will keep for a couple of days.

Dried apples

If you own an apple tree, this is an extremely useful way to deal with the fall glut. The fruit must be ripe, with a high enough sugar content to stop the apples from rotting.

Core the apples but otherwise leave them whole, with the skins on. Slice them on a mandolin or with a knife into very thin slices, all with a hole in the middle. Then simply thread the slices on to string and hang them up to dry in a drafty place; the temperature is not so important. In a few weeks they will be firm and chewy, and good, just as a snack. They can also be incorporated into cake batter, bread, pâtés, and salads.

Roll the dough out to a ¼in-thick rectangle, using a little extra flour to stop it sticking. Move onto a piece of parchment paper. Spoon the compote with the cranberries onto the middle third of the dough, leaving room either side. Using a sharp knife, slash the two areas of dough on either side of the filling 8–10 times each. Fold over the pieces of slashed dough, alternating the sides, to form a braided lattice over the filling.

Glaze the top with the egg and sprinkle on a generous layer of fine sugar. Bake until the cake is done and a lovely golden brown.

Old-fashioned apple trifle

This dessert is a good example of northern common sense! It's lovely, and made from simple ingredients – stale crumbs from either rye or normal wheat bread, and apples. It's cheap and maybe the best-loved apple dessert of all. The crab apple jelly or lingonberry jam is the finishing touch.

Scant ½ cup butter
½ cup brown sugar
6 cups stale bread crumbs
3¼ cups apple compote
 (page 192)

1¾ cups heavy cream, softly
 whipped
⅓ cup crab apple jelly or
 ¼ cup raw lingonberry
 jam (page 226)
SERVES 6

Melt the butter and sugar together in a heavy saucepan, then add the bread crumbs and stir over medium heat until crispy. Layer the crumbs and compote, ending with crumbs, in either a deep dish or individual glasses. Top with the whipped cream and blobs of jam or jelly.

Without the cream, the trifle will keep for several days in the refrigerator.

Very good apple cake

Or rather the apple cake to end all apple cakes: it's full of apples, as it's apples we want, not sponge (though in fact the cake works perfectly well with pears, plums, and all sorts of berries, too). The rice flour gives a very special consistency, light but fudgy. While the cake is easy to make, you must follow the recipe meticulously to get perfect results.

The quantities below make three large cakes, but you are welcome to reduce them—though since you are already at it, and your kitchen is a mess already, you might as well bake a couple of cakes. The cake will keep for at least 10 days in a cool place, and it also freezes very well.

Min. 5lb 8oz apples
3⅓ cups butter, plus extra
 for greasing
3¾ cups sugar
9 eggs
4 cups plain flour
Generous ½ cup rice flour
 or potato starch
1 tablespoon baking
 powder

2 teaspoons ground
 cinnamon
for the sugar crust
1 cup white or light
 brown sugar
Ground seeds from
 10 green cardamom pods
10 star anise, ground
MAKES 3 LARGE CAKES

Preheat the oven to 325°F. Quarter and core the apples, but do not peel them. Butter three large, loose-bottomed cake pans with a generous blob of soft butter.

Beat the butter and sugar together, preferably in a mixer, until the sugar has dissolved—be warned, this can take a long time. Then, when you're ready, mix in the eggs one at a time; make sure each one is well incorporated into the batter before proceeding to the next egg.

Sift the two flours and baking powder into the batter and mix thoroughly. Divide the mixture between the pans,

but be sure that it does not come higher than about 40 percent up the sides as you need to leave room for a lot of apples, plus space for rising. Now arrange the apples on top, squeezing them in well—the batter should be bursting with apples. Mix together the sugar and spices for the topping, and sprinkle over the cakes.

Bake in the oven until done. This may take anything from 35 minutes to an hour, depending on your oven, the pans, and the apples. Test the cakes with a skewer, and if it comes out clean they are done.

Crab apple

Crab apple trees grow in profusion all over Scandinavia. Fruit growers cultivate them in orchards to facilitate pollination, as crab apple trees draw hordes of bees to their abundant blossom, and they are used for their extremely hardy root stock. Others plant them simply to enjoy their beautiful display of white, pink, or cerise flowers in spring.

Crab apples are not widely used in the kitchen any more, but the small, slightly bitter fruits make an exquisite jelly, which is much more flavorful and intense than jelly from ordinary apples, and is often richly colored (depending on the color of the cultivar).

The procedure for making jelly is very much the same, whatever fruit you decide to make it from: you can use the same recipe for ordinary apples, black currants, red currants, gooseberries, medlars, and quince. The most important factor is a high level of pectin. Essentially a carbohydrate, pectin is transformed into sugar as the fruit ripens, which is why you must use unripe, tart fruit in order to make the jelly set. Most other fruit do not have enough pectin to make jelly unaided by commercial pectin. The latter is best avoided, as it suffocates the taste and often makes the jelly rubbery, instead of melting in your mouth.

here, I suggest you hang the fruit from the faucet and simply place the bowl in the sink. If you make a larger amount, you can tie the corners of the cloth to the legs of an upturned chair, with the seat resting on the table. Do not, under any circumstances, squeeze the bag; the juice must drip at its own speed. Leave overnight.

Once there is no more juice to come through, measure the contents of the bowl, then place in a large saucepan. Add 3¾ cups sugar per 4 cups. At this point, you should also put a small stack of saucers into your refrigerator to cool.

Boil the juice and sugar together vigorously, removing any scum. The setting point of the juice can be reached very fast, or may take 20 minutes of boiling. Check by dripping a small teaspoonful onto one of your cold saucers then replacing it in the refrigerator. Once it has cooled, run your finger through the jelly: if it runs, it's not finished, if it wrinkles, it is. If your jelly has not set after 20 minutes of boiling, it probably never will—but you will have a lovely syrup for desserts and pancakes, or for flavoring stews and marinades.

Pour the jelly into sterilized jars and let cool before putting the lids on. If you want to make sure that the jelly doesn't go moldy, add a little brandy or whisky to the jars beforehand and give them a shake (with the lid on, of course); remove, or drink, the contents before you add the jelly.

Crab apple jelly

This jelly is slightly bitter but tastes wonderful on buttered toast, as decoration for any dessert with apples, or served with venison and game.

4lb 8oz crab apples
Sugar

Wash the crab apples (or other fruit) and remove any blemished ones. Place in a non-reactive saucepan and barely cover with water. Bring to a boil and let the fruit bubble for around 20 minutes, or until it is soft, removing any scum from the top. Mash the fruit with a spoon or a balloon whisk.

Pour the fruity pulp into a colander lined with a very clean cloth or cheesecloth and place over a large bowl—the cloth must be big enough for you to tie a piece of string around it once it's full of fruit, so you can suspend the whole thing for the juice to drip through. For the amounts given

Pear

Pears are popular as a dessert fruit. We love eating ripe pears with delicious matured cheese, including blue cheese, and crispbread. (This is way better than eating cheese with the ubiquitous grapes, which can make the cheese taste like soap.) There is no real tradition of utilizing pears in the kitchen, except for a few highlights.

Pears will grow only in southern Scandinavia. In general, the pears we grow are the same as the rest of Europe, but we have a few very old cultivars, including the *gråpære* (or "gray pear"), a small, wonderfully perfumed, juicy pear which is perfect for pickling.

Pears in elderberry syrup

This is a very Nordic take on the French or Italian recipe for pears in red wine. It has a beautiful autumnal feel to it and a surprising, rich flavor. The elderberry cordial can be replaced with other strongly colored/flavored fruit juices such as cherry, blackberry, lingonberry, or black currant; just remember to adjust the sweetening.

4 large or 8 small slightly underripe pears	1 cup sugar
	1 cinnamon stick
2 cups unsweetened elderberry cordial (page 230)	Zest and juice of 1 lemon
	SERVES 4

Peel the pears, keeping them whole, and leaving the stalks on. Place in a deep, heavy-bottomed saucepan, then add the rest of the ingredients. Heat gently and let fruit simmer over a low heat until the pears are tender, turning them gently once in a while. The cooking time will vary a lot depending on the cultivar and ripeness of the fruit.

Take the pears out with a slotted spoon, then reduce the liquid to a thick syrup. Taste it for sweetness and add more sugar if required: this needs to be a sweet dessert, but not too sweet. Once it has cooled, pour the syrup over the pears in a pretty, deep serving dish. Serve them cold as they are, or with cardamom ice cream (page 23).

Pears preserved with lingonberries

These preserved fruit are my own childhood favorite, delicious eaten with whipped cream or ice cream. If you don't fancy preserving the pears in jars, you can simply simmer them in the syrup and eat them straight away, adding the lingonberries at the end of the cooking time.

5 cups sugar	4lb 8oz small hard pears
4 cups water	5 cups lingonberries
1 vanilla bean, split	

Begin by boiling the sugar, water, and vanilla bean together in a saucepan until the sugar has dissolved.

Peel the pears, keeping them whole, and leaving the stalks on. Pack them tightly into pickling jars (the sort with a rubber seal), and add some lingonberries. Cut up the vanilla bean and add a piece to each jar, then simply top up with the syrup. This should cover the pears, but leave a gap of ¾in at the top to allow room for boiling. If the pears are small and tightly packed, the amount of syrup you have made should be sufficient; if not, make some more, but without the vanilla bean.

Close the lids and put the jars in a cold oven. Turn the heat to 225°F and let the jars bake until the pears are done—they take on a glassy look—and the contents have been visibly boiling for at least 20 minutes. Turn off the oven and let cool.

Pears prepared in this way absorb benzoic acid from the lingonberries, which adds to the keeping quality.

Cherry

Wild cherries (*Prunus avium*), which are not indigenous to Scandinavia, were probably imported by travelers during the Iron Age. The trees took root and so did a taste for the cherries among the locals, who have been gathering them to eat fresh, or dried, ever since. Wild cherry trees are common in deciduous forests, while cultivated ones are found in many country gardens—though they grow to an enormous size so can rarely be accommodated in smaller gardens. Cultivated sweet cherries are the same species, bred for uniformity of taste and size. The cultivars we grow are almost all British.

The sour cherry (*Prunus cerasus*) is much hardier than its sweet cousin. It was imported to Britain by the Romans, from where it probably came to Scandinavia. Sour cherries grow on small, spindly trees that are much easier to accommodate—and also well worth growing—in small gardens. Their fragrant, cloud-like blooms are a wonderful sight in early spring.

Appearance and taste Wild cherries are sexually reproduced and they are extremely variable; some are large and resemble modern cultivars, while others have a pronounced almond taste, and some are wickedly sour. Modern sweet cherry cultivars can be huge or small, crisp or soft, early or late, yellow, dark red, or scarlet, and they are all good to eat fresh.

Sour cherries are the size of very large black currants and will dye you crimson all over. They come off the stem when you pick them, while sweet cherries come off the branch with their stem attached. The famous Marasca cherry, called *Stevnsbær* in Scandinavia, is an extremely tasty cultivar. Juice from sour cherry cultivars can be red or almost black, depending on the variety. Sour cherries are never eaten as a dessert fruit.

Health benefits Like all dark fruit, cherries are full of antioxidants, iron and, when fresh, lots of vitamin C.

Buying and storing Sweet cherries can be bought anywhere in the summer season, while sour cherries are hard to find. Frozen sour cherries are a very good substitute for fresh ones, if you want to cook with them.

Culinary uses Sweet cherries are generally eaten just as they are. Sour cherries are usually inedibly sour when fresh, but give a rich, almondy taste to all jams, liqueurs, cakes, and sauces when cooked. The traditional use for sour cherries is in a special sauce for *riz à la mande*, an almond-flavored rice pudding, and homemade cherry brandy—both of which are traditionally consumed on Christmas Eve. Wild cherries with an acid taste and dark flesh are fine to use in cooking as well.

Cherry brandy

This is a drink for Christmas. When the fruit is in season, fill a wine bottle with fresh, whole sour cherries. Add 1 cup sugar and fill the bottle with unflavored schnapps, dark rum, or vodka. Then simply sit back and wait for Christmas, when we traditionally drink cherry brandy with dessert on the December 24. It's also a wonderful addition to the spiced, hot Christmas drink *gløgg* (page 257).

Sweet cherry sauce

This is a classic sauce to be served with *riz à l'amande*, Christmas rice pudding with almonds (page 266). You can use fresh or frozen sour cherries, or alternatively a jar or can of preserved cherries. You will need about ⅓ cup of cherry sauce per head.

2¼ cups sweet/sour cherries (fresh or frozen), pitted
1 cup sugar
1–2 tablespoons cornstarch
2 Spanish almonds (optional)
A little lemon juice (optional)
SERVES 8–10

Put the fresh or frozen cherries in a large, wide saucepan. Heat the fruit until the juices run, then add the sugar, and boil vigorously until you have a beautiful, garnet-colored syrup holding juicy, whole cherries. When you are ready to eat, warm the sauce and stir in 1–2 tablespoons cornstarch mixed with enough cold water to form a thin paste. Boil for 5 minutes and serve.

The sauce, up to the stage when you add the cornstarch, can be prepared several days ahead. For a more pronounced almond taste, you can add a couple of finely grated Spanish almonds to the sauce as well. Or if the sauce seems rather insipid, add a spoonful of lemon juice. Neither of these measures should be necessary if you make your own sauce from scratch.

If you are using preserved cherries, you don't need to boil the fruit at all. Simply heat the syrup in a saucepan and add 1 tablespoon cornstarch (mixed to a paste with a little cold water), which should be sufficient for a ¾pt jar. Boil for 5 minutes, then add the cherries at the last minute. If all you can obtain are the Italian Amarena cherries, these are very sweet and definitely over the top as far as taste goes, but fine as a rather overwhelming substitute.

Cherry sauce for meat

This simple cherry sauce is perfect for broiled or pan-fried dark meat, such as duck, reindeer, elk, or venison, and it's a far better option than simply incorporating cherries into a gravy. The rest of the accompaniments could be potatoes, a celery and apple salad, and a celeriac mash with nutmeg.

Scant 1½ cups sour cherries, pitted
⅓–½ cup sugar
1 tablespoon lemon thyme leaves
2 tablespoons salted butter
SERVES 4

Heat the cherries, sugar, and thyme leaves in a wide saucepan, until the juices run. Let the fruit bubble gently to reduce the liquid to a rich syrup, then stir in the butter to make a glossy sauce.

Rhubarb

Rhubarb has become so naturalized in the Scandinavian climate that it is hard to believe that it arrived only during the 16th century. Originally, it was imported as a medicinal plant, and that is how it was regarded for centuries, until the Scandinavians began to eat it in the early 1800s (when sugar became more affordable). Two centuries is not nearly enough time to exhibit a truly Nordic touch in how we use rhubarb. Nevertheless, it is loved in the spring, its hardiness an important virtue when the ground is covered with snow for many months, as in the plant's native Russia and northern China.

How it grows Rhubarb is a superbly rewarding plant to grow. When the first shoots appear in spring it's like a miracle—red, tightly crinkled leaves thrusting through the ground like small skulls, waiting impatiently to be born. And rhubarb is a survivor, growing on for decades even in derelict gardens, becoming larger and larger if the soil is fertile, and it's happy even in dappled shade. Some varieties are grown for their abundance, others for their extreme hardiness. We prefer the early cultivars because the growing season is so short.

Appearance and taste There are many species of rhubarb which, technically, is a vegetable rather than a fruit. In Scandinavia we grow only one species, *Rheum rhabarbarum*, of which there are many fine varieties with intensely colored stalks.

The first stalks to appear are particularly treasured, and are prepared as if they were solid gold, with great care to keep their delicacy and aroma, and, just as important, their shape. They remain in perfect condition until the first strawberries arrive, and the two together are a match made in heaven. Then the rhubarb is left to grow, and picked again only from August onward for jams, chutneys, and cordial.

Health benefits Rhubarb has a reputation for being potentially dangerous, and it does have a high content of both malic and oxalic acids. If you eat it every day, it's probably not good for your teeth, but nobody does. The acid can be counteracted by eating the rhubarb with a generous blob of something white, fatty, and milky, which you probably would anyway, because the

Rhubarb is a revelation of spring freshness in the kitchen, its pinkness welcome after a fruit-bare winter, the acidity good for burning off the extra fat accrued during the cold months. Young, adventurous cooks are finally discovering the virtues of rhubarb, using it in main course dishes as well as for desserts. For most of us, it is simply a most delicious and gloriously versatile fruit. You'll find rhubarb in almost every garden, all over Scandinavia, even if it's not always used in the kitchen. Kids play with the giant leaves and pick the young shoots to suck, filling their mouth with a strange acidity.

texture and taste of rhubarb marry so wonderfully with cream, yogurt, ice cream, or crème fraîche. The more intensely colored varieties have a high content of anthocyan, a coloring which is an important part of the plant's immune system, and thereby also the immune system of the people eating it.

Culinary uses The arrival of rhubarb is a great gift in spring, and fills the gap before the first gooseberries and strawberries. Rhubarb has much of the same charm as gooseberries, and can be used in the same recipes. Very young, red rhubarb can be made into a delicious and very pretty fresh relish for fried fish, chicken, pork, and *frikadeller* if treated exactly as for the cucumber salad on page 146.

The juiciness of rhubarb varies according to its age: young rhubarb will spill a lot of juice, older, not so much. And some varieties are far sourer than others, so when cooking with rhubarb be prepared to adjust the sugar accordingly.

Rhubarb compote

Rhubarb compote is such a beautiful thing: firm, translucent, and silky sticks in syrup of the loveliest pink, and a far cry from the pink-green sludge that it can be if not cooked with care. A delicious, well-made compote is at the heart of many great rhubarb dishes. Eat it hot or cold, plain with cream or ice cream, and/or with sponge cake. Excess syrup tastes wonderful as a cordial.

The secret of beautiful rhubarb compote lies in the method. Cooking it to perfection in a saucepan is difficult, while in the oven it's easy: the rhubarb is not stirred, and the oven simply melts the fruit in whole pieces, in a sugary syrup, until it's tender. Another secret—the lower, very pale part of the stalk is the best—just cut it a little thinner. And do not bother to strip off the outer layers of older, woodier stalks: just cut the stalks in fine slices.

Rhubarb and sugar are the only basic ingredients required, but you can choose to spice it with up with one of the following flavorings suggestions.

18oz rhubarb, cut into
  2in pieces
1 cup sugar
One of the following
  (optional): 2in piece of
  angelica; 3–4 rose
  geranium leaves;

1¼in piece of fresh ginger,
  sliced; 1 cinnamon stick,
  1 stem of sweet grass,
  1 small bunch of
  woodruff, or 1 split
  vanilla bean

Mix the rhubarb, sugar, and a spicing of your choice (if using) in an ovenproof dish. Cover with aluminum foil and bake at 350°F for approximately 25 minutes. Test the fruit after 10 minutes, and turn it over very gently. When the fruit is cooked, test the sweetness. If you need to add more sugar, do not add this directly to the rhubarb. Gently pour off the syrup into a saucepan, then add extra sugar, and bring to a boil. Let the syrup cool, then pour it back over the rhubarb.

TIP
• By adapting the above recipe slightly, you can make a compote that is a wonderful spring accompaniment for fried fish, chicken, pigeon, or pork. It is made as above, but using only ¾ cup sugar, and adding 3 tablespoons cider vinegar. You can spice it up with a little chile if you wish.

Rhubarb tart

This is what to do with the very first young, pink rhubarb. The buttery dough and crisp meringue achieved with long, slow baking, are the perfect foil for the rhubarb's tenderness and tart flavor.

To make one large tart you will need a loose-bottomed tart pan, (10½in) or you will never get it out alive.

for the pie dough
Generous ½ cup butter
Generous 1½ cups all-purpose flour
¼ cup sugar
1 egg
for the filling
1 big bunch rhubarb

½ cup sugar
2 tablespoons potato starch or cornstarch
for the meringue
3 egg whites
1⅓ cups confectioner's sugar
SERVES 8

Mix the ingredients for the dough on your counter. First cut the butter with a big knife into marble-size pieces, then mix it with your hands, not a machine. You want a very crunchy crust so do not knead it, as it will make it tough. Just mix it sufficiently not to fall apart. Put it in a cool place for an hour or more.

Meanwhile whip the egg whites and confectioners' sugar to a very stiff meringue.

Preheat the oven to 275°F.

Roll out the dough to approx. ¼in and line your pan with it. It sounds simple, but it is not, the dough will be sticking to your counter and will not be very cooperative, even if this is a flexible pie dough. The trick is to use a handful of flour to roll it out with, and using the thin metal bottom of the pan to lift it off the counter, if it sticks. Turn it often as you go, and finally lift it off the counter with the pan bottom, and let it drop—with the dough—into the pan. Use scraps to make the edges thicker than the bottom. Leftover dough can be made into cookies.

Cut the rhubarb into 1¼in pieces, mix with the sugar and starch, and spread on the dough.

Put the meringue in a plastic food bag, cut a corner off the bag with scissors, and squeeze it onto the rhubarb in whatever pattern you prefer. Bake in the oven until the dough is baked through and the meringue is crisp and dry. Cool and serve with whipped cream.

Spiced rhubarb jam

Choose from the suggested flavorings to add spice to the jam.

2¼lb rhubarb
3 cups sugar
One of the following:
  ½ cup paper-thin slices of fresh ginger, 1 split vanilla bean, 2 cinnamon sticks,

5 bashed cardamom pods, 2 star anise, or 4in piece of angelica, cut into very thin slices

Mix everything together in a deep oven pan—you should end up with a double layer of fruit. Bake at 225°F until the rhubarb is tender and translucent, and the syrup condensed into a thick coating. You can turn the fruit gently during cooking, making sure it's evenly baked, but do not stir too much or the rhubarb will disintegrate.

Pour into sterilized jars and llet cool. Close when cold.

Rhubarb cordial

For this cordial you can use old, woody stalks, and even enormous, green stalks will provide a lovely rosy result. I don't give precise quantities here. Once you've picked your rhubarb, all you need to do is work out how much sugar you need: take 1¼ cups per 4 cups of juice as your starting point, but you may need double that.

Chop the rhubarb stalks up roughly, then place in a saucepan, push down well, and barely cover with water. Bring to a boil and let the fruit simmer for 10 minutes.

Mash the cooked rhubarb into threads using a balloon whisk, then transfer into a large cloth or piece of cheesecloth which you can tie to a faucet for the juice to drip into a bowl in the sink. It must drip, all by itself, until the pulp is dry; if you squeeze it, the juice will be cloudy.

The following day, bring the juice to a boil and add sugar as you wish—there are no rules, and of course the sourness of the rhubarb will vary. Add at least 1¼ cups, then take it from there. Pour the cordial into sterilized bottles, and store in a cool place, or freeze in plastic containers.

Plum

In southern Scandinavia we have a huge tradition of making pickles and jams with every possible variety of plums. We make no distinction between plums and gages; both are simply called plums, and both are prized and recognized as a delicacy. There is almost no commercial growing of plums in Scandinavia—it is surprisingly hard to find them in the stores even during the picking season in late August and September—but they are grown in most gardens, wherever possible.

Habitat Plums are at their northernmost limit in southern Scandinavia. The trees can grow very far north, but the blossom is ruined by the bitter frosts. We grow mainly old British, French, and German varieties, but in old gardens you can still find the Hungarian variety used for making slivovitz (plum brandy) in eastern Europe.

Cherry plums, also known as myrobalan (*Prunus ceracifera*), are relatively new to the north, being introduced in the mid-19th century from southern Europe. But they have spread so fast that it now seems incredible that they are not a native. Cherry plums are the very first trees to flower in spring—sometimes even before the end of February: the clouds of white blossom that cover vast areas for several weeks are an overwhelming sight, their sweet honey scent wafting through the cool air. The fruit is not generally appreciated, and they are mostly self-seeded, and show every possible color from bright canary yellow to deep purple.

Before the cherry plum invaded the countryside, northerners grew and collected a huge variety of damsons and bullaces. They make identical suckers, and are easy to propagate; I grow several old cultivars, including the "raisin plum," a small, incredibly sweet plum with a distinct raisin flavor, and others that are more like sloes, but good for jam. Many of these old varieties are almost extinct, but some work is being done to preserve them. These plums are perfect for primitive methods of preserving, such as drying, as their sugar and acid content is high enough for them to dry safely even in the cold northern climate.

Appearance and taste Cherry plums vary in size from cherry to gage, and the taste can be anything from deliciously apricot-flavored to dark plum, mealy, juicy, sweet, sour, or plain bland. But even if their virtues as a dessert fruit are not consistent, they all make the most intensely flavored jam, ketchup, and chutney. In general, the fair-skinned fruits have an apricot/gage taste, dark fruits more of a prune flavor.

While cherry plums, damsons, and bullaces are small, proper plums are a more manageable size, making it much easier to take out the pits. Apart from the omnipresent Victoria plum, which is not so good to cook with, the most common varieties include the Opal, originally a Swedish cultivar, which is the earliest variety to ripen in mid-August and is a small, blue, and sweet fruit that is best eaten fresh; and the Kirkes Blue, a plump, purple-skinned, green-fleshed and highly flavored British variety which ripens from mid-September. This plum is very good for jam and pickling, and the harvest is usually abundant. The best variety for most of the following recipes is the Italian prune plum—a huge, juicy, purple fruit with delicious amber flesh that tastes as sweet as honey; it ripens in late September or early October. Greengages are grown, and loved by aficionados, and eaten fresh or preserved whole.

Pickled plums in red wine

These pickled plums are a little cumbersome to make but taste exquisite and are definitely worth the effort. Eat with whipped cream or ice cream. They are also very nice with game or cheese.

4lb 8oz Italian prune or other firm-fleshed plum	Peeled zest of 1 lemon
	1 bottle red wine
10 cloves	10 cups sugar
2 cinnamon sticks	MAKES 6 REGULAR JARS

Prick each plum 5–6 times with a fork, then put into a sterilized jar. Add the spices and lemon zest. Put half the bottle of wine and 5 cups of the sugar into a saucepan and heat until the sugar has dissolved and the liquid is boiling. Pour this, still boiling, over the plums. Leave the fruit to macerate for two days in a cool place. Strain the syrup from the plums, and put this in the refrigerator.

Boil together the same amounts of wine and sugar as before to make an identical syrup, and pour over the plums. Leave them to macerate again for two days.

Mix the two syrups together in a saucepan and bring to a boil, removing any scum. Add the plums and bring them quickly to a boil. They must not actually boil, just be heated through. Pour the whole lot into a colander placed over a pan, and return the plums to the crock. Reduce the syrup until it is fairly thick, then pour it over the plums. Close the crock when the contents have thoroughly cooled.

The plums taste best when matured for a month, but they will keep almost indefinitely. When removing some of the plums, use a sterilized spoon to avoid contaminating the remainder and so causing them to spoil.

Plum chutney with licorice

This recipe, admittedly, is not particularly Nordic in origin, but its fruity, sweet-sour feel certainly is. It tastes very good with an array of cold cuts and cheeses, or with pork, venison, or reindeer.

The recipe is not very traditional for a chutney, as there is no onion, but it is undoubtedly delicious: the method of slowly baking the chutney in the oven produces perfect levels of caramelization and evaporation. You can use proper or cherry plums.

2¼lb plums (pitted weight)	2 bay leaves
1½ cups sugar	4 tablespoons licorice root, finely cut
Generous ¾ cup cider vinegar	
Generous ¾ cup red wine or apple juice	2–3 chiles
	2 whole mace
1 large cinnamon stick	5 long peppers
1 tablespoon coriander seeds	2 tablespoons mustard seeds
10 cardamom pods	MAKES ABOUT 3 JARS

Preheat the oven to 325°F. Mix everything together well in a deep oven pan, making sure that the fruit fits into a single layer. Place in the oven and let the fruit sweat, but keep a close eye on it. You must turn everything over once or twice, while the plums release their juices and while these evaporate. If the whole lot threatens to burn, turn down the heat. You'll need to adjust the sugar after 30–40 minutes. The level of sweetness may well be fine, but you might need to add much, much more sugar.

The chutney is finished when it looks nice and gooey, with the beautiful, almost whole plums lying in a rich, thick, spicy syrup.

TIP

• You can make a superb jam by using the same recipe but excluding the spices and vinegar—though both cardamom and cinnamon are delicious in a plum jam should you wish to try them. The baking method is perfect as there is so much water in plums that it's always a problem to boil them down in a saucepan without them burning or sticking; and the jam often becomes mushy because you have to stir it so much. The oven method leaves whole, amber pieces of caramelized plum flesh in your jam.

Baked plums

This is a wonderfully easy way to prepare plums for both sweet and main course dishes. Any kind of plum will do, but I like to use Kirkes Blue. The recipe is adaptable: simply allow 1¼ cups sugar for every 2¼lb of fruit.

Wash the plums, leaving them whole, then arrange in a single layer in an ovenproof dish. Scatter over the sugar, turning the fruit, then bake at 325°F. The plums should burst and be tender but still a little firm. In the bottom of the dish you should find the loveliest pool of garnet-colored, syrupy juice.

The plums can be eaten as they are, hot or cold, with duck, pork, venison, reindeer, or *frikadeller*, or as a dessert with yogurt, ice cream, or whipped cream. But finding ways to eat them will not be a problem: the almond flavor from the pits makes them absolutely irresistible.

Sloe

In spring, the indigenous blackthorn (of which sloes are the fruit) is one of the very first bushes to flower, displaying huge, creamy cushions of airy blossom on bare, black stems—a beautiful sight against a leaden, early spring sky. It appears to be everywhere, in woods, in hedges, as if the whole landscape were strewn with them. By the time fall comes, there are plenty of sloes for you to pick, with ample amounts left over to be eaten by the birds in winter.

Sloes are a cousin of the cherry, and they taste very much like damsons, of which they are probably a parent. They are a virtually black fruit with a purple-blue, waxy bloom and thin skin, and are not only bitter, but the epitome of tartness when they first ripen in October. However, once the first winter frosts have mellowed the taste to a rich, almondy sourness they are perfect for cordials and schnapps.

If you aren't able to pick fruit that has been through at least one night of frost, put the fruit in the freezer for a couple of days to improve the flavor. Sloe cordial can be made in the same way as the elderberry cordial on page 230.

Sloe schnapps

This rich, garnet-colored, almost cherry-flavored schnapps is great to drink on its own, but you can also use it to spice up stews and marinades. If you add sugar (as in the black currant liqueur on page 229), you will end up with a very interesting liqueur for desserts or cheese.

Fill a wide-mouthed bottle with sloes, then pour in unflavored schnapps or vodka and leave to macerate for a month. This will produce very intense schnapps that can be drunk as it is, or diluted with unflavored schnapps. Unlike many other flavorings for schnapps, sloes can be left in the alcohol, and in time the almond flavor from the pits will penetrate the drink and make it even better. For more information on making schnapps, see page 257.

Nothing sums up Scandinavian cuisine better than northern berries, which ripen slowly during the cool summers and are full of sweet, health-giving, and flavorful juiciness. Berries are the jewels in the crown of northern eating, adorning everyday meals—as lingonberries on the morning hot oatmeal or with veal, game, roasts, or fish, as blueberries simply eaten with cream, or as strawberries and raspberries in every possible cake and dessert during their brief season.

The abundance of berries with all their nutritional virtues has undoubtedly kept us healthy during long winters; and their acidity, sweetness, and tartness have balanced the fare of heavy meals and abundant animal fat over thousands of years. But berries offer far more than mere health hype: they are the focus of countless trips to heaths and woods, where the whole family gathers berries for the winter season, and their beauty is beyond compare. Absolutely no other food is so inviting as freshly picked berries—children should be allowed to gorge on these little globes of concentrated sunshine to their heart's delight. Some of them are unobtainable in the stores, or costly, and rightly so. Blueberries, lingonberries, wood strawberries, and cloudberries are still picked from the wild. The small and incredibly aromatic *åkerbär* or Arctic raspberry is found only on the high ground, but below tree level, in North America, Norway, Russia, Finland, or Sweden.

Berries are extremely inviting, and for good reason—the plants need to make delicious and irresistible fruit in order for animals and humans to eat them, thereby spreading the seeds further afield than they can do themselves. We have always known, by instinct and guidance from our taste buds, that berries are good for us, and we do not really need science to tell us that they are, and why.

berries

Strawberry

Scandinavians adore strawberries. During the short and rather hectic season—usually just four weeks—strawberries are eaten almost every day for dessert. We also make sure that we buy enough to eat on the way home and to have strawberries on top of the morning muesli or junket as well.

When the main season is over, there are still the wild wood strawberries, scattered over the forest floor and along country lanes all over Scandinavia. They produce unbelievably flavorful, small, dark berries. Children thread them like beads on a string, to avoid the ripe, soft berries getting mushy in small hands. These are the ultimate treat, eaten on a picnic, or gathered for a special meal. You can even be lucky and find enough to make a small jar of jam.

How it grows Professional growers in Scandinavia grow mostly less flavorful, but transport-friendly, modern cultivars, as is the case all over Europe. In modern large-scale thinking, strawberry quality is equal to a long shelf life. Many people do not agree, however, and grow their own or visit fruit farms to pick the smaller, more fragile and sweeter berries they remember from childhood. If you have been put off the idea of

growing your own strawberries because your garden is plagued by birds, you could try a very sweet, creamy white wood strawberry (a cultivar of *Fragaria vesca*), which is much harder to spot than its bright-red cousins.

Taste and appearance Northern strawberries are thin-skinned and juicy, and the cold climate and long summer days give extra sweetness and flavor. There are many wonderful local cultivars, from strawberries that are almost orange and look like cocks' combs, to huge midseason berries the color of pomegranate seeds and late berries that are blood-red all the way through. These old cultivars have been cherished through generations and still survive in private gardens. The small, dark strawberries, which are sweet but with a high acid level, and make the best jam, come at the end of the season.

Buying and storing Strawberries must be completely ripe for eating, with all the berries thoroughly colored, fresh, unblemished, and fragrant. Never keep them in the refrigerator, as this will take every bit of taste away. If you need to keep strawberries overnight, coat them with sugar. Do not wash strawberries. If you must, do it before hulling.

Culinary uses We northerners tend to eat strawberries very simply, with cream or ice cream, until the end of the season, when we grow just a little tired of them and prepare more complicated strawberry desserts. Late season is the time for everybody's summer favorite *rødgrød med fløde*, made when strawberries are on their way out but raspberries and black currants have started to appear. If you are very lucky, your birthday is in the summer. The strawberry layer cake, for which there are variations all over Scandinavia, could maybe compensate a little for the fact that all your friends are away on vacation.

Strawberry and elderflower birthday layer cake

We normally decorate the cake with candles and small flags, and usually write the name and age of the birthday girl or boy on top too. If strawberries are off season, blueberries, cloudberries, raspberries, raw sugared currants, blackberries, or even a rhubarb or gooseberry compote work just as well. If using store-bought elderflower cordial, add the juice of 1 large lemon to the cordial (home-made naturally has a lemony flavor).

Birthdays are often for a lot of guests, hence the two cakes, but you can always use just half quantities. The sponge will keep for two weeks in the refrigerator, and can be used for another day. It freezes well, too.

9 medium eggs	**for the filling**
1¾ cups sugar	2¼–3lb 5oz strawberries
1 vanilla bean	Sugar, to taste
Zest of 1 lemon	3 cups heavy cream
½ stick butter, melted	1¾ cups elderflower cordial
2–2½ cups all-purpose flour	(page 230)
2 teaspoons baking powder	SERVES 16–18
Confectioner's sugar	

Butter two cake pans measuring 9½in in diameter. Preheat the oven to 350°F.

Break the eggs into a mixing bowl and add the sugar. Split the vanilla bean and scrape the seeds into the bowl. Beat the sugar and eggs until frothy and pale; if you stop before the sugar is completely dissolved, the cake will not rise.

Gently blend the lemon zest and butter into the batter. Mix the flour and baking powder together and sift into the bowl. (If the eggs are very large, you may need 2½ cups flour.) Fold into the batter, then pour into the cake pans and level with a spatula. Bake until the cakes feel like a springy foam mattress and leave to cool in the pans.

For the filling, hull and slice the strawberries, keeping a handful of the prettiest aside for decoration. If the fruit is naturally sweet, you will need no extra sugar; if not, sprinkle generously with sugar to bring out the flavor. Whip the cream to a very soft consistency.

Using a long, sharp knife, divide both cakes into three or four layers each. Keep the upper layers aside, and put the bottom layers on to two cake stands. Soak with half or a third of the elderflower cordial. Scatter on some of the sliced berries followed by some of the whipped cream, and repeat for the other layers. Put on the top layers and press gently but firmly with your hands to make sure the cakes keep together, and become nicely soaked all the way through.

Wrap and put in a cool place for up to 2 days: the longer, the mushier and better. Unwrap and decorate with a dusting of confectioners' sugar and a scattering of the reserved whole strawberries.

Rose and strawberry jam

The petals from fragrant, old-fashioned roses—and especially *Rosa rugosa*, the wrinkled Japanese rose which grows like a terrifying weed all over the north—are perfectly coupled in this jam. The taste is almost indecently intense, and the rose petals add a delicious chewiness; eating it is an altogether "mouth-opening" experience.

Jam made this way is nicely set, without the need for pectin, and the short, hefty boiling preserves the taste. Be sure to gather roses that have not been sprayed, and pick the flowers in the morning, when the fragrance is at its highest level. You can use buds, and even blowsy, almost spent flowers, as long as the petals are in good condition. Clean the petals by spreading them out on a dish towel, then removing insects and stamens by hand; do not wash them.

2½ cups sugar

2lb strawberries, hulled

6 cups rose petals

MAKES 4–5 JARS

Heat the sugar in an ovenproof dish in the oven at 300°F for 5 minutes. At the same time, put the strawberries in a non-reactive heavy-bottomed pan and boil at full heat until the berries give up their juices.

Stir the hot sugar into the fruit. Keep the heat on high, and stir for some minutes until the juice thickens. Stir in the petals, which will collapse in a very short time. Boil until the petals are soft and well integrated in the jam and the strawberries have a cooked-through, jammy look, but are not too mushy.

Pour the jam into sterilized jars, cover with a clean dish towel and let cool. Seal when completely cold. The jam keeps well if stored in a cool, dark place.

Strawberries and cream crisp cones

This is the perfect platform for freshly cooked strawberry jam. The cones are made from a tuile batter, thin, crisp, eggy, and delicious. They are eaten filled with cream and strawberry jam, but I must admit that raspberry or cloudberry jam is just as nice. Whatever you do, do not make this for more than six people, and do not fill the cones in advance. They go soggy in a minute. The shaping of the cones takes some practice—the first are bound to be too thick or too thin, you will burn your fingers, or shape them into elephant's ears instead of cones. But it is definitely worth the struggle. If I were a child, I would wish that someone would cook something as delicious as this for me.

3 eggs	1¼ cups cream, whipped
The same weight each of butter, sugar, and all-purpose flour as the eggs	1¾ cups homemade strawberry jam
	SERVES 6

Cream the butter and sugar until the sugar is dissolved. Stir in the flour and eggs. Spread the batter on parchment paper with a rubber spatula, in very thin ovals, roughly 4 x 6in.

Bake for 5 minutes at 350°F, until they are browned slightly at the edges, and no more. Bake only a few at a time, as there must be time to shape them into cones, while the next batch is baking.

While they are warm, take the ovals off the paper and shape into cones. Place them into a bowl of sugar, or suspend them in small glasses, until cooled, when they will hold their shape. If they cool down prematurely, you can heat them very carefully until pliable again. When they are cold, you can stack them gently inside each other.

The cones are best the day they are made, but will keep for a couple of days in a airtight container. Put them on the table with the cream and jam, for people to fill themselves.

Summer compote

This wonderful and famous compote, called *rødgrød med fløde*, is basically a summer pudding without the bread—an intensely flavored, lightly set compote of mixed berries, with raspberries stirred in as it cools. Strewn with slivered almonds, then eaten with a thick blob of rich cream and a sprinkling of sugar to add crunch, this dessert is heaven on a long, light summer evening, and so special to the Nordic summer.

18oz strawberries, hulled	3 tablespoons cornstarch
18oz black- or red currants and/or gooseberries	4 cups raspberries
1¼–2¼ cups sugar	⅓ cup almonds, halved
	SERVES 6–8

Put the strawberries and the currants or gooseberries (don't bother topping or tailing these) into a wide, non-corrosive saucepan. The amount of sugar needed varies enormously with the berries, but try 1¼ cups to start with. Add absolutely no water! Heat the pan gently and boil until the berries begin to bleed. Lower the heat and let the fruit bubble away until the strawberries become jammy and the whole thing tastes like heaven.

Adjust the sugar: the compote should be sweet, but still a little tart, and you must leave room for a crunchy sprinkling of sugar when it's eaten! Dissolve the cornstarch in a little juice from the berries and stir into the compote, making sure that it's evenly distributed. Boil for another 5 minutes, remove from the heat, then stir in the raspberries and cool.

When the compote has cooled a little, pour it into a beautiful bowl and sprinkle generously with sugar to prevent a skin forming. When it is cold and set, decorate with the almonds. Eat cold with pouring cream.

Raspberry

Raspberries grow wild all over the northern hemisphere and in great abundance. Clearings and woods, where the soil is deep and well nourished, are sure to host prickly areas of wild raspberries, which taste incomparably better than domesticated ones. And you can pick as many as you want if you take the time for a fruitful picnic in the woods. A handful of raspberries is a wonderful thing simply eaten from a juice-stained hand, but it can also go a long way to add flavor to cakes and puddings. Furthermore, raspberries are full to the brim with antioxidants and, of course, vitamin C.

Appearance and taste Wild raspberries are small but richly flavored. This does not mean that home-grown raspberries are necessarily inferior; depending on the cultivar, they can be intoxicatingly sweet, juicy, and bursting with taste. But beware of modern cultivars with over-large berries: you will get lots of fruit, but your jam will be nondescriptly berry-ish and without the tart, distinct raspberry taste that you want.

How it grows Raspberries grow on canes, usually bearing fruit the year after initial planting. I grow many cultivars in my garden, including a fall-fruiting yellow variety which actually bears fruit twice, both in the summer and again from September to November—that is, if you ignore the garden "wisdom" of cutting back the canes after fruiting. They have a flavor all of their own, as the color indicates, of peach Melba.

Buying and storing If you are buying raspberries, they must be completely fresh, with absolutely no mold on them. Commercially grown raspberries are more resilient than home-grown ones, but generally raspberries do not keep for long and the taste can deteriorate very quickly, particularly if the fruit is warm or wet. If you keep raspberries for more than a few hours, you must put them in the refrigerator, but this will take away their taste, and you must return them to room temperature before eating them. Any surplus must be heavily dusted with sugar to prevent mold, which relieves them from the strain of the refrigerator, and are heaven on your morning muesli or yogurt.

Raspberries are well suited to freezing as they keep their taste well, but of course lose any firmness.

Culinary uses Raspberries are much loved by northern people, and may even be our best-loved berry for jam. The culinary uses for raspberries have no end, but it's not very often that you have the chance to tire of raspberries eaten raw with cream or ice cream, or made into *rødgrød*, fools, or jam. However, these cakes are well worth a try. The sponge and jam in the multilayer raspberry cake melt slowly into a fusion of rich marzipan taste, and it is to us what Christmas cakes are to the British. The pastry squares are quick to make and perfect for afternoon tea.

While strawberry jam tends to be best for toast, raspberry jam is exciting enough to be used in desserts and cakes too, as its flavor is much more pronounced.

Raspberry jam

It's easy to adapt the quantity to suit the amount of fruit you have available, or if preparing the jam to use in one of the following recipes.

2½ cups sugar
8 cups raspberries

Put the sugar in a heatproof bowl in the oven at 225°F.

Meanwhile, boil up the raspberries in a wide, heavy-bottomed pan, preferably copper as this transmits the heat

well—jam-making is, after all, a matter of keeping the heat up high for rapid evaporation.

As soon as the berries give up their juices, add the warm sugar. Stir over a very high heat for a few minutes, until most of the water is evaporated and the jam is dark ruby and perfect.

Decant into sterilized jars and seal when cooled.

TIP

• The most enjoyable way to sterilize jars is to use either brandy or whisky, whose flavors are compatible with all jams and preserves. Simply pour a small glassful of the liquor into the jars, put the lid on, and shake vigorously, then pour it into the next jar and repeat the process. You can drink what's left at the end.

Raspberry pastry squares

These delicious and homely-looking pastry squares are quick and easy to make, and are perfect for afternoon tea. Children love them and are quite capable of baking them themselves.

1¼ cups raspberry jam (page 216)

for the pastry
Scant 1 cup butter, chilled
¾ cup confectioner's sugar

2¼ cups all-purpose flour
2 egg yolks
A little rice flour, for rolling
Confectioner's sugar, dusting
MAKES 8–10

Chop the ingredients for the pastry on the counter with a large knife. When it resembles grated cheese, assemble the dough using the warmth of your hands. Do not knead it. Divide the pastry in half and form into two flat rounds. Chill for 1 hour.

Preheat the oven to 400°F. Using a little rice flour, roll out the pastry directly onto parchment paper to form two identical ¼in-thick squares. Place on a baking sheet and bake until cooked through and lightly golden.

While the pastry is still hot, spread the jam onto one of the squares. Leave the other to cool, then place it on top—the easiest way to do this is upside down, as you can pull off the paper once the pastry is in place. Gently press together.

The price you pay for this delicious, very crispy, and flaky dough is that it will crack in unexpected places when you cut the cake into squares, triangles, or whatever shape you prefer. It will keep for several days if wrapped in plastic wrap and stored in a cool place, though not the refrigerator as it gives cakes a nasty consistency and steals the taste. Dust with confectioner's sugar before eating.

Multilayer raspberry cake

This cake has amazing keeping quality. It is an everlasting and improving commodity, to serve in very thin slices, to countless guests.

It is not a traditional layer cake, but is made up of multiple very thin layers of Genoise (sponge) batter, layered with intensely flavored homemade raspberry jam. Forget store-bought jam, it won't do the trick. And another warning: if you can't be bothered to bake all the layers, you may as well choose another recipe as it's the multiple thin layers that make this cake so special. One more thing: the cake tastes best if you wait at least a week before eating it!

1½ cups butter
1½ cups sugar
6 medium eggs
3 cups all-purpose flour

1 teaspoon baking powder
Raspberry jam (page 216)
SERVES MANY!

Preheat the oven to 350°F.

Whisk the butter and sugar until white and foamy. Add the eggs one at a time, making sure that each is completely absorbed into the batter before adding the next one. Sift the flour and baking powder together, then add to the batter and blend carefully with a spatula until all lumps are gone.

Using a dinner plate, draw several circles on sheets of parchment paper (you can use the same paper several times). Place the paper on baking sheets and distribute the batter very thinly and evenly in the circles. Bake until lightly golden—it's a matter of minutes. Turn upside down when cooled a little, and remove the paper. Continue baking in batches until all the batter is used up.

Assemble the cake on a cake dish. Spread the sponge layers with a ¼in layer of jam, and sandwich together. When finished, press the whole thing down gently, but firmly. Wrap the cake and dish in several layers of plastic wrap and store in a cool place, where it will keep for ages.

Blueberry

Wild blueberries are abundant all over Scandinavia and are gathered in enormous quantities in summer and fall. The entire crop is picked in the wild, and they have been a favorite berry for millennia. True wild blueberries are far more delicious than the northern or bog bilberry and their cousin the giant American highbush blueberry. Blueberries keep well, as they contain a natural preservative, and have always been dried in the sun for winter use.

How it grows True blueberries (*Vaccinium myrtillus*) grow on acid soil in woodland and heaths and are abundant all over the north. The deciduous, low bushes with small, bright green leaves are very hard to grow in gardens as the plant lives in symbiosis with a fungus. The northern bilberry (*Vaccinium uliginosum*), another small bush with almost round, blue-gray leaves, requires the same conditions and grows all over Scandinavia. Highbush varieties, which are grown commercially, are easy to grow if you have acid, peaty, or sandy soil.

Appearance and taste Wild blueberries are smaller than the cultivated blueberries you buy in the stores, and also darker, appearing to be almost black with a hint of blue; most distinctively, they are dark all the way through, and will color everything a lovely dark purple—your teeth, tabletop, food, pancakes… They are much tastier and more intensely flavored than either the northern bilberry or indeed the American blueberry, which is dark purple on the outside but has pale green flesh. But you love what you can get, and commercially grown blueberries are still much better than no blueberries at all.

Buying and storing Blueberries picked in the wild are a superior thing, so buy them if you are lucky enough to find them, or pick your own, as many Scandinavian families do. They keep their taste well when frozen; in fact, frozen, ripe true blueberries are often the better option if you are going to use them in cakes, smoothies, and jam.

As blueberries keep so well, the ones you buy are often picked underripe, and sold when too old; since the taste disappears in time, it's worth checking that they are not dried out, and never buy if some are moldy.

Health benefits Blueberries have become very popular in the past years because of their medicinal qualities. They contain huge amounts of antioxidants, as well as vitamin C, and the color will replenish the color in pale eyes.

Culinary uses The taste of blueberries is rich and refreshing, equally good in main course dishes and desserts. They make a marvelous jam, and are traditionally served with thin crêpes, or as a filling in pies. They can be raw-sugared like lingonberries and eaten with game, cold cuts, and any dish in which lingonberries are used. But when you have picked your own, they are usually eaten in huge bowls, simply and deliciously with sugar and cream.

Curd cheese pancakes with blueberries

You can make the pancakes with a variety of fresh cheeses, including *skyr*, a fresh, unfermented cheese, much like fresh ricotta, quark, or fresh goat cheese. They work well with any of these.

2 cups blueberries
2 tablespoons sugar
for the pancake batter
3–4 eggs, depending on size
1 cup ricotta, quark, *skyr* or fresh goat cheese
¼ cup sugar

Finely grated zest of
  1 lemon
¼ stick butter, melted, plus
  extra for frying
Scant 1 cup all-purpose
  flour
SERVES 4

Warm the blueberries very gently with the sugar, until they begin to break open. Cool a little while you make the pancakes.

Separate the eggs, and whisk the whites until stiff. Mix all the other pancake ingredients together in a bowl, then gently fold in the whites.

When it comes to frying the pancakes, you'll need a large, heavy-bottomed skillet. We're after thick, American-style pancakes, so you should fit three in at a time. Fry the pancakes gently in butter, making sure you don't turn them over until they are properly set underneath; they are loose-textured and will break up if you turn them too soon.

Eat while hot with the warm blueberries.

Buttermilk ice cream with blueberries

This ice cream is very low in fat, but deliciously tart from the buttermilk and lemon. It's good with any kind of berry, but especially ripe blueberries. The taste is very close to the unique Nordic buttermilk dessert *kærnemælkskoldskål* (page 20). You can serve with cubes of palm sugar (not very Scandinavian but delicious!)

10 egg yolks
1½ cups sugar
4 cups buttermilk
2 cups crème fraîche
   (18% fat)

Juice and grated zest of
   1 lemon
Lots of blueberries, to serve

Whisk the egg yolks and sugar until the sugar has completely dissolved and the eggs are pale and fluffy. Mix in the rest of the ingredients, then either freeze in an ice-cream machine, which will give a creamier result, or put it in a large container in the freezer. If you go down the latter route, you'll have to give the ice cream a stir every half hour to break up the ice crystals. The ice cream is best eaten shortly after it's made, with a generous scattering of blueberries.

Gooseberry

Gooseberries are indigenous to northern Europe and northern Asia and thrive in the cool climate and rainfall of the north. In fact, hot summers and milder climates are no good for gooseberries. It is very difficult to buy fresh gooseberries in Nordic countries, so people generally have to grow their own if they wish to have a supply. The reward is one of the most delicious fruits you can grow this far north.

How it grows Gooseberries are a low-maintenance fruit; they grow happily in semi-shade but they detest fertilizing. They might grow more, but there is an instant pay-off as the fast growth attracts gooseberry mildew, a true killer. You also have to beware of caterpillars that can strip your bush to the bone in an instant. Apart from these threats, gooseberry cultivation is easy. The picking, however, is less so.

Appearance and taste The bush is covered with nasty thorns, the berries themselves are softly hairy and, on top of this, perfectionist housewives have a dogma about the virtues of topping and tailing them before eating, all of which may help to explain why gooseberries have fallen massively out of favor. What a shame it is that children no longer know the joy of crushing a sun-warmed gooseberry against their teeth, the sweet jelly exploding in sensations of exotic fruit, awakening their taste buds. There are many cultivars, all starting out green, but ripening to whitish, yellow, green or red according to variety; old cultivars tend to be sweeter and with more taste.

Health benefits Gooseberries contain vitamins A, B, and C.

Culinary uses Gooseberries are often used to make compote and jam, while they are green and unripe and the pectin level is high, but the crisp, ripe berries filled like chocolates with a fragrant, musky jelly are the real treat. Young, green gooseberries are lovely simply softened in a saucepan to make compote with a minimum of water, then sweetened to take away the tartness and finished with a piece of butter. Ripe berries will take a lot less sugar than the unripe ones, but you will need to add lemon juice at the end of the cooking time to make it set.

The amount of sugar used and the cooking time are the only differences between sauce, compote, and jam. Whichever you are making, always add the sugar after the berries have burst, otherwise they will float like punctured tennis balls in the syrup and never tenderize. On the other hand, gooseberries should not be cooked to a mush—a certain amount of structure is good in any gooseberry preparation. Don't bother to top and tail gooseberries, as you will go mad doing it; they will be nice and tender after cooking.

Gooseberry and elderflower jam

The blossoming of the elderflowers coincides perfectly with the appearance of the first green gooseberries. They are a match made in heaven.

10 cups unripe gooseberries	10 elderflower heads
4 cups sugar	Generous ¾ cup elderflowers, picked off the stalks

Put the washed gooseberries into a shallow, non-reactive saucepan, then cover the bottom of the pan with ⅙in water. Put the lid on and bring to a boil. Let the berries bubble gently until they burst, but take care that the fruit doesn't burn before they have released their juices.

Add the sugar and the elderflower heads, which you should tie together with string, with most of the green stalk removed. Let the fruit boil vigorously for 5 minutes, until most of the liquid has gone and the mixture looks jammy. Taste, and add more sugar if necessary. Remove and discard the bunch of elderflowers.

Stir in the little white elderflowers (without stalks) after you have removed the jam from the heat. Pour into sterilized jars and seal.

Gooseberry compote

This is made very much like the jam above, but with a shorter boiling time and less sugar. Stop boiling the berries once they are punctured and have collapsed, then add sugar to taste. You can serve the compote hot as a sauce or cold as a dessert with cream and sugar on top. The inclusion of elderflowers is optional, but the combined flavor goes wonderfully with fried fish and crispy pork.

Flaky pastry cakes with gooseberry-elderflower fool

These cakes are beautiful in all their simplicity and the filling can be changed with the season—use rhubarb, cloudberries, or even prunes instead of gooseberries.

2 sheets (4 x 8in) flaky pastry, made with butter	Generous ¾ cup gooseberry compote with elderflowers (see left)
1 egg, beaten, for glazing	**to finish**
for the gooseberry fool	2 cups undiluted elderflower cordial
Generous ¾ cup heavy cream	5 tablespoons confectioner's sugar
3 sheets of gelatin	SERVES 6

Preheat the oven to 400°F.

Cut the pastry sheets into three pieces each. Turn them over, glaze with egg, and place on parchment paper. Bake until golden. Cool.

Whip the cream. Soak the gelatin in cold water until soft, squeeze dry, then melt in a small saucepan with the water clinging to it. Dilute with a spoonful of compote, then stir into the rest of the compote. Mix in the whipped cream.

Split the pastry crusts, fill them with the fool, and serve them in a puddle of cordial, in deep plates. Dust the top with confectioner's sugar.

Cloudberry

The most sought-after berry in Scandinavia, the hardest to find, and the most expensive to buy must be the cloudberry, a beautiful, rich-flavored cousin of the raspberry. But still, the cloudberry is accessible and affordable, if not for every day.

How it grows *Rubus chamaemorus*, a slow-growing alpine and sub-Arctic species, is found all over the northern hemisphere. The cloudberry plant is small in comparison to its relative the raspberry, growing only to around 8in. The berries are easy to find as they have a stiff, upright stem, each boasting a single juicy berry. Their habitat, however, is less easy to locate as cloudberry plants are very picky and thrive only under perfect conditions: in acid, unfertile ground on high plains, living in symbiosis with a fungus that makes them almost impossible to grow industrially. The entire world crop is picked in the wild, though

efforts are being made to introduce cultivars that can be grown in otherwise barren areas in the north.

Appearance and taste The ripe, golden fruits are soft and juicy, with very hard seeds. They are rich in vitamin C, and this you can detect in their characteristic tart taste. They are one of the most delicious berries, with a perfect balance of sweetness and acidity, but strangely enough not to everyone's taste.

Buying and storing Cloudberries can be bought fresh in the season, in northern Scandinavia. Like lingonberries, they contain benzoic acid and are more or less self-preserving. But they are soft, and not easy to handle in trade. Cloudberries are generally bought either frozen (they keep their shape and taste very well when frozen) or already transformed into preserves, or used as an added flavor to numerous foods and drinks such as Finland's famous cloudberry liqueur (*Lakkalikööri*).

Culinary uses Cloudberries are used both in main course dishes, as a sauce or accompaniment for game, and in desserts of almost any kind. The tradition is simple: you don't need to create elaborate desserts with a berry as flavorful as a cloudberry. Usually they are made into fools or ice cream; eaten as a topping for pancakes, waffles, or vanilla ice cream; or layered in cakes—much as you would use raspberries, but with a completely different taste. You can use cloudberries instead of raspberries in all sorts of recipes, but note that cloudberry seeds are very hard, and numerous. If you are lucky enough to find fresh cloudberries, they can be made into a delicious jam, with a taste all of its own.

Cloudberry jam is made exactly as raspberry jam, and the multilayer raspberry cake, the strawberry birthday cake, the rye bread apple cake with berries, the strawberries and cream crispy cones, and the raspberry pastry squares are also good ways to exhibit the luxurious taste of cloudberries.

Cloudberries are sufficiently elegant and powerful to match main course dishes as well as desserts and they are also a perfect match for hard, mature cheese, either served beside it, or on toast with Jarlsberg or Västerbottenost.

Cloudberry fool

The exquisite taste of cloudberries is displayed if you turn them into a lively fool, by mixing as many fresh cloudberries and sugar to taste, or as much cloudberry jam, as you can afford into softly whipped cream. Eaten on its own, or with a cookie, this is a favorite Sunday dessert, especially in Norway.

Norwegian waffles

Combining cloudberry fool with these crispy waffles makes a popular Christmas dessert, though they are just as good with cloudberry jam and whipped cream.

These thin, crispy waffles (*krumkake*), which are bent while warm into a cone shape, were traditionally baked in a heavy, cast-iron double griddle, imprinting the surface with an intricate pattern of swirls. These days you can buy electric *krumkake* irons (generally sold in Norway and America's Midwest) on the internet. Alternatively, you can bake them in the oven, as for the crispy cones on page 214.

4 eggs	Generous ½ cup potato
1¼ cups light brown sugar	flour, or fine rice flour
Generous 1 cup butter, melted	Generous ⅓ cup cold water
Scant 1¼ cups all-purpose flour	SERVES 4–6

Whisk the eggs and sugar together until the sugar has dissolved. Cool the melted butter and then add to the egg mixture. Whisk in the flours, followed by the water.

Bake using a *krumkake* iron or in the oven as for the crispy cones on page 214. An ordinary waffle iron will miss the point.

While they are golden, shape them into cones. Place them into a bowl of sugar, or suspend them in small glasses, until cooled, when they will hold their shape. If they cool down prematurely, you can reheat them very carefully until pliable again. When they are cold, stack them gently inside each other. After cooling completely, they can be stored in an airtight container for a couple of days.

Åkerbär

The *åkerbär* or Arctic raspberry (*Rubus arcticus*) is rarer, smaller, and even more elusive than the cloudberry. The incredibly aromatic fruit is considered to be the tastiest berry in the world by the fortunate inhabitants of the extreme north. But this is only mentioned as a curiosity, as it cannot be found outside the Arctic regions of Scandinavia, except as a delicious liqueur, *Mesimarja*, from Finland.

The true *åkerbär* will grow only under the midnight sun, but as the berries are so good much work has been done in Sweden to produce a similar, but more tolerant cross. It resulted in the *aläkerbär*, the "al" meaning "for everybody." Its English name is "All field berry." It is a cross with the Alaskan *Rubus stellarcticus*, delivering more tolerance of growth, and a lovely fragrance in the rose-like, pink flowers. It will grow successfully all over Scandinavia, as long as the soil is acid. It is self-sterile, and you must plant at least two, but preferably more, of the existing five varieties. It blooms in early summer, and the berries ripen in late summer. It's not quite as good as the true *åkerbär*, but good enough. It will spread if not controlled.

Lingonberry

Lingonberries, also known as cowberries (in the UK) and mountain or lowbush cranberries, are a wild crop yet are a cornerstone of Nordic cooking, providing color, a lively taste, and all the antioxidants you need. They are a staple food in Sweden, in particular, where many children are brought up on a morning meal of hot oatmeal with lingonberry jam—good and nourishing on a cold winter's day. The children's stories by Swedish writer Elsa Beskow have made a lasting impression on generations of northerners, so that we are unable to think of lingonberries without visualizing her tales.

How it grows Lingonberries grow on small bushes in woodland and ripen in August and September. They are picked with a special, wide, fork-like tool, which can strip a bush in a few strokes.

Appearance and taste The small, round, and intensely dark red berries, similar in size to an elderberry, are shiny and rather hard-skinned when fresh. They are dryish and bitter to eat when raw but are transformed with the addition of sugar.

Buying and storing If you live in the right place, lingonberries are surprisingly inexpensive to buy. They contain benzoic acid in large amounts and keep extremely well, and they are even used to preserve other fruits. Simply discard any blackened berries and small leaves, rinse in a bowl of cold water and dry on paper towels.

Culinary uses The berries are not good to eat in their raw state, but with sugar they reinvent themselves, showing all the endless possibilities they contain, as a side dish or an accompaniment for almost anything. Their bitterness gives them a grown-up taste that's interesting with anything from game, roasts, and meatballs to fried fish or herrings. They are lovely as a pancake filling, on ice cream or rice pudding, or as a topping for the traditional curd cheesecake (page 20).

Raw lingonberry jam

This is the ultimate Nordic jam, a simple but delicious uncooked jam made only from lingonberries and sugar. The jam keeps forever, thanks to the berries' high level of benzoic acid, which acts as a natural preservative, and has maximum taste and health-giving vitamins and antioxidants, as the fruit has not been cooked. It is made at home (especially in Sweden where it is a winter staple), in huge quantities, in August and September when the lingonberries are in season.

Slightly mash the berries with an equal amount of sugar and stir from time to time for a couple of days, until the sugar has dissolved. Pour into sterilized jars and seal. There will be a lot of ruby-red lingonberry syrup in the jars—any surplus is lovely as a cordial.

The raw jam is perfect with apples in any form; the classic *æblekage* is a trifle made from stale bread instead of macaroons (page 226), and is especially delicious with raw lingonberry jam.

TIP
• While the uncooked version is the more flavorful, you can equally well make conventional jam with lingonberries; use the raspberry jam recipe on page 216.

Creamed rice with lingonberries

This is an everyday version of the Christmas evening dessert, *riz à l'amande* (rice pudding—page 266). It can be made from leftover salted boiled rice.

Approx. ¾ cup heavy cream
Seeds from ½ vanilla bean
Generous 2 cups salted
   boiled rice

3 tablespoons sugar
Generous ¾ cup raw
   lingonberry jam (page 226)
SERVES 4

Whip the cream with the vanilla seeds until very soft. Blend half of the cream with the rice and sugar, then carefully fold in the rest. You may need to add some more cream—the amount needed depends on the rice that you're using.

Serve in glasses, topped with the lingonberry jam.

Potato pancakes with bacon and lingonberries

A Nordic, and maybe more interesting, version of American pancakes with bacon and maple syrup. Good for breakfast or lunch.

6 medium potatoes,
   unpeeled, coarsely grated,
1 egg
1–2 tablespoons all-purpose
   flour
A few fresh thyme leaves
A little ground mace
Sea salt and ground pepper

15 very thick slices
   of bacon
Butter, for frying
1¼–1¾ cups raw
   lingonberry jam or raw
   sugared lingonberries
MAKES 10 LARGE PANCAKES

Mix together the batter ingredients. Fry the bacon slowly in butter until crispy and done, then keep warm.

Fry the pancakes in butter, taking care to stir the batter well between making each pancake. Fry at a low heat so that they cook through while also crisping up on the outside. Flip over only once, when the pancake is set. Make sure there is enough fat in the skillet, or the pancakes will burn.

Serve the pancakes with the bacon and jam.

Black currant

Black currants have their home in the north of Norway, their "gene center," which is where the genetic variation of the wild plants is most varied. They thrive in the cool climate all over Scandinavia, as long as they are grown in full sun, as their Danish/Norwegian name *solbær* ("sun berry"), implies.

How it grows Black currant bushes spread easily—their branches taking root wherever they touch the ground—and can grow to an impressive size; an old bush can reach 55 square foot.

Appearance and taste The berries are juicy, thick-skinned, and almost black, a deep purple on the outside, a rich, reddish purple inside. The most intensely flavored berry in the north, black currants are not to everyone's taste. But to us who love them, they are a marvel. The taste of fresh and cooked black currants is so different that you would not imagine it was the same berry, if you did not know. Fresh berries are more like blueberries, and have a definite fresh taste, much like the smell of fresh black currant leaves. Once cooked, they become more intense.

Buying and storing Black currants are best when freshly picked; they will keep for a day or two in the refrigerator, but the taste will deteriorate. They freeze well, and the taste stays more or less intact.

Health benefits Black currants are full of vitamin C, especially when raw. They also contain antioxidants, iron, and calcium, and plenty of essential minerals.

Culinary uses Black currants make wonderful jams and cordials, of course. The sourness and intensity of the berries forbid eating them raw, but an uncooked jam (like that made with lingonberries) is a beautiful thing with all kinds of pork, veal, venison, game, cheese, pancakes, and ice cream. Black currant jam is made like the raspberry jam on page 216.

You can make a purple fool by mixing equal amounts of fresh black currants and sugar, until the sugar has dissolved, mashing slightly, and then folding in double that amount of whipped cream. Black currants are also delicious made into ice cream. Whiz together 2 cups black currants and 1 cup sugar, and add it to the cardamom ice cream on page 223.

The leaves of black currants are like a magic wand of concentrated currant flavor that you can wave about, imbuing intensity to pickles, jams, cordials, and herbal teas. Black currant leaves are a classic ingredient in pickled beets and gherkins: add a few leaves to the jar before pouring over the hot liquid.

Black currant liqueur

For this all you need is black currants, sugar (2½ cups for every 2¼lb of fruit) and some dark rum.

Fill a sterilized bottle with fresh black currants, then add the sugar, plus 2 or 3 leaves as well if you have them. Top up with rum.

Let steep for 2 months and the liqueur will be ready for drinking. You can leave the berries in the rum, and eventually eat them. The liqueur is perfect for making rum toddy—simply add boiling water and a slice of lemon—or for sipping from small glasses with dessert or tea.

Black currant tea

Collect fresh, young black currant leaves and lay them out to dry in a drafty place out of the sun until crisp. Pack into jars. Tea can be made by simply adding these dried leaves to black tea, or infusing them on their own in boiling water. The tea is fruity and fragrant and good with a little lemon and sugar.

Red and white currants

The days of massive pickling and preserving are over, but most people in Scandinavia have a red currant bush in the garden and make a few jars of red currant jelly for the winter. The taste is not overwhelming, but nice and fresh, and it goes well with apple cakes and venison. Red and white currants come into their own while fresh, when the taste is most pronounced. This can be appreciated in *rysteribs* ("shaken currants"), a pantry standby in the late summer.

Shaken currants

Rysteribs is simply raw currants and almost as much sugar, stirred for a day until the sugar has dissolved. Leave whole, shiny berries in the rich red syrup.

It tastes delicious with *frikadeller*, fried fish and, in particular, with old-fashioned, apricot-fleshed, netted (or musk) melons. The melons' fragrant but bland flesh is a perfect match for the tartness of the berries. Cut a lid, as if for a Jack-o'-lantern, scoop out the seeds, and fill the cavity with the sugary scarlet berries. The *rysteribs* is also a wonderful filling for a layer cake (page 219), with whipped cream.

Elderberry

Elderberries are not the tastiest berries in the world, but they are so plentiful that they have to be considered, and they do make a very nice, cold-fighting cordial. The epitome of good, old-school housekeeping is having elderberry cordial for colds and flu in your well-stocked pantry.

If you have picked elderflowers in May (page 182), you'll know where to look for these tiny berries in early fall. The common elder (*Sambucus nigra*) produces great hanging bunches of juicy, purple-black berries. They are virtually tasteless when raw, but come into their own when cooked.

Culinary uses Elderberries are generally used to give other, less colorful jams and cordials a nice full color. This means that if you do not take precautions, your kitchen will be a nice uneven mauve after you've dealt with the berries. Cover everything with plastic and newspapers, or do the preparations outside.

Elderberry cordial

The cordial is not too sweet and is used as a toddy (with hot water, a little honey, and a slice of lemon) against all ills during cold and nasty Nordic winters. Some people even add rum or schnapps, if the victim is a grown-up. I like to call this recipe "elderberry catastrophe in your kitchen!"

Fill a 21pt non-corrosive saucepan with the elderberries—the long stalks should be stripped off, but the little ones can stay. Cover with water, then heat gently, and let simmer for half an hour. You can mash the berries to release more juice, and you will end up with a lovely, everlastingly purple wooden spoon.

For the next, dripping stage you will need an old, clean dish cloth and a large bowl. You can either put the fruit in a very large colander lined with the cloth, tie the corners of the fruit-filled cloth to the legs of an upturned chair, or tie the gathered ends of the cloth to a drawer handle. Leave the fruit to drip into the bowl until the next day.

When it is ready, you may choose to freeze the cordial straight away, and sweeten it when you are going to use it. Alternatively, sweeten the cordial to taste, then pour it into jars and sterilize them in the oven. To do this: screw on the lid (but not completely tight as there must be room for steam to escape), then bake in the oven at 225°F until you can see the cordial bubbling in the jars. Turn off the oven, screw the lids on tightly, and let the jars cool in the oven. Prepared in this way, the cordial will keep for ages. If you use proper sterilizing jars (with rubber rings), you can tighten the lids straight away, before putting them in the oven.

Elderberry soup

The elderberry cordial recipe can be converted into a wonderful, sweet elderberry soup—diluted only slightly, and served with raisins, purple-tinted slices of fresh or canned pear, and a blob of whipped cream. Lemon juice is essential to make it sparkle. This is eaten as an appetizer, not a dessert, as it is a dish so old that it comes from the tradition of eating oatmeal or a fruit soup as an appetizer to fill up the stomachs, and has never been moved to a modern position in the menu.

Rowanberry

Currant-sized, tart, and dry rowanberries are very popular with birds. They are inedible, and slightly toxic when raw, but no one in their right mind would eat them raw. The taste is pleasingly bitter, and extremely aromatic when cooked.

The rowan, or mountain ash (*Sorbus aucuparia*), is a small, deciduous tree that bears the vividly orange berries in August. A fast-growing, pioneer species that invades disturbed ground, the rowan will grow almost anywhere. Rowanberries from the species found in North America are not considered edible.

Culinary uses European strands of rowanberries can be extracted into cordials, and a delicious jelly. The berries are rich in pectin, so the jelly naturally sets well. It is beautiful with game and roast beef, with apples or simply on toast.

The berries are an important ingredient in the famous digestif *gammel Dansk*, which owes much of its taste and bitterness to rowanberries. The berries are a much-used ingredient in flavored schnapps.

The berry itself is not used as a fruit, because the dryness and seeds are not too interesting, though some species were formerly dried and used as we use raisins.

Cordial is made in the same way as the rhubarb cordial on page 205, and jelly like the crab apple jelly on page 197.

Blackberry

Blackberries are even more plentiful than raspberries, being an invasive weed throughout the north, where they thrive under all conditions. They have a nasty habit of spreading over abandoned homes, and every clearing in the woods, at an amazing pace. Their long, thorny stems drive their ends into the ground, where they take root and spread even further. You can of course buy small punnets of cultivated blackberries, but you are much better off collecting them in the wild: if you are prepared for the venture, in full indestructible picking gear, complete with boots and tough gloves, you can pick as many as you want.

Appearance and taste Blackberries may be a weed but are a marvel to eat when absolutely ripe. Store-bought blackberries are generally of the thornless and much less tasty kind, and are often underripe, while wild berries are huge and soft. To be perfect they must be so ripe that they actually drop into your hand when you merely give them a good stare. You can grow your own, but they are a dangerous thing to invite into your garden—a fact that tempts gardeners to plant the thornless varieties, with a less spreading habit, and much less taste.

Culinary uses Blackberries freeze well, so abundant pickings can be savored over a period of time. They also make perfect jam—use the raspberry jam recipe on page 216, though you must add a squeeze of lemon as blackberries lack acidity; they can be a bit bland on their own.

Apples and blackberries have a definite affinity for each other, which is fortunate as the two fruits are in season at the same time. You can add them to a simple apple compote (page 192), just scattered over the top. And vanilla-spiced baked apples taste wonderful with some fresh blackberries and cream.

Rye-bread apple cake with blackberries

The use of rye bread instead of white bread in all kinds of desserts is very Nordic, and very similar to the *pain perdu* of other countries. The bread is often grated, fried in butter and sugar until crispy, and eaten with apple compote or apple rings fried in butter, and cream.

This dish is called *arme riddere* ("poor knights") and is much loved, especially by children. In this recipe, the rye bread is incorporated into a meringue batter, layered with apples, cream, and lots of juicy berries. The cake is not very sweet, so you must make a fairly sweet compote.

7oz rye bread
⅔ cup hazelnuts or almonds
Butter, for greasing
6 medium eggs
1¼ cups sugar
1 teaspoon baking powder
Apple compote (made with
   5lb 8oz apples), well
   sweetened (page 192)

8 cups ripe blackberries
   and/or fall raspberries
2½ cups heavy cream
MAKES 1 VERY LARGE
CAKE, OR 2 SMALLER CAKES
(TO FEED 10)

Coarsely grate the rye bread and grind the nuts to a powder: both can be done in a food processor. Roast the nuts and bread together in a saucepan over a low heat,

turning with a spatula all the time, until the nuts smell toasted and delicious. Do not let them burn or the taste will become indelibly bitter. Let cool.

Grease two pieces of parchment paper with butter—the batter is so sticky that it will be difficult to get off unbuttered paper—and place on two baking sheets. (If your baking sheets are very small, you will need to use three.)

Preheat the oven to 400°F.

Whisk the eggs and sugar in a bowl until fluffy and pale. Mix the bread mixture with the baking powder, then add to the bowl and fold carefully into the egg mixture. Spread the batter evenly into two (or three) identical layers on the paper, with a maximum thickness of ¼in.

Bake the cakes for about 12 minutes, but keep an eye on them: they must be baked through and lightly browned, but no more. Let cool.

When you are ready to assemble the cakes, put them, paper-side up, on the counter and draw back the paper horizontally, nice and slowly. Next, decide whether you want one very large cake or two smaller ones. For one cake you simply cut each cake into two pieces, while for two cakes you must cut each cake into three or four oblong pieces.

Assemble the cake (or cakes) by sandwiching together the various layers using the compote and berries. Whip the cream and spread some over the top, and serve the rest separately. Decorate with as many blackberries and/or fall raspberries as you can possibly cram on.

You can wrap one of the cakes in plastic wrap and freeze it for several months, without the cream and berries.

TIP

• If you want to prepare in time for a party, you can assemble the cakes the day before and decorate with cream and berries at the last minute.

Rosehip

Rosehips, the berry-like fruit of roses, have always been eaten by man, and birds. They are regarded as a healthy treat and, especially in wartime and periods of famine, as an important source of vitamin C, but luckily they are also delicious.

How it grows Any rose cultivar with sizable hips can be eaten. The hips from *Rosa rugosa* are the most widely used, as the fruits are large and relatively easy to handle. But this rose is not indigenous to Scandinavia. It comes from Japan and is, in fact, a terrible weed, colonizing vast areas of sandy coastal ground.

Appearance and taste The hips of wild roses ripen in early fall and are usually scarlet. Some species have black or purple fruits. Inside the fruits is a large number of ivory seeds, used by children to tease each other as they itch terribly when they come into contact with soft skin.

The ripe rosehip is mushy, so hips must be picked just before ripeness if you want to use them for a jam, in which the fruit is kept in beautiful, translucent halves (see recipe, right). The taste is sweet and a bit bland. They are a little like overripe tomatoes, but will transform themselves with heat, sugar, and a little acidity from lemon or vinegar and will have a delicious taste all their own.

Buying and storing Fresh rosehips are not sold in grocery stores, but they can be picked for free almost anywhere. They freeze well, and the seeds are actually easier to extract when frozen. Dried rosehips are available in health-food stores and can be made into a delicious herbal tea or rosehip soup.

Health benefits Rosehips contain a lot of the vitamins C, D, and E, calcium and a load of antioxidants. They are even considered as a treatment for gout. Rosehip seed oil is rich in vitamin C and essential fatty acids, and is much used in skin care.

Culinary uses The velvety flesh is used for a very popular fruit soup, especially in Sweden, and also in drinks, cordial, jam, jelly, pickles, and as a filling in cakes. The seeds are not eaten, and must be taken out by hand if you are making jam. It's a bit cumbersome

and impossible if the fruit is overripe. If you want the fruits for soup or cordial, you can boil them in water as they are, with the seeds, and strain them from the liquid later.

With all rosehip preparations, it's essential to add a fragrant acidity, as rosehips need this to balance their mealy blandness. Cider vinegar adds an even more fruity ripeness, lemon juice an exotic note.

Rosehip jam

This is a beautiful jam—translucent scarlet fruits suspended in clear orange syrup, and with a taste so exotic it's hard to believe that the rosehips grow all the way to the Arctic Circle. The jam is very good on toast, and in cheese sandwiches.

Collect the hips from *Rugosa* roses, remove the remnants of the blossom, cut in half, and scoop out the seeds with a teaspoon. Rinse in a bowl of cold water, then dry.

4lb 8oz rosehips, rinsed
for the syrup
3 cups sugar
4 cups water
Generous ¾ cup cider
   vinegar

Pared zest of 1 lemon,
   in thin strips
to finish
Juice of 1 lemon

Boil the syrup ingredients in a large, non-corrosive saucepan. When the sugar has dissolved, drop in the rosehips and simmer until translucent. Take them out with a slotted spoon and divide among sterilized jars.

Reduce the syrup until thick and jammy, and stir in the lemon juice. Pour over the fruit, cool, then seal.

Rosehip soup

This soup is a magical comfort food in Sweden: reassuring, homely, health-giving, and loved by everyone for its velvety, delicious sweetness. It can be served as a dessert or snack or, as in the old tradition, as an appetizer. The soup can be made from any rosehip, even dried rosehips. The method is the same; just soak the dried hips overnight in cold water.

Boil the cleaned rosehips in water to cover, until soft, then purée in a food processor or mash with a whisk. Run the mixture through a sieve. Add sugar and lemon juice to taste, and eat the thick, orange soup hot or cold with a blob of whipped cream.

The soup can also be made from smaller rosehips, with seeds and all. Prepare as above, but pass the boiled hips through a very fine sieve, to extract the seeds, before adding the sugar and lemon.

Sea buckthorn

The fruit of the common sea buckthorn is a wonder berry, prized for its rich taste and medicinal properties. The fruit is high in polyunsaturated oils and carotene and contains 12 times as much vitamin C as oranges; you can almost taste it in the juice. It is also bursting with antioxidants.

How it grows Common sea buckthorn is found all over Europe and right across Asia as far as China. In Scandinavia it grows primarily on dry, windy ground in coastal areas and is tolerant of salt spray from the sea.

Sea buckthorn bushes are huge, resembling olive trees, with silvery green leaves and masses of bright orange berries in the fall. The sprays of berry-laden branches are a flower-arranger's dream. There are male and female plants (the latter bearing the berries), so if you grow sea buckthorn at home, you will need both to get the berries.

Sea buckthorn berries are the most time-consuming and difficult berry to pick: the berries do not drop off willingly and the ripe berries are very soft. The "thorn" in the plant's name is no joke. The easiest, but rather destructive, way of harvesting the berries is to cut the berry-laden stems and put them in the freezer. Once frozen, the berries come rattling off.

Appearance and taste Health-giving though they are, the best thing about sea buckthorn berries is their astringent but interesting fruity taste. With their smooth, golden skin, they look great too.

Culinary uses The berries make a lovely, rich, almost tropical-tasting jam and cordial, and are even finding their way into baby food. You can make the jam just as you would raspberry jam (page 216). You can also use the berries to flavor schnapps by steeping them in the unflavored spirit for a couple of months, then diluting to taste when serving. The berries are very good in ice cream, and in sauces for fish and venison.

Scandinavians love to bake. We have a special and great tradition of home-baking, for every good reason you can think of. In former times it was the only way to have bread. People lived in remote places, with farms scattered over vast areas. Store-bought bread from the city bakeries was out of reach for all but the rich. In the cities, the risk of fire was much too great to have domestic ovens. They were not introduced until around 1800, before which every home had open fires, but not ones you could bake bread in. Loaves were brought to the bakers to finish, as were big roasts and the Christmas goose. For the very poor, bread was not an option; they ate hot oatmeal and different forms of the oldest types of bread—flat, unleavened breads, made from rye and barley, that could be baked on a hot stone or upturned pan.

In the country the bread was baked at home, in huge, wood-fired ovens. The traditions vary, but the breads that have made Scandinavia famous stem from the wood-fired ovens. The Finnish mass oven was built in almost every home in northern Scandinavia. The ovens are still there—constructed from brick or local stone, around a chimney, in the middle of the house. Intricate systems of channels inside the ovens distribute heat to the entire house, and heat the water too. On the back are cozy, warm alcoves for the old people, and sometimes adjacent ovens in the main rooms. In the kitchen the fire heats a stove and two ovens: a low oven for drying and keeping things warm, and a baking oven. Not everything was heated at once; you could arrange the firewood and embers as you pleased.

breads & grains

Many households also had a wood-fired outdoor stone or brick oven, often built a bit away from the house, as the risk of fire was alarming in old wooden houses. These worked on the same principle: the wood was burnt to embers directly on the oven floor, and pushed aside when the oven was thoroughly hot. You then baked on the hearth, as long as you wanted, keeping a small fire going in the back. (On estates and at vicarages, the ovens were often built as a separate bakehouse, where less fortunate parishioners could bring their loaves and flatbreads to bake.)

Man has been baking bread in ovens like these for millennia, and they produce the best, crispest, and most flavorful bread—there is no comparison with anything baked in a modern oven. Often the fumes are scented with ling, or dried leaves, adding even more flavor.

Since ancient times, bread has also been baked in earth ovens, and still is in some parts of the world. In principle, this is a hole in the ground, clad with flat stones, and with a dome on top supported by wicker and clay. The best bread I ever baked was in such an oven, built in the Danish Antiquity center in Lejre, south of Copenhagen, where they have recreated a village from every age since the Stone Age. I was teaching Viking cooking, and brewing a soup with ingredients from that era in an enormous cauldron, on an open fire, to feed the museum guests. Bones from all kinds of domestic animals

and bunches of herbs were protruding from the surface, and down in the soup were cabbages, parsnips, water mint, caraway, and fava beans. The bread was made from emmer and sourdough and wrapped in huge leaves to keep it from scorching on the hot stones.

This type of oven was not necessarily used more than once a month—to heat a big oven was expensive—so the preferred breads were long-keeping, dense rye breads, whole grain loaves and a huge assortment of crispbreads. They were baked from whatever was at hand—cheap rye and barley or maybe oats; nowadays the crispbread is usually baked from wheat and rye because we have lost the taste for the rougher cereals as we have become richer. The

The Swedish AGA

Wood-fired Finnish mass ovens were the predecessors of the famous AGA, an institution in many British homes, but originally invented in 1922 by the Swede Gustav Dalén. He was a man of his time, an entrepreneur, starting the huge gas company AGA. In 1912 he was blinded by a gas explosion and, in the same year, received the Nobel Prize in Physics for a simple but effective sun-sensitive valve for lighthouses. The stove was an immediate success, and worked on the exact same principle as the old Finnish mass ovens, but was made of 1,323lb cast iron, fuel efficient, and much cleaner and easier to regulate than the old stoves. It can even serve as central heating. The stoves were produced in Sweden at first, but sold to an English company in 1857. Although quite popular in Britain, AGAS are still a rarity in the US.

Sourdough starter

Before baker's yeast was readily available, everybody baked with sourdough, and this is coming back, big time, as people are tiring of boring industrial bread and are reinventing bread-baking as a healthy and tasty way of relaxing. Our traditions are influenced happily and radically by the organic movement, craving better nourishment and no chemicals, and by the beautiful, long-leavened, chewy, crusty breads from southern Europe. And they're all the better for it: any tradition grows stale, if not under constant change. Small, organic bakeries are popping up everywhere, selling handmade rustic breads, made from stone-ground flour, of ancient wheats, lovingly crafted into delicious wholesome loaves—and sold at high prices. The tide really is turning on the bread front.

A live sourdough is the basis of all traditional breads and crispbreads baked from both wheat and rye. Sourdough is a mystery, but an easy one to live with; once you accept that you are not the only living creature in your house all you can hope for is mutual love. Control is out of the question: it has a life of its own, and all you can do is help it on its way.

It's simple enough. The basis is 2 cups of freshly milled, organic, wholemeal rye or wheat flour in a bowl. Add enough water to make a sludge. Put the bowl on your counter, cover it with a towel, and wait. Over the next five days you feed it with a little more flour and water, and watch. It will be invaded with all the good bacteria, yeasts, and lactic acids living with you. If harmful bacteria come along, the yeasts and lactic acid will take care of them. These little microbes will eventually help you ferment your bread. They eat simple sugars, and even more indigestible carbohydrates, and if you feed them refined, sifted flour they binge and die. They need wholemeal to keep them alive and well. Sourdoughs are never the same, and if you move households, your starter will change. It's made from the microbes living with you, and if you have frequent cleaning frenzies, you will have serious problems making a sourdough starter. If your water is chlorinated, this is a problem too, and you will need to buy clean bottled water for your starter.

The longer a sourdough lives, the more complex it will be, and the bread will be all the better for it. If not well fed, it can get too sour and smell of vinegar and sweaty feet.

This is cured by reviving it on the counter with a diet of more wholemeal, a teaspoon of unheated honey, and a spoonful of live yogurt. Wait a day or two, and it will be fully recovered. You have to use your starter frequently (read once a week) or it will be starved. You can feed it a little flour and water if you are not baking for a fortnight.

When you have made your dough, reserve some for next time, and it will quickly turn into a starter, but never, ever empty your container of sourdough. If you should forget to save some of the new dough, even a spoonful left in the container is enough to make a new one, with more water and flour. So, in principle, a sourdough is simply a piece of the dough you are working with, as it matures. But you do not have to wait; any piece of fresh dough can be used to ferment new dough, straight away. This admittedly sounds like just another worry, but trust me, it's worth it, and a lot easier than keeping a Tamagotchi alive. If you bake a lot, it makes sense to maintain both a wheat and a rye sourdough starter, but it's not really necessary, if you can accept some rye in your wheat bread and vice versa.

traditional breads are very good, though, and are returning to favor, as home bakeries are popping up like mushrooms after rain, all over Scandinavia.

When a large wood-fired oven is lit, the temperature is extremely high at first—ideal for crispbread and wheat breads. When the temperature drops, it's time to bake the rye breads that need a longer time at a lower heat. Last come the small cakes, and sometimes an extra drying of the crispbread. The flatbread is either dry or soft, and eaten like Middle Eastern breads, wrapped around smoked meats, *Surstrømming*, jam, or cheese.

Wheat

Habitat Wheat has been grown in Scandinavia since the Bronze Age, but not as much as barley, rye, and oats, which are much easier to grow in cold climates. The first wheats grown were grasses and primitive wheat, which all play a role in the ancestry of the modern bread wheat, emmer. This giant wheat species is sold under the name kamut, spelt, aegilops, and the special northern form of spelt, *Ølandshvede*. They have been grown all the way through agricultural history, but were more or less gone, except for being grown in remote mountainous areas, and by smallholders with stony, hardly arable land where they have survived modern agriculture, and modern wheat. Ancient wheat has had a huge comeback in the last 20 years, because of its hardiness, health benefits, and way of providing a stable but relatively low yield under difficult growing conditions. The old wheat types have a much higher nutrient content, a beautiful taste, and have, almost overnight, become immensely popular with Scandinavians concerned with environment and health.

Health benefits Until the 20th century, wheat was a luxury and bread baked from wheat was simply called cake. This has changed dramatically and so has the quality of both flour and bread. This, and the tasteless "cardboard" bread offered to us by the bread industry,

Wheat germ

The original principle for milling grain was invented when man first started to grow it in the fertile crescent in the Middle East, 10,000 years ago. Grinding grain between two stones is still the best way to make flour. The massive stones keep the temperature in the grain down, and keep the flavor and vitamins intact; the process grinds the germ inseparably into the flour. This gives fragrant, nourishing flour with a beautiful rich taste, and keeps all the valuable oils and nutrients intact, even when sifted. This was the state of the art, and fiddling with flour was already punishable with death by Roman times. However, the invention of the rolling mill in the late 1800s made it not only acceptable, but also respectable, to tamper with the daily bread. The milling principle is different—it crushes the grain, and thereby makes it possible to extract the germ from the flour. The germ has a crystalline consistency and a different density from the rest of the grain, and can be easily extracted from rolled grains. And since it was possible, it was done, suddenly adding years to the shelf life of flour, as milled germ oxidizes quite quickly so fresh flour keeps its maximum quality for only a few months. But the germ is an essential part of the nutrients in bread, full of essential oils, proteins, folic acid, and much more. It's like an egg yolk, sufficient to make the grain sprout and grow until it reaches up into the sun. The germ itself is very expensive, finding its way into pills, anti-wrinkle cream, muesli, and other foods. This is old news, but the extent of its significance is influencing our habits in Scandinavia, as consumers demand wholesome, natural food and rediscover old methods.

have made better home-baking a favorite pastime. And as a habit it's hard to quit. Once you have tasted home-baked bread, from stoneground flour, made with sourdough and time, there is no turning back.

This bread is brownish gray from the lactic acids in the germ, fragrant from long, slow fermentation and smells like a sun-baked wheat field in late summer; its obvious wholesomeness is very much present, and irresistible. Bread like this is expensive to buy, and easy to make at home, once you get the knack of it. And a long-leavened bread is easier to digest as the fermentation makes a lot of nutrients available to the human body that are not digestible if you eat bread that has been leavened for a short time.

Buying and storing The mills offering stoneground flour are all organic or biodynamic, which has a massive influence on the taste. There are many more varied nutrients in organic food and, as nutrients and flavor are more or less the same thing, it simply tastes better. When baking at home, using organic flour is the only way to make really flavorsome and nutritious bread. The flour has a much shorter shelf life than conventional flour, because the germ is still present, and must be kept dry, and only stored for about 3 months. Homemade wheat bread will keep in perfect condition for several days. Wheat bread must be kept in a bread box or sealable plastic bag, but never in the refrigerator, as this will make it dry in a matter of hours.

Culinary uses Scandinavia has a long and lively tradition of baking wheat breads. Even though wheat has been a cheap commodity for more than a century, the traditional breads baked with wheat are festive ones, enriched with butter and eggs, sweet and spicy from cardamom, lemon zest, and saffron. In the past, the daily bread was baked mostly from rye, but coarse breads from whole wheat, often blended with oats, sifted rye, and barley were common, all juicy, nutritious, and delicious.

In northern Scandinavia the bread is often spiked with fennel or anise seeds, in the south it's more usually spiced with caraway, but all three can be combined or replace each other, giving a lovely flavor to your bread. Adding fermented milk products is also popular; it gives a fine-grained texture and a mellow acidity, plus it keeps the bread fresher for longer. These breads are best on the day they are baked, but can be gently reheated. They are perfect with ham, kale, sausages, cheese, and vegetable soups.

Wicker baskets

Soft doughs will give you juicier bread, but unsupported they will also make very flat bread. The remedy for this is traditional wicker baskets, specially designed for raising the dough in the second rising. They give good support to soft dough, keeping it from spreading too much, and make a beautiful pattern on the finished bread. Remember to flour your basket extremely well before putting in the dough or you will never get it out again. Don't ever wash it; just shake off excess flour after using and dry out on top of the oven.

Sourdough bread and poppy seed buns

This recipe is for rustic, crusty, extremely aromatic bread, using ancient wheat, sourdough, and time.

It's also for buns covered in rich poppy seeds, giving a special aroma and nutty crust to them. Both are perfect with soups, and for sandwiches with smoked fish and cheese. In summer the weather is often too hot and humid to bake successfully with sourdough, and it turns very sour before it's properly risen; at this time you can replace it with ⅕oz (5g) organic yeast as a starter.

4 cups tepid water	1½ tablespoons salt
9oz sourdough starter	Black poppy seeds
15 cups spelt or *Ølands*	MAKES 2 LOAVES
wheat flour, sifted	AND 12–15 BUNS

Mix the water and sourdough starter in a large bowl. Mix in half of the flour and the salt. Mix with the rest of the flour, but hold back some of it—you can always add more, but the opposite is much more difficult. Knead well, by folding the dough again and again; don't punch it. After 10–15 minutes it should be tight and resist folding. If it is very heavy, blend in more water. The dough must be pliable and soft, not heavy. If you have problems with the dough sticking to your hands, flour your hands well, but do not put more flour into the dough. Let the dough rise in a covered bowl on your counter for 4–5 hours, until doubled in size. The time may vary hugely, depending on the strength of your starter.

Tip the dough gently on to a lightly floured counter. Don't punch or flatten the dough. Cut it in half and reserve one half for poppy seed buns. Take care that this dough is not covered in flour, or the poppy seeds will not stick.

Cut the first half in half again and gently fold the dough into two loaf shapes. Put on parchment paper and let them rise slowly in a cool place till doubled in size—this may take up to 12 hours. Cut the second half of the dough into 12–16 pieces and roll all over in a plate of black poppy seeds. The buns will be irregular, but this does not matter as long as they are about the same size. Put on parchment paper and let rise with the loaves (they will probably rise more quickly). Preheat the oven to 480°F and bake the bread on baking sheets for 10 minutes, then lower the heat to 375°F and bake through. Both buns and loaves are done if they give an empty-sounding thud when you knock on the bottom with your knuckle.

Anise-flavored bread with fresh cheese

This bread has a lovely flavor from the aniseed and is delicious with stews and great for sandwiches.

1½oz fresh yeast

2 cups tepid water

1 tablespoon coarse salt

6 cups stone ground wheat flour, sifted

Scant ¼ cup olive or canola oil, plus extra for shaping the breads

1 tablespoon anise seeds

1 cup fresh cheese or ricotta

for the glaze

½ stick butter

2 tablespoons honey

Makes 6 round breads

Dissolve the yeast in the water, then mix in the rest of the ingredients, reserving some of the flour. Knead well, and add the rest of the flour if necessary to form a very soft, pliable dough. Let the dough rise in a covered bowl. Place in either a cool place overnight (which will reward you with tastier, long-lasting bread) or on the counter. When the dough is absolutely foamy and bubbly tip it on to your counter; instead of using flour, oil the surface well with olive or canola oil. Shape the dough into 6 round breads. Put them on parchment paper, flatten to 1¼in all over and let them rise again on the counter. They should end up more flat than rounded, so flatten them in the middle if too high.

Preheat the oven to 425°F and bake the breads on baking sheets for 20 minutes, but keep an eye on them; when they are beautifully browned and light, they are done. Melt the butter and honey in a small saucepan and brush the breads lavishly with the glaze as soon as they are out of the oven, and maybe again when they have cooled a little.

Bread cakes

Breads like this are baked all across Scandinavia, with small variations, and are extremely popular. It's a festive bread that is soft, white, and slightly sweet to go with smoked meats and cheese, or butter and jam, or any meal. It's best when baked in a wood-fired oven, but also fine in an ordinary oven, especially if you bake it on a pizza stone. If you bake this bread with an ancient wheat, remember that it needs more water—or less flour.

⅓ cup butter

2 cups water

¾oz fresh yeast

1 teaspoon coarse sea salt

½ cup sugar

⅓ cup + 2 tablespoons rye flour

6 cups fine stone ground wheat flour, sifted

Makes 6

Melt the butter in generous ¾ cup of the water; then add the rest of the water and pour into a large bowl. Dissolve the yeast in the liquid. Add the salt and sugar. Stir in the rye flour and half the wheat flour. Stir in more of the flour to form a soft dough. Knead on the counter until soft and pliable. You may not need all the flour. Let the dough rise on the counter, until doubled in size.

Divide into 6 round balls, then roll out into ¼in-thick round "cakes." Make numerous incisions with a fork and let them rise until doubled again.

Preheat the oven to 480°F and bake the bread cakes in the middle of the oven, preferably on a pizza stone, otherwise on parchment paper on heated baking sheets, for 20 minutes. They should be quite pale, but done.

Rye

Habitat Until very recently rye was the staple grain across Scandinavia. It has been grown since the Bronze Age in damp, cold areas as it is more reliable than sun-loving wheat. Rye is a healthy crop, most often sown as a winter annual, giving precious ground protection in winter. The problem with rye for millennia, however, has been the ergot fungus, which thrives in damp conditions and very much resembles the grains, both in size and weight, so that even modern grain-rinsing machines have difficulty sorting them out. Ergot can easily be detected by the naked eye, but are laborsome to extract from the grain. The problem is that ergot is poisonous and a powerful hallucinogen, containing some of the same chemicals as LSD. The symptoms of ergotism are terrible: gangrene, convulsions, and craziness, just to name a few. Many claim that it may be the cause of the strange behavior that was identified as bewitchment during the witch hunts of the 16th and 17th centuries.

Culinary uses Rye bread has an amazing number of forms: from the fudgy, totally dense, black pumpernickel-type breads, baked for 24 hours, which are so good for mature cheese, smoked meats, and spicy jam, to long-leavened sourdough rye breads, which are the backbone of *Smørrebrød*, to light, crisp, rye *knäckebrød*, eaten with almost everything.

Rye used to be the main ingredient in rye bread, but modern people have juvenile tastes and prefer rye bread with almost no rye. If you want real rye bread, you have to bake it yourself, even in Scandinavia, and it's easy, once you master it. If I had to pick just one dish to be totally and undeniably Scandinavian, it must be rye bread pudding, made from stale rye bread, but other rye bread dishes come close. The crunchy granola-type topping so popular for eating on junket and yogurt is easily made from stale, grated rye bread, mixed with an equal amount of dark muscovado sugar. It's good, and it's also a bit of a challenge for your taste buds, if the slightly bitter caramel taste of rye is unfamiliar to you. Grated dry rye bread is also the basis of the beautiful apple rye bread cake on page 232.

Just a short while ago nothing went to waste, and the Nordic take on the *pain perdu* idea is a gorgeous apple trifle made from grated rye bread, fried until crisp in butter and loads of brown sugar, topped with an avalanche of apple compote and whipped cream; it's surprisingly good—actually it's a favorite of mine.

Rye bread is perfect for the salty fish preparations of Scandinavia, giving a solid, slightly sour, and beefy background for everything smoked and cured that would overwhelm a soft white bread. Its malt is beautiful with beer, and the contrast to anything sweet, such as apples, raisins, and prunes, is amazing.

The Swedish have a slightly different rye bread tradition from the rest of Scandinavia; they prefer a sweetened rye bread. The rest of us like it as a salty, coarse sourdough—that is, if we like it at all.

Home baking is popular even with men, and in most households rye bread seems to be a male thing. Kneading a huge rye dough is tough: it's stiff and heavy, and completely unlike a wheat dough. Just a hundred years ago the kneading in the bread factories was done by men, tramping around in the dough with their feet. It is actually beneficial to the dough—clean feet are full of helpful enzymes, and the bread is all the better for it.

Malt is an important part of the complex rye bread taste, either as a small fraction of malt flour, malt syrup, or simply malt coffee, which is brewed like coffee and used instead of water, malt beer, or dark ale. You can use all of them, or try different variations to suit your taste.

In the following recipes, wheat flour can be substituted for spelt or other old wheats, or simply by more rye flour. I suggest you try the recipes as they are the first time, to get the consistency and baking time right, and then alter as you wish.

Health benefits Rye flour is almost always whole grain, which means it contains the germ, but you must buy it freshly milled or it will be stale. It is often coarser than wheat flour, and this is good for you. Apart from that, the nutrients in rye and wheat are much the same.

Buying and storing Read the label: if a bread contains rye, sourdough, and salt, it's good; if it's mostly wheat, no sourdough, and additives galore, it's not good. Rye bread is best kept wrapped in a sealable plastic bag in the fridge. Home-baked bread can be wrapped in a clean, damp dish towel inside a sealable plastic bag to keep the crust moist. Rye bread will keep for weeks in the refrigerator. Dry bread can also be made into one of the delicious options above.

Mix all the ingredients thoroughly in a large bowl. Rest the dough for 30 minutes on the counter to allow the flour to absorb the water (different brands absorb at different speeds). Now comes the moment to estimate whether the dough will need a little more water, a little more flour, or is perfect. This will be difficult the first time you make it. It must be soft but stiff, and you must be able to put a finger in it with no effort. If in doubt, keep it on the drier side.

Butter 1 large or 2 smaller loaf pans well and fill with the dough, but leave ¾in at the top for the bread to rise. With a spatula, level the surface until smooth. Let rise in a cool place, covered with a damp dish towel, for 12 hours.

Preheat the oven to 325°F. Prick each bread 20 times, all the way to the bottom, with a wooden skewer just before putting it in the oven. This is to prevent a thick, impenetrable crust forming, and a giant hole beneath it, as the bread lets out steam. The tiny holes act like multiple chimneys. Bake for 1¼ hours. Cool the bread by wrapping in a clean, damp dish towel.

24-hour pumpernickel with orange

This type of bread has multiple variations; this one is not sweet, but filled with dried fruit. It's perfect with eggs or cheese, for a hearty breakfast, or just as a snack with butter. It will keep for 3 months wrapped in a damp dish towel and plastic food bag in the refrigerator. You can swap the spelt flour for rye only, and use other dried fruits and nuts. But try this before experimenting.

2 cups sourdough starter
2½ cups malt beer
3¾ cups water or malt coffee
7 cups whole grain rye flour
2¾ cups spelt flour
Generous ¾ cup
   golden raisins
Generous ¾ cup dried
   cranberries—no added
   flavoring
1¾ cups pumpkin seeds

1¼ cups poppy seeds
1¾ cups flax seed
5 tablespoons coarse salt
1 tablespoon malt syrup or
   chestnut honey
2 tablespoons ground, dried
   orange peel
⅔ cup candied orange peel
Butter, for greasing
MAKES 4 BREADS

Mogens' rye bread

This is as simple as a rye bread gets, but still maintains its quality as a real rye bread. It's in one go, and set to ferment and rise in the pan. It's good bread to start with, as it's always successful, and the taste is great. It also has the advantage that it can be cut into slices as soon as it's cooled – unlike most rye breads, which need a day to rest.

1¼ cups sourdough starter,
   freshly made or dough
   from your last rye bread
2 cups cracked rye
2 cups whole grain rye flour
2¾–3¼ cups water or beer
2 cups wheat flour

2 tablespoons malt syrup
1 tablespoon coarse salt
1 cup seeds, such as
   sunflower, flax, or poppy
Butter, for greasing
MAKES 1 LARGE OR
2 SMALL BREADS

Jon's rye bread

This is a traditional rye bread, baked over two days. The first day you mix in all the grains and seeds, to give them time to absorb the water, and mature the dough; the next day you add the rest of the ingredients.

The result is a fragrant bread, complex in flavor. The nutrients are easily digested, as in time enzymes in the grain break down the flour to make the nutrients available to the body that you can simply not digest if you eat bread that has not had time to mature.

for the starter dough
10½oz sourdough starter
7oz cracked grains and
  seeds, such as rye,
  sunflower, flax, poppy
3½oz rye or wheat flour
1¼ cups lukewarm water
1 teaspoon coarse salt
2 teaspoons honey

for the bread dough
the starter dough
1½lb rye flour
2 tablespoons coarse salt
2 teaspoons honey
2¼ cups lukewarm water
¼ stick butter, for brushing
MAKES 2 X 1LB 10OZ
BREADS

Day 1 Mix all the starter dough ingredients in a big bowl. Let the dough rest overnight, covered with a wet dish towel.

Day 2 Mix all the bread dough ingredients in a mixer or on the counter. Knead well. Reserve 10½oz dough as the starter for your next batch of bread.

Mix all the ingredients thoroughly. Butter 4 loaf pans, or line them with parchment paper.

Divide the dough evenly between the pans. Smooth the surface with a wet spatula. Cover the dough with a fitted piece of parchment paper. Wrap the pans in several layers of aluminum foil, taking care that this is not torn. Bake at 100°F for 12 hours, then for another 12 hours at 200°F. By this time the breads should be fragrant and dark brown from the slow caramelizing, and feel like they are firm and done all the way through. Try not to cut them as they will have to pull themselves together for a day, to distribute the moisture evenly through the bread; if they are still spongy, they may need a couple of hours more, especially if the oven temperature is not accurate. Be careful not to tear the foil as it will cause the bread to dry out and be inedible. While they are still warm, wrap in wet—not damp—dish towels, and then in a plastic food bag. Cool.

The sustainable solution to the problem of using aluminum foil is a heavy-duty wooden frame with a fitted metal lid. The frame is placed directly on the baking pan. This is very useful if you grow fond of rye bread, but a bit expensive, and you will probably need more than one.

Grease two rye bread pans lavishly with butter. Divide the dough between them and, using a spatula and a little water, smooth the surface. Let breads rise for 3 hours on the counter.

Preheat the oven to 325°F and bake the breads for 2 hours. Turn them out of the pans, brush all over with melted butter, and bake for another hour, out of the pans. Cool, wrap in damp dish towels and a plastic food bag, and wait until the next day to cut.

Swedish *limpa* with scalded rye

This is a soft, moist, slightly sweet Swedish *limpa*. It can be studded with lingonberries—just add a jar of lingonberry jam on day two. It's eaten with everything, though I prefer the unsweetened rye bread for fish. The scalding gives a special chewy texture and a juicy interior. Measure the flours in a measuring jug.

for the starter dough

4 cups water

6 cups rye flour

2 teaspoons coarse salt

1.5 tablespoons cider vinegar

3 tablespoons sourdough starter

1 tablespoon ground, dried orange peel

for the bread dough

1¼oz fresh yeast

Generous ⅓ cup tepid water

⅓ cup malt syrup

1 teaspoon sugar

Candied orange peel from ½ Seville orange, chopped

5½ cups wheat flour

for the glaze

1 tablespoon malt syrup

1 tablespoon warm water

MAKES 2 ROUND LOAVES

Day 1 Boil the water and cool a little, then scald the rye in a big bowl. When it has cooled to finger warm, add the remaining ingredients. Knead in a mixer until smooth. Let it stay in the bowl on the counter, covered with a wet dish towel, until the next day.

Day 2 In a large bowl, dissolve the yeast in the water, then mix with the starter dough. Add all the other ingredients to the mixture. Knead until the dough is not too sticky, adding a little more flour if absolutely necessary. Let it rise for 1 hour.

Shape into two round loaves and put on parchment paper. Dust with flour and, using a sharp knife, cut a lattice on top of the breads. Let them rise again, until very fluffy.

Preheat the oven to 350°F. Mix the syrup and water together to make the glaze. Brush the loaves with the glaze and bake on a baking sheet in the lower half of the oven for 1–1½ hours. Knock the bottom of the bread with a knuckle after 1 hour—if it sounds hollow, it's done. Otherwise bake a little longer.

10½oz sourdough starter
½ oz yeast
1¼lb wheat flour
14oz rye flour, sifted
1 tablespoon coarse sea salt
2½–2¾ cups buttermilk
2 tablespoons caraway
seeds
MAKES 2 LOAVES

Mix all the ingredients together in a large bowl. Tip the dough on to a floured counter and knead well for 20 minutes, by hand. Let it sit on the counter and rise until doubled in size. This may take 6–12 hours, depending on the sprightliness of the sourdough.

Shape into loaves, and let them rise in two wicker baskets (page 241). Leave until extremely fluffy and spongy. Preheat the oven to 350°F. Turn the loaves on to a heated baking sheet and bake for about 35 minutes. Knock on the bottom of the loaves with a knuckle and if they sound hollow, they are done. If not, bake a little longer.

Either the first or second rising period should be in a cool place, whichever suits your schedule best.

Vörtbrød

Vörtbrød is an ancient type of spiced dark bread, baked with *vört* or wort, which is unfermented beer. It's still eaten for Christmas, especially in Sweden. In former times beer was brewed for all occasions and the daily drink was a very light beer, drunk with all meals by everyone, including the children, as drinking water was unsafe. Several types of beer were brewed for Christmas: a quickly fermented lighter beer and a special sweet Christmas beer, heavily spiced with licorice, which is still available today and is drunk with rice pudding—children love it as it is rich and sweet and contains very little alcohol. Very strong beers are also brewed for Christmas and Easter, which are released on certain dates from the breweries, and a lot of people in Denmark, where there are no alcohol laws, consider this an unofficial festive day, and take the day off to try out the new beers. In the rest of Scandinavia strong beer, wine, and alcohol can only be bought in special stores, as a means of trying to preventing alcoholism. I will not be the judge of whether it's an effective measure…

It's virtually impossible to buy real *vörtbrød*; often what's on sale is just a spiced plain loaf, maybe made with beer instead of the *vört*. But home-brewing is

Rye and wheat "sourbread" with caraway seeds

This is an age-old bread, made from sourdough and a mixture of sifted rye and wheat flour. It's made more or less the same way from eastern Europe through to Russia, Germany, and all of Scandinavia. Even Portugal has similar bread in the north, but without the caraway. It's served with sausages and hearty soups. The caraway adds a very interesting flavor, but if you hate caraway, omit it. The consistency is spongy and dense as rye does not have as high a gluten content as wheat, but it holds moisture well and the bread is good for a week. The taste is complex and it works with both sweet and savory toppings. In Scandinavia it's traditionally eaten with shrimp, mature cheese, smoked cheese, and smoked salmon. If you have difficulty finding sifted rye flour, buy a bag of rye flour and sift it yourself.

becoming immensely popular now, and perhaps it's time for a revival of this ancient, tasty bread.

Use a dark, richly flavored ale or stout for this bread, if you are not the proud owner of a brewery.

If dark malt is out of reach, you can use the roast coffee substitute available in health-food stores, which is also made from malt, and maybe roasted chicory, which is also nice in bread.

1oz fresh yeast or 7oz sourdough starter	dark malt
1¾ cups tepid full-fat milk	Generous ⅓ cup dark beer or wort
1 teaspoon coarse sea salt	Scant ½ cup raisins
½ cup malt syrup or honey	18oz rye flour
1 tsp ground cinnamon	9oz wheat flour
½ tsp ground cloves	Beaten egg, to glaze
2 tbsp roasted,	Makes 1 loaf

Dissolve the yeast in the milk (or mix the starter with the milk, if using). Mix with all the other ingredients, except the flours. Finally add the flours and knead until smooth. Let the dough rise until doubled in size.

Shape the dough into a braided loaf on a floured counter. Let it rise again, until it has a light and marshmallow-like texture.

Preheat the oven to 400°F. Brush the loaf with beaten egg and bake for about 35 minutes. Wait until absolutely cool before slicing. One of the risings should be done in a warm place and one slowly in a cool place—you can choose which way round.

Øllebrød with malt syrup and stout

Øllebrød translates as "beer bread" and is either a dessert or a warming winter breakfast. Easy to make and with the added value of using up stale rye bread, it's an extremely simple dish, relying on a rich malt flavor in a sweet context, which must be a combination otherwise seen only in sweet dark beer, not in anything edible. It's delicious and very filling—children love it. It's made in winter—in summer you can use the stale bread for a cake. This recipe emphasizes the malt by using stout and malt syrup. If this is too much for you, try using beer and sugar instead.

18oz dry rye bread	1¼ cups heavy cream, softly whipped
1⅓ cups stout or malt beer	Serves 5–6
Malt syrup, to taste	
Sugar, to taste	

In a thick-bottomed pot, soak the bread in cold water overnight. Pour the beer into the bread pot and boil slowly, while whisking to dissolve lumps. After 10 minutes it should turn into a completely smooth, lump-free oatmeal. You may need to add more water. Season with malt syrup until slightly sweet, but there must be room for a thick dusting of sugar on top. Eat while warm, with generous amounts of whipped cream. Leftovers can be reheated with more water.

Mämmi

Mämmi takes the malt concept a step further; it's a concoction so unique that it exists only in Finland. It's a rich, chocolate brown, fudgy dish made from rye flour and ground malted rye, sweetened with molasses. The flours are boiled and slightly fermented, and then baked in a dish until set. It's traditional for Easter, but available year round, in such good quality that I must admit I have never made it from scratch. Eat it warmed, with cream and sugar, or ice cream. I absolutely love it.

Crispbread

I was given this recipe, along with several others for this book, by Nik Märak, a fabulous Sami woman and master baker. She teaches baking in Stockholm, but returns every year to her native Jokkmokk, a small Sami town in northern Sweden on the Arctic Circle, to bake with family and friends for the annual Sami Market in February. You can use a mixture of flours as long as the flour weight adds up to 3 cups.

¾ oz fresh yeast	1¾ cups sunflower seeds
1¾ warm water	⅔ cup sesame seeds, plus
1¼ cups rye flour	extra for sprinkling
1¾ cups wheat flour	2 tablespoons honey
2 teaspoons coarse sea salt	MAKES AROUND 45

Preheat the oven to 400°F. Dissolve the yeast in the water, add the remaining ingredients, and knead to a smooth dough. Roll out the dough as thinly as possible on your counter, dusting with flour so it doesn't stick. Sprinkle with the extra sesame seeds. Cut into squares or triangles as you wish. Bake on parchment paper on a baking sheet for 10–15 minutes, or until lightly browned and crisp.

When the crispbreads are done, turn off the heat and let them dry out in the cooling oven.

Crispbread with sourdough

This crispbread is made with sourdough and yeast, and all four of the Nordic grains. You can change the proportions or bake it with only one grain and it will still turn out just fine. If you want to hang it from the ceiling on a string, in the traditional manner, you must make a hole in the middle of each bread with a small glass. You roll out the dough to cover the entire baking sheet, and then cut it on the sheet, and break it up after it's baked, or follow the recipe. The spicing can be varied with anise, fennel seeds, and more poppy seeds to cover the surface. The recipe comes from Rosendal's Trädgård in Stockholm, an oasis on the island of Djurholmen, with a nursery, organic gardens and store, and a famous café in one of the old greenhouses.

for the starter dough	for the crispbread dough
2 cups milk	
1oz fresh yeast	1½ teaspoons coarse salt
3 tablespoons honey	14oz flour from a mix of
1 cup rye flour	wheat, rye, barley, and oats
½ cup spelt or wheat flour	MAKES 14 ROUND
Scant ¼ cup sourdough starter	CRISPBREADS

For the starter, heat the milk to finger temperature, then add the yeast and honey and stir until dissolved. Transfer to a large bowl. Add the flours and sourdough to the milk and knead into a smooth dough. Cover with a clean dish towel and let it rest on the counter for 2 hours.

Preheat the oven to 425°F. Add all the other ingredients to the starter and knead into a dough. Divide into 14 round buns. Roll the buns into very thin rounds. Prick all over with a fork and bake in the oven, two at a time, on a baking sheet for 5 minutes.

When all the breads are baked, lower the heat and return the breads to the oven for another 7–10 minutes until golden and crisp.

More grains

Oats

Oats are newer to the north than wheat, but only by a few thousand years. They were cultivated in the north from the Bronze Age, and were widely enjoyed by the Celts. Oats are still most popular in areas where the Celtic culture was once dominant: Ireland, Scotland, and central Europe. The Romans disregarded oats, and so did everybody wealthy enough to do so, until a hundred years ago. Oats were regarded as animal fodder, and the main part of the harvest is still used for animal feed.

The poor have been eating them all along, and oats have probably played an important part in human survival since the Bronze Age. Oats grow well on damp, cold ground and yield more than most grain in the Scandinavian climate. Until a century ago oats were the most widely grown grain in Scandinavia.

Appearance and taste An oat field is a rare and pretty sight these days, the nodding, pendulous seeds gently rustling in the summer breezes; no other crop has a color like the blue-green of the immature oats. They are always sold either as whole rolled oats, or cracked and then rolled into smaller flakes. The whole rolled oats are far superior in taste, and for cooking. Rolled oats are usually slightly roasted, which brings out their delicious nutty flavor.

Buying and storing Check oats before buying, as they are high in useful fatty acids, and these will turn rancid over time. Rancidness is not always easy to detect, but this is a skill worth acquiring, as rancid fats are extremely harmful and taste really bad. Oats should smell like a newly harvested, sun-warmed field; if they don't, don't buy.

Culinary uses Oats have a beautiful nutty taste and can be added to any cookie, crispbread, or bread dough—up to 10 percent oats will not affect the rising and will add body to the bread.

Oats are often used instead of almonds and nuts, and share some of the same cooking qualities, as in the following cookie recipe. They work beautifully in pie dough, where you can replace half of the flour with oatmeal. They are also good as a coating on fried

fish and vegetables. The Scandinavians are fond of hot oatmeal, and even though lots of grains can be used for this, rolled oats are the preferred one. If you can get hold of giant rolled oats, the hot oatmeal will have a delicious chewiness, if the oats are left to soak in milk or water overnight and boiled swiftly in the morning. Just add a tiny amount of salt, eat with lingonberries, and you will be prepared for any Arctic weather.

Crisp oat caramel cookies

These are absolutely delicious with tea or coffee, or with a dessert with berries. You can replace the almonds with more oats, but it's very nice with the two kinds of nuttiness together. Generously space the cookies on the parchment paper and let cool a little before removing them from the parchment paper, but do so before completely cooled or they will break.

½ cup raw sugar

¼ cup corn syrup

Generous ½ cup butter

Scant ¼ cup heavy cream

⅔ cup almonds

1½ tablespoons flour

½ teaspoon baking powder

Grated zest of 1 lemon

½ teaspoon ground
   cardamom

Generous ½ cup whole
   rolled oats

Boil the sugar, syrup, butter, and cream together until the entire surface is filled with small bubbles. Don't stir. Let the caramel cool and transfer to a large bowl.

Preheat the oven to 350°F. Chop the almonds and mix, with the rest of the ingredients, into the cooled caramel to form a batter. Put the batter on parchment paper lining a baking sheet, a spoonful at a time, to make little mounds. They will be runny when heated, so take care not to crowd the tray. Bake for 8–10 minutes.

Barley

Barley is an ancient grain in the north, and the most widely grown now. It has a multitude of uses: malting for beer, malt syrup, animal fodder, and as human food. It was the grain used for bread before wheat was common—and affordable—and it's highly nutritious.

Bread baked from barley is the oldest type, such as flatbread baked on a hot stone or griddle, as it is still done in many parts of the world. As leavened breads became popular, barley bread was eaten only by the poor, because its gluten content is very low and a bread baked from barley alone is extremely heavy. However, a bread of up to 25 percent is fine—and it will have an interesting grassy but pleasant taste.

Crispbreads and flatbreads baked with part barley or all barley are still made in Scandinavia, and they are delicious. The four-grain crispbread (page 250) is good baked with all barley.

Pearl barley (polished barley grains) is currently a very fashionable food. It's cooked like rice and has a special flavor that is very nice in salads, as in the ancient wheat salad (page 186) or as a risotto-style dish.

Smørgås-Smørrebrød

Bread in the north is eaten not only with the meal, with soups and stews, but also in the open-face sandwiches that are eaten for lunch every day, even if Italian-type *panini* are becoming popular.

Open-face sandwiches are an art form and, if you meet them in restaurants, often far too lavish. The everyday open-face sandwiches are delicious, but leaner in appearance, often just a piece of rye bread with liver paste and a pickled gherkin or beet on top, a simple rye and sausage sandwich with raw or toasted onion, or a herring on rye with fresh apple and onions. The best are often the simplest: boiled new potatoes on rye with chives and mayonnaise, while egg and tomato or potato and herrings are classics as well.

It's normal to use leftovers from dinner the night before for the next day's open-face sandwiches; all kinds of roasts topped with pickles, or pickled red cabbage, *frikadeller* with cucumber salad, chicken with mayonnaise and gherkins, fried fish with lemon and a sprinkling of salt, or leftover fried fish soused and eaten with a mountain of raw onion rings on rye. The best open-face sandwiches are made this way, and Scandinavian meals are very often put together to accommodate lovely open-face sandwiches for the next day.

There are strict rules for which bread is used for what topping, but generally it's safe, and delicious, to use rye bread. Herrings of any conceivable sort are always eaten on rye; smoked salmon, shrimp, and prawns always on toast or sourbread; most meat is on rye, even if *rullepølse* is occasionally served on wheat bread. Cheese is usually on wheat bread, but very strong, mature cheese and blue cheese are mostly eaten on rye bread.

Then there is the question of which spread to use. With cured herrings, sausage, and most pork toppings it's usually rendered, spiced fat from pork or pork/duck/goose. Most others are with butter. Leftover sauce is also used as a spread, and it's good.

Another specialty is the "salads"—not really salads, but mayonnaise-based concoctions, like the Italian salad (page 144). They are not eaten on their own but as a topping for ham and other salted pork. However, red herring salad is eaten on its own on rye with egg.

Remoulade is used as a topping for both fried fish and roast beef sandwiches on rye. There are many salads to choose from; the most spectacular to foreign eyes probably being the mackerel salad—canned mackerel in tomato sauce, eaten with mayonnaise—and it's actually quite good.

Crispbread is eaten with everything: smoked fish, cheese, jam, smoked meat, and sausage; the heavily spiced toppings are usually on rye crispbread, lighter ones on wheat.

Other peculiarities are the Scandinavian fondness for cheese and jam together, and the frequent use of raw egg yolks, used for tartare sandwiches on rye with capers and horseradish, with mature cheese, blue cheese, smoked herring, and mackerel—delicious.

Soft wheat flatbreads are used as a basis for smoked meat, cheese, the Norwegian goat's cheese *Myseost*, and jam—the bread and toppings are rolled up tightly. You will find numerous dishes and suitable toppings suggested for eating on open-face sandwiches throughout this book, all listed in the index.

If you want to serve Scandinavian open-face sandwiches you can make them yourself, and provide 3–4 per person for a meal, or serve the ingredients separately so people can help themselves. Finished sandwiches are rarely served in private homes, but it's nice when someone has taken the care to make them for you.

Try a herring or two, a smoked fish or shrimp salad, a sandwich with liver paste or pork with crackling, and maybe a chicken salad. In summer, try a potato sandwich with mayonnaise and chives. Serve with beer, schnapps, and a cake to finish.

Scandinavian Christmas is a colorful mixture of old pagan rituals and imports from all over Europe and Christianity. The past is very much present in all the yuletide traditions that flourish under a veneer of Christian lore. This hotchpotch nevertheless represents a real Scandinavian Christmas.

The buzzword is the untranslatable *hygge*, meaning coziness, only much more. The important point of all the gatherings and traditions is that there is *hygge*, an amiable spirit of warmth, tradition, relaxation, and well-being, all put together in a single word that every Scandinavian understands.

Naturally, everybody is aware that Christmas celebrates the birthday of Christ, and an extraordinary number of Scandinavians fill the churches during this time. However, in reality, the Christian aspect is just another tradition among others. The early Christians cleverly placed the birth of Christ on top of the ancient yuletide festivities, to make sure that the population would celebrate His birthday. Yule was originally a pagan festival celebrating the longest night of the year by lighting as many candles and oil lamps as you could afford, and eating, drinking, and fighting and warding off the evil spirits by keeping watch during the night.

Yuletide was not for the faint-hearted, and this is what Christmas is still about for the majority of adult Scandinavians. Every workplace, institution, school, association, and society—which Scandinavians are so fond of—has its own Christmas lunch; this often involves substantial orgies of food, but is more about drinking and having a good time. Special trains and buses carry the victims safely home, and for most people December is a month of extremely busy weekends.

festive food

Over the centuries, hundreds of traditions associated with Christmas have been imported from all over Europe, among them the Christmas tree from Germany, Christmas cards from England, nativity plays and little decorative figurines from Italy, and various foods that gradually become new, firm traditions. The *Nisse* or *Tomte*—little people living on farms, where they keep an eye on everything and help with the livestock—are a very important part of the lore at yuletide. They demand respect and are not always good-natured. You have to keep the *Nisse* happy, and put a bowl of creamed rice with cinnamon in the attic for them to share with the cat. They are everywhere, with their red, pointed hats and long beards, and some of them even have families.

The children's Christmas is, to be truthful, mostly about Christmas presents, making decorations and homemade presents, doing nativity plays at school, and a month-long countdown to the big event. In northern Scandinavia there is always snow for Christmas, so here building snowmen, sledding, and making snow lamps are also very much part of the festival. Many families fell their own Christmas tree and decorate it with red apples, pepper cookies, and a mix of homemade Christmas decorations—little, cleverly constructed baskets to hold sweets, nuts, baubles, and fairy hair.

In Scandinavia, Christmas Eve is the big night. Families gather to eat the Christmas dinner, and dance around the Christmas tree, singing carols and more secular songs about *Nisse* or *Tomte*. Often, a member of the family dresses up as Santa Claus and delivers the gifts in a huge sack, the children usually scared, but fascinated. There are stars made of birch shavings in the windows, three-armed candles on the table representing the three wise men, and everything is decorated in red, green, and white. Finally, the gifts are shared, while sweets, dried and fresh fruit, and nuts are eaten, and everybody can relax.

The celebratory meals continue after Christmas Eve. On 25 and 26 December there are family lunches, and here the focus is on the food. Elaborate and often very traditional arrays of herrings and smoked meat, salads and relishes, breads, pies and desserts, cookies and candy are involved. This is where young Scandinavians learn to appreciate traditional foods, often served only at Christmas.

Along with all the other traditions, family and friends gather for informal *gløgg* parties, where hot mulled wine spiced with everything Christmassy and spiced cookies or delicious sweet apple dumplings (*æbleskiver*) are consumed. All of these sweet things are often followed by cold beer and open-face sandwiches, for people to assemble themselves from an assortment of sausages, smoked fish, ham, and cheese.

In Scandinavia, as elsewhere, the traditional foods are offered in ready-made versions in every store, and sometimes they are quite good. But if you want the taste of real traditions, you will, I'm sorry to say, have to make them yourself, as generally there is absolutely no comparison. Also, when you rely on the store-bought versions, there is a tendency to have too much of everything, and the delicacies, meant to be special treats, are reduced to being merely a symbol of what Christmas is about, rather than the real thing.

Traditional *gløgg*

The traditional *gløgg* is made from red wine, and a reduction of spices boiled in water to a concentrate, sweetened and spiked with schnapps and often port wine. The mixture is heated, but must not boil, and is served in tall glasses with raisins soaked in schnapps, and blanched almonds. It can be lovely, even if you tend to have too much of it during Christmas.

The spice mix for *gløgg* must be made from whole spices; they have more flavor and will yield clear, pretty syrup, which will keep for a long time in the refrigerator. The alternative method is to steep all the spices and zest in rum or schnapps for a fortnight, then add directly to the wine. Both methods are fine. You can add raisins or almonds to either version. If using raisins, plump them up in extra rum or schnapps for a day, then add at the last minute with the almonds.

for the spice mix	1¾ cups unflavored
1 tablespoon cloves	schnapps (optional)
2 cinnamon sticks	2 bottles red wine
1 tablespoon whole allspice	1¾ cups port
½ teaspoon black	¾ cup sugar
peppercorns	⅔ cup raisins
1 blade of mace	⅔ cup blanched almonds
Grated zest of 1 orange	SERVES 10

Either, steep the spices and peel in the schnapps for a couple of weeks. Sieve. Heat the wine and port and sweeten to taste, adding the schnapps at the last minute. Or, boil the spices with 4 cups of water for an hour, or until reduced to 2 cups. Sieve, sweeten the flavored water to a syrup, and add to the heated wine and port. Put raisins and almonds in the glasses, if you wish, pour on the *gløgg* and serve.

White *gløgg*

This is a fresher and slightly different version, made from white wine or hard cider and differently spiced. Simply follow the method given for the recipe above.

2 bottles white wine or	1¾ cups rum or white port
hard cider	Sugar, to taste

Generous ¾ cup raisins,	½ nutmeg, grated
soaked in schnapps	20 whole black peppercorns
for a day	2 cinnamon sticks
Generous ⅓ cup whole	4 allspice berries
blanched almonds	1 teaspoon coriander seeds
for the spice mix	½ a bay leaf
4 star anise	Peel of 1 lemon
4 thick slices fresh ginger	SERVES 10

Schnapps

There are very few Scandinavian traditions not involving schnapps, or *aquavit* as it is also called. It's a clear spirit, made from potatoes, or sometimes grain. The spicing is what sets it apart from other similar spirits. When bought ready-made it is usually scented with caraway or gale (*Myrica gale*, also known as bog myrtle), which grows wild in bogs all over Scandinavia. There is, however, a very lively tradition of making your own flavored schnapps, and in some families it's a passion. Schnapps is usually unsweetened, but if you flavor it with green walnuts, sloes, or cherries, it will have a pleasant taste that is delicious with sweet foods.

The most popular flavorings for schnapps are: St John's wort (which yields beautiful, ruby-red schnapps thanks to the tiny oil glands in the yellow leaves), basil leaves, angelica root and leaves, blueberries, dill flowers and leaves, rose petals and rosehips, lingonberries, crab apples, juniper berries, sweet woodruff, heather, young fir, and spruce shoots. Any culinary herb, with a few exceptions such as horseradish and mustard, will give a pleasant flavor. The general rule is to steep the fresh herbs or ripe fruit in the schnapps for a fortnight or more, but basil, sloes, berries, and walnuts, for example, can be left in. Then use these precious drops to flavor another bottle of schnapps, either as a single flavor or blended.

Sweet breads

We have a treasure trove of sweet yeast breads and cakes in Scandinavia. Every country, town, and household has its favorites. Baking sweet breads, cookies, and cakes for festive occasions is a firm tradition, and the pride of every old-fashioned housewife. Even now, buns, cakes, and cookies for special occasions are made at home: buns with raisins for birthdays; cinnamon rolls for Sunday afternoon tea; *brunsviger,* a giant yeast cake topped with brown sugar and cinnamon, which forms deep cavities of fudgy filling when baked; or the traditional Swedish saffron-flavored Lucia buns. And they all have confusingly different recipes, but I have made it easy for you, so that just one basic dough can be transformed into any of them.

Cardamom is a favorite flavoring for any sweet bread in Scandinavia, and it's far superior if you grind your own from the seeds inside the green pods. The combination of cardamom with lemon zest is beautiful, and the scent wafts through the air, telling every nostril in the neighborhood that it is a very special day.

1 oz fresh yeast
1¾ cups tepid milk
Scant ½ cup butter, melted
1 egg
1–1½ cups all-purpose flour
Generous ⅓ cup sugar
1 teaspoon coarse sea salt
1 teaspoon ground cardamom
Grated zest of 1 lemon
Beaten egg, for glazing

Dissolve the yeast in the milk, add the rest of the ingredients (except the egg), holding back a quarter of the flour, to add if necessary. Knead well to make a sticky dough. Let the dough rise in a cool place till doubled in size. From this point on you can make whatever you want from it.

The shaped dough is put in a warm place to rise again, until big and fluffy, and then glazed with beaten egg and baked at 400°F for a surprisingly short time. Small breads and buns needs only 8–12 minutes.

Lucia buns

These lovely, saffron-scented, sweet buns (*lussekattor*) are named after the Christian martyr Lucia, the patron saint of the blind and the Sicilian town of Syracuse. She was killed in AD 303 on December 13, which was the shortest day in the Julian calendar, and as her name means "light" in Latin, her day was a festivity of the returning light, held in the depths of winter.

Since the 17th century, there has been a tradition in Sweden of eating these buns in the early morning on December 13 while watching the sun come up. The ceremonial Lucia processions of young girls with spruce wreaths with lit candles in their hair, waking up the family while singing hymns, is only a century old, but is extremely popular, and has spread to the rest of Scandinavia.

The origin of the buns is unclear, but the symbolism of their beautiful shapes, which look like Celtic signs used to decorate cauldrons and jewelry from the Iron Age, is pre-Christian—though the original names were changed in the Christian era. The most common swirled half-cross and cross are much more like the prehistoric sun cross than a Christian one. The Lucia celebration has nothing to do with Christmas, even if these buns make any Scandinavian feel very Christmassy. They are served with morning coffee or afternoon tea, with butter.

Make the sweet bread dough as on page 258, adding 1/50oz (0.5g) powdered saffron with the milk. After the dough has risen the first time, shape into *lussekattor*, as in the photograph opposite; the dough should make around 18 buns. Place on parchment paper, glaze with beaten egg, and decorate with raisins or currants. Let the buns rise until doubled in size or more. Bake at 400°F until golden and just baked through.

Birthday buns

These buns with raisins are so good with hot cocoa, butter, and a child-friendly, mild cheese; they are always served first, before the layer cake.

Using the sweet bread recipe, mix ⅔ cup or more of raisins into the dough while shaping the buns after the first rising. Place on parchment paper, glaze with egg, and let them rise until doubled in size. Bake at 400°F until golden. The quantities are enough for 18–24 buns.

Cinnamon rolls

These are extremely popular all over Scandinavia, especially with the Swedish tradition of *fika*, meaning coffee and some sweet bread, at any time of day.

1 quantity sweet bread dough (see page 258)	1½ tablespoons ground cinnamon
1 egg, beaten	2 teaspoons ground cardamom
for the filling	
⅔ cup soft butter	MAKES 25
1½ cups sugar	

Make the dough. After the first rising, roll the dough into a thin square on a lightly floured counter. Mix the filling and spread on the dough. Roll it up and cut into ½in-thick slices.

Place on parchment paper and glaze with the egg. Let rise until extremely fluffy, then bake at 400°F until golden.

Danish pastry dough

This is the basis for another lot of cakes and pastries, a very rich, delicious dough, rolled with butter to a semi-flaky pastry, known to the rest of the world as Danish pastry. In Denmark, however, it's called Viennese bread, as the first baker who made it in Denmark came from Vienna. It is served any time, but is rarely made at home. It is possible, even if it's a little more difficult than ordinary pastry, and worth every minute you spend on it. The recipe for the basic dough is given first, with recipes for three different fillings below.

1oz fresh yeast	4 cups all-purpose flour
Generous ¾ cup lukewarm milk	1 teaspoon ground cardamom
2 eggs	Grated zest of 1 lemon
½ cup sugar	¾ cup butter

Dissolve the yeast in the milk, then mix in the rest of the ingredients (except the butter) to form a dough. Knead it well, until smooth and shiny. Let the dough rise in a warm place for 2 hours, or until doubled in size. Roll on a lightly floured counter to a very thin, large rectangle.

Cut the butter into very thin slices and place on two-thirds of the dough. Fold the butterless third over the buttered section, and fold again into a tight package, ensuring the butter is enclosed in the pastry. Roll this out, and fold again four to five times. The butter will disappear, and the dough will appear layered. If the butter starts to break through the layers, chill the dough in between rollings.

From this point, you can make several different pastries.

Danish pastries

If you want to make Danish pastries, roll out the dough above to a very thin, long rectangle. Make a filling with ½ cup sugar, ½ stick butter, a grated apple, and a handful of raisins. Fold the dough so it does not meet in the middle, and shape into a giant pretzel, or wreath, on parchment paper. Glaze with a beaten egg, and scatter sugar and flaked hazelnuts over the surface. Let it rise till doubled in size and bake at 350°F until golden brown. Serve in wedges. Alternatively, you can fill it with a stiff vanilla custard.

Flaky pastry Christmas cake

This Christmas cake is a rich pastry filled with candied peel, almonds, and raisins, and is traditionally eaten for afternoon tea or with a glass of *gløgg*.

1 quantity Danish pastry dough	⅓ cup blanched almonds, chopped
⅔ cup raisins or currants	½ cup sugar
1 cup chopped candied peel	Melted butter, to glaze
	MAKES 1 LARGE CAKE

Roll out the dough to a very thin rectangle and scatter the dry ingredients over the surface. Roll into a tight roll and place it as a loose swirl in a buttered cake pan. Let it rise in a warm place till more than doubled in size. Glaze with melted butter and a sprinkling of sugar. Bake at 325°F for an hour, but try to pierce it with a wooden skewer after 45 minutes. If no dough sticks, it's done.

Chistmas buns

Proceed exactly as for the Christmas cake above, but slice the roll into 12 pieces and fold into buns. Let rise until very fluffy, glaze with beaten egg, then bake until golden.

Carnival buns

Carnival buns are exquisite, filled with whipped cream or a crème patissière, and glazed with confectioner's sugar. Roll the pastry dough as above. Shape into round buns, glaze with a beaten egg, and let them rise in a warm place until more than doubled in size. Bake at 350°F until golden brown. Let cool and then cut the buns open. Remove a little of the middle, and fill with sweetened whipped cream and jam. Put the top back on, then dust with confectioner's sugar, or go all the way with a glaze made from lemon juice and confectioner's sugar.

Carnival

The annual carnival (*fastelavn*), just before Lent, is a tradition from pagan times. In the dark ages it was a wild and rebellious feast, and rightly feared by the authorities. People dressed up, roles were switched, and peasants could become king for the day, for as long as it lasted. The church has never approved of this feast either. It is an absolutely secular event, celebrating the coming of spring, and a binge before the 40 days of Lent.

In Scandinavia, both grown-ups and children celebrate by dressing up in costume, and hitting the "cat in the barrel"—a Scandinavian *piñata*, a giant barrel filled with oranges and sweets. (Until the 1930s, it contained a live black cat that was beaten to death in the barrel, a symbol of evil, to be dealt with before the new season.) Everybody lines up, fairies and princesses, dinosaurs and buccaneers, with freezing blue knees and lips in the snow. Whoever manages to hit the bottom out of the barrel, so all the sweets spill out, is crowned the "cat queen," and the one who grounds the final board of the barrel is the "cat king;" both are given paper crowns and sometimes special privileges. The children often go on trick-or-treat visits around the neighborhood.

The only surviving culinary traditions are the two carnival buns described here, and they are both delicious.

Semler

This Swedish pastry bun is eaten for the carnival period before Lent, a massive mouthful of almondy filling and whipped cream (you will need 2 cups heavy cream).

Bake as for the birthday buns (page 259) but omit the raisins. When they are cooled, cut in half, remove the soft inner part, and transfer to a bowl. Discard a third and soften the rest with some of the heavy cream. Mix with 7oz marzipan to a soft, sticky consistency, and return to the buns. Whip the remainder of the cream and use to decorate the top of the buns. Finish with a dusting of confectioner's sugar. These quantities will make 18 buns.

Christmas cookies

In the old days, cookies were eaten all year round—they were always offered with a cup of coffee. But times have changed, and very few find the time to bake regularly, or have the necessary ingredients and spices to hand. Cookies now mean Christmas, and this is kept up, even in busy families. Children enjoy baking them, and it's a firm tradition in most homes to set aside a weekend day to a baking binge, messing up everything, glazing the entire kitchen with cookie dough. At our house the dogs, keyholes, boots, and even the bathtub are mysteriously decorated with silver balls and caramel.

Cake pans are filled with spicy, crispy cookies, to be eaten along with dried fruits and nuts, and coffee and *gløgg*. They are also hung in little woven paper baskets on the Christmas tree. The pepper cookies are a decoration in themselves, pierced with a hole before baking, glazed or unadorned, to be dangled on the tree. Cookies are popular gifts too, and many children bake them to give away to family and friends.

Choosing which cookies to include here was difficult as there are hundreds of delicious Christmas cookies, and everybody has their favorites. For this book I have chosen ever-popular examples, and as they are much the same all over Scandinavia, there is enough to please everyone, I hope.

Vanilla-almond fluted cookies

This is, in my opinion, very, very good cookie dough. It can be made into the traditional wreath-shaped cookies, which involves an old-fashioned meat-grinder with a star-shaped hole, to make the long, fluted sausages, which are then shaped into wreaths. Or simply roll lengths of the dough and twist to a coil and cut, or it can be cut into rounds, squares, or whatever you fancy. Whichever you choose, the more surface area you can procure, the crisper the cookies will be.

3⅓ cups blanched almonds	1¼ cups sugar
1–2 vanilla beans, finely chopped	½ cup butter
2 cups all-purpose flour	2 eggs
1 teaspoon baking powder	MAKES 30–40

Run the almonds and vanilla beans through the food processor until they resemble fine bread crumbs. Put all the ingredients into a bowl big enough to hold everything, and knead to a smooth dough. Let it rest in a cool place until the next day.

Now run the dough through the meat-grinder, without the knife attached, but with the disc with a star-shaped hole in it. If this is unavailable, any hole will do. You will need two people to do this, one to receive the long strands of cookie dough and shape them on parchment paper and one to crank the handle and feed the grinder.

Bake at 350°F until pale golden.

Brown caramel cookies

With their slightly bitter tinge, these cookies are for grown-ups. The recipe also involves precision, the dough starting off as a caramel, to which the rest of the ingredients are added, which means the dough-making is definitely not kids' stuff, but the cutting and baking are. The cookies have a very special porous crispness due to the potassium carbonate, or potash, used (available from chemists). This recipe makes a lot of cookies, but the dough keeps well wrapped in the refrigerator, and also freezes well. It's a good idea to bake them as they are needed, and not in one big batch—they are at their best when freshly baked and the smell coming from the oven is enchanting.

Alternatively the dough is amazing used in a layer cake with paper-thin layers, assembled at the very last minute with sweetened whipped cream.

2½ cups sugar	¼oz ground cloves
Generous ¾ cup corn syrup	¼oz ground ginger
2¼ cups salted butter	1 blade of mace, ground
½oz potash	2 cups candied peel from
Scant ¼ cup beer	a cedrate (a large lemon
Scant 1 cup blanched	relative), or other candied
almonds, roughly	peel, cut into ½in dice
chopped	Grated zest of 1½ lemons
½oz ground cinnamon	8 cups all-purpose flour

Melt the sugar, syrup, and butter in a heavy-bottomed saucepan. When it boils, remove from the heat and let cool. Dissolve the potash completely in a little beer: it emits a foul odor, but this disappears in a short while.

When the sugar mixture has cooled slightly, mix in the potash, almonds, and spices. Cool some more, until just below room temperature. Mix in the candied peel, grated zest, and flour. If you do not follow these instructions carefully, the dough will separate, or it will become a solid caramel, and you will have to start over by melting it again.

Roll the dough into fat sausages, wrap in several layers of parchment paper and plastic wrap and cool completely in the refrigerator. Cut into slices as thin as you can manage with a very sharp knife. Bake on parchment paper at 350°F until the cookies are just baked through. The crispness comes when they are cooled. If they do not crisp up, bake them some more; but they must not burn or they will be indelibly bitter. Store in airtight containers.

Klejner

The recipe for this cookie is a far older heirloom, dating from the Middle Ages, and is a very typical example of a primitive, pre-cooking-range biscuit. It is deep-fried in fat like many similar cookies from around the world, and is crispy, and deliciously scented with cardamom and lemon zest. The name stems from the German word *klein*, meaning "small."

6 eggs

1¼ cups sugar

Generous 1 cup soft butter

1 teaspoon ground
   cardamom

Grated zest of 2 lemons

4 tablespoons heavy cream

8 cups all-purpose flour

Palm oil or pure fat,
   for frying

Stir the eggs, sugar, butter, cardamom, and zest to a batter. Add the cream and flour and mix until smooth. Let rest for an hour or two in a cool place.

Place a stack of large plates in the freezer. Meanwhile, roll out the dough to a thickness of ⅛in. Cut the dough with a special cutter—this is a fluted wheel probably obtainable only in Scandinavia, but a ravioli cutter that makes wavy edges will do just fine; the biscuits should be rhomboids roughly 1¼ x 2¼in. When this is done, make a 1¼-long incision in the middle of each cookies and then draw one pointed end through the center hole: this will give extra surface and therefore crisper cookies. When you have

completed a few, put the cookies immediately onto the chilled plates while you finish the rest, as they are much easier to handle when slightly stiff. Put the plates in the refrigerator if your kitchen is warm.

Heat the palm oil or fat in a stable and heavy skillet, or a friteuse. When it's hot, fry the cookies a few at a time or they will stick together. Once they are light and golden, take them out with a slotted spoon and put on paper towels to cool. Exactly how many to fry at a time and at what exact temperature is a matter of experience. If they fry too slowly, they will absorb too much oil; if too fast, they will brown before they are cooked through. Store in airtight containers.

Pepper cookies

If you know Astrid Lindgren's world-famous children's books, you will recognize these Swedish cookies known as *pepperkakor*, which actually contain black pepper. The lovely crispy and spicy cookies are cut out of a thin layer of dough and then decorated with royal icing. The cookie cutters in Scandinavia are in the shape of fat men and women, the mythical creatures *Nisse* or *Tomte*, pigs, reindeer, and the only really scary animal in Nordic Christmas lore, the horned billy goat. In earlier times this was another apparition of the devil himself, but nowadays is just a harmless goat made of straw used to decorate the house or placed by the front door. Hearts, stars, and bells are popular shapes, too.

The dough is very easy to make, and can also be shaped into *pebernødder* ("pepper nuts"), small, round, crispy cookies the size of a hazelnut. They are always extremely popular with children, and easy to shape even for a two-year-old.

Generous 1 cup soft butter

2½ cups sugar

Generous ¾ cup heavy
cream

Generous ¾ cup corn syrup

2 tablespoons baking powder

4 teaspoons ground ginger

4 teaspoons ground
cinnamon

4 tablespoons cocoa
powder

4 teaspoons ground
cardamom

2 teaspoons ground
black pepper

Approx. 8 cups plain flour

Royal icing, to decorate

MAKES MANY, MANY
COOKIES!

Blend the butter and sugar in a mixer, or in a big bowl. Stir in the cream, followed by the rest of the ingredients except the flour. Add the flour until the dough is no longer sticky, and no more. Knead it well, then let the dough rest in the refrigerator until the next day.

Preheat the oven to 350°F.

Roll the dough to a very thin sheet (⅙in thick is fine), and cut into shapes. Remember to pierce holes in the cookies destined for hanging. Arrange on parchment paper until the last scrap is used. Bake in the oven until golden.

Decorate with royal icing. The traditional way is to frame the cookie, make buttons, shoes, and so on, and to write the family's names on heart-shaped cookies and hang them in the windows on red ribbons.

Honey cakes

These cakes are very old. Similar cakes were made in ancient Egypt, and the tradition has survived in some form all over Europe. Honey cakes have a special history in the Danish city of Christianfeld. The Danish king gave a Moravian congregation from Holland the right to build a city in southern Jutland in the 18th century. They built an entire and extremely beautiful city in just a few years, all of which is preserved, and well worth a visit. They were also master bakers, and in time Christianfeld has become famous for its honey cakes (as well as its sausages).

So honey cakes are, if not only a Nordic, then also a Nordic-Baltic, Russian, German-Polish tradition. As with so many other foods, nobody owns the copyright. There has been trade since ancient times, and traditions, both good and bad, have spread, been altered, and loved throughout a vast area. This also accounts for the

incredible variety in recipes for honey cake, especially in the spicing, though everybody agrees to the citrus peel, cinnamon, cloves, allspice, and ginger. Aniseed is used in Germany and Poland, but usually not in Scandinavia.

The ancestor of all honey cakes is basically made by mixing fresh honey, harvested in summer, with rye flour. The lactic acids present in both honey and grain will get it going. The dough is left to ferment until Christmas, when eggs and spices are added. This kind of honey cake is still made, and the long fermentation gives it a very special flavor. The last of the batch is always kept to add to the new harvest next summer. If you have the patience, you can improve your own honey cake by fermenting it, if not for months, then a couple of weeks.

The cakes are obvious symbols of life and resurrection and were offered at christenings and marriages, and given as Christmas presents since the Middle Ages.

1½ cups honey

2½ cups muscovado sugar

1¼ cups water

2½ lb wheat flour or 50%
sifted rye flour and 50%
wheat flour

2 eggs

2 teaspoons baking soda

2 teaspoons ground ginger

2 teaspoons ground cinnamon

2 teaspoons ground, dried
Seville orange peel

2 teaspoons ground allspice

Grated zest of 2 oranges,
or Seville oranges

Generous 1½ cups raisins
or currants

MAKES 1 LARGE OR
2 SMALLER CAKES

Melt the honey, sugar, and water in a saucepan big enough to hold everything. Let cool, then stir in the flour. Cover the pan in plastic wrap and leave in a cool place. From here, you mature the dough for a week or two, if you have the patience, or else, proceed straight away.

Preheat the oven to 300°F.

Stir the rest of the ingredients into the dough and spread it in either a buttered baking sheet or two buttered round cake pans. Smooth the surface and bake for about 40 minutes. The baking time depends on the thickness of the dough, the oven, and other unpredictable circumstances, so after 30 minutes insert a wooden skewer; if no dough sticks to it, the cake is done. Don't overbake it as it's far better if a little underdone and fudgy in the middle. Cool and wrap.

Cakes like these will keep indefinitely, and the finished honey cake will only improve by maturing a little; it will keep in a quite delicious condition for 6 months. If absolutely dry, and this may happen to smaller honey cakes, put them in the oven at 275°F, pour a glass of water into a hot pan below the cakes, and wait for the steam to rise. Close the oven door, turn off the heat, and let the cakes resurrect for 10 minutes. Or you can moisten them by putting them in a closed container with a sliced raw potato.

Kransekage

This is the ultimate party cake for the grand celebration, for births, marriages, and New Year's Eve. It is decorated according to the occasion, often with flags, sugared flowers, or a little figurine of a new-born baby, newlyweds, or the number of the anniversary on top.

The cake can be bought everywhere before New Year, but your own is bound to be of better marzipan made from flavorful Spanish almonds and no apricot kernels. It's easy enough if you take your time. Choose the version of the recipe that suits, depending on whether or not you make your own marzipan.

cake with homemade marzipan

18oz almonds, weighed after peeling
2–4 Spanish almonds
2¼–2¾ cups superfine sugar, to taste
4–5 egg whites, according to size

cake with bought marzipan

2–4 Spanish almonds
2¼lb high-quality, low-sugar marzipan, made from almonds
½ cup superfine sugar, or to taste
4–5 egg whites, according to size

Serves 10–12

If you are making your own marzipan, begin by blanching the almonds: soak them in hot water for an hour, then pop them out of their skins. Grind the almonds to a fine powder in a meat-grinder or food processor. If you use an old-fashioned meat-grinder, you will need to grind the almonds twice, the second time with the sugar.

Knead the almond flour with the sugar and egg whites until smooth. Taste the marzipan, as it may need more sugar.

If are using ready-made marzipan, grate the Spanish almonds and mix with the rest of the ingredients to a smooth dough. Heat the finished marzipan dough in a very thick-bottomed saucepan, at a very low heat. Knead with a wooden spoon until the mixture is a little warmer than body heat.

Preheat the oven to 400°F.

On three sheets of parchment paper, draw rings that will fit onto one another to form a tall spire, the top being a half-sphere. In the end, this is much easier than making the rings freestyle, but by all means do what you please. When this is accomplished, the dough will have cooled a little, and you can shape it into rings with wet fingers, using the paper pattern as a guide. They should be 1¼in thick at the bottom, and 1–1¼in high, pointed or round as you please. Bake until barely browned on the top—they must be pale. Cool on the parchment paper. Assemble when cooled with a small amount of royal icing, in a zigzag pattern across every ring, all the way round; this will make the mound stick together.

Christmas rice pudding with almonds

Rice pudding itself is eaten frequently during the winter as a main course, dusted with cinnamon and sugar and with a generous blob of butter melting in the middle. It's solid winter fare, and filling, but not for very long—we usually have evening tea with some bread and cheese later on.

Eating rice at Christmas is a tradition from a time when everything imported, like rice and spices were luxuries. This almond rice pudding, (*riz à l'amande*) is relatively new, a bourgeois revival of the peasant hot oatmeal, and in the country it's still usual to eat ordinary creamed rice for Christmas Eve dinner, either as an appetizer, as in former times, or as a dessert. It's an age-old custom to make sure the resident *Nisse* is well fed during Christmas. Lots of people, including my family, put a bowl of hot rice pudding in the attic on Christmas Eve, just to make sure.

Riz à l'amande is lovely, and very rich, and actually not the kind of dessert I would normally recommend you eat after a heavy Christmas dinner of goose, duck, or roast pork. Tradition must not be tampered with, though, so in my family we usually eat it for breakfast the next day, in order to be able to go through with the traditional dance around the Christmas tree.

We have a tradition, similar to that of hiding money or some other treat in the Christmas pudding, of including one whole almond in the dessert. This takes skill, as there is always someone most in need of winning the "almond gift," and you have to make sure—very discreetly—that the right person gets it. The thing not to do is make a huge bowl of *riz à l'amande* and put the whole almond in at random. It always ends up in the last spoonful, even if this is not statistically possible, and everybody gets a stomach ache from eating too much. Instead, serve the pudding in individual glasses, in small portions. The gift can be anything, but often it is a homemade piglet, made from marzipan, with rosy painted ears and snout.

The classic accompaniment is hot cherry sauce, a glass of cherry brandy, or a fine tawny port.

for the creamed rice	to finish
1 vanilla bean	¼ cup heavy cream
Scant ¾ cup round pudding rice or risotto rice	1⅓ cups peeled Spanish almonds
Approx. 4 cups milk (maybe ¾–1¼ cups more, depending on the rice)	¼ cup sugar
½ teaspoon salt	3 Spanish almonds, finely ground
	Sweet cherry sauce (page 201)

SERVES 8–10

When it comes to making creamed rice, it's all about the right saucepan. It must be thick-bottomed, or the rice will definitely burn. Slash the vanilla bean lengthwise, then put all the rice ingredients in the pan. Bring to a boil, while stirring, and then turn down the heat to a minimum.

From now on, do not stir unless absolutely necessary, as you want whole, chewy rice, covered in creamy milk, not rice sludge. Let it simmer until the rice is only just done, no longer. (You may need to add more milk, depending on the rice you use.) It will finish cooking during cooling. The cooking may take 45 minutes, maybe less.

If the rice is taking up much-needed space on the stove, you can make an old-fashioned hay box instead. Fill a wooden box with hay—or crumpled newspapers and towels—and put the pan in after it has first come to the boil. Remember to cover the lid with lots of towels. Let the pan sit until the rice is succulent and swelled. This will make a better rice pudding, and is also effective with dried beans and peas and meat that otherwise would use a lot of power.

If you are familiar with risotto, you can choose to make the rice pudding risotto-style. Use the same ingredients as above, but use risotto rice. Heat the milk in a separate pan, and patiently stir it into the rice a ladleful at a time, adding more as soon as it is absorbed by the rice.

Whichever method you use, cool the creamed rice immediately: even if it's warm, it must go directly in the refrigerator, unless of course you intend to eat it as is. And a warning: the creamed rice must be absolutely cold before you add the cream, or you will end up with a disgusting bowl of inedible, smelly, cheesy rice.

Whip the cream, but only until soft. Chop the Spanish almonds, remembering to reserve one whole almond; and be sure to leave a few deceptively large pieces among the others. Fold half of the cream, all the sugar, and both the chopped and ground almonds into the rice. Mix well, ensuring there are no lumps. Fold in the rest of the cream, then cover the entire bowl with plastic wrap—nothing absorbs refrigerator odors like this pudding. Put the rice in the refrigerator immediately.

Serve in individual glass dishes, in one of which you have concealed the whole almond, so that you can present that dish to the appropriate diner. Hand the cherry sauce round separately.

Apple dumplings

These apple dumplings (*æbleskiver*) are eaten at every possible occasion during December, and often also in November. They are delicious, light, and fluffy when home-baked, though most people buy them ready-made.

There are different ways to make the dumplings, but, as with doughnuts, the ones made with yeast are the best. You will need a special dumpling pan, with seven half-spherical cavities in it, to produce absolutely round and right dumplings; you can buy one on the internet.

The only other necessary implement is a fork or skewer for turning the dumplings around—it must be able to hold the dumpling and then let it go easily. Everyone has his or her own favorite; often an old battered fork with a prong missing is the best. Serve the dumplings with jam and a small heap of confectioner's sugar.

½oz fresh yeast	plus extra for greasing
1 cup lukewarm whole milk	½ teaspoon ground
3 eggs, separated	cardamom
1 tablespoon sugar	Grated zest of 1 lemon
Generous 1½ cups all-purpose flour	3 apples, unpeeled, cut into small dice
Scant ⅓ cup butter, melted,	MAKES 25 DUMPLINGS

Dissolve the yeast in the milk. Whisk in the egg yolks and sugar until the sugar has dissolved. Whisk in the flour, followed by the melted butter, cardamom, and lemon zest. Finally, beat the egg whites until stiff and fold them into the batter. Let this rise in a warm place until foamy and light.

Heat the dumpling pan and place a little piece of butter in each hole. When the butter is golden, fill the cavities with batter. When the outer ⅛in of each dumpling is cooked and bubbling all round, this is when the outer shell can hold a quick half-turn, while the center is still runny and will flow out to form the other half-sphere. Apple dumplings must be round, and this is the tricky part—you will need to practice.

Before turning, place a teaspoonful of apple dice in each dumpling. Turn the dumplings over several times to make them completely round, but do not despair—they will be lovely even if they look a little deflated.

index

Note: page numbers in **bold**
refer to photographs.

A

AGAs 238
Almond
    vanilla fluted cookies 262,
        262
    Christmas rice pudding
        with 266–7, **266**
anchovy
    and duck fat, with liver
        paste 122–3, **123**
    Jansson's temptation 87, **87**
    Northern 86–7
    sunny eye sandwich 87
angelica 185, **185**
    with rhubarb soup 185
anise flavored bread with
    fresh cheese 243, **243**
apple 190–6, **190**
    beet, and celeriac salad 158
    with braised pork 192–3
    with Brussels sprouts salad
        135
    burning love 153–4, **153**
    cake, with potato crust and
        cranberries 194–5
    caramelized onions, and
        crisp pork slices 193, **193**
    caraway seeds and beet
        salad 151, **151**
    and celeriac soup, with
        turbot and shellfish
        49–50
    compote 192, **192**
    crème fraîche, and onions,
        with herring 77, **77**
    dried 194, **194**
    dumplings 267, **267**
    and horseradish compote
        192
    old-fashioned trifle 195
    and prunes, with braised
        heart 124, **124**
    rye bread cake, with
        blackberries 232–3, **233**
    syrup 192
    syrup, berries and fresh
        goat cheese 16, **17**
    very good cake 195–6, **196**
    walnut and celery salad
        193–4, **194**
Arctic char 34, 39
asiers, pickled, with dill
    flowers 146–7, **147**
asparagus 140–2, **140**
    and chicken stew 92–3, **92**
    Italian salad 144
    and poached eggs, with
        chervil soup 176

salad, with new potatoes
    142, **142**
soup 141
white 140–2

B

bacon 101
    crispy, and thyme, with
        cabbage soup 138–9, **139**
    and lingonberries, with
        potato pancakes 227, **227**
    with winter pea soup 144–5,
        145
barley 252
bear 114
beef 110–12
    lindström 112, **112**
    and potato stew 111, **111**
beer
    eel braised in 37
    vörtbrød 248–9
    wild boar braised in 119,
        119
beet 148–51, **148**
    celeriac, and apple salad 158
    pickled, with cardamom 151
    pickled, with horseradish
        179, **179**
    salad, with apple and
        caraway seeds 151, **151**
    salad, with fresh smoked
        cheese 150, **150**
    terrine, with horseradish
        149–50, **149**
berries 210–35
    apple syrup and fresh goat
        cheese 16, **17**
Beskow, Elsa 226
birthday buns 259
birthday layer cake,
    strawberry and
    elderflower 213, **213**
bisque, shore crab 65–6, **66**
black grouse 120
blackberry 232–3, **232**
    with rye bread apple cake
        232–3, **233**
black currant 228–9, **228**
    liqueur 229
    summer compote 215, **215**
    tea 229
blood 124–5
blueberry 210, 220–1, **220**
    with buttermilk ice cream
        221, **221**
    with curd cheese pancakes
        220–1, **221**
boletus 163–4
brandy, cherry 200
bread & grains 236–53
    barley 252

oats 251–2
rye 232–3, 239, 241, 244–50
wheat 238–45, 248–9, 253
brill 48
broccoli 133
Brussels sprouts 133
    salad with apple 135
buns
    birthday 259
    carnival 260, **260**
    Christmas 260
    Lucia 258–9, **259**
    sourdough bread and
        poppy seed 242, **242**
butter 18
buttermilk 18
    dessert 18, 20
    dressing, with green salad
        22
    ice cream with blueberries
        221, **221**
    and sweet grass cream with
        rhubarb jelly 18–19, **19**

C

cabbage 132–4
    caramelized white 137, **137**
    pointed head, with dill 139,
        139
    rolls (kåldolmar) 138, **138**
    soup, with crispy bacon
        and thyme 138–9, **139**
    see also red cabbage
cake
    apple, with a potato crust
        and cranberries 194–5
    bread 243, **243**
    Easter lamb 13, **13**
    flaky pastry, with
        gooseberry-elderflower
        fool 223, **223**
    flaky pastry Christmas 260
    honey 264–5, **264**
    kransekage 265, **265**
    raspberry multilayer 219,
        219
    rye bread apple, with
        blackberries 232–3, **233**
    strawberry and elderflower
        birthday layer 213, **213**
    very good apple 195–6, **196**
calabrese 133
calf's offal 124, 126–7
caper
    and lemon, with salted leg
        of lamb 108–9, **109**
    mayonnaise 57
    sauce 33
    sauce, with salted breast of
        veal 113
    sauce, with salted veal
        tongue **126**
caramel
    brown, cookies 262

crisp oat cookies 251–2, **251**
caraway seeds
    and apple, with beet salad
        151, **151**
    with red cabbage salad
        136–7
    with rye and wheat
        "Sourbread" 248, **248**
cardamom ice cream 23
carnival (fastelavn) 261
carp 34
cattle 110, 126
cauliflower 133, 134
celeriac 157–9
    apple and beet salad 158
    and apple soup, with halibut
        and shellfish 49–50
    root chips 159, **159**
    root vegetables with
        elderflower and lemon
        159, **159**
    soup with cardamom 158,
        158
celery 157
    apple and walnut salad
        193–4, **194**
cep 162
chanterelle 162
cheese 14, 15–17
    curd cheese pancakes with
        blueberries 220–1, **221**
    fresh, with anise flavored
        bread 243, **243**
    fresh goat, with berries and
        apple syrup 16, **17**
    fresh smoked, with beet
        salad 150, **150**
    goat, horseradish and
        mashed pea 144, **144**
    and jam 253
    summer smoked salad 16,
        16
cheesecake, Swedish 20–1
cherry 200–1, **200**
    brandy 200
    sauces 201
chervil 176, **176**
    and chives, with egg sauce
        11
    soup, with poached eggs
        and asparagus 176
chicken 90–3
    and asparagus stew 92–3, **92**
    with parsley and curdled
        sauce 173, **173**
    salad 93
    slow-roast, and peas with
        tarragon 174, **175**
    soup, with dumplings 91, **91**
    stew, with tartlets 92–3, **92**
chips, root 159, **159**
chives 186, **186**
    and chervil, with egg sauce
        11

chocolate, with dark elk stew
118, **118**
Christmas 122, 128, 134, 190–1,
225, 254–67
buns 260
cookies 261, **261**
flaky pastry cake 260
mustard 105, **105**
rice pudding with almonds
266–7, **266**
Swedish ham, with
mustard crust 105, **105**
chutney, plum, with licorice
208
cinnamon rolls 259, **259**
cloudberry 210, 224–5, **224**
fool 225
Norwegian waffles 225
cod 42, **42**
with pork fat 42
salt 72–3, 74
salted mousse 74, **74**
and sons 42
cod's roe 52–3
boiled 53
cod and sons 42
coley 42
compote
apple 192, **192**
gooseberry 223
rhubarb 203, **203**
summer 215, **215**
conch 49–50
cookies
brown caramel 262
Christmas 261, **261**
crisp oat caramel 251–2, **251**
klejner 263, **263**
pepper 263–4
vanilla-almond fluted 262,
262
cooperative movement 14,
100
coot 120
braised wildfowl 121, **121**
cordial
elderberry 230
elderflower 182
rhubarb 205, **205**
rowanberry 231
crab
common 64, **64**
gratin 64
Kamchatka king 57, 65
shore crab bisque 65–6, **66**
crab apple 197, **197**
jelly 197
crackling 102, 125
cranberry, with potato crust
apple cake 194–5
crayfish 60–1, **60**
with dill flowers 61, **61**
party (*kräft kala*) 61
cream 22–3

buttermilk ice cream with
blueberries 221, **221**
cardamom ice cream 23
dressing, with green salad
22
horseradish 145, **145**, 179, **179**
lemon creams 23
rømmegrød 22
and strawberry crispy cones
214–15, **214**
sweet grass and buttermilk,
with rhubarb jelly 18–19,
19
crisp bread 238–9, 250, **250**,
252–3
with sourdough 250
cucumber 146–7, **146**
mustard-dill-pickle 147, **147**
pickled asiers with dill
flowers 146–7, **147**
salad, with dill 171, **171**
sweet-and-sour salad 146

D
dab 49
dairies 14
dairy 14, 100
Dalén, Gustav 238
dandelion greens 186, **186**
Danish pastries 260
deer 114, **114**, 115–17
dill 170–1, **170–1**
creamed potato 154
with cucumber salad 171, **171**
flowers, with crayfish 61, **61**
flowers, with pickled asiers
146–7, **147**
gravad fish 78–9
loads of, with lamb stew
170–1, **170**
mayonnaise 57
mustard-cucumber-pickle
147, **147**
with pointed head cabbage
139, **139**
dough, Danish pastry 260
duck 94–9
braised wildfowl 121, **121**
poached and salted 98, **98**
roast 96–7
wild 120, 121
duck fat 95, 125
and anchovies, with liver
paste 122–3, **123**
dumplings
apple 267, **267**
with chicken soup 91, **91**

E
Easter 10, 11
lamb cake 13, **13**
eel 37, **37**
braised in beer 37
smoked 80, 81

egg 8–13
dirty, with seven greens
12–13, **12**
omelette with ramsons 180,
180
poached, asparagus and
chervil soup 176
sauce, with chervil and
chives 11
sun over Gudhjem 82, **82**
sun (*solæg*) 11
eider duck 120–1, **121**
elderberry 230, **230**
cordial 230
soup 230, **230**
syrup, pear in 198, **199**
elderflower 182–4, **182–3**
-gooseberry fool, with flaky
pastry cakes 223, **223**
cordial 182
and gooseberry jam 223
jelly 184, **184**
and lemon, with root
vegetables 159, **159**
spiced salt 182–3
and strawberry birthday
layer cake 213, **213**
with veal scaloppini 184,
184
elk 118
dark stew, with chocolate
118, **118**
elvers 37
emmer 240
ergot/ergotism 244

F
fallow deer 115
false morel 164
fastelavn (carnival) 261
fat 125
duck 95, 122–3, **123**, 125
goose 95, 125
pork 42, 125
fatty acids 35, 40, 44, 52
fenalår (mutton dish) 108
fish
fresh 24–51
baked on a plate 28, **28**
boning 27
buying 34
directory 35–51
filleting 27
flatfish 27, 48–53
freshwater fish 34–9
gutting 26–7
newspaper fish 30, **30**, 34
oven-baked whole fish
27–8
perfect crispy fried fish
28–9, **29**
plank fish 29, **29**, 34
pre-salting 27
preparation 26–7

round fish 26–7
saltwater fish 40–7
scaling 26
stock 31
storing 34
mustard sauce for 32
preserved 70–87
buying/storing 73, 76
cured fish 84–5
dried fish 72–4
gravad fish 78–9, **78**
salted fish 75–9
smoked fish 80–3
fish roe 52–5
fish cakes 30–1
Norway haddock herbed 41,
41
flatbread 239, 252, 253
flatfish 27, 48–53
roe 52, 53
flounder 49
pan-fried 50
fool
cloudberry 225
gooseberry-elderflower,
with flaky pastry cakes
223, **223**
fruit 188–209

G
game 114–21
Gammalost (cheese) 15
Gammel Dansk 231
garfish 46, **46**
garlic
-saffron mayonnaise 57
baked, with mushroom
soup 165, **165**
giblets 96–7
gizzards 97
gløgg
traditional 257
white 257
goose 94–9
poached and salted 98, **98**
roast 96–7
salted, with yellow split pea
soup 98–9, **99**
wild 120
goose fat 95, 125
gooseberry 222–3, **222**
-elderflower fool, with flaky
pastry cakes 223, **223**
compote 223
and elderflower jam 223
and elderflowers, with
broiled mackerel 44, **45**
summer compote 215, **215**
grains
ancient, and Nordic herb
salad 186–7, **187**
see also breads & grains
gratin, crab 64
gravad fish 34, 78–9, **78**, 84–5

gravy, for duck/goose 97
gray mullet 47, **47**
grouse 120
gule ærter (yellow split pea
    soup) 95

H
haddock 42
    Norway 41, **41**
hake 42
halibut 48–9
    and shellfish, with celeriac
        and apple soup 49–50
    smoked 80, 81
ham 104–5, **104**
    Christmas mustard 105, **105**
    home-salted 104
    Swedish Christmas, with
        mustard crust 105, **105**
headcheese, Scandinavian
    128, **128–9**
heads 126–8
    mock turtle 126–7
    Scandinavian headcheese
        128, **128–9**
heart 124
    braised with apples and
        prunes 124, **124**
herbs 168–87
herring 40, 43, **43**
    clay pot 43
    fried salted, with
        caramelized onions 77, **77**
    Matjes 76
    mustard gravad 84–5
    with onions, apples, and
        crème fraîche 77, **77**
    red herring salad 76
    roe 52, 53
    salted 75–7, **75–6**
    scania spiced 85
    silllåda 43
    soused, with mustard herbs
        84
    sun over Gudhjem 82, **82**
Hollandaise sauce 32–3
honey cakes 264–5, **264**
horn of plenty 162
horseradish 178–9, **178**
    and apple compote 192
    with beet terrine 149–50, **149**
    cream, with smoked
        salmon 179, **179**
    cream, with summer pea
        soup 145, **145**
    creamed 98, **98**
    and goat cheese, with
        mashed pea 144, **144**
    with pickled beets 179, **179**
hunting 114, 118–20

I
ice cream
    buttermilk, with

blueberries 221, **221**
    cardamom 23
    "Iceland Diamonds" 76

J
jam
    and cheese 253
    gooseberry and elderflower
        223
    raspberry 216–17, **217**
    raw lingonberry 226, **226**
    rose and strawberry 214, **214**
    rosehip 234
    sea buckthorn 235
    spiced rhubarb 204
Jarlsberg 15
jellied stock 101
jelly
    crab apple 197
    elderflower 184, **184**
    rhubarb, with buttermilk
        and sweet grass cream
        18–19, **19**
    rowanberry 231, **231**
Jerusalem artichoke
    and mussels 69
    and potato pancakes with
        løjrom 54–5, **55**
junket 16, 21

K
kærnemælkskoldskål
    (buttermilk dessert) 18,
    20
Kaffeost (coffee cheese) 15
kåldolmar (cabbage rolls) 138,
    138
kale 132–4
    creamed 135
    salad, with lemon dressing
        134
kalvdans (pancake) 20
kebabs, grilled venison 117
kidneys and curdled sauce,
    with roast veal 112–13, **113**
klejner (biscuits) 263, **263**
klipfisk (saltfish) 72
    with lots of trimmings 74, 74
kransekage 265, **265**

L
Lagerlöf, Selma 94, 120
lamb 108–9
    offal 124, 126
    pinnekött 108, 109
    salted leg of, cooked with
        capers and lemon 108–9,
        109
    stew, with loads of dill
        170–1, **170**
långfil (fermented cow's milk)
    18
langoustine 57, 59, **59**, 126–7
laxpudding (salmon pudding)

35
lemon
    and capers, with salted leg
        of lamb 108–9, **109**
    creams 23
    dressing, with kale salad
        134
    and elderflower, with root
        vegetables 159, **159**
lemon sole 49
licorice, with plum chutney
    208
limpa, Swedish, with
    lingonberries and
    scalded rye 247, **247**
lindström, beef 112, **112**
ling 42
lingonberry 210, 226–7, **226**
    with creamed rice 227, **227**
    pear preserved with 198
    potato pancakes with bacon
        and 227, **227**
    raw jam 226, **226**
    and scalded rye, with
        Swedish limpa 247, **247**
liqueur, blackcurrant 229
liver 122–3
    paste 122–3
    paste, with duck fat and
        anchovies 122–3, **123**
    pâté 97
lobster
    black 58, **58**
    Norway (langoustine) 57, 59,
        59, 126–7
løjrom, with Jerusalem
    artichoke and potato
    pancakes 54–5, **55**
lovage 177, **177**
    pesto 177, **177**
Lucia buns 258–9, **259**
lumpfish roe 52, 54
lutefisk 73

M
mackerel 44, **44**
    broiled, with gooseberries
        and elderflowers 44, **45**
malt 244
    syrup and stout, with
        øllebrød 249, **249**
mämmi 249
Märak, Nik 250
marbling 110–11
Martin, St 95, 96
marzipan, homemade 265
mayonnaise 93
    caper 57
    dill 57
    saffron-garlic 57
    for shellfish 56–7
meat-grinders 88
meatballs, Scandinavian
    101–2, **102**

medisterpølse (sausages) 106–7
milk 14, 15, 18
    see also sour milk products
milk-cap 163
milling 240
mock duck 103, **103**
mock turtle 126–7
molluscs *see* shellfish and
    molluscs
monkfish 46, **46**
morel 162, 164
mousse, salted cod 74, **74**
mushrooms 160–7, **161–3**
    creamed, on toast 165
    directory 162–4
    dried 166, **166**
    picking 163
    pickled, in vinegar and
        olive oil 166–7, **167**
    raw salad 167
    salted 166
    soup, with baked garlic 165,
        165
mussel 49–50, 68–9, **68**
    and Jerusalem artichokes
        69
    Northern soup 69
    oystered vegetables 156
    salad 69, **69**
mustard
    -dill-cucumber pickle 147,
        147
    Christmas 105, **105**
    crust, Swedish Christmas
        ham with 105, **105**
    gravad herrings 84–5
    sauce 78–9
    sauce, for fish 32
    sauce, simple 32
mutton 108–9
    fenalår 108
Myseost (*Mesost*) (cheese) 15,
    253

N
nettle 181, **181**
    waffles 181, **181**
Norway haddock 41, **41**
    herbed fish cakes 41, **41**
Norwegian waffles 225

O
oats 251–2
    crisp oat caramel cookies
        251–2, **251**
obesity 18
offal 100, 122–9
øllebrød with malt syrup and
    stout 249, **249**
omelette, with ramsons and
    other herbs 180, **180**
onion
    apples and crème fraîche,
        with herring 77, **77**

caramelized, and apples, with crisp pork slices 193, **193**

caramelized, with fried salted herring 77, **77**

open-face sandwiches *see* smørrebrød

orange

with 24 hour pumpernickel 245–6, **246**

Seville, with sugar-salted salmon 36, **36**

organic produce 10, 14, 90, 94, 100–1, 111

ovens 238–9

oyster 49–50, 67

oystered vegetables 156

shucking 67

oyster mushroom 162

P

pagans 254

pan-frying 50

pancakes

curd cheese, with blueberries 220–1, **221**

kalvdans 20

potato, with bacon and lingonberries 227, **227**

potato and Jerusalem artichoke, with *løjrom* 54–5, **55**

parsley 172–3, **172**

and curdled sauce, with chicken 173, **173**

sauce, and new potatoes, with crispy pork slices 172–3, **172**

parsley-celery 157

partridge 120

pastry

carnival buns 260, **260**

chicken stew with tartlets 92–3, **92**

Christmas buns 260

Danish pastries 260

flaky cakes, with gooseberry-elderflower fool 223, **223**

flaky pastry Christmas cake 260

raspberry pastry squares **218**, 219

rhubarb tart 204, **204**

semler 261

pâté, duck/goose liver 97

patties, beef 112, **112**

peas 143–5, **143**

dried 143

green split 143

Italian salad 144

mashed, with goat cheese and horseradish 144, **144**

summer soup, with horseradish cream 145, **145**

tarragon and slow-roast chicken 174, **175**

winter soup, with bacon 144–5, **145**

yellow split 98–9, 143

pear 198, **198**

in elderberry syrup 198, **199**

preserved with lingonberries 198

pearl barley 252

pepper cookies 263–4

perch 34

pesto, lovage 177, **177**

pheasant 120–1

pickle, mustard-dill-cucumber 147, **147**

pigeon 121

pigs 100, 104, 122

offal 100, 124, 126, 128, **128**–9

pike 34, 38–9, **38–9**

quenelles 38, 39

rissoles 38–9

pike-perch (zander) 34, 39

pinnekött (stick meat) 108, 109

plankefisk (plank fish) 29, **29**, 34

plum 206–8, **206**

baked 208, **208**

chutney, with licorice 208

pickled, in red wine 207, **207**

poisonous foods 162–4

pollock 42

poppy seed and sourdough bread buns 242, **242**

porcini 164

pork 100–3, **100**

braised, with apples 192–3

cabbage rolls 138, **138**

crisp slices, with caramelized onions and apples 193, **193**

crisp slices, with parsley sauce and new potatoes 172–3, **172**

mock duck 103, **103**

perfect roast 102–3

sausages 106–7, **106–7**

Scandinavian meatballs 101–2, **102**

yellow split pea soup with salted goose 98–9, **99**

pork fat

with cod 42

spiced 125

potato 152–4, **152**

bashed neeps 155

and beef stew 111, **111**

burning love 153–4, **153**

caramelized 153

crust apple cake, with cranberries 194–5

dill creamed 154

and Jerusalem artichoke pancakes with *løjrom* 54–5, **55**

mashed 153–4, **153**

new, with asparagus salad 142, **142**

new, and parsley sauce, with crispy pork slices 172–3, **172**

pancakes, with bacon and lingonberries 227, **227**

warm salad 154, **154**

Potkäse (pot cheese) 15

powan 34, 39

roe 54

prune and apples, with braised heart 124, **124**

ptarmigan 120

puffin 120

pumpernickel, 24 hour, with orange 245–6, **246**

Q

quenelles 38, 39

R

rakefisk 79

ransoms 180, **180**

and other herbs, with omelette 180, **180**

raspberry 216–19, **216**

Arctic (*Åkerbär*) 210, 225

jam 216–17, **217**

multilayer cake 219, **219**

pastry squares **218**, 219

summer compote 215, **215**

ray 51

red cabbage 133, 134

pickled 136

salad, with caraway seeds 136–7

red deer 115

red wine, pickled plum in 207, **207**

red currant 229, **229**

shaken currants (*Rysteribs*) 229, **229**

summer compote 215, **215**

reindeer 114, **114**, 115–16

renskav 116

suovas 114, 115

remoulade 32

rhubarb 202–5, **202**

compote 203, **203**

cordial 205, **205**

jelly, with buttermilk and sweet grass cream 18–19, **19**

soup, with angelica 185

spiced jam 204

tart 204, **204**

rice

creamed, with lingonberries 227, **227**

pudding with almonds, Christmas 266–7, **266**

rimmid lax (cured fish) 79, **79**

rissoles, pike 38–9

rødgrød med flød (summer compote) 215, **215**

roe deer 115

rømmegrød (porridge-like dish) 22

root chips 159, **159**

root vegetables with elderflower and lemon 159, **159**

rose and strawberry jam 214, **214**

rosehip 234–5, **234**

jam 234

soup 235, **235**

rowanberry 231, **231**

cordial 231

jelly 231, **231**

rullepølse (sausages) 107, **107**

russula 163

rye 241, 244–50

24 hour pumpernickel with orange 245–6, **246**

bread apple cake with blackberries 232–3, **233**

bread cakes 243, **243**

crisp bread 250, **250**

Jon's rye bread 246–7, **246**

mämmi 249

Mogens' rye bread 245, **245**

øllebrød with malt syrup and stout 249, **249**

sourdough starter 239

Swedish limpa with lingonberries and scalded rye 247, **247**

vörtbröd 248–9

and wheat "Sourbread" with caraway seeds 248, **248**

Rygeost (cheese) 15, 16

Rysteribs (shaken currants) 229, **229**

S

saffron-garlic mayonnaise 57

salad 253

beet, with apple and caraway seeds 151, **151**

beet, with fresh smoked cheese 150, **150**

Brussels sprouts with apple 135

celeriac, apple, and beet 158

celery, apple, and walnut 193–4, **194**

chicken 93

cucumber, with dill 171, **171**

green, with cream or
buttermilk dressing 22
Italian 144
kale, with lemon dressing
134
mussel 69, **69**
of Nordic herbs and
ancient grains 186–7, **187**
raw mushroom 167
red cabbage, with caraway
seeds 136–7
red herring 76
shrimp 63, **63**
summer smoked cheese 16,
16
sweet-and-sour cucumber
146
warm potato 154, **154**
salmon 34, 35–6, **35**
pudding (*laxpudding*) 35
roe 52, 54
smoked 80, 81, 83
smoked, with horseradish
cream 179, **179**
sugar-salted, with Seville
orange 36, **36**
salsify (oyster plant) 156
oystered vegetables 156
salt
elderflower spiced 182–3
Nordic herb 187, **187**
salt fish (*klipfisk*) 72
with lots of trimmings 74,
74
salted fish 75–9
Sami people 114, 115, 125, 250
sandwiches
open-face *see smørrebrød*
sunny eye 87
sausage 106–7, **106–7**
blood 124–5
medisterpølse 106–7
rullepølse 107, **107**
yellow split pea soup with
salted goose 98–9, **99**
Scandinavian headcheese 128,
129
schnapps
sloe 209
traditional *gløgg* 257
schnaps (*aquavit*) 257
scorzonera 156
oystered vegetables 156
sea buckthorn 235, **235**
sea kale 134
sea trout roe 54
semler (pastry) 261
sheep 108, **108**
shellfish and mollusks 26,
56–69
buying/storing 57
directory 56–69
mayonnaises for 56–7
shrimp 62–3, **62**

Baltic 62–3
North Sea 57, 62–3
salad 63, **63**
silllåda (herring) 43
skate 51
skyr (milk product) 18
sloe 209, **209**
schnapps 209
smørgås/smørrebrød (open-face
sandwich) 10, 11, 15, 16, 32,
44, 52, 53, 54, 63, 74, 76, 77,
81, 82, 84, 85, 87, 93, 95, 97,
101-2, 106, 107, 122, 125,
128, 136, 139, 144, 146, 147,
149,152-153, 157, 178, 180,
192, 253, **253**
smoked cheese 16
smoked fish 80–3
cold-smoked 80–1
hot-smoked 80–1, 83
sun over Gudhjem 82, **82**
snipe 120
solæg (sun egg) 11
sole 49
soup
asparagus 141
cabbage, with crispy bacon
and thyme 138–9, **139**
celeriac, with cardamom
158, **158**
celeriac and apple, with
turbot and shellfish
49–50
chervil, with poached eggs
and asparagus 176
chicken, with dumplings
91, **91**
elderberry 230, **230**
mushroom, with baked
garlic 165, **165**
Northern mussel 69
rhubarb, with angelica 185
rosehip 235, **235**
shore crab bisque 65–6, **66**
summer pea, with
horseradish cream 145,
145
winter pea with bacon
144–5, **145**
yellow split pea, with salted
goose 98–9, **99**
sour milk products 18–21
sourdough 238
bread and poppy seed buns
242, **242**
with crisp bread 250
rye breads 244
rye and wheat "Sourbread,"
with caraway seeds 248,
248
starter 239
sour cream 22
spelt 240
24 hour pumpernickel with

orange 245–6, **246**
sprouting broccoli 133
stew
beef and potato 111, **111**
chicken, with tartlets 92–3,
92
chicken and asparagus
92–3, **92**
dark elk, with chocolate
118, **118**
lamb, with loads of dill
170–1, **170**
stock
fish 31
goose 95
jellied 101
stockfish (*tørfisk*) 72, 73
stout and malt syrup, with
øllebrød 249, **249**
strawberry 212–15, **212**
and cream crispy cones
214–15, **214**
and elderflower birthday
layer cake 213, **213**
and rose jam 214, **214**
summer compote 215, **215**
wood 210, 212
stuffing, for duck/goose 97
suovas (dried reindeer) 114, 115
surströmming (herring dish) 79
swede 155, **155**
bashed neeps 155
sweet breads 258, **258**
sweet grass 186, **186**
cream with buttermilk and
rhubarb jelly 18–19, **19**
sweetbreads (offal) 123
fried 123, **123**
syrup
apple 192
elderberry, pear in 198, **199**

T
tails 126
tarragon 174, **174**
with slow-roast chicken
and peas 174, **175**
tart, rhubarb 204, **204**
tartlets, with chicken stew
92–3, **92**
tea, blackcurrant 229
terrine, beet, with
horseradish 149–50, **149**
tjälknöl (venison) 114, 116, **116**
tørfisk (stockfish) 72, 73
toast, creamed mushrooms
on 165
tongue 126
salted veal with caper sauce
126
trichinella 101
trifle, old-fashioned apple 195
trout 34
roe 52

V
vanilla-almond fluted cookies
262, **262**
Västerbottenost (cheese) 15
veal 110–13
cabbage rolls 138, **138**
roast, with curdled sauce
and kidneys 112–13, **113**
salted breast of, with caper
sauce 113
salted tongue, with caper
sauce 126
scaloppini, with
elderflower 184, **184**
vegetables 131–59
vendace roe 52, 54–5, **55**
potato and Jerusalem
artichoke pancakes with
løjrom 54–5, **55**
venison 114
grilled 117, **117**
roast leg of 116–17, **117**
tjälknöl 114, 116, **116**
vörtbrød 248–9

W
waffles
nettle 181, **181**
Norwegian 225
walnut, celery, and apple
salad 193–4, **194**
wheat 238–45, 248–9, 253
and rye "Sourbread" with
caraway seeds 248, **248**
wheat germ 240
whey 15, 18
white sauce 122–3
white currant 229, **229**
whiting 42
wicker baskets 241
wild boar 114, 119
braised in beer 119, **119**
wildfowl 120–1, **120**
braised 121, **121**
wolf 114
wood sorrel 186, **186**
wood pigeon 121

Y
yellow split pea 143
soup, with salted goose
98–9, **99**
yogurt 18
yuletide 254